DATE DUE

GAYLORD M-2   PRINTED IN U.S.A.

D0962225

DICTIONARY-HANDBOOK TO
HYMNS FOR
THE LIVING CHURCH

DONALD P. HUSTAD

with

**The History of Hope Publishing Company
and Its Divisions and Affiliates**
by George H. Shorney, Jr.

Hope Publishing Company
Carol Stream, Illinois 60187

© Copyright 1978 by Hope Publishing Company
All rights reserved
Item code:
ISBN: 0-916642-09-7
Dewey Decimal Classification: 783.9
Library of Congress catalog card number: 77-75916

To Ruth—
who did much of the first research and all of the typing—
with my love

FOREWORD

The publishing of *Dictionary-Handbook to Hymns for the Living Church* is a significant occurence in the life of the evangelical community, and hopefully a sign of increasing maturity in our approach to hymn singing. So far as we know, it is the first attempt to produce a companion to an inter-denominational hymnal which contains a large body of what have been called "gospel songs."

Like most dictionaries and encyclopedias, a hymnal handbook is derived in large part from information accumulated by others during the past; in hymnology this covers a period of approximately one hundred and fifty years. The list of references in the back of this volume gives the sources that have been consulted in preparing material on the hymns that are common to many groups within the Christian community. Our purpose has been to provide basic data on these older hymns and their writers. For each selection, we have tried to identify the author, the composer, the adapter or arranger, the date of writing or first publishing and the volume in which it first appeared, and to give a brief account of any specific events connected with its writing. We have also endeavored to explain the significance of the tune name, if any.

For each author, composer, adapter or arranger, we have made an effort to record the birth/death places and dates as well as the individual's training, professional activity, and particular contribution to hymnody. It has not been our purpose to clarify debated points in hymnic history. That material can be found in the many books included in the reference list. We have simply tried to give correct information based on a concensus of the sources; when there is disagreement, we have made a choice by investigating the latest evidence or by evaluating the comparative dependability of each source.

Our task has been particularly challenging in the area of gospel hymnody. Unfortunately, most hymnologists have tended not to take that *genre* or its craftsmen seriously. Even more regrettably, gospel song poets and composers—and their supporters—have failed to leave an adequate record of their contributions to the church. "Hymn story" books have appeared in profusion, but careful research and reporting that can be quoted as history is hard to find. To be honest, the management of Hope Publishing Company is a bit embarrassed because some of the missing information involves songs whose copyrights they have controlled for years. This fact may be better understood when it is remembered that many hymns came to them second- or third-hand through the acquisition of other companies and their holdings.

In *Hymns of Our Faith,* William J. Reynolds made a major contribution toward bridging this "knowledge gap." Furthermore, each year new theses and dissertations produced in our universities and seminaries are filling in more of the details. This dictionary-handbook also makes its own modest contribution to hymnic information. Our research has been directed particularly toward the hymns that have not been mentioned in earlier companions, as well as the contemporary works that are published for the first time in *Hymns for the Living Church.*

We have received assistance from many hymnologists as well as from today's authors and composers. These individuals have been particularly helpful:

John S. Andrews, Sub-librarian, University of Lancaster, England.

Frank W. Birkenshaw, Music Editor, Marshall, Morgan & Scott, Ltd., London.

Alton Bynum, Gordon College, Wenham, Mass.

Keith Clark, Clark Hymnological Library, Houghton, N.Y.

Gertrude Dye, Copyrights Department, The Rodeheaver Company, Winona Lake, Ind.

Harry Eskew, Editor, *The Hymn,* Hymn Society of America.

Andrew J. Hayden, Tonbridge, Kent, England.

Alan Luff, Secretary, The Hymn Society of Great Britain and Ireland.

Bernard Massey, Editor, *The Bulletin,* Hymn Society of Great Britain and Ireland.

Robert F. Mountain, Mathieson House, Chingford, London, England.

Martha Powell, Music Librarian, Southern Baptist Theological Seminary, Louisville, Ky.

William Watkins Reid, Former Editor, *The Hymn,* Hymn Society of America.

William J. Reynolds, President, Hymn Society of America.

Erik Routley, Westminster Choir College, Princeton, N.J.

Gordon R. Sayer, The Evangelical Library, London, England.

It is hoped that some readers will be able to identify the individuals about whom we have given scant information, and will bring their own knowledge to our attention. It is in this manner that research goes on and the omissions are eliminated.

Personally, I am grateful to the owners of Hope Publishing Company, who have allowed me to assist in compiling six of their hymnbooks during the past twenty-five years, and whose vision has made this dictionary-handbook possible. It is appropriate that in the opening pages, George Shorney, Jr. has given an account of the family's publishing activities that link them historically to such famous persons as E. O. Excell, C. H. Gabriel, Fanny J. Crosby, Ira D. Sankey, James McGranahan, Philip P. Bliss, Hubert P. Main and William B. Bradbury.

Of course, a book like this is not written simply to add to the material of hymnology. A hymn is a living bit of poetry with music; it accomplishes the purpose of its writers only if it is an instrument of the church—an effective declaration of God's truth or a meaningful response to that truth. A hymnal handbook achieves its best destiny when it is used by ministers and church musicians to help make this happen. It is for them and their ministry that this book is presented.

Donald P. Hustad, Senior Editor
Hope Publishing Company

February 1, 1977

THE HISTORY OF
HOPE PUBLISHING COMPANY
and Its Divisions and Affiliates

THE BIGLOW & MAIN COMPANY

Although the Hope Publishing Company of Chicago was established in 1892, the company's historical roots can be traced back to 1861. By virtue of the 1922 acquisition of the Biglow & Main Company of New York, Hope became the successor to one of the most important and prestigious 19th century publishers of sacred music in America.

It all began in 1833 when William Batchelder Bradbury (1816–1868), grandson of John Bradbury, one of the signers of the Declaration of Independence, began his studies at the Boston Academy of Music. The Academy was founded and directed by Lowell Mason (1792–1872), acknowledged father of church music and music education in America, and his English immigrant collaborator, George James Webb (1803–1887). Mason exerted a tremendous influence over young Bradbury, who became his protégé and close personal friend. Mason was not only a teacher, but a pioneer publisher through his own firm, Mason Brothers, New York. He personally edited or helped compile over 80 songbook collections and composed over one thousand hymn tunes. An undated manuscript signed by Lowell Mason and evidently given to Bradbury is today on display at the Hope Publishing Company's offices in Carol Stream, Illinois.

William Bradbury was fascinated by all aspects of music. He paid no heed to his friends who counseled that "becoming a professional musician would lead to a shiftless and unrewarding life style." In 1840 he took a job as organist in the First Baptist Church of Brooklyn and in 1841 became music director at the Baptist Tabernacle in New York City where he established singing classes patterned after Mason's Boston Academy. In that same year, Charles Walden Sanders of reader-and-spelling-book fame suggested to Bradbury that they collaborate in publishing a "juvenile music book." The result was Bradbury's first publication, *The Young Choir*, for which he wrote all the music. A second volume appeared in 1843 entitled *School Singer, or Young Choir's Companion*. These books were published by Dayton and Saxton of New York. In 1844 William Bradbury and Thomas Hastings (1784–1872) published the first of four volumes which they compiled together. Entitled *The Psalmodist*, it was the young musician's first commercial success.

Bradbury's parents came from humble circumstances, but in his first seven years as a composer, editor and compiler, he was able to set aside enough money to take his wife and children on a two-year European tour.

1

This included visits to London, Ghent, Antwerp, Brussels, Bruges and Cologne. The enterprising young man and his family spent almost a year in Leipzig, "the land of song." Bradbury's son recalled that in Leipzig they were quartered just three doors away from the illustrious but gravely-ill Felix Mendelssohn (1809–1847). He remembered watching the police spread sawdust on the cobblestones in front of the home (the week before the maestro died) to deaden the sound of the wooden carts lumbering down the street.

The piano Bradbury rented for his private use in Leipzig had belonged to Mendelssohn. Astute enough to recognize its increased value, Bradbury purchased the piano and shipped it back to his New York studio when he returned in 1849.

In Berne and Zurich, he attended many music festivals and concerts and met Franz Liszt, Hector Berlioz and Clara and Robert Schumann. Near the end of his stay, Bradbury returned to Leipzig where he studied harmony with Professor Moritz Hauptmann.

Back in this country and still exuberant from his travels, Bradbury and Hastings issued a new collection called, not surprisingly, *The Mendelssohn Collection*. He also began to travel throughout America conducting "Musical Conventions for singers and those interested in music." In 1850 Bradbury accepted the position of choir director at the Broadway Tabernacle in New York City and continued his editing and composing. In 1854 with his brother, Edward G. Bradbury, he acquired an interest in a piano manufacturing firm, which was later known as "Lighte & Bradbury." That firm was dissolved in the early 1860's in favor of the "Bradbury Piano Company." Around the turn of the century the business was acquired by the Knabe Piano Company, and today the Bradbury piano is still available and manufactured by the Aeolian Corporation of Memphis, Tennessee.

Most of Bradbury's compositions and collections were planned for youth and intended to be used in Sunday Schools. His *Oriola*, released in 1859, laid the foundation and established the pattern for later publishing successes. In this same year, Bradbury and his assistant, Sylvester Main, edited and published their first congregational hymn and tune book, *Cottage Melodies*, which was later taken over by Biglow & Main. This hymnal contained 320 standard hymn tunes with two or three appropriate texts for each tune.

By 1861 Bradbury had extricated himself from the day-to-day operation of the piano business which was now handled by his brother. Having achieved fame and fortune as an editor, compiler and composer, he decided to go into the publishing business himself. It was in this year that he founded the William B. Bradbury Company, New York. The company's first songbook was entitled *The Golden Chain,* which was the beginning of a series of very successful books. Within the next seven years, eleven collections appeared including *Golden Shower* (1862), *Golden Censer* (1864), *New Golden Chain* (1866) and *New Golden Shower* (1866). The eleven books alone sold over three million copies; *Fresh Laurels* (1867) and *New Golden Censer* (1870) reputedly sold over one million each. All of these books were pocket size (5"x6") with 130 to 160 pages and a retail price of 25¢ each.

2

Bradbury's most famous tune is the familiar setting to "Jesus Loves Me" which first appeared in the *Golden Shower*. The tune "Woodworth," commonly used with "Just As I Am," first appeared in *The Mendelssohn Collection* and the tune "Bradbury," composed for "Savior, Like a Shepherd Lead Us," was published in *Oriola*. "Olive's Brow" first appeared in *The Shawm* (1853) and "He Leadeth Me" in *The Golden Censer*. Other favorites include "Aletta" (1858), "Sweet Hour" (1861), "The Sweetest Name" (1861), "Even Me" (1862) and "Solid Rock" (1863). Though all of these tunes were written more than one hundred years ago and most of them were intended as songs for children, they are still favorites in most American churches. In his 1973 dissertation on the life and works of William B. Bradbury (written at Southern Baptist Theological Seminary, Louisville, Kentucky), Alan B. Wingard says:

> "As a composer his (Bradbury's) success rested on the simplicity and sweetness of his songs and their adaptability to the popular demands of Sunday Schools . . . These songs were concerned mainly with a love for the Sunday School, a love for Christ, and an anticipation of heaven. They were in the spirit and language of the people."

Beginning in the 1850's, Bradbury's offices were located in the Ponton Hotel at 425 Broome Street (corner of Crosby, one block east of Broadway) in New York City. He also used 421 and 427 Broome Street, and this location served as a showroom and warehouse for the popular Bradbury pianos. During the 1860's, the Broome Street editorial offices were a meeting place for many of the celebrated authors and composers of that time. It was here, in 1864, that Bradbury challenged the successful, blind-from-infancy, 44-year-old musician and poet, Fanny Jane Crosby (1820–1915), to write her first hymn poem. It was entitled "Our Bright Home Above" ("We are going, we are going, To a home beyond the skies, Where the fields are robed in beauty, And the sunlight never dies"). Set to music by Bradbury, this hymn appeared in *The Golden Censer*. Bradbury was delighted with Fanny's first effort and, recognizing her potential value to his publishing company, promised, "While I have a publishing house you will always have work." Fanny Crosby thus became part of the "trio" which included Josephine Pollard and Mary Ann Kidder and produced the bulk of the poems which the company's composers set to music. As a rule, they received $2.00 for each poem which then became the property of the company.

In 1866, just a year after the Civil War cannons were silenced, Bradbury became gravely ill. Recognizing the necessity of putting his house in order, he turned to his trusted assistant, Sylvester ("Vet") Main (1819–1873), whose son, Hubert, had recently entered the business. In order to obtain the financing necessary to take over the publishing enterprise, Main became associated with Lucius Horatio Biglow (1833–ca. 1910), a wealthy young merchant.

The Biglow & Main Company was thus formed in 1867 as "successors to William Bradbury" and was so identified on its letterhead and its publications for the next twenty years. With L. H. Biglow and Sylvester Main as the managing partners, the ailing Bradbury was named Music Editor. He served in that capacity until January, 1868 when he died of "consumption brought on by overwork." At his funeral held in the Presbyterian Church in Montclair, New Jersey, Fanny Crosby's first hymn, "Our Bright Home Above," (with Bradbury's music) was victoriously, if tearfully, sung. Bradbury's relationship with America's best-known gospel song writer was to be continued by his successors, the Biglow & Main Company, for the next half century.

Earliest Biglow & Main publications carry the addresses of 76 East 9th Street (at Madison Avenue), New York, and 145 State Street, Chicago. In 1869 the Chicago address changed to 81 Randolph Street. By 1906 the New York office had moved to 135 Fifth Avenue (corner of 20th Street) and the Chicago address was merely listed as Lakeside Building (corner Clark and Adams).

L. H. Biglow, the company's president, was always simply referred to as "Biglow" and his interests were in the operating rather than the editorial end of the business. Little else is known about this man whose firm bears his name. Sylvester Main, Biglow's original partner, was musically inclined and established close personal relations with the great hymn writers of the day. A prominent member of the Norfolk Street Methodist Church, he was also much in demand as a soloist in the churches of New York City.

Sylvester Main's greatest legacy to the publishing company was his son, Hubert Platt Main (1839–1925). It was the younger Main's editorial acumen that guided the company through its golden years. A first-rank composer in his own right, he was the most enterprising and resourceful of the gospel song publishers of his day. His knowledge of contemporary American hymns and hymn writers was comprehensive, and after his death, the extensive and valuable Hubert P. Main collection of music and books was donated to the Newberry Library in Chicago. His work in publishing had begun with Bradbury during the Civil War and extended well into the twentieth century.

Writing under several versions of her own name and almost two hundred pseudonyms, Fanny Crosby supplied the lyrics of one-third to one-half of the contents of many of Biglow & Main's publications. In all, she wrote almost six thousand poems for Bradbury and Biglow & Main, the most famous of which were "Rescue the Perishing," "Safe in the Arms of Jesus," "Some Day the Silver Cord Will Break," "Pass Me Not, O Gentle Savior," "More Like Jesus Would I Be," "Blessed Assurance, Jesus Is Mine," "To God Be the Glory," "I Am Thine, O Lord," "Jesus, Keep Me Near the Cross," "All the Way My Savior Leads Me," "Praise Him! Praise Him," "Redeemed, How I Love to Proclaim It," "A Wonderful Savior Is Jesus My Lord" and "When My Life Work Is Ended."

Although competitors were numerous during the fifty years that Hubert P. Main was active, he knew and published the works of most all of that era's gospel hymn composers. These included George F. Root (1820–1895), Adoniram J. Gordon (1836–1895), Anna Bartlett Warner (1820–1915), Philip P. Bliss (1838–1876), Daniel W. Whittle (1840–1901), Phoebe Palmer Knapp (1839–1908), William F. Sherwin (1826–1888), Chester G. Allen

4

(1838–1878), Annie Sherwood Hawks (1835–1918), Elizabeth Payson Prentiss (1818–1878), Lydia Baxter (1809–1874), William J. Kirkpatrick (1838–1921) and John R. Sweney (1837–1899). In 1880, Kirkpatrick and Sweney went into business for themselves, publishing some fifty songbooks with the John J. Hood Company of Philadelphia. These publications also included major contributions from the pen of Fanny Crosby.

"Hugh" Main also maintained invaluable editorial relationships with James McGranahan (1840–1907) and Robert Lowry (1826–1899). Lowry was a spellbinding Baptist preacher whose first love was music and he succeeded Bradbury as music editor of Biglow & Main in 1868. The undisputed leader of these hymnists was Ira David Sankey (1840–1908), songleader and soloist with evangelist Dwight Lyman Moody (1837–1899). Sankey returned from his first trip to England in 1875 to combine his 16-page Moody-Sankey songbook (*Sacred Songs and Solos*) with Philip Bliss' and Daniel W. Whittle's *Gospel Songs*. The result was a collection entitled *Gospel Hymns and Sacred Songs* published jointly by Biglow & Main and the John Church Company, Cincinnati, Ohio. This was the first of six successful volumes (later combined in *Gospel Hymns 1–6 Complete*), all published before the turn of the century. Bernard Ruffin, in his fascinating book, *Fanny Crosby* (United Church Press, 1976), says that "Biglow & Main of New York and the John Church Company of Cincinnati were among the nation's largest publishers of hymns and from the late 1860's Fanny (Crosby) completely dominated the hymnals published by the New York firm." It was in 1876 that Moody and Sankey first met Fanny Crosby and from then on she became one of their chief resources for new material for their songbooks. When L. H. Biglow retired in 1895, Hubert Main persuaded Ira D. Sankey to become president of the firm, a position he held until his death in 1908.

George Coles Stebbins (1846–1945), for many years one of Dwight L. Moody's associates, was also one of Biglow & Main's co-editors, as was the many-talented industrialist-banker, William Howard Doane (1832–1915). A devout Baptist, Doane became Fanny Crosby's most frequent and most successful collaborator. In the forty-seven years that they worked together, Doane set over one thousand of her lyrics to music.

Each Christmas, it was Fanny's practice to send a verse to her friends at the "store" (Biglow & Main). Only one of these still survives and, although undated, it was probably written around the turn of the century. The "honored president" in the poem refers, no doubt, to Ira D. Sankey and "brother Hugh" to Hubert P. Main; "Louie Glatz and dear Miss Dyer" must have been faithful employees. The use of the word "patrons" in the Victorian sense is totally consistent with Fanny Crosby's understanding of her relationship with her publisher.

> Honored president, I hail thee,
> And my loyal brother Hugh,
> Round my heart you both are clinging,
> With affection firm and true.
> Louie Glatz and dear Miss Dyer,
> Happy greetings one and all,

While I sing my yearly carol,
And your treasured names recall.

Lo, again a mighty chorus
Wakes the earth and fills the sky,
Peace, good will to every nation,
Glory be to God on high.
And we look, by faith directed,
To the pure transcendent morn,
When in Bethlehem of Juda
Our Redeemer Christ was born.

Merry Christmas, Merry Christmas,
All my friends and patrons dear!
May our Father's richest blessing
Rest upon the coming year;
And at last beyond the river
May we join the ransomed throng,
In the bright, the bright forever,
In the summer land of song.

Affectionately dedicated to my friends at the store

With love
Fanny J. Crosby

Ira Sankey's son, I. Allan Sankey (1874–1915), joined the firm in the late 1890's and succeeded his father as president in 1908. The Sankey heirs ran the firm for the next fourteen years. However, they were unable to exert or obtain the kind of editorial and managerial expertise needed to provide the continuity necessary for economic survival in the twentieth century.

In 1922 the assets of Biglow & Main were purchased by Hope Publishing Company, who continued to distribute the Biglow & Main publications still in print. The "assets" included more than 1000 unpublished poems of Fanny Crosby, of which Hope released 120 in 1977 in a new book of hymn poems entitled, *Fanny Crosby Speaks Again.*

Sixty years after her death, Fanny Jane Crosby was posthumously inducted into the Gospel Music Hall of Fame at the Dove Awards program held in Nashville at the Grand Ole Opry House, October 29, 1975. There being no surviving family, the award was accepted on her behalf by George H. Shorney, Jr., president of Hope Publishing Company.

An important publication released by Hope Publishing Company through its Biglow & Main affiliate was the *Inter-Church Hymnal* (1930). A 512-page worship hymnal edited by Dr. Frank Morgan, it was intended for use in the newly-emerging "community churches." The book had a forty-year life and was the fore-runner of the publications of the Agape division of Hope.

In 1933 the Biglow & Main Company was merged with the E. O. Excell properties which had been purchased by the Hope Publishing Company in 1931. The major publications of Biglow & Main and their compilers include the following:

Alleluia, The (1880) M. W. Stryker and H. P. Main
Bradbury Trio, The (1870) William B. Bradbury (Includes *New Golden Chain, New Golden Shower* and *New Golden Censer*)

Bright Jewels (1860) Robert Lowry

Brightest and Best (1875) Robert Lowry and W. H. Doane

Chapel Hymnal, The (1882) Sigismond Lasar

Christian Praise (1920) M. W. Stryker

Church Hymns and Gospel Songs (1898) Ira D. Sankey, James McGranahan and George C. Stebbins

Church Praise Book, The (1881) M. W. Stryker and H. P. Main

Church Song (1890)

Evangeliums Lieder 1 & 2 (1897) Walter Rauschenbusch and Ira D. Sankey

Gospel Hymns and Sacred Songs (1875) Ira D. Sankey and P. P. Bliss

Gospel Hymns No. 2 (1876)

Gospel Hymns No. 3 (1878)

Gospel Hymns No. 4 (1883)

Gospel Hymns No. 5 (1887)

Gospel Hymns No. 6 (1891)

Gospel Hymns 1–6 Complete (1895)

Hallowed Hymns New and Old (1907) I. Allan Sankey

Inter-Church Hymnal, The (1930) Frank A. Morgan

Mission Hymnal (1910)

New Golden Censer (1870) William B. Bradbury

Northfield Hymnal (1904) George C. Stebbins

Sacred Songs and Solos (1881) Ira D. Sankey

Sacred Songs Nos. 1 & 2 (1899) Ira D. Sankey, James McGranahan and George C. Stebbins

Select Songs (1885) F. N. Peloubet

Selected Gospel Hymns (1920) compiled from the contents of *Gospel Hymns 1–6 Complete*

Standard Hymns and Spiritual Songs (1917) H. P. Main and I. Allan Sankey

Winnowed Songs (1890) Ira D. Sankey

Young People's Songs of Praise (1902) Ira D. Sankey

THE E. O. EXCELL COMPANY

Edwin Othello Excell (1851–1921) was the son of the Reverend J. J. Excell, a minister of the German Reformed Church. Born and raised in Chicago, young Excell was a big and powerful man with a passion for music. He had a tenor voice of rare beauty and marvelous range. By his twentieth birthday, he was teaching voice in country singing schools, and was soon serving as songleader for many evangelists. For twenty years, he was associated with Sam Jones and near the end of his career he worked with Gipsy Smith.

In 1878 E. O. Excell began publishing songbooks and his company was located in The Lakeside Building in Chicago's Loop, where Biglow & Main later had offices. In 1911 he moved to 410 South Michigan Avenue. Excell was a craftsman who insisted on a quality product. He soon had the largest, most extensive collection of engraved music plates in the country, as well as a valuable copyright library. With these resources, he developed a very lucrative business by offering the services of his firm on a contract basis. He could provide editorial assistance, beautiful engraved metal plates of thousands of hymns, access to copyrighted material (both his and others, through exchange agreements), as well as printing and binding when needed.

Although Excell published a limited number of titles under his own name, he became the largest publisher's agent in the country, supplying many denominations with all of their songbook and hymnal needs. This kind of phantom publishing relieved him of the problems and attendant costs of advertising, distribution and sales promotion. He could deliver 50,000 songbooks to the Southern Methodists in Nashville, and return to Chicago the next day with the bill paid in full. In 1915 Excell entered into an editorial relationship with the Hope Publishing Company. That was negotiated by Hope's president, George Henry Shorney, and provided major hymnals in each of the next four years. *Joy to the World* and *Eternal Praise* produced during those years replaced the earlier *Pentecostal Hymns* series as Hope's leading publications. Other independent companies such as Robert Coleman in Dallas and John T. Benson in Nashville also made extensive use of Excell's editorial services.

On June 10, 1921, E. O. Excell died after a long illness. His wife and two sons ran the business for the next ten years but with disappointing results. In 1931 Hope Publishing Company purchased the Excell properties and in 1933 merged this newly acquired company with its Biglow & Main affiliate. The new division became the Biglow-Main-Excell Company which was maintained as a separate, wholly-owned corporation. Through the ensuing years, a number of Hope and Tabernacle publications were also released under the Biglow-Main-Excell name.

In 1968 installation of a modernized accounting system necessitated the consolidation of Biglow-Main-Excell, Tabernacle Publishing and Hope Publishing into a single corporation. Regrettably, the Biglow-Main-Excell Company did not survive this merger as a viable entity and its remaining publications were phased out during the next few years.

The major independent publications of E. O. Excell (and their compilers) include the following:

American Church and Church School Hymnal (1927) W.E.M. Hackleman
American Junior Church School Hymnal (1929) Edward R. Bartlett and Dean McCutchan
Coronation Hymns (1910) E. O. Excell
Excell Hymnal, The (1925) Hamp Sewell, W.E.M. Hackleman and E. O. Excell
Excell's School Songs Nos. 1 & 2 (1892)
Inspiring Hymns (1914) E. O. Excell
International Praise (1902) E. O. Excell
Make Christ King (1912) E. O. Excell and William E. Biederwolf
Praiseworthy (1916) E. O. Excell
Triumphant Songs Nos. 1 & 2 (1889) E. O. Excell
Triumphant Songs No. 2 (1889) E. O. Excell
Triumphant Songs No. 3 (1892)
Triumphant Songs No. 4 (1894)
Triumphant Songs Nos. 3 & 4 (1894)

Triumphant Songs No. 5 (1896)
Wonderful Jesus and Other Songs (1927) Gipsy Smith and E. Edwin Young

TABERNACLE PUBLISHING COMPANY

In 1916 A. M. Johnson, a wealthy Chicago insurance executive, financed the publishing of a 128-page gospel song and chorus choir book entitled *Tabernacle Praises*. The book was an extension of the ministry of Paul Rader, pastor of The Moody Tabernacle (now known as The Moody Church), his music director, Arthur McKee, and their talented music assistants, Richard J. Oliver and Lance B. Latham. Shortly thereafter, a second publication, *Tabernacle Hymns* (256 pages), was released. It was edited by McKee and Daniel B. Towner, then Director of the Moody Bible Institute Music Department. The success of these songbooks led to the establishment of the publishing company. Since Johnson's motives were entirely philanthropic, the enterprise was organized as a not-for-profit corporation. Located at 29 South LaSalle Street, Johnson obtained the services of Arthur W. McKee as president, Kenneth Mullins as secretary and Victor B. Cory* as manager.

In 1920 after the death of Charles M. Alexander, a Moody-educated songleader who worked worldwide with Evangelists R. A. Torrey and J. Wilbur Chapman, the Tabernacle Company acquired control of the American rights on Alexander's large copyright library. This provided the bulk of the contents for their new publication, *Tabernacle Hymns Number Two* (1921). Additional titles to follow included *Greatest Hymns, Tabernacle Choir, Living Gospel Songs and Choruses, Special Revival Hymns* and *Standard Songs of Evangelism,* plus the imported editions of some of Alexander's Conference Hymnals used in the Chapman-Alexander campaigns in England and Australia.

In 1921 Rader resigned from The Moody Tabernacle and founded The Chicago Gospel Tabernacle three miles north near Lake Michigan. No doubt this contributed to the unsettled state of affairs of the Tabernacle Publishing Company, which, despite salable products, a strong bargaining position in the industry (copyrights), a tax free shelter, plus the booming prosperity of the 1920's, was forced to close its doors. In 1926 Mr. Johnson sold his publishing interests to his Chicago neighbors, the Hope Publishing Company. Up to that time, the Tabernacle Company had released the following volumes, listed here with their editors:

Alexander's Conference Hymnal (1919) Charles M. Alexander
Greatest Hymns, The (1924) George C. Stebbins and R. A. Torrey
Hymns from the Heart (1926) Mr. and Mrs. James H. Larson
Living Gospel Songs and Choruses (1925)
Praises in Song (1923) Raymond T. and A. J. Richey
Rader Campaign Carols (1921) Lance Latham and Clarence Jones
Special Revival Hymns (1924) Harry E. Stores, Bob Jones and E. E.
    Young
Standard Songs of Evangelism (1926)
Tabernacle Choir (1922) Richard J. Oliver and Lance B. Latham

*Cory, with his wife, Bernice, founded Scripture Press of Wheaton, Illinois in 1934.

Tabernacle Hymns (1916) D. B. Towner and Arthur W. McKee
Tabernacle Hymns No. 2 (1921)
Tabernacle Praises (1916) Arthur W. McKee

As a part of the acquisition contract, Victor Cory spent the next year at Hope's offices assisting in the transition. He was of invaluable help in sorting out the problems and giving the company new life in its new surroundings. Two years later, in 1929, *Tabernacle Hymns Number Three* was published and in the next decade it outsold the total of all previous publications of the company. This book, which is still in print today, has been one of the company's all-time best sellers.

In the twenty years that followed, song leader Wesley Nehf served as an editor for the company and he and Hope's new president, Gordon D. Shorney, compiled *Tabernacle Hymns Number Four,* which included a number of "arrangements" by Fred Jacky, music director of the famous "Hymns of All Churches" radio broadcasts. Published in 1941, this book was caught in the paper shortage of World War II and was, consequently, never widely distributed until 1946.*

The last in this hymnbook series, *Tabernacle Hymns Number Five* (1953), was edited by Gordon Shorney and Donald P. Hustad, who was then Director of the Sacred Music Department of Moody Bible Institute. With 384 pages, it was slightly larger than its predecessors, but was still considered a secondary book (used in Sunday School or in evening services) rather than a full size hymnal.

Under Hope's editorial direction, Tabernacle also published *Tabernacle Choir Nos. 2, 3 and 4* (1944, 1958 and 1967) and the spiral paperback "pocket songbook," *Let's Sing* (1960).

It was not until 1967 under editors Don Hustad and John F. Wilson that a full size 512-page Tabernacle hymnal, *Favorite Hymns of Praise,* was produced. This book was well received and was the backbone of the company's line of hymnals for the next decade. The Tabernacle hymnbooks have been designed principally for the church where the gospel song is still important musical fare. All of the Tabernacle hymnals have been fully orchestrated and made available in either round or shaped notes.

Hope Publishing Company held the Tabernacle Publishing Company as a separate corporation until 1968 when it was merged into the parent corporation. However, the name "Tabernacle" has a long and respected history, and it continues to be used for certain publications.

HOPE PUBLISHING COMPANY

The roots of the parent company may be traced to a little group of families that for many generations lived in the corner of West Somerset, England. Related by blood or marriage, the Dates, the Shorneys and the Kingsburys lived on farms on the sides of the lovely Quantock Hills. In 1870 after the failure of his small milling business, Henry Stoate Date

*During the depression and through World War II, all the Tabernacle songbooks were made available in paper covers.

emigrated to the United States, arriving in Chicago with no friends and only $19 in his pocket! In a letter to his parents, with whom he had left his wife and five children, he wrote: "I have great cause to thank God and take courage. Seven months ago all seemed dark and no way of escape for me . . . but I am fully satisfied I am in the right place. The country suits me better than England. I refer to the form of government and go-ahead way they have here . . . more chances to strive. I will have my dear wife and children with me before very long."

His words were prophetic and he was soon joined by his family. They settled in Chicago just months before the great fire (1871) that destroyed much of the city, but fortunately they were not in its path. The four sons became successful business men and one of them, Henry Shepherd Date (1858–1915), became the founder of the Hope Publishing Company.

Henry, who was known as "Harry," was a frail man of almost dwarf-like proportions physically, but a giant spiritually. "All of us could not go to college and become silver trumpets," he declared. "Many of us are not even ram's horns, but I am content to be whistling in the service of the Lord." He studied to be a Methodist evangelist and became very active in campground gatherings. He was in demand as a speaker at young people's meetings in DesPlaines, Illinois, and throughout the midwest. As president and organizer of the Young People's Alliance (later called Epworth League), he felt the need of an appropriate gospel song book that could be sold at a popular price, so he decided to publish such a book himself. In 1892 he rented a one-room office (199 Randolph Street) to house his secretary, a portable pump organ and the advance pages (64 pages) of the songbook he was compiling. Not having the funds to complete the larger hymnal, he released the small paperbound songbook, which was advertised as a sample of the soon-to-be-released 224 page *Pentecostal Hymns.*

"I had very limited funds but a great deal of hope," Date later said. "In fact all I had was hope and that is how the company got its name." Things were about to change, however, and soon orders for the little booklet were pouring in from all over the country. The following year, the complete book was held up on purpose because of the fear that its publication would interfere with the highly profitable business generated by the sale of the "Advance Pages."

When *Pentecostal Hymns* was finally released in 1893, three things had been achieved. First, its wide advance publicity assured its success. Second, capital had been provided to publish and promote the book. Third, the Hope Publishing Company was on its way to become one of the foremost independent inter-denominational publishers of church music in the twentieth century.

In 1893 Hope's founder and first president moved the company to larger quarters at 56 Fifth Avenue along Chicago's lakefront. Date very early decided to concentrate on music publishing and to avoid investing in engraving, printing or binding equipment. The company has observed that policy to this day.

With the business growing faster than he could manage it, "Harry" turned for help to an English cousin, George Henry Shorney (1864–1919), who had come to America in 1884. A deacon in the Windsor Park Baptist

Church, Shorney had been profoundly influenced by the ministry of Ira Sankey, Dwight L. Moody's song leader. At the time, George was employed in the wholesale division of Marshall Field and Company but he would frequently drop in to lend Date a helping hand during his noon hour. As business continued to grow, George resigned his position at Field's and became manager of the Hope Publishing Company in 1894. Two years later, another boyhood friend from Somerset, Francis G. Kingsbury, was employed as errand boy, his chief occupation being to push a two-wheeled cart loaded with mail through the heavy traffic to the post office. Like Date, Kingsbury was a Methodist. In the same year, the company moved again to 167 Wabash Avenue.

By 1898 a second volume in the *Pentecostal Hymns* series was released and the company address changed again, to 84 Wabash Avenue. In 1899 *Pentecostal Hymns 1 & 2 Combined* (412 pages) was published; this was the company's first hardbound hymnal to become a best seller. It was carried in the catalog for the next thirty-three years. *Winnowed Anthems Nos. 1 & 2 Combined* (224 pages) was a hardbound choral collection compiled by M. L. McPhail in 1899 and this title was a part of the Hope catalog until 1962, when it was finally allowed to go out of print.

These early successes paved the way for another move (in 1901) to larger quarters at 228 Wabash Avenue. In 1902 the company was incorporated in the state of Illinois with Henry Date as president, George H. Shorney as treasurer and general manager, and Francis G. Kingsbury as secretary. In 1909, the officers, all of whom were living in the western suburbs, decided to move their company away from the noise and confusion of the loop, then called "Smoke City," and bought a half a block of property fronting on West Lake Street in Austin. On this site facing the "L" tracks, they built a three-story brick building which adequately provided for the needs of the company for the next sixty-three years.

It was during these years just after the turn of the century that George Shorney was invited to Bridgeport, Connecticut, to meet Fanny Crosby. Knowing of his eldest son Herbert's interest in trains, he took him along on the overnight journey. This meeting with that saintly woman made a profound impression on the young lad, who twenty years later would join his father's firm and was eventually to become Hope Publishing Company's fifth president.

By 1913 the payroll had grown to include 35 people and favorable copyright arrangements had been negotiated which permitted three major hymnals to be released during the next four years. Two years later, Hope acquired the Will L. Thompson Music Publishing Company of East Liverpool, Ohio. In that same year, Henry Date, founder and president, died. Just four years later, in 1919, George H. Shorney, who succeeded Date as president of the firm, succumbed to pneumonia at the age of fifty-four. "Frank" Kingsbury, the new Hope president, was left with a thriving business but a dearth of executive personnel. In 1920 he persuaded George Shorney's son, Gordon Dudderidge Shorney (1899–1964), to come into the business. At the time, Gordon was studying to become an engineer. He was a big man with a big heart and had just won his varsity letter in football as a sophomore tackle at the University of Wisconsin. Of strong Christian commitment, Gordon, like his older brother, Herbert, was a lifetime member of the First Baptist Church in Oak Park, the community in which they both lived.

Gordon Shorney shared his father's interest in all the church's activity, including its music. In a 1922 letter to Ira Sankey's widow, he recalled his mother, Elva, telling him that, as a youngster she stood in line for several hours in the rain in Plymouth, England, just to hear the world-renowned American evangelistic team of Dwight L. Moody and Ira D. Sankey. She was not disappointed.

However, 1922 was a year of mixed blessings for Hope. On one hot summer evening, several members of the shipping room stayed after hours for an unauthorized hand of poker. Evidently a cigarette was not properly extinguished and soon after midnight a good portion of the building had been gutted by fire. This set-back was only temporary, however, and the company was soon back in business. In this same year, Frank Kingsbury negotiated the purchase of the valuable George C. Stebbins copyrights. Months later, he signed the papers acquiring the Biglow & Main Company. In 1923 he also obtained an assignment of the William J. Kirkpatrick songs. These agreements assured Hope of a strong copyright position for many years to come, and put the company in a position of internal strength.

Management recognized the need to focus its attention on some common industry problems. At the invitation of Frank Kingsbury, Hope's president, representatives of ten independent publishers met at the Greenbrier Hotel, White Sulphur Springs, West Virginia, on November 5, 1925. The outcome of that meeting was the founding of the group which is today known as the Church Music Publishers Association. In the early days, membership was limited to non-denominational publishers who had unique and common problems in the handling of their hymn and gospel song copyrights. The group met annually through the years and developed strong personal relationships between friendly competitors. Today the association represents virtually all of the major publishers of American church music and has provided a representative forum for their industry-wide problems and concerns.

The year 1926 was an important milestone at Hope for several reasons. As mentioned earlier, the Tabernacle Publishing Company was acquired that year. Frank Kingsbury, who had just reached his fiftieth birthday and had lost both of his partners in their mid-fifties, decided to retire. Kingsbury's final legacy to the company was the release of *Hymns of Praise Nos. 1 and 2 Combined* (1926) which he personally compiled. This 464-page hymnal utilized for the first time within the covers of one book the newly-acquired songs of Robert Lowry, Robert Harkness, Haldor Lillenas, Henry Barraclough, Mrs. C. H. Morris, Will L. Thompson, Daniel B. Towner, James McGranahan, P. P. Bliss, Ira D. Sankey, Fanny Crosby, as well as the songs of Charles H. Gabriel, George Stebbins, M. L. McPhail, James Black and William Kirkpatrick, already under Hope's control. The fact that this book is still in print fifty years later attests to its widespread popularity.

Frank Kingsbury's retirement in 1926 gave the Shorney family an opportunity to purchase his interest and to obtain majority control of the company's stock. Gordon Shorney succeeded Kingsbury as president, a position he was to hold for the next thirty-eight years. Gordon's brother, George Herbert Shorney (1895–1976), who was known as "Herb," was persuaded to leave a position with the Ryerson Steel Company to join Gordon in guiding the destiny of the Hope Publishing Company. Gordon handled the editorial affairs, and Herbert the manufacturing and operating end of the business. A team of able administrators, their steadying influence guided the company through the difficult depression years and the equally difficult years of World War II.

In 1931 shortly after the stock market crash, Hope acquired the E. O. Excell Company. No sooner had the sale been consummated than a run on the nation's banks began. In the midst of the panic, Herb Shorney, being concerned about meeting the company's payroll, cancelled a luncheon appointment and went down to the bank to withdraw all of the company's funds. Two hours after his visit, the bank closed its doors permanently. The decade of the thirties was certainly the most difficult in Hope's history. Almost overnight, sales were cut in half as thousands of Americans were fed in soup lines. Stringent cost cutting methods were adopted and many titles in the various catalogs were discontinued.

Unwilling to fold their tents, the Shorney brothers took important steps to expand their publishing horizons. Up to this time, all their hymnals had been planned as the "second hymnbook" in a church—used for Sunday school, evening services or other activities where gospel songs were the significant music. Admittedly, for many churches, it was their only hymnal. As recounted in the "E. O. Excell Company" story, the 512-page *Inter-Church Hymnal* (1930) was released as the first complete worship hymnal by the Biglow-Main-Excell affiliate. For forty years it was used by many community and "united" churches who had no denominational affiliation, and was also found in hospitals, and army base chapels.

In 1935 Hope released its first "fully classified" major hymnal. That publication was entitled *The Service Hymanl* and was intended for use as the sanctuary hymnal in evangelical churches. Containing a large body of historic hymnody as well as many newer gospel songs, it was compiled and edited by Gordon Shorney and William M. Runyan (1870–1957), who was then associated with the Moody Bible Institute. The book is still widely used today. In that same year, the company joined the American Society of Composers, Authors and Publishers (ASCAP) and the company's membership has been with that Society ever since.

William Runyan, the composer of "Faithfulness," the tune for "Great Is Thy Faithfulness," and many other distinguished hymn tunes, assigned all of his songs to Hope in 1943. Runyan, who had served the company as music editor and advisor for twenty-two years, retired in 1949.

In 1950 Gordon Shorney obtained the editorial services of the young and talented Director of Moody's Sacred Music Department, Donald P. Hustad (1918–   ). A versatile musician, who is known both as a performer and an educator, Don compiled or helped edit the following major hymnals:

Tabernacle Hymns Number Five (1953)
Worship and Service Hymnal (1957)
Youth Worship and Sing (1959)

Crusader Hymns (1966)
Favorite Hymns of Praise (1967)
Hymns for the Living Church (1974)

During these years, he also edited and arranged over twenty different organ and choral collections, which became the core of the company's backlist during the sixties and seventies. Although he was primarily an educator, Hustad served for several years as the organist for the Billy Graham Crusades. He is now the V. V. Cooke Professor of Organ at Southern Baptist Theological Seminary, Louisville, Kentucky, and continues his part-time editorial relationship with the company. He is also the author of this dictionary-handbook.

In 1958 the Shorney brothers welcomed the third generation to the business when George H. Shorney, Jr. (1931–   ), the son of G. Herbert Shorney, joined the firm. George worked under his Uncle Gordon's tutelage in product development. Committed to choral music, George developed a catalog of anthems featuring works of many of the best-known contemporary composers of music for the church. They include: Richard Avery, John Ness Beck, Eugene Butler, Emma Lou Diemer, Philip R. Dietterich, Walter Ehret, Sib Ellis, Richard E. Gerig, Hal Hopson, Donald P. Hustad, Charles Kirby, Theron Kirk, Robert Kreutz, Phillip Landgrave, Austin C. Lovelace, Donald S. Marsh, Jane M. Marshall, Vaclav Nelhybel, Kent Newbury, Lloyd Pfautsch, Maxcine Posegate, Robert Powell, Joe Ridenour, Walter Rodby, Joseph Roff, Natalie Sleeth, David Smart, G. Alan Smith, Leonard Van Camp, Robert Wetzler, Elwyn A. Wienandt, David H. Williams, Malcolm Williamson, Shirley Whitecotton, John F. Wilson, Alec Wyton, Carlton R. Young and Gordon Young.

With the death of Gordon Shorney in 1964, G. Herbert Shorney assumed the presidency and his younger son, William Gordon Shorney (1936–   ), came into the business. Bill, who had been employed at the Irving Trust Company in New York, worked with his father in the finance and operating end of the business. Under Bill's direction, the entire operation was modernized, streamlined and computerized. He also restructured Hope's trade policies, providing a new and positive image with music dealers and bookstores across the country.

The Wendell P. Loveless copyrights had been acquired by Hope in 1960. Recognizing the need to better utilize the existing copyright library as well as to develop salable new publications, John F. Wilson (1929–   ) was added to the staff in 1966 as a full-time resident editor. Wilson had been an educator, serving first on the music faculty of the Moody Bible Institute and later as Director of the Music Department at Marion College in Marion, Indiana. A talented and creative composer, he started and directed the Hope record division, and personally composed a string of successful cantatas and musicals for church and school. In 1977 Wilson was promoted to the position of Executive Editor with responsibility for all of the company's publications.

1968 saw the formation of Somerset Press with Walter Rodby (1917–   ) as editor. A nationally recognized music educator and choral conductor, Rodby helped broaden the company's base of operations.

Somerset's goal has been to provide quality publications for music education and, to date, the catalog has specialized in choral music for elementary, junior high and high school levels.

In 1970 management was again reorganized. G. Herbert Shorney became Chairman of the Board and George was named Hope's sixth president. At the same time, Bill was elevated to the position of Vice President.

The following year, the Agape division was formed under Editor Dr. Carlton R. ("Sam") Young (1926–   ). Editor of *The Methodist Hymnal* (1966), Young had also served as the director of music publications for Abingdon Press. Later he was associate professor of church music at Southern Methodist University in Dallas, Texas, and he is presently chairman of the Department of Music, Scarritt College, Nashville, Tennessee. Agape, through this new catalog, offered an alternative to Hope's line by serving the more liturgically oriented church. The distinctive small hymnal, *Ecumenical Praise* (1977), edited by Young, Dr. Austin C. Lovelace (1919–   ), Dr. Erik Routley (1917–   ) and Dr. Alec Wyton (1921–   ), exemplified this focus.

Since 1974, a small number of gospel song arrangements have been released by yet a new division, Faith Publications. None of the present divisions—Tabernacle, Somerset, Agape or Faith—are independent; they are all part of Hope Publishing Company and the names are used simply to give identity to various musical styles.

In 1972 Hope closed its Chicago doors at 5707 West Lake Street and moved thirty miles west to the city of Carol Stream (population 4,500) just north of Wheaton, Illinois. Here the third generation Shorneys designed and built a modern one-story brick and glass office and warehouse.

The company's new publishing program was now in full gear and the options offered by the various divisions helped to expand the business. In 1974 Thomas Blum (1947–   ), a young college student just back from Vietnam, was appointed General Manager of the operating division.

In 1976 at the age of 81, G. Herbert Shorney died. He had been active in the business through the summer of his last year, a total of 51 years. One of his great joys was having his sons join him in the business to which he devoted his life.

Hope's management, the officers of the company, since 1892 have shared several similarities. All were primarily businessmen and not musicians. Most had worked in other industries before joining Hope. All shared a personal commitment, love and concern for the music of the church. Professional composers and editors were retained as needed. Attorneys Frank Sweat and Donald L. Vetter both served as corporation counsel for over 20 years and Vetter is still active in that capacity. Ownership has been limited to those actively involved in the business. The company has been fortunate that such ownership has been passed from generation to generation without acrimony and the very existence of such a family legacy can only be viewed as a blessing beyond all reasonable expectations.

George H. Shorney, Jr.
President, Hope Publishing Company

HOPE PUBLISHING COMPANY EDITORS
(WITH YEARS OF SERVICE)

1894–1912	Elisha A. Hoffman (first music editor)
1896–1920	M. L. McPhail (specialized in choral music)
1900–1912	William J. Kirkpatrick (compiled children's songbooks)
1904–1915	Daniel B. Towner (compiled Sunday School books)
1908–1912	Thoro Harris (compiled organ collections)
1910–1914	Charles H. Gabriel (compiled Sunday School books)
1915–1921	Edwin O. Excell (soloist at George Shorney's funeral)
1922–1932	George C. Stebbins (Patron Saint of gospel music)
1926–1937	Lance B. Latham (first served as Editor for Tabernacle publications)
1927–1949	William M. Runyan (reviewed all manuscripts for over twenty years)
1930–1931	Frank Morgan (compiled *Inter-Church Hymnal*)
1935–1953	Fred Jacky (orchestrator of numerous hymnals)
1938–1960	Wesley Nehf (served as Editor for Tabernacle publications)
1950–	Donald P. Hustad (Senior Editor who has served the company longer than any other editor)
1966–	John F. Wilson (Executive Editor and creative director of the company's new publishing program)
1968–	Walter Rodby (Editor of the Somerset Press division)
1971–	Carlton R. Young (Editor of the Agape division)

HOPE PUBLISHING COMPANY RELEASES (CHRONOLOGICAL)

The following is a list of major publications of the Hope Publishing Company and its subsidiary companies, with their compilers or composers. Most all are hymnals and songbooks, although several representative works in other categories are also listed. Not counting octavos (of which there are presently 750 active titles), sheet music, plays, pageants, orchestration books, etc., the complete list of Hope songbook titles from 1892 through 1977 numbers 290.

Title	Editor or Compiler	Year Published	Out of Print
Pentecostal Hymns (Advance Pages)	Henry Date	1892	1894
Pentecostal Hymns No. 1	Henry Date	1893	1906
Gospel Song Sheaf, The	F. E. Belden	1894	1909
Winnowed Anthems, No. 1	M. L. McPhail	1896	1918
Pentecostal Hymns 1 & 2 Combined	Henry Date	1899	1932
Winnowed Anthems 1 & 2 Combined	M. L. McPhail	1899	1962
Sacred Songs for Little Voices	William Kirkpatrick	1900	1949
Uncle Sam's School Songs 1 & 2 Combined	Langley & Towner	1904	1940
His Last Week	Strong, Barton & Soares	1905	1972
Sunny Songs for Little Folk	Henry Date & George Shorney	1908	1965
Sunday School Voice No. 1	Charles Gabriel	1910	1931
Sacred Songs for Little Voices No. 2	William Kirkpatrick	1912	1945
Joy to the World	E. O. Excell	1915	1932
Eternal Praise	M. Lawrence & E. O. Excell	1917	1935
Hymns and Sacred Songs	G. H. Shorney & E. O. Excell	1918	1932
Songs of Hope	E. O. Excell	1920	1933
Hymns of Praise	F. G. Kingsbury	1922	1935

Title	Author	1925	1948
Hymns of Praise No. 2	F. G. Kingsbury	1925	In Print
Hymns of Praise Nos. 1 & 2 Combined	F. G. Kingsbury	1926	In Print
Tabernacle Hymns No. 3	Gordon Shorney	1929	1969
Inter-Church Hymnal	Frank A. Morgan	1930	In Print
The Service Hymnal	William Runyan & Gordon Shorney	1935	1970
Devotional Hymns	William Runyan & Gordon Shorney	1935	1969
Hymns for Christian Service	Herbert & Gordon Shorney	1936	In Print
Tabernacle Hymns No. 4	Wes Nehf & Gordon Shorney	1941	1971
Songs & Choruses for Fishers of Men	Mary Clarke	1942	In Print
Tabernacle Hymns No. 5	D. P. Hustad & Gordon Shorney	1953	In Print
Worship and Service Hymnal	D. P. Hustad & Gordon Shorney	1957	In Print
Let's Sing	George Shorney	1960	In Print
Ensemble Music for Church and School	Wesley Hanson	1964	In Print
Crusader Hymns	Donald P. Hustad & Cliff Barrows	1966	In Print
A Time to Sing	D. P. Hustad & John Wilson	1967	In Print
Favorite Hymns of Praise	D. P. Hustad & John Wilson	1967	In Print
A New Now	John F. Wilson	1971	In Print
Songbook for Saints & Sinners	Carlton R. Young	1971	In Print
Folk Songs for Weddings	John F. Wilson	1972	In Print
Genesis Songbook, The	Carlton R. Young	1973	In Print
Folk Encounter	John F. Wilson	1973	In Print
Hymns for the Living Church	Donald P. Hustad	1974	In Print
Let George Do It	Marti McCartney & John Wilson	1975	In Print
Dove Songbook, The	John F. Wilson	1975	In Print
Exodus Songbook, The	Carlton R. Young	1976	In Print
I Believe	John F. Wilson	1976	In Print
Ecumenical Praise	Young, Routley, Lovelace, Wyton	1977	In Print
The Small One	Grace Hawthorne & John Wilson	1977	In Print
Festival Hymns and Processionals	Vaclav Nelhybel	1977	In Print
Dictionary-Handbook to Hymns for the Living Church	Donald P. Hustad	1977	In Print

MAJOR COPYRIGHT ACQUISITIONS
OF HOPE PUBLISHING COMPANY

(This is primarily a list of the authors and composers whose works were obtained. The list of selections is only representative.)

Assignments from many other important composers are held in the company's vaults. Because the bulk of their songs are identified with other publishers or because the assignment is not considered a major acquisition, they are not listed above. Some of these include Bentley D. Ackley, George S. Schuler, Hart P. Danks, Margaret Clarkson, Thoro Harris, Oswald J. Smith, David G. Danielson, Paul Hutchens, Leonard Volk, Kenneth H. Wells, Arthur Pankratz, Herman Voss, Geraldine Beryl Alden, Warner R. Cole and Ray Repp.

1897–1906	James M. Black (1859–1938) "When the Roll Is Called Up Yonder"
1902–1916	Elisha A. Hoffman (1839–1929) "I Must Tell Jesus," "Leaning on the Everlasting Arms"
1905–1925	Mrs. C. H. Morris (Lelia N. Morris) (1862–1929) "What If It Were Today," "Let Jesus Come Into Your Heart"
1915	Will L. Thompson (1847–1909) "Jesus Is All the World to Me," "Softly and Tenderly"
1917	Charles H. Gabriel (1856–1932) "O That Will Be Glory for Me"
1922	George C. Stebbins (1846–1945) "Have Thine Own Way, Lord," "Take Time to be Holy"
1922	Fanny J. Crosby (1820–1915) "To God Be the Glory," "Blessed Assurance"
1922	Ira D. Sankey (1840–1908) "Under His Wings," "Faith Is the Victory"
1922	P. P. Bliss (1838–1876) "Hallelujah, What a Savior," "Wonderful Words of Life"
1922	Hubert P. Main (1839–1925) "The Bright Forever," "We Shall Meet Beyond the River"
1922	James McGranahan (1840–1907) "I Will Sing of My Redeemer," "Showers of Blessing"
1922	Robert Lowry (1826–1899) "Shall We Gather at the River," "I Need Thee Every Hour"
1922	William H. Doane (1832–1915) "To God Be the Glory," "Pass Me Not, O Gentle Savior"
1923	William J. Kirkpatrick (1833–1921) "Cradle Song," "Lead Me to Calvary"
1925	Henry P. Morton (–) "The Touch of His Hand on Mine"
1925	Charles Albert Tindley (1851–1933) "Leave It There"
1926	Henry Barraclough (1891–) "Ivory Palaces"
1926	Robert Harkness (1880–1961) "We Will Follow Thee"
1926	Lance Latham (1894–) "Only Jesus"
1926	Charles M. Alexander (1867–1920) Copyright proprietor, not a composer
1926	Daniel B. Towner (1850–1919) "Grace Greater Than Our Sin," "At Calvary"

continued

1926	Haldor Lillenas (1885–1959) "Wonderful Grace of Jesus"
1926	Harry D. Clarke (1888–1957) "Into My Heart," "Believe on the Lord Jesus Christ"
1928	John R. Sweney (1837–1899) "More About Jesus," "Tell Me More"
1931	Edwin O. Excell (1851–1921) "He Died for Me," "Count Your Blessings"
1931	Gipsy (Rodney) Smith (1860–1947) "Songs of Praises"
1931	E. Edwin Young (1895–) "Jesus Revealed in Me," "Not Dreaming"
1931	Elton M. Roth (1891–1951) "In My Heart There Rings a Melody"
1934	W. Stillman Martin (1862–1935) "God Will Take Care of You"
1935	Harry D. Loes (1892–1965) "All Things in Jesus"
1943	William Runyan (1870–1957) "Great Is Thy Faithfulness"
1945	Roger M. Hickman (1888–1968) "Saved, Saved, Saved"
1945	Albert S. Reitz (1879–1966) "Wonderful, Unfailing Friend"
1946	Grant C. Tullar (1869–1950) "Face to Face with Christ My Savior"
1951	Albert Ketchum (1894–) "Why Do I Sing about Jesus"
1960	Wendell P. Loveless (1892–) "Trust in the Lord," "Precious Hiding Place"
1967	Billie Hanks, Jr. (1944–) "Lonely Voices"
1969	Kent Schneider (1946–) "The Church Within Us"
1975	Tedd Smith (1927–) "There's a Quiet Understanding"
1975	Fred Kaan (1929–) "Help Us Accept Each Other"
1975	Malcolm Williamson (1931–) "This Is My Father's World"
1976	Christopher Coelho O.F.M. (1932–) "Divided Our Pathways"

NOTES ON THE HYMNS AND TUNES

1. Holy, holy, holy! Lord God Almighty

This paraphrase of Revelation 4:8–11 was written for Trinity Sunday by Reginald Heber, while he was vicar of Hodnet, Shropshire, England. The hymn first appeared in *Hymns of the Parish Church of Banbury* (third edition, 1826), the year of Heber's death. The next year it was published in his posthumous volume entitled *Hymns, Written and Adapted to the Weekly Service of the Year*.

NICAEA. The tune was written expressly for the hymn by John B. Dykes. It first appeared along with six other tunes by Dykes in *Hymns Ancient and Modern*, 1861. The tune name refers to the Council of Nicaea which convened a.d. 325 and affirmed the doctrine of the Trinity in refutation of the Arian heresy.

2. Almighty Father, strong to save

The Navy Hymn, "Eternal Father, Strong to Save," written in 1860 by William Whiting, has been revised many times—by its first publishers (the compilers of *Hymns Ancient and Modern*, 1861), by the author himself in the Appendix to *Psalms and Hymns for Public Worship*, 1869, and by others. It is a prayer for safety on the high seas.

In the *Missionary Service Book*, 1937, Whiting's first and fourth stanzas were retained, with slight alterations, and a second and third stanza covering travelers by land and air were added by Robert Nelson Spencer. This is the hymn that appears here.

MELITA. The tune was composed by John B. Dykes for the Whiting hymn and first published in the original musical edition of *Hymns Ancient and Modern*, 1861. The name refers to the island (now called Malta) where St. Paul was shipwrecked, as mentioned in the King James version of Acts 28:1.

3. God, our Father, we adore Thee!

This hymn first appeared in America in *Hymns of Grace and Truth,* published by Loizeaux Brothers (New York, 1904), and included only the three stanzas written by George W. Frazer. The third stanza, addressed to the Holy Spirit, was written by Alfred H. Loizeaux in 1952 for the hymn's appearance in *Tabernacle Hymns, No. 5* (Hope Publishing Company, Chicago, 1953). Loizeaux has said that Frazer probably did not include a "prayer to the Holy Spirit" because many of the Plymouth Brethren (a group of which they were both members) saw no scriptural precedent for directing worship to the Holy Spirit. Loizeaux added: "Personally, I do not hold invariably to this rule and thought that the hymn would be more complete with a stanza addressed to the Holy Spirit."

BEECHER. The tune (also called "Zundel") was composed in 1870 by John Zundel, Henry Ward Beecher's organist at the Pilgrim Congregational Church in Brooklyn, New York. It was written for "Love Divine, All Loves Excelling" and published in *Christian Heart Songs, A Collection of Solos, Quartettes and Choruses of All Meters,* 1870.

4. Come, Thou Almighty King

For more than a hundred years the authorship of this hymn, originally titled "an hymn to the Trinity," was attributed to Charles Wesley, an idea that is strongly debated by Armin Haeussler in *The Story of Our Hymns.* It appeared first with George Whitefield's *Collection of Hymns,* ca. 1757. It is now thought that the hymn was an imitation of the English national anthem, "God Save Our Gracious King," and for this reason the author chose to remain anonymous. For many years, these words were sung to the same tune, which we know as "America."

ITALIAN HYMN. The tune appeared for the first time with this text, in *The Collection of Psalm and Hymn Tunes Sung at the Chapel of the Lock Hospital,* 1769. Its name is derived from the nationality of the composer, Felice de Giardini. In the hymnals of Great Britain, the common tune name is "Moscow," presumably for the city in which the composer died.

5. Father of heaven, whose love profound

Soon after 1800 a number of small hymnbooks were published in Staffordshire, England for the use of local churches. The first to leave the press was *A Selection of Psalms and Hymns for Public and Private Use,* Uttoxeter, 1805. The Rev. Edward Cooper, one of several editors, contributed two hymns, including this one. It is based on the litany, consisting of three original stanzas, plus a doxology first added in *Hymns Ancient and Modern,* 1861.

QUEBEC. The tune was named "Whitburn" when it first appeared in J. Grey's *A Hymnal for Use in the English Church,* 1866. It is said that in 1861 the *Penny Post* in London sought a tune for John Keble's "Sun of My Soul" and for a whole year received settings from many readers. The tune regarded as the best was unsigned. Sir Henry Baker finally claimed authorship after it was republished anonymously in Bishop Bickersteth's compilation in 1871. He had composed it in 1854, while still an undergraduate student at Exeter, Oxford.

6. Holy Father, great Creator

This "Hymn to the God of Christians" by Alexander Viets Griswold was first published in his *Prayers Adapted to Various Occasions of Social Worship,* 1835. It has been sung by American Episcopalians and has appeared in their hymnals since 1874.

REGENT SQUARE. The tune was composed by Henry Smart for the English Presbyterian hymnal *Psalms and Hymns for Divine Worship* (London, 1867), which he edited. It was named for the Regent Square Presbyterian Church, known as the "cathedral of Presbyterianism in London."

7. Praise ye the Father!

Elizabeth Charles published two volumes of poems in 1858 and 1859. It is believed that this Trinity hymn appeared in one of them. It has no rhyme, which is unusual for this date of writing.

FLEMMING. The tune was composed in 1811 by Friedrich Flemming as a male-voice setting of part of Horace's ode "Integer Vitae." It has long been a favorite of college glee clubs and other men's groups in the United States, England and Germany. As a hymn tune, it appeared in the 1875 edition of *Congregational Psalmist* and the second series (1876) of the *Bristol Tune Book.*

8. Glory be to God the Father!

This hymn of Horatius Bonar was written specifically for *Psalms and Hymns for Divine Worship,* 1867, a compilation for the English Presbyterian Church. However, it appeared first a year earlier in the writer's own volume, *Hymns of Faith and Hope,* 1866. In some churches the first stanza is sung at times in place of the traditional Doxology.

FREUEN WIR UNS ALLE. Written in the Aeolian mode, this melody was set to Michael Weisse's "Freuen wir uns all in ein'" in *Ein Neu Gesengbüchlen,* 1531, and is attributed to him.

9. Holy God, we praise Thy name

The hymn is a metrical paraphrase of the first line of the Latin "Te Deum" (*ca.* 4th century). It appeared first in German in Maria Theresa's

Katholisches Gesangbuch (Vienna, *ca.* 1774). Four years later it was included in altered form in Ignaz Franz's *Gesangbuch*, and is attributed to him. The English translation by Clarence A. Walworth is dated 1853 in *Evangelical Hymnal*, 1880. However, its first authenticated appearance is in the *Catholic Psalmist* (Dublin, 1858).

GROSSER GOTT, WIR LOBEN DICH. The full history of this tune may be found in Wilhelm Bäumker's *Katholische deutsche Kirchenlied*, Vol. III, pp. 285–87. It first appeared *ca.* 1774 in *Katholisches Gesangbuch*. The present form of the melody was developed by J. G. Schicht in *Allgemeines Choralbuch* (Leipzig, 1819). In another version the tune appears as "Hursley" (see No. 559). The tune name is the first phrase of the German hymn.

10. All glory be to God on high

Based on the *Gloria in Excelsis Deo*, the angels' song recorded in Luke 2:14, this hymn originated in a "Low German" rendering of the text in four stanzas of seven lines by Nikolaus Decius. According to Julian's *Dictionary of Hymnology*, it first appeared in the Rostock *Gesangbuch*, 1525, and later (in "High German") in V. Schumann's *Gesangbuch*, Leipzig, 1539. From the latter, Miss Catherine Winkworth made her translation for the *Chorale Book for England*, 1863.

ALLEIN GOTT IN DER HÖH. The tune name is the first line of the hymn in "High German." The music was probably adapted by Nikolaus Decius from an old Gloria tune of an Easter Mass.

11. A mighty fortress is our God

Once called the "Marseillaise of the Reformation," this chorale is now sung by all Christians the world over. It was first published in Klug's *Geistliche Lieder*, 1529. Martin Luther wrote it, probably at the time of the Diet of Speyer, when the German princes made their formal protest against the attacks on their liberties and hence gained the name "Protestants."

This translation, written by Frederick H. Hedge in 1852, first appeared in W. H. Furness's *Gems of German Verse* (Philadelphia, 1853), and later the same year in *Hymns for the Church of Christ*, edited by Hedge and F. D. Huntington.

EIN' FESTE BURG. The tune (whose name is derived from the first words of the German hymn) was probably developed along with the text. It first appeared in *Kirchen Gesänge* (Nuremberg, 1531) and later in the second edition of Klug's *Gesangbuch*, 1535. It is probably the work of Martin Luther himself, and may have been adapted from an earlier source. The present version is based on the arrangement and harmonization of J. S. Bach.

12. Praise the Lord, His glories show

Henry F. Lyte's paraphrase of Psalm 150 first appeared in his *Spirit of the Psalms*, 1834. The Alleluias were first added to fit the tune "Llanfair" (see No. 27) to which the text is often sung in England.

GWALCHMAI. The tune was composed by Joseph David Jones and published in Stephen's *Llyfr, Tonau ac Emynau*, 1868. Gwalchmai was a Welsh bard who lived in the 12th century.

13. Sing praise to God who reigns above

Johann Jakob Schütz's hymn, "Sei Lob und Ehr dem hochsten Gut," was first published in his *Christliches Gedenckbüchlein*, 1675. Frances E. Cox's translation was printed in *Lyra Eucharistica*, 1864 and in her own *Hymns from the German* the same year.

MIT FREUDEN ZART. "Bohemian Brethren" is another name for this tune, after the Bohemian Brethren's *Kirchengesänge*, 1566, in which it first appears in print. The melody may be much older, from German or French folk sources.

14. Rejoice, ye pure in heart

This processional hymn by Edward H. Plumptre, written for a choir festival in May, 1865 at Peterborough Cathedral, first appeared in eleven stanzas. The same year, Novello published it as a choral piece and it also appeared in the second edition of Plumptre's *Lazarus, and Other Poems*. It also was included in the Appendix to *Hymns Ancient and Modern*, 1868.

MARION. Named for the composer's mother, this tune was written by Arthur H. Messiter in 1883. It was first printed in the *Hymnal with Music as Used in Trinity Church* (New York, 1889), a collection edited by Messiter.

15. Begin, my tongue, some heavenly theme

Isaac Watts' hymn was included in his *Hymns and Spiritual Songs*, Book II, 1707, where it is entitled "The faithfulness of God in His promises," and consists of nine four-line stanzas.

LAND OF REST. The tune is a traditional melody collected and arranged by Annabel Morris Buchanan in her *Folk Hymns of America*, 1938. Mrs. Buchanan states that she first heard it as a child from her grandmother, Sarah Ann (Love) Foster, who sang it to the lines, "O land of rest, for thee I sigh"; it appeared with those words in J. R. Graves' *Little Seraph*, 1873. The tune may well be of Scottish or North of England origin, and was widely sung throughout the Appalachian region. Mrs. Buchanan is of the opinion that the Negro spiritual "Swing Low, Sweet Chariot" may be derived from it.

16. O Splendor of God's glory bright

The original Latin hymn "Splendor paternae gloriae" has been ascribed to St. Ambrose. In its complete form it is a morning hymn to the Holy Trinity and a prayer for help and guidance throughout the day. Its reference to Christ as "Light" was a favorite image in this period of Christian history. The earliest manuscript containing the hymn is *ca.* 890, but it dates much earlier. The English translation is a composite from many sources.

WINCHESTER NEW. The tune was first published in *Musicalisch Handbuch der geistlichen Melodien*, 1690 with the hymn "Wer nur den lieben Gott." It appeared in England in the *Foundery Tune Book* of 1742, probably introduced by John Wesley, and was called "Winchester New" in George Whitefield's *Divine Musical Miscellany*, 1754. This arrangement by William H. Havergal is from *Old Church Psalmody*, 1847.

17. Praise the Lord! ye heavens, adore Him

This is a free version of verses from Psalm 148 in which all the hosts of heaven and earth join in a magnificent chorus of praise to God. The first two anonymous stanzas were first found in a pamphlet appended to copies of the musical edition of *Psalms, Hymns, and Anthems of the Foundling Hospital*, 1796, compiled by Thomas Coram, an English merchant captain and philanthropist. In later life, Coram devoted his time and money to support a children's hospital, in which musical activity was very significant.

The third stanza is the work of Edward Osler, published in 1836 in his journal *Church and King* and in Hall's *Mitre Hymn Book*. It appeared as part of this hymn in the Cooke and Denton *Church Hymnal*, 1853.

AUSTRIAN HYMN. The tune is said to be based on a Croatian melody. Franz Joseph Haydn adapted it for the poet Hauschka's nationalistic hymn "Gott, erhalte Franz, den Kaiser" and it was first performed for the emperor's birthday on February 12, 1797. It is still recognized as a German patriotic song.

18. Praise the Lord who reigns above

Based on Psalm 150, the text first appeared in *A Collection of Psalms and Hymns*, 1743 edition, published by John and Charles Wesley. It was frequently credited to Augustus Toplady during the 19th century, and has not appeared in standard hymnals as often as it deserves.

AMSTERDAM. The source of the tune is J. A. Freylinghausen's *Geist-reiches Gesangbuch* (Halle, 1704) from which John Wesley adapted six tunes. This one appeared in *Foundery Collection*, 1742, the first Methodist hymnal.

19. Ye servants of God, your Master proclaim

The year 1744 was one of great tension, confusion and unrest in England. The Wesleys and their Methodist followers were persecuted, because they were accused of trying to overthrow the throne. This hymn was No. 1 in a collection published that year and entitled *Hymns for Times of Trouble and Persecution*. It was written by Charles Wesley and was based on Psalm 93:1–4 and Rev. 7:11–12.

HANOVER. The tune first appeared in *The Supplement to the New Version of Psalms* by Dr. Brady and Mr. Tate (6th ed., 1708). Although it was early ascribed to Handel, hymnologists now believe that it was written by William Croft. It was named "Hanover" at a time when Handel was assumed to be the composer, and George III (of the house of Hanover) was on the British throne. Handel was court-conductor at Hanover (in Germany) in 1710–11.

20. All people that on earth do dwell

Of all the English psalm versions now in use, this is the oldest. Based on Psalm 100, it was one of 25 paraphrases contributed by William Kethe to the Anglo-Genevan psalters of 1561. Very few changes have been made in the text throughout history; a fifth stanza Doxology—"To Father, Son and Holy Ghost"—is omitted here.

OLD HUNDREDTH. The melody is the best-known and most widely used of all psalm tunes, and is attributed to Louis Bourgeois. In the French Genevan Psalter of 1551 it is set to Psalm 134. In English books, it has always appeared with Psalm 100, beginning with William Kethe's version in *Four Score and Seven Psalms of David*, Geneva, 1561.

21. O worship the King, all glorious above

This hymn version of Psalm 104 is Sir Robert Grant's adaptation of an earlier setting by William Kethe which appeared in *Fourscore and seven Psalmes*, 1561. It was first printed in *Christian Psalmody*, 1833, edited by Edward Bickersteth.

LYONS. The tune was introduced to English congregations through volume two of William Gardiner's *Sacred Melodies* (London, 1815), and in America through Oliver Shaw's *Sacred Melodies* (Providence, 1818). It has been credited to Johann Michael Haydn, though its exact source cannot be identified.

22. Stand up and bless the Lord

Based on Nehemiah 9:5, the hymn was written by James Montgomery for the Red Hill Wesleyan Sunday School Anniversary observed in Sheffield, England on March 15, 1824. The second line originally was "Ye children of His choice." Montgomery gave the hymn wider use by changing it to "Ye people..." when it appeared in his *Christian Psalmist,* 1825.

ST. MICHAEL. The original melody is the tune for Psalm 101 in the French Genevan Psalter, 1551. First known in England as the "Old 134th," it had many variants in later English and Scottish psalters. Largely forgotten in the 17th and 18th centuries, William Crotch revived and adapted the melody for use in his *Psalm Tunes,* 1836, and named it "St. Michael."

23. Come, we that love the Lord

This hymn first appeared in Book Two of Isaac Watts' *Hymns and Spiritual Songs,* 1707 under the heading "Heavenly Joys on Earth." The original text had at least ten stanzas and they were altered to their present form by the 1709 edition.

ST. THOMAS. This is only a fragment of a 16-line tune, "Holborn," in Aaron Williams' *Collection,* 1763, and was no doubt written by him. The present shortened form (sometimes called "Williams") was first used in his *New Universal Psalmodist,* 1770.

24. Let all the world in every corner sing

On his deathbed George Herbert handed a manuscript to his lawyer, Edmond Duncon, requesting that his brother read it and let it be published "if he thought it would be of advantage to any soul—if not, to burn it." *The Temple,* with this "Antiphon" was published the following year (1633), and is Herbert's principal literary work. "Antiphon" indicates the form of the poem, a refrain beginning and ending each stanza. Herbert's poetry was not intended for public worship, but the Wesleys used some forty of the selections in their *Hymns and Sacred Poetry,* 1739.

ALL THE WORLD. Robert Guy McCutchan composed the tune for this text. No doubt he had antiphonal treatment in mind, with the first and last phrases (the "antiphon") sung by the congregation, and the remainder by a soloist or choir. It first appeared in *Methodist Hymnal,* 1935 under McCutchan's pen name, John Porter.

25. Joyful, joyful, we adore Thee

According to the author's son, this text was written in 1907 while Henry van Dyke was visiting Williams College in Massachusetts as a guest preacher. Evidently inspired by the beautiful Berkshire Mountains, he presented the manuscript to the college president (Garfield) one morning at the breakfast table, suggesting that it be sung to Beethoven's "Hymn to Joy." It was included in van Dyke's *Poems,* 3rd ed., 1911, and in *The Hymnal* (Presbyterian) that same year.

HYMN TO JOY. This is an adaptation of the principal theme of the final movement of Beethoven's Ninth Symphony, first performed in Vienna in 1824. The arrangement commonly used as a hymn tune was made by Edward Hodges, and appeared in Tuckerman's *Trinity Collection of Church Music,* 1864. However, it had appeared in other versions and with other texts, at least since 1846.

26. Praise, my soul, the King of heaven

This hymn of praise was published first in author Henry Francis Lyte's *Spirit of the Psalms,* 1834, a collection of over 280 paraphrases of individual psalms. Lyte wrote the hymns for his congregation in the small fishing village of Lower Brixham, Devonshire, where he was curate from 1823 until his death. Slight changes have been made in the text through the years; in this hymnal, the editors have changed "thy" to "your" (st. 1) and "ye" to "you" (st. 4).

LAUDA ANIMA. The tune (whose name is Latin for "Praise, my soul") was composed for this text by John Goss. It was first published in Robert Brown-Borthwick's *Supplemental Hymn and Tune Book,* 3d ed. with new Appendix, 1869.

27. Let the whole creation cry

This hymn originally had ten stanzas and is an imitation of Psalm 148. It was written by Stopford A. Brooke, an Anglican clergyman and was included in *Christian Hymns,* published in 1881 for his congregation.

LLANFAIR. This simple Welsh melody is from an 1817 manuscript book of the Welsh singer Robert Williams, though he may not have written it. The arrangement by John Roberts is from Joseph Parry's *Peroriaeth Hyfryd,* 1837. "Llanfair" is only the first part of the long name of Williams' home locality in Montgomery County, Wales.

28. Come, Thou Fount of every blessing

Robert Robinson wrote the hymn in 1758 for the festival of Whitsunday (Pentecost). The lines reveal a deep gratitude to God for saving him from a life of dissipation, and were written while he was a pastor in Norwich, England. The text was first published in *A Collection of Hymns, Used by the Church of Christ in Angel-Alley, Bishopsgate*, 1759.

The original version contained an allusion to a Biblical reference (I Samuel 7:12) to Mt. Ebenezer, and has often been criticized as "not meaningful to contemporary congregations." At the request of the editors, Miss Margaret Clarkson made the present adaptation for *Hymns for the Living Church;* her words explain the original Biblical allusion.

NETTLETON. "Hallelujah" was the first name of this tune, in John Wyeth's folk hymn collection, *Repository of Sacred Music*, 1813. It has been attributed both to Wyeth and to Asahel Nettleton, a 19th century New England evangelist. It has also been suggested that a friend of Nettleton composed the tune and named it in his honor.

29. Give to our God immortal praise

This is thought to be the best of Isaac Watts' three versions of Psalm 136, and it appeared in his *Psalms of David imitated in the Language of the New Testament*, 1719. The hymn was a favorite in Billy Graham's crusades in Britain, 1954–1967.

WARRINGTON. The melody first appeared in Ralph Harrison's *Sacred Harmony*, 1784 with his name as composer. It was undoubtedly named for the Warrington Academy where the composer studied.

30. Lord of all being, throned afar

This poem, which Oliver Wendell Holmes titled "A Sun-day Hymn," was first published in the *Atlantic Monthly* in December, 1859 at the end of the last essay in the entertaining, stimulating series "The Professor at the Breakfast Table." The date "1848" has traditionally been given for the text, and it may have been written that early.

MENDON. The tune appeared in the Supplement of Samuel Dyer's *Third Edition of Sacred Music*, 1825, and was named "German Air." Lowell Mason changed it to "Mendon" (a town in Worcester County, Mass.) when it appeared in the second edition of *The Choir*, 1833.

31. Praise Him, O praise Him

Mary Lou Reynolds wrote these words at the request of her husband, William J. Reynolds. The three stanzas were written one evening in 1970 and went to the engraver the next morning.

PASCHALL. To provide a new hymn for a pamphlet ("New Hymns for the 70's") he was preparing for Broadman Press, William J. Reynolds first wrote the tune and asked Mrs. Reynolds to provide the text.

The tune is named for Dr. H. Franklin Paschall, pastor of First Baptist Church, Nashville, Tenn. When he first submitted the music, Dr. Reynolds gave it the name "Raymer," and it was so identified in the early printings of the hymnal.

32. How great Thou art

The following account appears in detail in *Crusade Hymn Stories* (Hope Publishing Company, 1967). The original of this hymn was written *ca.* 1885 by Carl Boberg, a Swedish preacher, editor and statesman. It appeared in a German version ("Wie gross bist Du") in Estonia in 1907, and in a Russian translation by Ivan S. Prokhanoff in 1912. S. K. Hine, a British missionary in western Ukraine, made this English translation of the Russian over a period of years and it first appeared in a Russian gospel magazine in 1949. The song was popularized through its use in Billy Graham crusades.

O STORE GUD. This is a Swedish folk melody, to which Boberg's text was first sung, and was first printed in *Sanningsvittnet,* 1891. The name consists of the first words of the original Swedish hymn.

33. My God, how wonderful Thou art

Originally titled "The Eternal Father," these words were first published in Frederick W. Faber's *Jesus and Mary,* 1849, and later in his *Hymns,* 1861 edition.

DUNDEE. Bearing the name "French Tune," this melody was first used in *The One Hundred Fifty Psalms of David,* published by Andro Hart in Edinburgh, 1615. It was one of twelve "common tunes" that could be used with different hymns. The Scottish name "Dundee" was associated with the tune when it appeared in this version in Ravenscroft's *Psalmes,* 1621.

34. God, my King, Thy might confessing

This text by Richard Mant first appeared in his *Book of Psalms, in an English Metrical Version,* 1824. It is based on Psalm 145.

STUTTGART. The tune is believed to be an adaptation of a melody by Christian Friedrich Witt first published in his *Psalmodia Sacra, oder Andächtige und schöne Gesänge* (Gotha, 1715). It was one of 25 different settings for the hymn, "Sollt es gleich bisweilen scheinen," and was eventually the one preferred above all others. The present arrangement by Henry Gauntlett, and the tune name, are from *Hymns Ancient and Modern*, 1861.

35. Immortal, invisible, God only wise

Walter Chalmers Smith's poem was first published in his *Hymns of Christ and the Christian Life* in 1867. It is based on the doxology in I Timothy 1:17. A number of changes were made in the original text when it was included in Garrett Horder's *Congregational Hymns*, 1884.

ST. DENIO. The tune (sometimes called "Joanna") first appeared with a hymn text in John Robert's *Caniadau y Cyssegr*, 1839 and was called "Palestina." It is based on a traditional Welsh ballad "Can Mlynedd i 'nawr" ("A Hundred Years from Now"), which was identified in the *Welsh Folk Song Journal*, Vol. 1, 1911.

36. The God of Abraham praise

This text was written by Thomas Olivers while staying in the home of John Bakewell in Westminster, London in 1770. It was inspired by hearing the "Yigdal" sung in the Great Synagogue, Duke's Place, London. Olivers commented that he had given it a "Christian character" with his reference to the Holy Trinity. It was first published in a leaflet, "A Hymn to the God of Abraham," *ca.* 1770.

LEONI. The tune is one of seven traditional melodies for the "Yigdal." It is named for its transcriber, Meyer Lyon, the cantor of the Great Synagogue who wrote it out for Olivers. Its origin is unknown but it is thought to be related to Spanish and Basque melodies. The Wesleys included both words and music in their *Pocket Hymn Book*, 1785.

37. Great is Thy faithfulness

The text was written by Thomas O. Chisholm in 1923. According to him, there were no special circumstances which caused its writing—just his experience and Bible truth. The hymn first appeared in *Songs of Salvation and Service*, 1923, compiled by William M. Runyan. It is the unofficial "school hymn" of Moody Bible Institute in Chicago, with which Dr. Runyan was associated for a number of years.

FAITHFULNESS. The tune was written by William M. Runyan for these words. The name "Faithfulness" was chosen by him when it appeared in *Baptist Hymnal*, 1956.

38. When all Thy mercies, O my God

These words formed the conclusion of an essay on gratitude by Joseph Addison. The poem was first published in the *Spectator,* August 9, 1712.

BELMONT. *The Historical Companion to Hymns Ancient and Modern* gives three possible antecedents for this melody. Most authorities agree that it is probably from William Gardiner's *Sacred Melodies,* 1812, a collection of tunes to which English hymns have been set.

39. God is love; His mercy brightens

The text first appeared in Sir John Bowring's second collection, *Hymns: as a Sequel to the Matins,* 1825. Originally the first verse was repeated at the end, but this practice ceased with the *Leeds Hymn Book,* 1853.

CROSS OF JESUS. See "Cross of Jesus, cross of sorrow," No. 153.

40. To God be the glory

This text was one of the new gospel songs written by Fanny Crosby and published in the collection, *Brightest and Best,* 1875, compiled by William Doane and Robert Lowry. Other songs in the collection were included in the more-famous *Gospel Hymns* series published by Ira D. Sankey and consequently became widely-known; "To God Be the Glory" was not included, and so was little known in America. Sankey introduced the song in Great Britain during his 1873–74 tour with D. L. Moody, and included it in his *Sacred Songs and Solos,* published in England. It was printed in the *Greater London Crusade Song Book* for the Billy Graham Harringay Crusade in 1954 and introduced in the Nashville, Tennessee crusade the same year. Since then, this long-forgotten American gospel song has become very popular in its homeland.

TO GOD BE THE GLORY. William H. Doane wrote the tune for this text, as he did for many of Fanny Crosby's poems.

41. Children of the heavenly Father

In 1858, while Carolina ("Lina") Sandell (later Berg) was taking a boat trip with her father, he fell overboard and she saw him drown. After she lost her earthly father, she found comfort in writing hymns that express the care of her heavenly Father. That same year, 14 of her hymns were published, including this one. It appeared with this tune in the Swedish-American hymnal, *Sionsharpan,* 1890. The translation of Ernst W. Olson was prepared for *Augustana Hymnal,* 1925.

A devotional study of the text by the author of this handbook appears in *Crusade Hymn Stories*.

TRYGGARE KAN INGEN VARA. It is a European custom to use the first text line as the tune name. *Song Book for Sunday Schools* (Stockholm, 1871) marked the first known appearance of this tune in print. It was long thought to be a Swedish folk melody, but some have suggested it may be of English origin, brought to Sweden in the Pietist movement of the late 19th century.

42. God be with you till we meet again
This text was written by Jeremiah E. Rankin while he was the pastor of the First Congregational Church in Washington, D.C. There was no specific reason for its writing; he simply wanted to interpret the derivation of "good-bye" from "God be with you." It was first published with this tune in *Gospel Bells*, 1880, edited by J. W. Bischoff, Otis F. Presbrey and Rankin.

GOD BE WITH YOU. The tune was written at the request of the author (Jeremiah Rankin) by William G. Tomer, who was then director of music at the Grace Methodist Episcopal Church in Washington, D.C. It has persisted as a favorite, despite criticism that it is "maudlin and repetitious." The traditional refrain has been omitted in several recent hymnals.

43. Praise to the Lord, the Almighty
This text, based on Psalms 103 and 150, is one of about 60 hymns written by Joachim Neander during his short life. Neander is widely regarded as the best poet of the Reformed Church in Germany and this is his best known hymn, published in his *Glaub-und Liebesübung*, 1680. The present translation by Catherine Winkworth appeared in her *Chorale Book for England*, 1863.

LOBE DEN HERREN. The tune ("Praise the Lord") is an adaptation of a melody which appeared in *Stralsund Gesangbuch*, 1665 and is thought to be an old secular air. Neander chose it for his words in their first printing. The present version appeared with Catherine Winkworth's translation and was harmonized by Sterndale Bennett and Otto Goldschmidt.

44. Unto the hills around
The text is a metrical version of Psalm 121, often referred to as the "Traveler's Psalm," and it is dated 1877 in *Church Hymnal for the Christian Year*. It was written by John Douglas Sutherland Campbell, before he became a public figure. *Companion to the Song Book of the Salvation Army* says it

is one of the few versions of Psalm 121 which give the correct rendering of the opening verse of the Psalm, that is, that "the hills themselves are not the source of our help; they symbolize the futility of expecting help from such sources."

SANDON. Written by Charles Henry Purday for the hymn "Lead Kindly Light," this tune appeared in *Church and Home Metrical Psalter and Hymnal,* 1860, which Purday edited. "Sandon" is an old English residence name.

45. The Lord's my Shepherd, I'll not want

This metrical paraphrase of Psalm 23 is taken from the Scottish Psalter of 1650 (*The Psalms of David in Meeter*) which was called the "Prince of Versions" because it contained the best of the psalters in existence at that time. It is still in use and remains the only version officially authorized by the Church of Scotland. The text is said to be a composite of seven extant versions of the psalm, including one by William Whittingham.

CRIMOND. The music first appeared in the *Northern Psalter,* 1872 and is now one of the most popular tunes for these words. The melody has been ascribed to David Grant, but research has determined that it was written by Jessie Seymour Irvine, daughter of a minister in Crimond, a parish in the northeastern part of Aberdeenshire, Scotland. She supposedly gave the tune to Grant for harmonization, and this is how the mix-up occurred. In the *Scottish Psalter,* 1929 the tune was assigned to Miss Irvine, and this has been quite generally accepted.

A full discussion of this text and tune may be found in *The Baptist Hymn Book Companion* (London: Psalms and Hymns Trust, 1967, rev. ed.)

46. The King of love my Shepherd is

This text was written by Henry W. Baker and appeared with this tune in the 1868 Appendix to the first edition of *Hymns Ancient and Modern,* 1861. It will be recognized that it is more a free paraphrase than a strict metrical version of the 23rd Psalm. The third stanza was said to be the last expression of the author, on his deathbed.

DOMINUS REGIT ME. The tune name, which means "The Lord rules me," is the Latin title for Psalm 23. The music was composed by John B. Dykes for this text, and the hymn was sung at the composer's funeral in 1876.

47. God moves in a mysterious way

The text appeared anonymously in John Newton's *Twenty-Six Letters on*

Religious Subjects, 1774 under the subtitle, "Light shining out of Darkness." In *Olney Hymns,* 1779 it was properly credited to William Cowper. It has been described as the finest hymn on God's providence ever written.

DUNDEE. See "My God, how wonderful Thou art," No. 33.

48. O God, our help in ages past

This paraphrase of Psalm 90 appeared in nine stanzas in Watts' *Psalms of David Imitated in the Language of the New Testament,* 1719 under the title "Man frail and God eternal." The original hymn began with "Our" and John Wesley changed this to "O" in his *Psalms and Hymns,* 1738. "Our" is still used frequently.

ST. ANNE. Set to Psalm 42, the tune first appeared anonymously in *A Supplement to the New Version of Psalms by Dr. Brady and Mr. Tate . . . the Sixth Edition, Corrected and Much Enlarged,* 1708. Croft is listed as composer in Philip Hart's *Collection* (London, 1720), and he was organist at St. Anne's Church, Soho, London, for which the tune is named.

49. A pilgrim was I and a-wandering

This gospel song paraphrase of Psalm 23 was written by John W. Peterson and Alfred B. Smith in Montrose, Pa. in 1958. Mr. Peterson tells the story:

> One day while improvising at the piano in my Montrose, Pennsylvania studio, Alfred B. Smith, with whom I was associated at the time, walked in. For no particular reason that I can remember, we started to develop a new song. I would come up with a thought—then Al. In a short time "Surely Goodness and Mercy" was born. I had never worked with another writer in such a manner to compose a song. Later Al and I wrote two or three other numbers like that. That was the last of it.

Alfred B. Smith remembers more about the initial inspiration for the song. He adds a humorous touch:

> It was written after receiving a letter from one of the descendants of P. P. Bliss telling of Bliss's first country school teacher, named Miss Murphy, whom he dearly loved. It told of her teaching the class (before they could read or write) to memorize the 23rd Psalm. When the part "surely goodness and mercy" was reached, little Philip thought it said "Surely good Miss Murphy shall follow me all the days of my life." This little incident focused our thoughts on the phrase which became the heart and title of the song.

SURELY GOODNESS AND MERCY. The tune name is the traditional title of the song. The completed composition was first published in *John Peterson's Folio of Favorites,* 1958. (Singspiration, Grand Rapids, Mich.)

50. Let us, with a gladsome mind

Written in 1623 when author John Milton was only 15 years old, this psalm paraphrase was published in his *Poems in English and Latin,* 1645. It is one of Milton's 19 poetic versions of various psalms, and is based on verses 1, 2, 7 and 23 of Psalm 136.

MONKLAND. John B. Wilkes, organist at Monkland, gave this version of the music to his vicar, Henry W. Baker, editor of *Hymns Ancient and Modern,* 1861. Its source is uncertain. In the archives of the Moravian church in London, a manuscript volume of hymn tunes ascribes the tune to John Antes. A longer variant can be found in chorale form in Freylinghausen's *Geistreiches GesangBuch,* 1704.

51. I will sing of the mercies of the Lord

The text is taken verbatim from Psalm 89:1, with repetitions.

MERCIES. The music from the pen of an unknown composer appeared in United States' youth groups about 1960. This arrangement by Donald Hustad, one of the first to appear, was released in the booklet, *Let's Sing* (Hope, 1960).

52. God of concrete, God of steel

Responding to the need for hymnody using the major symbols of modern life, Richard G. Jones wrote this text in Sheffield, England in 1962. It was copyrighted in 1966 and first published in *Hymns and Songs,* 1969, by Epworth Press.

NEW HORIZONS. Francis Westbrook wrote this tune in 1968 in London for a Sunday School hymn book of the Methodist Church, which never materialized. The editorial committee of *Hymns and Songs,* 1969 decided to use the tune when the hymn "God of Concrete, God of Steel" was included in their volume.

53. All things bright and beautiful

Like most of the hymns of Mrs. Cecil Frances Alexander, this text was written to make biblical truth understandable to young minds. It appeared in her *Hymns for Little Children,*1848, and is based on the phrase in the Apostles' Creed describing God as "Maker of heaven and earth."

ROYAL OAK. The traditional tune was named for a tree at Boscobel, Shropshire, England, in which King Charles II took refuge following the Battle of Worcester in 1651. The melody was originally called "The

Twenty-Ninth of May" and was sung to words honoring Charles' restoration to the throne, May 29, 1660. It was arranged by Martin Shaw in *Song Time,* 1915.

54. The spacious firmament on high

These words appeared in the August 23, 1712 edition of *The Spectator* (London) at the close of Joseph Addison's article entitled "An Essay on the Proper Means of Strengthening and Confirming Faith in the Mind of Man." The text is a paraphrase of Psalm 19:1–6.

CREATION. The tune is an adaptation of parts of the chorus "The heavens are telling" from Haydn's oratorio *The Creation,* 1798. Its use as a hymn tune is generally confined to American hymnody. However, it was an Englishman, William Gardiner, who first arranged the melody for Addison's text, in *Sacred Melodies from Haydn, Mozart, and Beethoven* (London, 1812). By 1848, in *The National Psalmist,* it had assumed much of its present form.

55. For the beauty of the earth

The inspiration for this hymn came one day when Folliott S. Pierpoint viewed the beauty around him from a hilltop near Bath, England. It was first published in Orby Shipley's *Lyra Eucharistica,* 2nd ed., 1864. Its original title "The Sacrifice of Praise" is significant in that the hymn was originally written for the Eucharist. Changes in the text have made it suitable for general use.

DIX. The source of the tune was a melody by Conrad Kocher in his collection of German hymns, *Stimmen aus dem Reiche Gottes,* 1838. William H. Monk adapted the melody for William Dix's hymn "As with gladness men of old" in *Hymns Ancient and Modern,* 1861. The tune was named for the author of that text.

56. God of everlasting glory

This is an unusual type of hymn for John W. Peterson to write, and it is best explained by him:

> When I was compiling Singspiration's *Great Hymns of the Faith* (1965), it seemed to me there was a dearth of objective hymns of praise with contemporary texts. I thought and prayed about it. In time the words came with a reference to such up-to-date things as space travel and atomic research. Of course, the climax of praise in this hymn is reached in the final verse, written some three years later, where reference is made to the person and work of Christ.

BRETON ROAD. Though the hymn was written especially for *Great Hymns of the Faith*, it was first published in *Singspiration Annual*, Vol. 3, 1965. John Peterson says of the tune name: "It is the name of the street leading to the Ridgemoor area where we lived in Grand Rapids, Michigan."

57. I sing the almighty power of God

This text appeared in the first hymnal written exclusively for youth— *Divine Songs Attempted in Easy Language, for the Use of Children*, 1715. The book was in print for more than 100 years, and was the "fountainhead of English children's hymnody." In this collection, author Isaac Watts titled the hymn "Praise for Creation and Providence."

FOREST GREEN. This is an English folk tune as adapted by Ralph Vaughan Williams for the *English Hymnal*, 1906. Its name is associated with Forest Green, Surrey, England, and the melody was originally called "The Ploughboy's Dream."

58. This is my Father's world

Written by Maltbie Davenport Babcock during his first pastorate in a Presbyterian church in Lockport, New York, this poem was inspired by his early morning walks when he would say he was going out "to see my Father's world." It was published posthumously with other writings of Babcock in a small book called *Thoughts for Everyday Living*, 1901. The hymn is only a short cento of the complete poem, which emphasizes the fatherhood of God.

TERRA BEATA. The tune, whose name means "Blessed Earth," was written by Franklin L. Sheppard for the above text. He believed it was inspired by a traditional English melody he learned from his mother as a boy. The tune is also called "Terra Patris," related to the hymn's first line.

59. All creatures of our God and King

The original text is said to have been written by Francis of Assisi during the last months of his life when he was suffering intense pain and was almost blind. Known as "Canticle of the Sun," it is thought to be the oldest religious poem extant in the Italian language. It expresses St. Francis' intense love of all creation. William Draper paraphrased the hymn for use at a Whitsuntide (Pentecost) festival at Leeds, England sometime between 1899 and 1919; it was not published until 1926 when it appeared in a collection of Draper's hymns and in *School Worship*.

LASST UNS ERFREUEN. "Lasst uns erfreuen" is the beginning of the first line of an Easter hymn in *Geistliche Kirchengesäng,* 1623, for which this melody is used. It is thought to have been derived from a folk tune.

60. Come, Christians, join to sing

Originally titled "Come, Children, Join to Sing," this hymn appeared in *Sacred Melodies for Sabbath Schools and Families,* 1843, edited by author Christian Henry Bateman. For many years the book was Scotland's "Sabbath School hymnal." The first line has been changed to make the hymn available to all age groups.

MADRID. The origin of the tune and its name are unknown, though some publications date it "17th century." In 1825 and 1826 it appeared in Philadelphia in arrangements by Benjamin Carr for piano solo, and for solo with chorus and accompaniment. The tune also appeared in *A Collection of Metrical Versions, etc.* by M. Burgoyne (London, 1827) with the title "Spanish Chant." This arrangement by David Evans appeared in *The Revised Church Hymnary,* 1927.

61. At the name of Jesus

An invalid for the last 25 years of her life, Caroline Noel wrote many hymns to bring comfort to others who were suffering. This one was written as a processional hymn for Ascension Day and is based on Philippians 2:5-11. It first appeared in Miss Noel's book, *The Name of Jesus, and Other Verses for the Sick and Lonely,* 1870.

KING'S WESTON. The tune was composed for this text by Ralph Vaughan Williams for *Songs of Praise,* 1925. It is named for a country house and park on the River Avon, near Bristol, England.

62–63. All hail the power of Jesus' name

This text by Edward Perronet consisted originally of eight stanzas, the first of which appeared in the November, 1779 issue of the *Gospel Magazine,* Toplady's journal. The remaining seven stanzas appeared in the April, 1780 issue. Often revised and altered, the version most frequently used is by John Rippon and appeared in his *Selection of Hymns from the best authors,* 1787.

DIADEM. James Ellor, a hatmaker by trade, directed the music at the Wesleyan Chapel, Droylsden, near Manchester and wrote this melody in

1838 at the age of 19. The tune is typical of the florid style of the period and is named for the phrase "royal diadem" in the first stanza.

CORONATION. This is the tune most often used with this text in America, and it was composed by Oliver Holden in 1792 and first published in his *Union Harmony,* 1793. The tune name refers to the words "Crown Him."

MILES LANE. The tune was published anonymously with Edward Perronet's first stanza when it first appeared in the *Gospel Magazine,* November, 1779. In April, 1780 composer William Shrubsole was credited when the entire hymn appeared in Stephen Addington's *Collection of Psalm Tunes.* "Miles Lane" was the name given by Addington, who was minister of Miles' Lane Meeting House, London. This is the tune commonly used with the text in Great Britain.

64. In Thee is gladness
The German hymn, "In dir ist Freude" by Johann Lindemann, is one of two significant poems published in his *Decades Amorum Filii Dei* (Erfurt, 1598). Catherine Winkworth's translation appeared in her *Lyra Germanica,* 2nd series, 1858 and also her *Chorale Book for England,* 1863.

IN DIR IST FREUDE. The first printing of Lindemann's German hymn included this tune, adapted from a madrigal by Giovanni Giacomo Gastoldi da Caravaggio, printed in Venice beginning in 1591. The tune was originally set to the words "A lieta vita" and is mentioned in Burney's 18th century chronicle, *A General History of Music.*

65. O could I speak the matchless worth
Under the title "Praise of Jesus," this text first appeared in Samuel Medley's *Hymns: The Public Worship and Private Devotions of True Christians, Assisted in Some Thoughts in Verse: Principally Drawn from Select Passages of the Word of God,* third edition, 1789.

ARIEL. The music is of unknown origin, though one researcher says it "comes from Mozart." Lowell Mason arranged it and is so credited in the *Boston Academy Collection of Church Music,* 1836. It is evidently one of the many tunes he adapted from European sources.

It is interesting to speculate on the origin of the tune name "Ariel." The name appears several times in the Old Testament, and Lowell Mason often used biblical sources. In medieval folklore, Ariel was a "light, graceful spirit of the air," and John Milton (in *Paradise Lost*) identified him as one of heaven's rebellious angels. One might guess there is some connection between "Ariel" and another angel mentioned in the full hymn (in the words "and vie with Gabriel while he sings"), but omitted in this version.

66. Take the name of Jesus with you
This text was written in 1870 by Lydia Baxter, who was an invalid for many years. Her sickroom became a center of inspiration, and this song was widely used in the Moody-Sankey campaigns.

In *Forty True Stories of Famous Gospel Songs*, Ernest K. Emurian tells of Mrs. Baxter's deep understanding of the name of Jesus, gathered from her study of the Bible.

PRECIOUS NAME. William H. Doane wrote the music for Lydia Baxter's words. The song first appeared in *Pure Gold*, edited by Doane and Robert Lowry in 1871.

67. Fairest Lord Jesus
Although it is known to have been written at least fifteen years earlier, the original German text ("Schönster Herr Jesu") was first published in the *Münster Gesangbuch*, 1677. The anonymous English translation of this Roman Catholic hymn first appeared in Willis' *Church Chorals and Choir Studies* (New York, 1850). A fourth stanza was added by Joseph A. Seiss in 1873, and appeared as part of his full translation in *The Sunday School Book* of the American Lutheran General Council (Phila., 1873).

CRUSADER'S HYMN. The tune first appeared with the German text in a book of Silesian folk songs, *Schlesische Volkslieder* (Leipzig, 1842). It was first published in America in *Church Chorals and Choir Studies* (New York, 1850). The name refers to the erroneous tradition that German knights sang the hymn on their way to capture Jerusalem in the 12th century.

68. How sweet the name of Jesus sounds
The words by John Newton were written while he was curate at Olney, Bucks, England. There, together with William Cowper, he produced the memorable volume *Olney Hymns*, 1779, containing 280 hymns by Newton and 68 by Cowper. This hymn was entitled "The Name of Jesus" in the collection and was based on a line from the Song of Solomon 1:3, "Thy name is as ointment poured forth."

ST. PETER. Alexander Reinagle's melody was originally set to a version of Psalm 118 in his *Original Psalm Tunes, for Voice and Pianoforte*, ca. 1836. It was named "St. Peter" in his *Collection of Psalm and Hymn Tunes,* 1840, after St. Peter's-in-the-East, Oxford, where the composer was organist.

69. All glory to Jesus, begotten of God

This hymn of praise to Christ was written by John W. Peterson in Montrose, Pennsylvania and first published in *Chorister* magazine, Vol. 2 (Singspiration) in September, 1957. Mr. Peterson has written:

> In our times and throughout the church's history, the enemies of the gospel have directed their attacks at the person and work of Christ, particularly the deity of our Lord. This hymn was written with those attacks in mind and is, in a word, a declaration of faith in His person as God the Son.

RIDGEMOOR. John W. Peterson chose this name for his tune and says that it is "the name of the area in which my family and I lived during our years in Grand Rapids, Michigan."

70. Join all the glorious names

Originally with twelve stanzas, this text by Isaac Watts was first published in Book I of his *Hymns and Spiritual Songs,* 1707 under the caption "Offices of Christ." It is said to be one of the most impressive and exalted hymns that Watts ever wrote.

DARWALL. Sometimes called "Darwall's 148th," the tune was originally written by John Darwall for Psalm 148 in Aaron Williams' *New Universal Psalmist,* 1770. It is the lone survivor of the 150 tunes written for the complete psalter.

71. The great Physician now is near

The theme of this hymn was suggested by a railroad accident in which there were a large number of fatalities. Several medical men were on the train, and they were instrumental in saving the lives of many who would otherwise have been among the casualties. The text, which author William Hunter titled "Christ the Physician," appeared in his *Songs of Devotion,* 1859.

GREAT PHYSICIAN. The tune was written for the text by John Stockton. It appeared in *Joyful Songs, Nos. 1, 2 and 3 Combined,* 1869, and gained wide usage after appearing in Bliss and Sankey's *Gospel Hymns and Sacred Songs,* 1875.

72. My Jesus, I love Thee

These words were written by William Ralph Featherstone (possibly when he was converted) at the age of 16. He sent the hymn to his aunt, Mrs. E. Featherstone Wilson, in Los Angeles, and she suggested it be published. It first appeared anonymously in England in the *London Hymn Book*, 1864. Shortly thereafter, it was included in American hymnals.

GORDON. Adoniram J. Gordon composed the music for the text, which he found in the *London Hymn Book*. It first appeared in *The Service of Song for Baptist Churches*, 1876, compiled by S. L. Caldwell and Gordon.

73. O Jesus, King most wonderful!

This cento (like "Jesus, the very thought of Thee") is a selection of verses from Edward Caswall's translation of "Jesu, dulcis memoria," a famous Latin poem usually attributed to St. Bernard of Clairvaux. The translation appeared in Caswall's *Lyra Catholica*, 1849.

SERENITY. The musical setting was taken from a longer love song, "Waft, ye Winds," written by William Vincent Wallace in 1856. Its earliest appearance as a hymn tune adaptation by Uzziah C. Burnap may have been in Robinson and MacArthur's *The Calvary Selection of Spiritual Songs*, 1878. The same year it was printed in *The Hymnal of the Methodist Episcopal Church with Tunes*.

74. Shepherd of eager youth

This is one of the earliest Christian hymns (*ca.* 200) and was appended to *The Tutor*, a treatise by Titus Flavius Clemens, known as St. Clement of Alexandria, with the title "Hymn of the Savior Christ." Henry M. Dexter's translation was done in 1846, first in prose and then in poetry. It was first sung in the Manchester, N.H. church in which Dexter was ordained to the Congregational ministry, and first printed in the *Congregationalist*, December 21, 1849.

ITALIAN HYMN. See "Come, Thou Almighty King," No. 4.

75. Love divine, all loves excelling

This hymn appeared under the heading "Jesus, show us thy salvation" in Charles Wesley's pamphlet *Hymns for those that seek, and those that have Redemption in the Blood of Jesus Christ*, 1747. It had appeal from the beginning because so few hymns in those days expressed "the love of God." It also presents the Wesleyan doctrine of "Christian perfection" through an experience of "sanctification."

BEECHER. See "God, our Father, we adore Thee," No. 3.

76. We sing the boundless praise

When author Donald P. Hustad was helping compile *Worship and Service Hymnal*, 1957 for Hope Publishing Company, he was associated with Joseph C. Macaulay and Harry D. Loes on the faculty of Moody Bible Institute, Chicago, Illinois. Dr. Macaulay wrote these words "in his desire to maintain the note of praise in modern evangelical hymnody" and Mr. Loes set them to music. They first appeared in the hymnal mentioned above.

BOUNDLESS PRAISE. Joseph C. Macaulay has written us about his relationship with Harry D. Loes, composer of this music:

> Mr. Loes had very high regard for my lyrics, and urged me to have them set to music. He then encouraged me to develop my own music talent, and became my first teacher in composition.

77. Awake, my soul, to joyful lays

This text by Samuel Medley first appeared in J. H. Meyer's *Collection of Hymns* for Lady Huntingdon's Chapel, Cumberland Street, Shoreditch (London, 1782). The first line is sometimes sung "in joyful lays."

LOVINGKINDNESS. The tune (whose name is the Old Testament word meaning "steadfast love") was included in William Caldwell's *Union Harmony*, 1837. It is one of at least 42 tunes written by him.

78. Praise the Savior, ye who know Him

Typical of Thomas Kelly's hymns in its use of an unusual meter, this text appeared in his *Psalms and Hymns extracted from Various Authors*, 2nd ed., 1806, entitled "Praise of Jesus." It was significant in the Moody-Sankey campaigns of 1873–75 in Great Britain, and is still a favorite of evangelicals in the United States and around the world.

ACCLAIM. In Sankey's *Gospel Hymns No. 5* (New York, 1887) and *Sacred Songs and Solos* (London, 1873) this text appears with another tune that is called a "German melody." However, in the enlarged edition (1903) of the latter book, this melody appears with no identification. Through the years it has also become known as a "traditional German melody," and is named for the character of the text.

79. We come, O Christ, to Thee

E. Margaret Clarkson wrote this text in the summer of 1946 after Stacey Woods, Chairman of Inter-Varsity Christian Fellowship, had asked her to provide a hymn for students. It was first sung at Inter-Varsity's first American missionary conference, held in Toronto in December, 1946. It was first published in *Hymns,* 1947, an Inter-Varsity publication.

DARWALL. See "Join all the glorious names," No. 70.

80. I greet Thee, who my sure Redeemer art

This poem by the great Reformer, John Calvin, first appeared in the French Psalter, 1545 entitled "Salutation à Jésus-Christ." The first English translation of record is by Elizabeth Lee Smith and it appeared in 1868 in Philip Schaff's compilation, *Christ in Song.* The full poem and a detailed argument for the hymn's authorship is found in Armin Haeussler's *The Story of Our Hymns.*

TOULON. The tune "Toulon" is an abridged form of the "Old 124th," first used in the Genevan Psalter, 1551 and commonly used in English psalters. It is probably named for the French city, Toulon. It appeared slightly altered with the name "Montague" in *The National Psalmist,* 1848, edited by Lowell Mason and George Webb.

81. All praise to Him who reigns above

These stanzas by William H. Clark appeared in *Hymns of the Christian Life,* 1891, compiled by R. Kelso Carter and A. B. Simpson. The refrain was one of those "wandering choruses" that was appended to many different sets of words; it also appeared in Ralph E. Hudson's *Songs for the Ransomed,* 1887 with the stanzas of "O for a thousand tongues to sing."

BLESSED NAME. This may be one of those "folk hymn" tunes that emerged from 19th century campmeetings. The arrangement by William J. Kirkpatrick appeared with the text in *Hymns of the Christian Life,* 1891, compiled by R. Kelso Carter and A. B. Simpson. An earlier arrangement by Ralph E. Hudson is described above.

82. Friends all around us are trying to find

The widow of Harry Dixon Loes has written that her husband was inspired by a sermon of Dr. Paul Rader in Moody Church with the theme, "All that I want is in Jesus." The song was first sung in a youth group at Moody Church in 1915, the year Mr. Loes graduated from Moody Bible

Institute. Dr. Rader first held the copyright and published the song in *Tabernacle Hymns*, edited by Arthur McKee and D. B. Towner (Tabernacle Publishing Company, 1916).

OKMULGEE. Harry Dixon Loes' tune for his own text is named for Okmulgee, Oklahoma, where he served as minister of music at the First Baptist Church for eleven years, 1927–29 and 1930–39.

83. Jesus, the very thought of Thee

This hymn is thought to be one of the most beautiful in the English language. The translation was derived by Edward Caswall from the Latin poem "Jesu, dulcis memoria," attributed to Bernard of Clairvaux. It first appeared in Caswall's *Lyra Catholica*, 1849. (See also Nos. 73 and 91, two more centos from the Latin poem.)

ST. AGNES. The tune was composed by John B. Dykes for this text and was first published in Grey's *Hymnal for Use in the English Church*, 1866. In order to differentiate between this tune and another used in England, it is sometimes called "St. Agnes, Durham." One of the early Christian martyrs, St. Agnes was beheaded in 304 A.D. at the age of thirteen.

84. Come and praise the Lord our King

These anonymous words appeared with an arrangement of the tune in Great Britain about 1964. They were published in *Youth Praise* (London: Falcon Books, 1966).

MICHAEL'S BOAT. The tune comes from the historic folk song, "Michael, Row the Boat Ashore." It was published in *Slave Songs of the United States* (N.Y., A. Simpson and Co., 1867) in the section "Southeastern Slave States," and has been characterized as "a spiritual used by (American) blacks who wanted to colonize Africa."

85. Crown Him with many crowns

Matthew Bridges wrote the words of stanzas one and four in 1851 and published them with three others in the second edition of his *Hymns of the Heart* under the title "On His Head Were Many Crowns." The hymn was revised and additional stanzas written by Godfrey Thring for his *Hymns and Sacred Lyrics*, 1874; stanzas two and three are Thring's.

DIADEMATA. The tune (whose name means "crowns") was written for this hymn by George Elvey and appeared in the Appendix to the first edition of *Hymns Ancient and Modern*, 1868.

86. Christ has for sin atonement made

This hymn, both text and tune, were written by Elisha Hoffman and first appeared in *Gospel Hymns No. 6*, 1891, published by Biglow and Main.

BENTON HARBOR. The editors of *Baptist Hymnal*, 1956 named the tune for the city of Benton Harbor, Michigan, where Hoffman was once pastor of the First Presbyterian Church.

87. I love Thee, I love Thee

The author of this text is anonymous, though it has been credited to John Adam Granade, the "Billy Sunday of the early 1800's." It appeared in *The Christian Harmony, or Songsters Companion,* compiled by Jeremiah Ingalls in 1805. Its infrequent appearances in American hymnals include those in *Free Methodist Hymnal,* 1910 and *Baptist Hymnal,* 1956.

I LOVE THEE. The composer of this melody is also unknown. George Pullen Jackson says it is of the "Lord Lovel" family of tunes. In its first appearance in Ingalls' *Christian Harmony,* 1905 it was named "Charity."

88. I've found a Friend

This text written by James G. Small, a Scottish Free Church minister, first appeared in *The Revival Hymn Book,* 2nd series, 1863 and then in Small's *Psalms and Sacred Songs,* 1866. It was originally entitled "Jesus, the Friend."

FRIEND. The tune was composed by George C. Stebbins in January, 1878 and was first published in *Gospel Hymns No. 3,* 1878.

89. Majestic sweetness sits enthroned

This text first appeared in John Rippon's *A Selection of Hymns from the Best Authors,* 1787. It was written by Samuel Stennett, an English Baptist pastor, and was originally titled "The Chiefest Among Ten Thousand; or, the Excellencies of Christ." It is based on Song of Solomon 5:10–16.

ORTONVILLE. Written for these words by Thomas Hastings in 1837, this music first appeared in his book, *The Manhattan Collection,* 1837. The suffix "ville" indicates that it is named for a town.

90. O for a thousand tongues to sing

Charles Wesley wrote this text on May 21, 1739 to commemorate the first anniversary of his "spiritual birth." The first stanza of the full 18-stanza hymn began "Glory to God, and praise and love." It first appeared in *Hymns and Sacred Poems,* 1740.

AZMON. The tune first appeared anonymously in Lowell Mason's *The Modern Psalmist,* 1839. It was one of many melodies picked up by Mason on a tour of Europe for the purpose of obtaining materials from distinguished composers for future publications. Among the composers visited was Carl G. Gläser. In *The Sabbath Hymn and Tune Book,* 1859, Mason called this tune "Denfield" and credited it to "C. G." Later he named it "Azmon," a name mentioned in Numbers, chapter 34.

91. Jesus, Thou Joy of loving hearts

This text (like Nos. 73 and 83) is taken from "Jesu, dulcis memoria," a long devotional poem attributed to Bernard of Clairvaux. The cento was translated by Ray Palmer for the *Sabbath Day Hymn Book,* 1858.

QUEBEC. See "Father of heaven, whose love profound," No. 5.

92. I know of a Name

No information can be found about Jean Perry or this text. Evidently it was given to Mabel Johnston Camp who set it to music for publishing.

THAT BEAUTIFUL NAME. The tune name is the traditional title of the song. Mabel Johnston Camp's daughter-in-law, Mrs. John Camp, tells this story about the music:

> "Rev. Norman B. Camp found some torn scraps of music in a waste basket beside Mrs. Camp's desk. He patiently fit the pieces together and in time realized what a lovely melody his wife had written, and then persuaded her to publish it."

Words and music appeared together in *The Voice of Thanksgiving No. 2,* 1916, published by Fleming H. Revell for Moody Bible Institute. It is said that publication of the book was delayed until Mrs. Camp could complete the editing of this music from her bed in the Henrotin Hospital on LaSalle Street in Chicago.

93. Deep in my heart there's a gladness

Albert A. Ketchum wrote this song while he was a student at Moody Bible Institute, Chicago in the early 1920's. He sold it to a fellow-student, Harry D. Clarke, who published it in *Gospel Truth in Song, No. 2,* 1922. The copyright was not filed until 1931.

For years this song was considered to be only a "special" and was sung as a solo or a duet. In 1967, editor Donald P. Hustad included it in *Crusader Hymns,* and since that time it has had wide use with choirs and congregations.

KETCHUM. Although Albert A. Ketchum wrote a number of hymns in the 1922–23 period, this is the only one to achieve wide use. The tune name memorializes him.

94. Worthy is the Lamb

Stephen Leddy wrote this song in 1963, while he was a student in Baylor University, Waco, Texas. He says:

> I was sitting in my dormitory room just looking at my school textbooks, when my eyes ran across a book entitled *Worthy Is the Lamb,* by Ray Summers. The title "stood out" and I felt an inspiration to put a song to those words. The result (in an hour or so) was this hymn.

WORTHY LAMB. The title and tune name are derived from Revelation 5:12, "Worthy is the Lamb that was slain to receive power, and riches, and wisdom, and strength, and honor, and glory, and blessing."

Stephen Leddy's words and music were first published in *A Time to Sing* (Hope Publishing Co., 1967).

95. Hail, Thou once despised Jesus

Attributed to John Bakewell, one of the lay preachers associated with the Wesleys, this text first appeared in *A Collection of Hymns Addressed to the Holy, Holy, Holy Triune God, in the Person of Christ Jesus, Our Mediator and Advocate,* 1757. It was altered in Martin Madan's *Collection of Psalms and Hymns,* 1760 and also in Toplady's *Psalms and Hymns,* 1776.

IN BABILONE. This traditional Dutch air is from *Oude en Nieuwe Hollantse Boerenlities en Contradanseu, ca.* 1710 and is similar to the tune "Vruechten" in *The Oxford Book of Carols.* It was arranged by Julius Röntgen and included in *The English Hymnal,* 1906.

96. Praise Him! praise Him!

Fanny Crosby's text was first published by Biglow and Main in *Bright Jewels,* 1869, edited by W. B. Bradbury, W. H. Doane, W. F. Sherwin and Chester G. Allen. It was originally titled "Praise, Give Thanks."

JOYFUL SONG. The tune was written by Chester G. Allen for the first publication of these words and was first called "Allen."

97. There is no name so sweet on earth

George Bethune's text honoring the name of Jesus was early ascribed to "E. Roberts." Julian's *Dictionary* says that Hubert P. Main identified it as Bethune's. It was apparently written in 1858.

THE SWEETEST NAME. The title "Sweetest Name" was given to this tune of William B. Bradbury in *The Mennonite Hymnary*, 1940 and *Baptist Hymnal*, 1956. In *Baptist Hymnal*, 1975 it is called "Golden Chain," the name of the book published by Bradbury in which this text and tune first appeared in 1861.

98. O Savior, precious Savior

This text was written by Frances Havergal at Leamington, England in November, 1870 and was first published in her volume *Under the Surface*, 1874.

MUNICH. The original chorale melody was found in the *Neuvermehrtes Gesangbuch*, 1693 and is one of many tunes used for the text "O Gott, du frommer Gott." Felix Mendelssohn adapted it for the aria "Cast thy burden upon the Lord" in his oratorio *Elijah* (1847), and this hymn tune is based on Mendelssohn's version.

99. Jesus! what a Friend for sinners

This interesting hymn by the Presbyterian evangelist J. Wilbur Chapman quotes many phrases from Charles Wesley's "Jesus, Lover of my soul." It might also be called a sequel to Isaac Watts' "Join all the glorious names," with its large number of names for Christ. It was published with this tune in 1910 in *Alexander's Gospel Songs, No. 2* (Revell).

HYFRYDOL. The tune by the Welsh composer Rowland H. Prichard was harmonized for this text by Robert Harkness, pianist in Dr. Wilbur Chapman's evangelistic campaigns. "Hyfrydol" is discussed with No. 102, "Come, Thou long expected Jesus."

100. O come, O come, Emmanuel

The liturgical practice from which this hymn developed reaches back to the seventh century, possibly earlier. The text is derived from the seven "Great O's" (antiphons) which were said before and after the *Magnificat* in the office of Vespers, on successive days from December 17 to 23. The English translation (originally "Draw nigh, draw nigh, Emmanuel") first appeared in John Mason Neale's *Hymnal Noted*, 1851.

VENI EMMANUEL. The tune (whose Latin name means "Come, Emmanuel") is an adaptation or a composite of plainsong phrases taken from settings of the *Kyrie*. Thomas Helmore included this arrangement in the *Hymnal Noted, Part II* (London, 1854) and indicated that it was from a French Missal in the National Library at Lisbon, Portugal.

101. Let all mortal flesh keep silence

This text is based on the "Cherubic Hymn" from the Liturgy of St. James of Jerusalem, which was used in Eastern churches as early as the fifth century and is still associated with Orthodox worship. The present translation was made by Gerard Moultrie for the second edition of Shipley's *Lyra Eucharistica*, 1864.

PICARDY. The tune is a traditional French carol, included in *Chansons populaires des provinces de France*, IV (1860). The adaptation as a hymn tune appeared in the *English Hymnal*, 1906.

102. Come, Thou long expected Jesus

This text was first published by its author Charles Wesley in a small compilation of 18 poems, *Hymns for the Nativity of Our Lord*, 1744.

HYFRYDOL. The tune was composed by the 20-year-old Rowland H. Prichard about 1830, and was first published in his *Cyfaill y Cantorion*, 1844. The tune name means "Good cheer."

103. O come, all ye faithful

Seven different manuscripts found in widely-separated parts of Europe contain this hymn. All bear the signature of John Francis Wade, who made his living in the mid-eighteenth century by copying and selling plainchant and other music. In Dom John Stephan's *Adeste Fideles; a study on its origin and development*, 1947, sufficient evidence is presented for crediting the authorship to Wade. These stanzas are based on a translation by Frederick Oakeley made in 1841 and printed in Murray's *Hymnal*, 1852.

ADESTE FIDELES. The tune name is taken from the opening words of the original Latin hymn. The melody appeared in manuscript with this text in *Cantus Diversi*, a volume compiled by John Wade in 1751 for use in Roman Catholic homes and institutions. The present arrangement was published in *Essay on the Church Plain Chant*, 1782 by Samuel Webbe, organist at the Portuguese embassy in London; hence the tune is sometimes called "Portuguese Hymn."

104. It came upon the midnight clear

This is one of the first carol-hymns written in America. The work of Edmund H. Sears, a Unitarian minister, it was first published in the *Christian Register,* December 29, 1849.

CAROL. Richard S. Willis' tune was originally used with "See Israel's gentle Shepherd stand." It is an adaptation of Study No. 23 in Willis' *Church Chorals and Choir Studies,* 1850.

105. What Child is this, who, laid to rest

The text is taken from a longer Christmas poem, "The Manger Throne," written by William C. Dix *ca.* 1865. He was inspired after reading the Gospel lesson for Epiphany Day—Matthew 2:1–12.

GREENSLEEVES. The melody "Greensleeves" is a traditional English folk tune. In Chappell's *Popular Music of the Olden Time,* 1855–59, it is associated with a great variety of texts. It has been used with the carol "The old year now away is fled" since about 1642.

106. Hark! the herald angels sing

This text by Charles Wesley first appeared in *Hymns and Sacred Poems,* 1739 beginning "Hark! how all the welkin rings." In succeeding years it underwent many alterations, appearing in its present form in George Whitefield's *Collection of Hymns for Social Worship,* 1753.

MENDELSSOHN. The music was adapted from the second movement of Felix Mendelssohn's *Festgesang,* Opus 68, composed in 1840. The hymn setting was made by William H. Cummings and published in Chope's *Congregational Hymn and Tune Book,* 1856. It has become the recognized tune for this hymn.

107. Gentle Mary laid her Child

Joseph S. Cook's text won first prize in a carol competition sponsored by the *Christian Guardian.* It first appeared in the Christmas, 1919 issue of that magazine, printed by the Methodist Book and Publishing House, Toronto, Canada.

TEMPUS ADEST FLORIDUM. The tune is from the historic collection *Piae Cantiones* compiled by Theodoricus Petrus of Nyland, Finland in 1582. For many years it was used with Neale's "Good King Wenceslas." The present harmonization was made by Sir Ernest Macmillan for the *Hymnary* *of the United Church of Canada* (1930), in which this text and tune appeared together for the first time.

108. The first Noel, the angel did say

This carol is thought to be about three hundred years old. "Nowell" is the old English spelling and refers to the joyous expression of greeting to celebrate the birth of Christ. The present text is taken from the nine original verses published in William Sandys' *Christmas Carols Ancient and Modern,* 1833.

THE FIRST NOEL. The traditional tune for this text appeared with it in William Sandys' *Christmas Carols Ancient and Modern,* 1833. Its source is unknown, but it is thought to date from the 17th century. The present harmonization by John Stainer is from Bramley and Stainer's *Christmas Carols New and Old,* 1871.

109. Once in royal David's city

Cecil Frances Alexander wrote these words to illustrate and interpret the phrase of the Apostle's Creed, "Who was conceived by the Holy Ghost, born of the Virgin Mary." It first appeared in her *Hymns for Little Children,* 1848.

IRBY. Henry J. Gauntlett composed the tune for the text and it first appeared in his *Christmas Carols,* 1849. He also prepared this four-part setting for *Hymns Ancient and Modern,* 1861. "Irby" is the name of a village in Lincolnshire, England.

110. Angels from the realms of glory

James Montgomery wrote this poem for the Christmas Eve edition of his paper, *The Sheffield Iris,* in 1816. He revised it in 1825 and published it in his *Christian Psalmist.* In this form it has become universally popular.

REGENT SQUARE. See "Holy Father, great Creator," No. 6.

111. From heaven above to earth I come

This text, originally containing 15 stanzas, was based on a popular Christmas song of the day, "Aus fremden Landen komm ich her." Martin Luther wrote it for his small son Hans, for a Christmas Eve family celebration. It first appeared in Luther's *Geistliche Lieder*, 1535, usually referred to as Klug's *Gesangbuch*. The translation by Catherine Winkworth appeared in her *Lyra Germanica*, 1855.

VOM HIMMEL HOCH. The tune is thought to have been composed by Luther, or adapted from an existing folk melody. It was set to his Christmas hymn in Schumann's *Geistliche Lieder*, 1539 and identified by the opening words of the German text.

112. Away in a manger

This text has long been attributed to Martin Luther. However, an exhaustive study by Richard Hill entitled "Not so far away in a manger, forty-one settings of an American Carol," (*Music Library Assn. Notes*, Dec. 1945) discloses that the text was probably written by an anonymous author in Pennsylvania during the 19th century. The hymn was first published in a collection authorized by the General Council of the Evangelical Lutheran Church in North America, *Little Children's Book*, 1885.

CRADLE SONG. This is one of the most popular tunes used with this text in Great Britain. It was published in America in 1895 in a pamphlet of seven songs entitled *Around the World with Christmas: A Christmas Exercise*, with words arranged by E. E. Hewitt, and music by John R. Sweney and William J. Kirkpatrick. Kirkpatrick is credited with writing it, but it has enough "elegance" to be a folk melody.

113. Angels we have heard on high

It is thought that this anonymous French macaronic (vernacular and Latin) carol "Les anges dans nos campagnes" dates from the 18th century. The first publication in which it is known to have appeared was *Nouveau recueil de cantiques*, 1855. It has become one of America's best known and loved Christmas carols, though the author of the English translation is also unknown.

GLORIA. The traditional French melody was usually associated with this historic carol, although it was used with another text in R. R. Chope's *Carols for use in the Church*, 1875. The present version of text and tune appeared in *Carols Old and Carols New*, 1916, edited by Charles L. Hutchins.

114. As with gladness men of old

During his recovery from an illness, William Chatterton Dix wrote this hymn after reading the Gospel lesson for that particular day in the

Epiphany season. It was published in *Hymns of Love and Joy,* a small personal collection, and then in the first edition of *Hymns Ancient and Modern,* 1861.

DIX. See "For the beauty of the earth," No. 55.

115. Go, tell it on the mountain
No attempts were made before 1840 to collect the songs of the American Negro. George Pullen Jackson states that the spirituals had their roots in the campmeeting music and gospel songs, which in turn had their beginnings in the folk music of the British Isles which was perpetuated in Appalachia. Others present strong evidence that many American black "call and response" chants have been heard in African usage.

These stanzas for this traditional spiritual were written by John W. Work, Jr., who arranged the piece for the Fisk (University) Jubilee Singers and published it in *Folk Songs of the American Negro,* 1907.

GO TELL IT. The music continues to appear in different versions of both melody and harmony. It has been pointed out that the stanza melody resembles the white spiritual "We'll march about Jerusalem" and the refrain echoes George F. Root's "Tramp, tramp, tramp, the boys are marching."

116. Good Christian men, rejoice
This text, a free rendering of the old German-Latin carol "In dulci jubilo," first appeared in John Mason Neale's *Carols for Christmastide,* 1853. The earliest existing form of text and tune is in Leipzig University, Ms. No. 1305, *ca.* 1400. The first published version is that in Klug's *Gesangbuch,* 1535.

IN DULCI JUBILO. The tune accompanied the text in the above-mentioned manuscript. It was published, much in its present form, in Klug's *Gesangbuch,* 1535.

117. Silent night! holy night!
The original text "Stille nacht, heilige nacht" was written by Joseph Mohr, assistant priest in St. Nicholas Church in Oberndorf, Upper Austria. It was first sung on Christmas Eve, 1818. Because of an organ breakdown, previous plans for the Christmas Eve service had to be abandoned. Mohr asked the organist Franz Grüber to set this text to music for choir, two voices and guitar. This English translation by John Freeman Young, second bishop of the Episcopal Diocese of Florida, first appeared in Hollister's *The Sunday-School Service and Tune Book,* 1863.

STILLE NACHT. The tune is believed to have been written by Franz Grüber just a few hours before the Christmas Eve service of 1818. The organ repair man, Karl Mauracher of Zillerthal, heard it and passed it on to others; otherwise it might well have been forgotten. The earliest manuscript, dated 1833, is the composer's arrangement for chorus, orchestra and organ.

118. Shepherds came, their praises bringing

This text was written *ca.* 1410 and first appeared, with this tune, in Triller's *Schlesich Singebüchlein aus Gottlieder Schrifft,* 1555. It was translated by George B. Caird in 1944 and first appeared in *Congregational Praise* (London, 1952).

QUEM PASTORES LAUDAVERE. Named for the first line of the German-Latin text, this carol was found in a 14th century manuscript. The present version was arranged by Ralph Vaughan Williams and appeared in the *English Hymnal,* 1906.

119. While shepherds watched their flocks by night

A collection of sixteen hymns titled *A Supplement to the New Version of the Psalms,* 1700, compiled by Nahum Tate and Nicholas Brady, included this text. The hymn by Tate is the only one to have survived in common use.

CHRISTMAS. Its name derived from association with the text, the tune is adapted from the closing aria of Act II of Handel's opera *Siroe,* composed in 1728. The hymn tune version first appeared in Weyman's *Melodia Sacra,* 1815, set to Psalm 132.

120. Joy to the world! the Lord is come

Isaac Watts' paraphrase of the second half of Psalm 98 first appeared in his *Psalms of David Imitated in the Language of the New Testament,* 1719. It bore the caption, "The Messiah's Coming and Kingdom."

ANTIOCH. The music first appeared in Lowell Mason's *Modern Psalmist* (Boston, 1839) with the notation "from Handel." It cannot be traced with any degree of certainty, though some have pointed out a resemblance to phrases in "Comfort Ye" and "Lift Up Your Heads" in *Messiah,* 1742.

121. O little town of Bethlehem

This text was inspired by Phillips Brooks' visit to the Holy Land in 1865. He was rector of Holy Trinity Church in Philadelphia and wrote this much-loved carol for the children in his Sunday School. It was sung in their Christmas service in 1868, and included in *The Church Porch*, 1874, a Sunday school hymnal.

ST. LOUIS. The tune was written at Brooks' request by the organist of Holy Trinity Church, who also was the Sunday School superintendent. Lewis Redner composed the tune and it was first sung on December 27, 1868. Tradition has it that Redner had delayed fulfilling his assignment and that the tune came to him during the night before Christmas. Text and tune appeared together for the first time in *The Church Porch*, 1874, edited by Dr. William R. Huntington. It has also been suggested that the tune name is a "play" on Redner's first name and was chosen by Phillips Brooks.

122. Of the Father's love begotten

Most of Aurelius Clemens Prudentius' fourth century poems were written for personal devotional use. However, they have been freely drawn upon to provide the Western Church with some of its finest hymns. One of his major works *Cathemerinon*, in a section called *Hymnus omnis horae*, contains this hymn, "Corde natus ex Parentis." Parts of the hymn were sung at the service of Compline in the Christmas season in certain English churches. The translation by John Mason Neale appeared in *The Hymnal Noted*, 1854 and was altered by Henry W. Baker in a trial edition of *Hymns Ancient and Modern*, 1859.

DIVINUM MYSTERIUM. The tune is a plainsong melody found in many European manuscripts from the 12th to 15th centuries set to the text "Divinum Mysterium." It was a Sanctus "trope"—a musical interpolation in the medieval liturgy. This melody was associated with Neale's text in *The Hymnal Noted*, 1854, and C. Winfred Douglas made the present arrangement which first appeared in *The Hymnal*, 1940.

123. Little Baby Jesus, born in Bethlehem

Blaine H. Allen wrote the words and music of this song in November, 1966 in Hayward, California. It was one of twelve new songs recorded in a Christmas album. It was included in the folk songbook, *Now* (Hope Publishing Company, 1969). This is its first appearance in a standard hymnal.

YULE SPIRITUAL. The name of Blaine Allen's tune was chosen by the editors of *Hymns for the Living Church* to signify the message of the text and the style of the music.

124. Thou didst leave Thy throne

This text based on Luke 2:7 ("there was no room for them in the inn") was written for the choir and children of the parish school at St. Mark's, Brighton, England by Emily E. S. Elliott. Her father was rector of the parish. It was first sung in 1864 from leaflets, and later printed in the *Church Missionary Juvenile Instructor,* 1870 and in Miss Elliott's *Chimes for Daily Service,* 1880.

MARGARET. The tune (also called "Elliott," for the author) was composed by Timothy R. Matthews for these words, and named by the composer for reasons unknown. It was first published in *Children's Hymns and Tunes,* 1876.

125. We would see Jesus; lo! His star is shining

John Edgar Park produced this hymn poem at the suggestion of Grace W. Conant, who was helping to prepare a hymnal for Pilgrim Press and wanted a hymn based on the biblical phrase "We would see Jesus." These first words had been used in another hymn (see No. 425), but the remainder was written by Park as an expression of "youth and promise and sunshine . . . and an inner glimpse of the Young Man of Nazareth living and moving among us." It first appeared in *Worship and Song,* 1913, edited by Ms. Conant and B. S. Winchester.

HENLEY. Lowell Mason composed this tune, which first appeared as a setting for "Come unto Me, when shadows darkly gather" in *The Hallelujah,* 1854.

126. Amen, Amen!

Although this is identified as a "traditional spiritual," we are tempted to believe that it is more contemporary, because the art of improvisation is still very much present in black-church worship and similar expressions began to appear about 1950. This version of the text is by John F. Wilson, resident editor for Hope Publishing Company since 1966. In 1970 it was released as a choral octavo and then in the folk hymnal *A New Now,* 1971.

AMEN. The music arrangement of the traditional spiritual is also by John F. Wilson.

127. Who is He in yonder stall?

This text was written by Benjamin R. Hanby and was published in *The Dove, a Collection of Music for Day and Sunday Schools* (Chicago, 1866). For many years the song appeared with at least ten stanzas, each only one line long. Donald Hustad introduced the present version in *Worship and Service Hymnal,* 1957.

LOWLINESS. The tune was composed by the author for the words. The name is derived from the sentiment of the hymn's stanzas, which are in dramatic contrast to the refrain.

128. One day when heaven was filled with His praises

There is no information available concerning the writing of this hymn by J. Wilbur Chapman. The evangelist handed two poems (including this one) to Charles H. Marsh to be set to music. At the time (*ca.* 1908) they were working together in a Bible conference in Stony Brook, Long Island, New York.

CHAPMAN. Charles H. Marsh wrote the music for this text at the request of J. Wilbur Chapman, the author. In *Hymns of Our Faith,* William J. Reynolds quotes a letter from the composer in which he tells of a conflict regarding the ownership of the copyright. When the issue was settled, the copyright was controlled by The Rodeheaver Company, but Hope Publishing Company has special privileges pertaining to its use. The complete song was first published by Praise Publishing Company in 1911 in *The Message in Song.*

129. Who is this boy?

The anonymous first stanza telling of "the boy Jesus" was found by Hope Publishing Company's editor, John F. Wilson, in an anthem. He added stanzas two and three to present Christ crucified and resurrected. The song was first performed by the children's choir of the First Methodist Church, La Grange, Illinois under Wilson's direction, and later published in *A Time to Sing* (Chicago: Hope Publishing Co., 1967).

MOUNTAIN VIEW. John F. Wilson named his tune in remembrance of his first teaching position (1950–52) at the Mountain View Bible College in Didsbury, Alberta, Canada.

130. Tell me the story of Jesus

This text was written by Fanny J. Crosby and first appeared in *The Quiver of Sacred Song,* 1880, compiled by William J. Kirkpatrick and John R. Sweney, and published in Philadelphia by John J. Hood.

STORY OF JESUS. The music was composed by John R. Sweney and has appeared with the above text since it was first published in *The Quiver of Sacred Song,* 1880.

131. All glory, laud and honor

The original Latin text by St. Theodulph of Orleans is thought to have been written while he was in prison at Angers about 820 or 821. From the tradition that, when King Louis the Pious passed the prison he heard Theodulph sing the hymn and afterward set him free—the hymn has often been used in Palm Sunday processionals. The original Latin consisted of 78 lines from which this cento is taken. In its present form John Mason Neale's translation appeared in *Hymns Ancient and Modern*, 1861. Its first printing was in the *Hymnal Noted*, 1854 with the first line "Glory, and laud, and honor."

ST. THEODULPH. The tune was composed by Melchior Teschner in 1613 for "Valet will ich dir geben," a hymn of consolation written by Valerius Herberger. It was published in *Ein andachtiges Gebet* (Leipzig, 1615). It was set to the above text and called "St. Theodulph" in *Hymns Ancient and Modern*, 1861.

132. Ride on! ride on in majesty

This Palm Sunday hymn was written by Henry Milman, an Anglican clergyman and professor of poetry at Oxford. It was first published in Reginald Heber's posthumous volume, *Hymns Written and Adapted to the Weekly Service of the Church Year*, 1827, and designated for "The Sixth Sunday in Lent."

WINCHESTER NEW. See "O Splendor of God's glory bright," No. 16.

133. Alone Thou goest forth, O Lord

Peter Abelard wrote the original Latin text, "Solus ad victimam procedis, Domine" *ca.* 1100 as a Good Friday office hymn and published it in his *Hymnarius Paraclitensis*, 1129 for the use of his wife Heloise's Convent of the Paraclete. (See biographical sketch.) The paraphrase-translation was made by F. Bland Tucker in 1938 for use in the *Hymnal 1940*.

BANGOR. Named for the ancient city of Bangor in Wales, this melody was long popular in Scotland as a psalm tune. It was published in William Tans'ur's *A Compleat Melody: or Harmony of Sion*, 1734 set to Psalm 101. In *The Hymnal Companion*, an interesting folk tale credits the humming of this tune with the naming of the fledgling town of Bangor, Maine in 1781.

134. Hosanna, loud hosanna

All of Jeannette Threlfall's poems were written at "idle moments." This, her best-known hymn, was first published in her volume, *Sunshine and Shadow*, 1873.

ELLACOMBE. The melody first appeared in the *Gesangbuch der Herzogl,* (Württemberg, 1784). It came into English usage from an 1833 Mainz *Collection* edited by Xavier Ludwig Hartig, who dated the tune 1700 but gave no source. *Hymns Ancient and Modern* (1868 ed.) brought it into wide use in Great Britain. It bears the name of a village in Devonshire, England.

135. He was wounded for our transgressions

Thomas O. Chisholm sent the first stanza of this hymn to Merrill Dunlop suggesting that he might like to write music for "the chorus." Mr. Dunlop acquiesced but, realizing the hymn was not a "chorus-type," asked Chisholm to add other stanzas. Three more were supplied and the complete text appeared in *New Songs of a Christian,* 1941, a collection by Dunlop.

OAK PARK. The tune was named after Oak Park, Illinois, the Chicago suburb in which its composer Merrill Dunlop has lived for many years.

136. O sacred Head, now wounded

Originally ascribed to the twelfth century church leader, Bernard of Clairvaux, the Latin hymn "Salve caput cruentatum" was just one cento from a long poem addressed to seven parts of the body of the crucified Christ. Paul Gerhardt's free German translation "O Haupt voll Blut und Wunden" first appeared in *Praxis Pietatis Melica,* 1656. James W. Alexander translated the Gerhardt version into English and this appeared in *The Christian Lyre,* 1830.

PASSION CHORALE. The tune was set to a German love song in Hans Leo Hassler's *Lustgarten Neuer Deutscher Gesang,* 1601. It first appeared as a hymn tune in *Harmoniae Sacrae* (3rd ed., Görlitz, 1613) set to "Herzlich thut mich verlangen." It was set to the above Gerhardt text in Crüger's *Praxis Pietatis Melica* and has been coupled with it (and its translations) ever since; this association has given it its name. The present harmonization by J. S. Bach is found in his *St. Matthew Passion,* 1729.

137. What wondrous love is this

It is generally agreed that the author of the text is unknown, though *The Hesperian Harp,* 1848 attributes the original words to Alexander Means, a Methodist preacher in Oxford, Georgia. It appeared in a number of 19th century hymnals, including *The Sacred Harp,* 1844.

WONDROUS LOVE. Appearing in Billy Walker's *Southern Harmony,* 1835, this tune has the characteristics of traditional Anglo-American folk melodies of Elizabethan tradition. George Pullen Jackson, in *The Story of the*

Sacred Harp, 1844–1944, has pointed out its resemblance to a tune used for 250 years with a song about the pirate, Captain Kidd.

138. There is a green hill far away

Cecil Frances Alexander's hymn was first published in her *Hymns for Little Children* in 1848. It was intended to teach the meaning of the fourth article of the Apostles' Creed, "Suffered under Pontius Pilate, was crucified, dead, and buried," and was written as Mrs. Alexander sat by the bedside of a sick child.

GREEN HILL. Its name derived from the hymn's first line, this music was written by George C. Stebbins in 1878 and first appeared that year in *Gospel Hymns No. 3,* edited by Ira D. Sankey, James McGranahan and Stebbins. When published this way, the original hymn's fifth stanza becomes the refrain.

139. 'Tis midnight; and on Olive's brow

These words by William B. Tappan appeared in his *Poems,* 1822 entitled "Gethsemane," and also in *Lyra Sacra Americana,* 1868 and later in many hymnals.

OLIVE'S BROW. Written for the text and named for the end of the first phrase, this music by William B. Bradbury first appeared in *The Shawm* (New York, 1853) compiled by Bradbury and George F. Root.

140. In the cross of Christ I glory

Based on Galatians 6:14, this text was written by John Bowring. Tradition has a disputed story that Bowring was inspired by a view of the cross on the spire of the fire-gutted St. Paul's Church in the Portuguese colony of Macao, on the coast of China. The words appeared in his *Hymns,* 1825 and the opening line was inscribed on his tombstone.

RATHBUN. Composed by Ithamar Conkey in 1849 while he was organist and choirmaster of the Central Baptist Church in Norwich, Connecticut, the tune was named in honor of his soprano soloist, Mrs. Beriah S. Rathbun; the interesting story appears in *Guide to the Pilgrim Hymnal.* The music first appeared in Greatorex's *Collection of Psalm and Hymn Tunes,* 1851.

141. Lift high the Cross

This processional hymn is unique in that it begins and ends with the refrain. It was written by George W. Kitchin and Michael R. Newbolt and was included in the 1916 Supplement to *Hymns Ancient and Modern*.

CRUCIFER. Sydney H. Nicholson's tune was written for this text and appeared with it in the 1916 Supplement to *Hymns Ancient and Modern*. A "crucifer" is one who carries a cross in ecclesiastical processions.

142. Deep were His wounds, and red

This poem was submitted for publication in *The Lutheran Companion* in 1953 by William Johnson, an obscure writer-farmer in Minnesota. Ernest E. Ryden, editor of the magazine, was at that time serving on the commission that was preparing a new hymnal that would be used by several Lutheran bodies. Impressed by the text, Ryden sent it to Leland B. Sateren for a musical setting. The hymn and tune appeared together in the *Service Book and Hymnal*, 1958.

MARLEE. The tune was composed for the text by Leland B. Sateren at the request of Ernest E. Ryden, as narrated above. The tune name is an acrostic, composed of the first three letters of the names of the composer's two sons, Mark and "Lee" (Leland, Jr.).

143. Glory be to Jesus

The Italian antecedent of this text ("Viva! Viva! Gesù!") was found in an 1837 edition of Galli's *Raccolta di Orazione e pie Opere colle Indulgenze*. Earlier (1815) Pope Pius VII had granted a 100-day indulgence to all who used the hymn. The translation by Edward Caswall first appeared in his *Hymns for the Use of the Birmingham Oratory*, 1857, entitled "Hymn to the precious blood."

WEM IN LEIDENSTAGEN. Friedrich Filitz' tune appeared first in his *Vierstimmiges Choralbuch*, 1847 set to the words "Wem in Leidenstagen."

144. Ask ye what great thing I know

The German hymn by Johann Schwedler, "Wollt ihr wissen was mein Preis?" (based on I Cor. 2:2 and Gal. 6:14), was first published after the author's death in the *Hirschberger Gesangbuch*, 1741. This most-used English translation by Benjamin H. Kennedy first appeared in his collection of 1863, *Hymnologia Christiana*. Its first appearance in America was in the Dutch Reformed publication, *Hymns of the Church*, 1869.

HENDON. Henri A. C. Malan's tune was first published in his own collections in France, probably in 1827. Lowell Mason is credited with bringing it to America and he included it in his *Carmina Sacra,* 1841. Hendon is a village in Middlesex, England; Malan may have visited there.

145. Were you there when they crucified my Lord?

This text is anonymous, and also appears as "Have you heard how they crucified, etc." George Pullen Jackson lists as the earliest-known printed source, *Old Plantation Hymns,* compiled by William E. Barton in 1899. Tradition ascribes its origin to black slaves who interpreted biblical stories in spontaneous song.

WERE YOU THERE? The tune also is anonymous. It first appeared in its present form in Frederick J. Work's *Folk Songs of the American Negro,* 1907. The folk melody was long known in the mainly-white upper Cumberland region of Tennessee, and may have had earlier British antecedents.

146. I saw One hanging on a tree

The full hymn by John Newton begins "In evil long I took delight," but the first stanza is usually omitted. It appeared in *Olney Hymns,* 1779 and tells the story of the transformation in Newton's life when he was converted. As such, it parallels "Amazing grace! how sweet the sound," another hymn by Newton.

EXCELL. Edwin O. Excell wrote this tune for Newton's words, using one of the stanzas for the refrain. They were published together in 1916 in his *Praiseworthy.* The song's copyright was filed in 1917.

147. Go to dark Gethsemane

This text by James Montgomery portrays four of the final incidents in the life of Jesus—His agony in Gethsemane, trial, crucifixion and resurrection—and draws lessons for Christian living. First published in 1822, the present text is the second and much-revised form which appeared in Montgomery's *Christian Psalmist,* 1825 under the heading "Christ, our example in suffering."

REDHEAD. The tune is named for its composer, Richard Redhead. It first appeared in his *Ancient Hymn Melodies and Other Church Tunes,* 1853, where it bears only the Roman numeral LXXVI. Consequently, it is sometimes called "Redhead 76."

148. When I survey the wondrous cross

This text by Isaac Watts, possibly based on Galatians 6:14, has been acclaimed by some as "the finest hymn in the English language." It first appeared in his *Hymns and Spiritual Songs*, 1707 and was intended to be sung principally at Communion services. The original was altered somewhat and appeared in the enlarged edition of the same work in 1709.

HAMBURG. The music was written by Lowell Mason in 1824 and appeared in the third edition of the Boston *Handel and Haydn Society Collection of Church Music*, 1825. Mason indicated that "Gregorian plainsong" was the source of the tune.

149. Rock of Ages, cleft for me

A single four-line stanza of this text (containing parts of the present first and third stanzas) first appeared in the *Gospel Magazine* published by Augustus Toplady in 1775. It came at the end of an article titled "Life—a Journey," a message of hope for all who had fallen into sin. The complete poem appeared in the same magazine in March, 1776 with the heading "A living and dying Prayer for the Holiest Believer in the World." The same year it was No. 337 in Toplady's *Psalms and Hymns*.

TOPLADY. The tune was composed for these words in 1830 by Thomas Hastings, and appeared with the title "Rock of Ages" in *Spiritual Songs for Social Worship*, 1831, edited by Hastings and Lowell Mason. The name was changed (to memorialize the text's author) and the rhythm was altered in Mason's *Sabbath Hymn and Tune Book*, 1859. The editors of *Hymns for the Living Church* recommend "Redhead," No. 147 as an alternate tune for these words.

150. My Lord has garments so wondrous fine

These words were written by Henry Barraclough in 1915 as a versification of the outline of a sermon of Dr. J. Wilbur Chapman, with whom he served as pianist in evangelistic campaigns.

The place was the Presbyterian conference grounds in Montreat, N.C. and the sermon was based on Psalm 45:8, "All thy garments smell of myrrh, and aloes, and cassia, out of the ivory palaces, whereby they have made thee glad." After an evening service, Henry Barraclough wrote the stanzas and refrain. The next morning the new hymn was sung as a duet in the Montreat conference session.

The hymn was published in 1915 in *Alexander's Hymns, No. 3* (Marshall Brothers, London) and also in the Sunday School hymnal of the Presbyterian Church in the U. S. (Southern).

MONTREAT. Henry Barraclough composed the music for his words. The tune name memorializes the place where the hymn was written—Montreat, North Carolina. Evangelist Billy Graham lives on the mountain nearby.

151. Beneath the cross of Jesus

This text is a part of a poem published anonymously in Edinburgh, Scotland in 1872 in *Family Treasury*, a Scottish Presbyterian magazine. The editor added a comment that the hymn expressed "the experience, hopes and longings of a young lady lately released." The reference was to Miss Elizabeth C. Clephane, who had died three years earlier at the age of 39.

ST. CHRISTOPHER. Frederick C. Maker composed the music for this hymn and it first appeared in the supplement to the *Bristol Tune Book,* 1881. The tune was presumably named for a third century martyr.

152. Ah, holy Jesus, how hast Thou offended?

The first source of this text, long attributed to St. Augustine, is now recognized as the writings of Jean de Fecamp, published 400 years after his death in a 15th century devotional book entitled *Meditationes sanctorum patrum.* The hymn version (in German) by Johann Heermann first appeared in his *Devoti Musica Cordis, ca.* 1630. The English translation by Robert D. Bridges (derived from both the Latin and German) appeared in his *Yattendon Hymnal,* 1899.

HERZLIEBSTER JESU. The music was composed by Johann Crüger and was found in his famous *Gesangbuch,* 1640. It may be based on the tune for the 23rd Psalm in the Genevan Psalter, 1562 and/or on "Geliebter Freund" in Schein's *Cantional,* 1627. Its title is derived from the beginning of the German version of the hymn.

153. Cross of Jesus, cross of sorrow

William J. Sparrow-Simpson wrote the libretto for John Stainer's cantata *The Crucifixion,* 1887, of which this hymn is a part.

CROSS OF JESUS. John Stainer's tune "Cross of Jesus" appears with this hymn in *The Crucifixion.* In that choral work, it was evidently intended to be sung by the congregation.

154. King of my life, I crown Thee now

No information is available on the writing of this hymn by Jennie E. Hussey. It first appeared in *New Songs of Praise and Power, No. 3* (Hall-Mack Company, 1921).

DUNCANNON. The tune was written for these words by William J. Kirkpatrick and was named for his birthplace, Duncannon, Pennsylvania.

155. "Man of Sorrows," what a name

The text and tune were both written by Philip P. Bliss and first appeared in *The International Lessons Monthly,* 1875, and then in *Gospel Hymns No. 2,* 1876.

HALLELUJAH! WHAT A SAVIOR! The music was written for this text by the author. The tune name, "Hallelujah! What a Savior" is a title commonly given to the poem. The tune is also sometimes called "Gethsemane."

156. Alas! and did my Savior bleed?

Isaac Watts' well-known hymn first appeared in his *Hymns and Spiritual Songs, Book II,* "Composed on Divine Subjects," July, 1707. It appeared under the heading "Godly Sorrow Arising from the Sufferings of Christ." The last phrase of stanza one "For such a worm as I" is frequently changed; the editors have chosen "For sinners such as I."

MARTYRDOM. The tune "Martyrdom" first appeared in leaflet form in the late 18th century. It was set "in triple time" in R. A. Smith's *Sacred Music Sung in St. George's Church* (Edinburgh, 1825) where it was called an "old Scottish melody." After Hugh Wilson's death, a lawsuit declared him to be the rightful owner of the copyright, but the magazine *Choir* (July, 1934) traced similarities in structure which indicate that Wilson may have adapted it from a traditional secular air, "Helen of Kirkconnel." In this arrangement, the editors have returned to Wilson's "common time."

157. I know that my Redeemer liveth

Jessie B. Pound's words appeared first in 1893 in an Easter cantata entitled *Hope's Messenger,* by James H. Fillmore. They were presented as a congregational hymn in *The Praise Hymnal,* 1896, compiled by Gilbert J. Ellis and Fillmore.

HANNAH. James H. Fillmore's tune appeared with the above text in his cantata, *Hope's Messenger* (Fillmore Music House, Cincinnati, 1893.) "Hannah" (Lockwood) was Fillmore's mother's given name; hence the tune name.

158. I serve a risen Savior

In *Forty Gospel Hymn Stories,* George Sanville (editor for the Rodeheaver Company) tells the story of the writing of this text and tune by Alfred H. Ackley. In 1933 a young Jew had asked him, "Why should I worship a dead Jew?" and Ackley had witnessed, "But Jesus lives!" The song first appeared in *Triumphant Service Songs* (Chicago: Rodeheaver Co., 1933).

ACKLEY. The tune was named for the composer, A. H. Ackley, by the editors of the *Baptist Hymnal,* 1956.

159. Jesus lives and so shall I

Based on John 14:19, "Because I live, ye shall live also," Christian Gellert's text "Jesus lebt, mit ihm auch ich" was published in his *Geistliche Oden und Lieder* (Leipzig, 1757). The first appearance of this hymn in the United States was in the *Plymouth Collection,* 1855; the translation there (as here) was by J. D. Lang and first appeared in *Aurora Australis* (Sydney, 1826).

ZUVERSICHT. The tune (named from the last line in German, "Dies ist meine Zuversicht") appeared in the *Rungsche Gesangbuch* without the name of the composer. In the 1668 edition of *Praxis Pietatis Melica* the initials "J.C." (Johann Crüger) appeared.

160. O sons and daughters, let us sing

"L'aleluya du jour de Pasques" (The Easter Alleluia) was written in Latin by Jean Tisserand, a Franciscan monk who died in 1494 in Paris. It was first discovered in a small untitled book printed some time between 1518 and 1536. John Mason Neale translated the poem for his *Medieval Hymns and Sequences,* 1851. It has frequently been altered during the years of its use.

O FILII ET FILIAE. "O Filii et Filiae" (the first line in Latin) is a traditional French tune, probably contemporary with the text and always associated with it. The composer is unknown, but its first appearance has been traced to *Airs sur les hymnes sacres, odes et noels,* 1623.

161. The strife is o'er, the battle done

The Latin antecedent of this hymn has been traced to the *Symphonia Sirenum Selectarum* (Cologne, 1695), where it appears anonymously. In the original version, two "Alleluias" begin each stanza. Francis Pott translated it about 1859 and published it in his *Hymns Fitted to the Order of Common Prayer,* 1861.

VICTORY. The music is an adaptation of the opening phrases of "Gloria Patri et Filio" from Palestrina's *Magnificat Tertii Toni,* 1591. William H. Monk arranged it for the original musical edition of *Hymns Ancient and Modern,* 1861. The title comes from the second phrase, stanza one of the English text.

162. Now the green blade riseth

John M. C. Crum wrote these Easter words for the old French tune traditionally associated with the Christmas carol "Noël nouvelet." They appeared in *The Oxford Book of Carols* (London, 1928), edited by Percy Dearmer, Ralph Vaughan Williams and Martin Shaw. In the United States, they were first included in *Methodist Hymnal,* 1964.

FRENCH CAROL. Martin Shaw arranged the historic French melody to accompany the new Easter text by Crum.

163. Christ the Lord is risen today

Entitled "Hymn for Easter Day," this text of Charles Wesley was first included in *Hymns and Sacred Poems,* 1739. It was altered and published in Martin Madan's *Collection of Psalms and Hymns,* 1760, a famous volume that influenced English hymnals for more than 100 years.

EASTER HYMN. *Lyra Davidica* (London, 1708), a collection of twenty-two tunes, included this anonymous melody. Since its first appearance, it has been frequently revised. In essentially the present form, it is found in Arnold's *Compleat Psalmodist,* 1741.

164. Come, ye faithful, raise the strain

From the pen of John of Damascus, the most important of the early Greek hymnists, this is the first Ode of the Canon for Low Sunday. John Mason Neale translated four of these odes into English. The text was first published as part of an article on Greek hymnody in the *Christian Remembrancer,* April, 1859, and later in Neale's *Hymns of the Eastern Church,* 1862.

ST. KEVIN. The tune was written for this text but appeared unnamed in *The Hymnary* (London, 1872), edited by its composer, Arthur S. Sullivan. It was given this name in Sullivan's *Church Hymns with Tunes,* 1903. St. Kevin was an Irish hermit who lived in the Vale of Glendalough (Valley of the Two Lakes), Ireland. He is credited with having established a monastery.

165. Low in the grave He lay

Robert Lowry wrote the text and tune in 1874 while he was pastor of a Baptist Church in Lewisburg, Pennsylvania and a professor of rhetoric in Bucknell University.

CHRIST AROSE. The complete hymn of Robert Lowry was first published in *Brightest and Best,* 1875, edited by William H. Doane and Lowry.

166. I know that my Redeemer lives

This text appeared anonymously in George Whitefield's *Psalms and*

Hymns, Extracted from Different Authors, 1775. Authorship was verified in the posthumous collection of Samuel Medley's lyrics, entitled *Hymns: The Public Worship and Private Devotions of True Christians, Assisted in Some Thoughts in Verse: Principally Drawn from Select Passages of the Word of God* (London, 1800).

LASST UNS ERFREUEN. See "All creatures of our God and King," No. 59.

167. Jesus Christ has triumphed now!

Hymns for the Living Church was ready to go to press in late 1973 when it was discovered that a previously selected hymn on the resurrection was unavailable because of copyright restrictions. As associate editor of the hymnal, John F. Wilson was assigned the task of finding a replacement or writing one himself. This contemporary hymn was the result.

RESURRECTION. John F. Wilson wrote music for his words, and the tune name is the oft-repeated word which dominates the refrain.

168. The day of resurrection

In the original Greek, this hymn is the first ode of the "Golden Canon" by John of Damascus. In Orthodox churches it is sung at midnight on Easter Morn as the congregation, on a given signal, light their candles filling the darkened church with light. The translation is a free setting by John Mason Neale and first appeared in his *Hymns of the Eastern Church,* 1862.

LANCASHIRE. The tune was written for a missionary festival held at Blackburn, Lancashire, October 4, 1835 to celebrate the 300th anniversary of the Reformation in England. On that occasion it was used with the hymn "From Greenland's icy mountains." Composer Henry Smart was organist at Blackburn at the time and named the tune for the county. It first appeared in *Psalms and Hymns for Divine Worship,* 1867.

169. "Welcome, happy morning!"

The complete Latin poem by Venantius Fortunatus, "Tempora florigero rutilant distincta sereno," portrays the coming of spring as a symbol of the new life that came to the world with Christ's resurrection. This paraphrase by John Ellerton of the Easter cento "Salve, festa dies" was first published in 1868 in Brown-Borthwick's *Supplemental Hymn and Tune Book.* It is often used as a processional hymn.

HERMAS. Frances R. Havergal wrote this music for her words, "Golden Harps Are Sounding." It was first published in W. H. Havergal's *Psalmody*

(London, 1871). The tune was named for Hermas, one of the friends of St. Paul (Romans 16:14).

170. Good Christian men, rejoice and sing

Cyril A. Alington wrote the text for this tune while he was Head Master at Eton. It was first published in *Songs of Praise,* 1931.

GELOBT SEI GOTT. The tune was set to the hymn "Gelobt sei Gott' in Melchior Vulpius' *Ein schön geistlich Gesangbuch* (Weimar, 1609) and is possibly of folk origin. It was introduced into English hymnody with Alington's words in *Songs of Praise,* 1931.

171. Thine is the glory, Risen, conquering Son

The French hymn, "A toi la gloire" (dated 1884) by Edmond Budry, pastor in Vevey, Switzerland, was first published in the *Y.M.C.A. Hymn Book* (Lausanne, 1904). It was translated into English by Richard B. Hoyle in 1923 and appeared in *Cantate Domino,* 1925, the hymnal of the World's Student Christian Federation. In England the first line is sung "Thine be the glory."

MACCABEUS. The hymn tune is adapted from a chorus in the original version of Handel's oratorio *Joshua,* 1748. The music was transferred from *Joshua* to *Judas Maccabeus* in 1751 and there it has remained, set to the words "See, the conquering hero comes."

172. Hark! ten thousand harps and voices

Thomas Kelly's hymn of praise to "Christ the King" first appeared in his *Hymns on Various Passages of Scripture* (2nd ed., 1806). It was originally titled "Let all the angels of God worship Him" (Hebrews 1:6).

HARWELL. Lowell Mason added the "Hallelujahs" and the "Amen" to Kelly's text when he set the hymn to music in 1840. It appeared in his *Carmina Sacra,* 1841.

173. Hail the day that sees Him rise

This "Hymn for Ascension Day" is by Charles Wesley and appeared with ten stanzas in the Wesley brothers' *Hymns and Sacred Poems,* 1739. The "Alleluias" were added in G. C. White's *Hymns and Introits,* 1852.

LLANFAIR. See "Let the whole creation cry," No. 27.

174. Alleluia! sing to Jesus

These words by William Chatterton Dix were written in 1866 and first appeared in *Altar Songs, Verses on the Holy Eucharist, No. 7*, 1867. The original title was "Redemption by the Precious Blood," based on Revelation 5:9.

HYFRYDOL. See "Come, Thou long expected Jesus," No. 102.

175. Look, ye saints! the sight is glorious

Thomas Kelly's majestic coronation paean for the second advent of Christ is considered to be one of the best of his 765 hymns. It first appeared in the third edition of his *Hymns on Various Passages of Scripture*, 1809 and is based on Revelation 7:9–15 and 11:15, "And he shall reign forever and ever."

REGENT SQUARE. See "Holy Father, great Creator," No. 6.

176. The head that once was crowned with thorns

This is primarily an Ascension Day hymn based on Hebrews 2:9, 10. It was first published in author Thomas Kelly's *Hymns on Various Passages of Scripture*, 5th ed., 1820.

ST. MAGNUS. The melody was first published anonymously in Henry Playford's *Divine Companion* (1707, 2nd ed.). It has been attributed to Jeremiah Clark because of its similarity and adjacency to three "psalms" credited to him in the volume. The tune is named after St. Magnus Church, located near the old London Bridge.

177. Rejoice, the Lord is King

This text first appeared in Charles Wesley's *Hymns for Our Lord's Resurrection*, 1746. The refrain is based on Philippians 4:4, "Rejoice in the Lord alway: and again I say, Rejoice." The hymn has been recommended for processionals on Easter Day.

DARWALL. See "Join all the glorious names," No. 70.

178. It may be at morn

This second coming hymn by H. L. Turner first appeared in Ira D. Sankey's *Gospel Hymns, No. 3*, 1878 with the scripture reference John 14:3, "I will come again, and receive you unto myself."

CHRIST RETURNETH. James McGranahan wrote the tune for this text and they appeared together in *Gospel Hymns, No. 3*, 1878.

179. Jesus may come today
This song by Henry Ostrom appeared for many years under the pseudonym "George Walker Whitcomb." Dr. Ostrom said that he felt greater freedom to use the hymn in his evangelistic campaigns when he was not listed as author. Words and music were first introduced at a conference session of the Seibert United Evangelical Church of Allentown, Pennsylvania.

CROWNING DAY. The music by Charles H. Marsh was composed for this text. They were copyrighted in 1910 and published together in *The Message in Song* (1911, Praise Publishing Company).

180. Jesus is coming to earth again
Both words and music were written by Lelia N. (Mrs. C. H.) Morris. The song first appeared in *The King's Praises No. 3*, compiled by H. L. Gilmour, George W. Sanville, William J. Kirkpatrick, and Melvin J. Hill, (Phila.: Praise Publishing Company, 1912).

SECOND COMING. The tune name was given first in *Baptist Hymnal*, 1956.

181. The King shall come when morning dawns
This text, of unknown Greek Orthodox origin, was translated by John Brownlie and first appeared in his *Hymns from the East, being Centos and Suggestions from the Service Book of the Holy Eastern Church*, 1907.

KENTUCKY HARMONY. The traditional melody was apparently first published in *Kentucky Harmony*, 1816. It appears in that historic book with the name "Consolation" and is credited in the index to an unknown author "Dean."

182. Marvelous message we bring
Author-composer John W. Peterson says that this "second advent" song was written expressly for the first volume (1957) of the *Songster* choir magazine he edited, which was published for several years by "Better Choirs" and later by the Singspiration Company.

COMING AGAIN. Customarily John W. Peterson has written music for his own words, and that is true of this song which sometimes appears with the title "Coming Again."

183. Christ is coming! let creation
The *Handbook to the Mennonite Hymnary* calls this "a Scottish hymn setting forth the glowing hope and expectation of the coming of Christ in glory." It is based on Revelation 22:20, was written by John R. Macduff and published in his *Altar Stones*, 1853.

UNSER HERRSCHER. Sometimes called "Neander" after its composer, Joachim Neander, the tune originally appeared with the hymn "Unser Herrscher, Unser König" in the 1680 edition of the *Glaub- und Liebesübung*.

184. Lift up your heads, pilgrims a-weary
This is the best-known hymn of Mabel Johnston Camp, but little is known about its writing. It was first released in *The Voice of Thanksgiving*, 1913, published by Fleming H. Revell for the Moody Bible Institute in Chicago.

CAMP. Mrs. Mabel Johnston Camp wrote tunes for her own texts and this is one of her best.

185. Lo, He comes with clouds descending
In writing this hymn Charles Wesley was inspired by an earlier work of John Cennick, published in 1752. The text on the Second Advent was first published in the Wesleys' *Hymns of Intercession for All Mankind*, 1758. The present version appeared with alterations by Martin Madan in his *Collection of Psalms and Hymns*, 1760, and is a combination of the earlier texts.

REGENT SQUARE. See "Holy Father, great Creator," No. 6.

186. In the glow of early morning
Winfield Macomber's text is one of the early "second coming" hymns in the present tradition. It was written about 1888 and later appeared in *Hymns of the Christian Life, No. 2*, 1897, edited by R. Kelso Carter and A. B. Simpson, under the title "Christ Is Coming."

MACOMBER. The tune name honors the author-composer, who lived only thirty-one years and served as a heroic missionary in Africa.

187. Breathe on me, Breath of God

In Edwin Hatch's text, the Holy Spirit is addressed as "Breath of God" (from John 20:22). The hymn was first printed in a pamphlet "Between Doubt and Prayer" (1878), and later in Dr. Allon's *Psalmist Hymnal,* 1886.

TRENTHAM. The tune was written by Robert Jackson, who was born at Trentham, Staffordshire, England. It was composed for Henry W. Baker's "O perfect life of love" and was first printed in *Fifty Sacred Leaflets,* 1888 or 1894. (Equally trustworthy sources give both dates!)

188. Come, Holy Ghost, our souls inspire

"Veni, creator Spiritus," the Latin original of this hymn, dates back to the ninth or tenth century and is often credited to Rabanus Maurus, Archbishop of Mainz. It has had wide liturgical use for a thousand years. The translation by John Cosin was taken from his *Collection of Private Devotions in the Practice of the Ancient Church,* 1627. Bishop Cosin composed this hymn for the coronation of Charles I in 1625, at which he officiated.

MENDON. See "Lord of all being, throned afar," No. 30.

189. O spread the tidings 'round

Frank Bottome wrote this "Holy Spirit" hymn and it was published with this music in *Precious Hymns for Times of Refreshing and Revival* (1890 edition), selected by Thomas Harrison and published by John J. Hood, Philadelphia, Pa.

COMFORTER. The tune is by William J. Kirkpatrick, who worked with John R. Sweney in editing the above-mentioned collection. It is named after the title given to the Holy Spirit in John 14:16, 26 (KJV), and featured prominently in the text.

190. We are gathered for Thy blessing

Lance B. Latham was assistant in music at Moody Church in Chicago when the pastor, Paul Rader, wrote this hymn. Dr. Latham says:

> Paul Rader knew the value of prayer, and in this lasting hymn expressed his proved experience.

Latham, who at 83 only recently retired from a 40-year pastorate, added his personal conviction:

> God's plan of working through prayer has not changed with the modern times.

Evidently the hymn was first written about 1916, revised in 1920, and officially copyrighted in 1921.

TABERNACLE. Paul Rader conceived the melody for his words and they were harmonized by his music assistant, Lance B. Latham. According to Latham, it was written in Rader's home on Fullerton Avenue in Chicago. The complete hymn was first published in *Tabernacle Praises, No. 1,* and the revised form appeared in *Tabernacle Hymns, No. 2, 1921.* The tune name has many associations with this hymn and its author. The Moody Church was once known as a "tabernacle"; Dr. Paul Rader encouraged the founding of the Tabernacle Publishing Company (long an affiliate of Hope Publishing Company) in 1916; and finally, Rader founded the Chicago Gospel Tabernacle in 1922.

191. Spirit of God in the clear running water

Miriam Therese Winter began to write biblical folk hymns in 1965, and this was one of her first. It was recorded that year in the now-famous album "Joy Is Like the Rain" and published by Vanguard Publishing Corporation, New York under the same title in 1966.

MEDICAL MISSION SISTERS. Miss Winter's tune is named for the Society of Catholic Medical Missionaries with which she has served since 1955.

192. Joys are flowing like a river

Manie Payne Ferguson wrote this hymn about 1900 after coming into the Wesleyan experience of "holiness" or "entire sanctification," called by some the "filling of the Spirit." The third stanza was then her testimony:

> Like the rain that falls from heaven,
>   Like the sunlight from the sky,
> So the Holy Ghost is given,
>   Coming on us from on high.

The song first appeared in *Pentecostal Hymns, No. 3* (Hope Publishing Company, 1902). In this book, the author is named as "Mamie" Payne Ferguson.

BLESSED QUIETNESS. The tune name is the traditional title of the hymn; in the first printing it was "Holy Quietness." The melody was written by W. S. Marshall and arranged for publication by James M. Kirk. However, *Pentecostal Hymns, No. 3* credits the arrangement to T. C. O'Kane, one of the book's editors.

193. Gracious Spirit, dwell with me

This text by Thomas Toke Lynch is from his collection *The Rivulet:*

Hymns for Heart and Voice, 1855. Because of certain doctrines included in this book, a fierce controversy arose in his congregation. Typical of him, when the conflict was at its height he responded quietly, "The air will be all the clearer for the storm. We must conquer our foes by suffering them to crucify us, rather than by threatening them with crucifixion."

REDHEAD. See "Go to dark Gethsemane," No. 147.

194. Holy Spirit, Light divine

The editors of *Hymns for the Living Church* have adapted the well-known "Holy Ghost, with Light divine" by Andrew Reed, because of today's preference for the title "Holy Spirit" instead of "Holy Ghost." The original hymn was included in Reed's *Supplement to Watts' Psalms and Hymns,* 1817 and was titled "Prayer to the Holy Spirit" (sic).

MERCY. This melody was early associated with Charles Wesley's "Depth of mercy, can there be"—hence the tune name. It was arranged by Edwin P. Parker from Louis Gottschalk's piano piece, "The Last Hope," 1854.

195. Hover o'er me, Holy Spirit

Elwood H. Stokes' prayer to the Holy Spirit was copyrighted in 1879. It appeared in *The Quiver of Sacred Song* (John J. Hood, publishers, 1880), edited by John R. Sweney and William J. Kirkpatrick.

FILL ME NOW. Under the title "Fill Me Now" this tune by John R. Sweney appeared with this text. In *Songs of Redeeming Love,* 1880 and 1882 (ed. by Sweney, C. C. McCabe, T. C. O'Kane and Wm. J. Kirkpatrick), the tune is also suggested for "Come, Thou Fount."

196. O Breath of Life

The *Anglican Hymn Book,* 1965 dates Bessie P. Head's hymn *"ca.* 1914," and it probably appeared first in leaflet form. It was included in Mrs. Head's *Heavenly Places and Other Messages,* 1920 and in the *Keswick Hymn Book* of 1936. This stanza is omitted in *Hymns for the Living Church:*

> O Heart of Christ, once broken for us,
> 'Tis there we find our strength and rest,
> Our broken contrite hearts now solace,
> And let Thy waiting Church be blest.

SPIRITUS VITAE. Mary J. Hammond wrote the music for these words, and it is named from the first words of the first stanza, "O Breath (Spirit) of Life."

197. Come, Holy Spirit, heavenly Dove

This hymn by Isaac Watts based on Romans 5:5 appeared in his *Hymns and Spiritual Songs*, 1707 under the heading "Breathing after the Holy Spirit: or, Fervency of Devotion Desired." Numerous alterations have been made to the text; Watts himself made some changes in a second edition. Four of the five original stanzas are used here.

ST. AGNES. See "Jesus, the very thought of Thee," No. 83.

198. Spirit of God, descend upon my heart

This text, written by a London clergyman, George Croly, was not included in his *Psalms and Hymns for Public Worship*, 1854 as many handbooks claim. Its first appearance seems to be in the work of a contemporary, Charles Rogers' *Lyra Britannica*, 1867.

MORECAMBE. The tune was written in 1870 by Frederick Atkinson as a setting for "Abide with Me," and was first published in leaflet form. G. S. Barrett and E. J. Hopkins included it in their *Congregational Church Hymnal* (London, 1887). Morecambe is a well-known town on Morecambe Bay in west England.

199. Brethren, we have met to worship

In *Hymns of Our Faith*, William J. Reynolds says:

> In many early collections George Atkins is credited as being the author of this hymn. However, no information has been found concerning either the hymn or the author.

From the style of the text and tune we may presume that it was produced in the camp meeting tradition of the early nineteenth century. It was brought back into use through its inclusion in *Baptist Hymnal*, 1956.

HOLY MANNA. George Pullen Jackson has pointed out that, while the melody of lines 1, 2 and 4 are identical, the third phrase's tune has appeared independently with other words, such as "Come, ye sinners, poor and wretched."

The tune name is derived from the words "holy manna" in stanzas one, two and three.

200. The Church's one foundation

This text was written by Samuel Stone because of his admiration for the noble defense of the faith by Bishop Gray of Capetown, South Africa. The controversy arose from Bishop John William Colenso's book *The Pentateuch and Book of Joshua, Critically Examined*. The hymn appeared first in Stone's

Lyra Fidelium: Twelve Hymns on the Twelve Articles of the Apostles' Creed, 1866, where it contained seven stanzas. The present hymn with five stanzas appeared with the tune "Aurelia" in the 1868 Appendix to *Hymns Ancient and Modern.*

AURELIA. Samuel Sebastian Wesley's tune first appeared in *A Selection of Psalms and Hymns* (London, 1864) edited by Wesley and Charles Kemble. It was originally set to "Jerusalem the Golden." Wesley's wife suggested the tune name, taken from "aureus," Latin for "golden."

201. Built on the Rock the church doth stand

Nicolai F. S. Grundtvig's hymn was published in his *Sang-Värk til den Danske Kirke* in 1837. It was translated by Carl Doving and appeared in the *Lutheran Hymnary,* 1913. The present version was adapted by Fred Hansen and appeared in the *Hymnal for Church and Home,* 1927.

KIRKEN DEN ER ET. Ludvig Lindeman's tune, written for this text, first appeared in W. A. Wexel's *Christelige Psalmer,* 1840. It has been noted to have the characteristics of Norse folk music, of which Lindeman was an avid scholar, collector and publisher. "Kirken den er et gammelt hus" literally means "The church, it is an old house."

202. Jesus, with Thy Church abide

A "litany" is a ceremonial prayer with a series of supplications and a common response, such as "We beseech Thee, hear us." This "Litany of the Church" first appeared in Thomas B. Pollock's Appendix to *Metrical Litanies for Special Services and General Use,* 1871. It originally had 18 stanzas and was rewritten for the revised edition of *Hymns Ancient and Modern,* 1875.

LITANY OF THE PASSION. The tune by John Bacchus Dykes was set to another poetic litany—"Litany of the Passion"—in the revised edition of *Hymns Ancient and Modern,* 1875, and from this takes its name.

203. I love Thy kingdom, Lord

This text was inspired by Psalm 137:5, 6 and is perhaps the oldest hymn written by an American which has remained in continuous use. The author, Dr. Timothy Dwight, revised *The Psalms of David* by Isaac Watts in 1800 and added 33 of his own paraphrases and hymns, including this one. It is apparent from stanza one that Dwight equates the "Kingdom" with the Church universal; stanza four interprets "Zion" similarly.

ST. THOMAS. See "Come, we that love the Lord," No. 23.

204. There's a quiet understanding

Tedd Smith says that he wrote this folk hymn in September, 1972.

> After a Billy Graham Crusade meeting in Oakland, California, I was invited by a few friends to attend a communion service. There were about twelve of us in attendance, most meeting for the first time. As we sat in a circle on the floor sharing communion, the feeling of being strangers disappeared and there seemed to come this quiet understanding of each other, a feeling of being with brothers and sisters and sensing the oneness Christ promised whenever two or three gather in His name. I went back to my room and wrote "There's a Quiet Understanding" as a benediction to a meaningful evening.

Mr. Smith copyrighted the song in 1973.

QUIET UNDERSTANDING. Tedd Smith's words and music were first published as a choral octavo in 1974 by Hope Publishing Company. This is the hymn's first appearance in a standard hymnal.

205. Renew Thy church, her ministries restore

This hymn appeared as part of the Baptist Jubilee Advance, a five-year denominational program. It was written specifically for the second year's emphasis on "The Renewal of the Church: Imperative to Evangelism." It was composed while author Kenneth Cober was traveling across the country on trains and planes in denominational work, and was sung for the first time at the American Baptist Convention in May, 1960.

ALL IS WELL. While this tune is said to be a traditional English melody, it may very well be American in its origin. Researchers reveal that it appeared as early as 1844 in *The Sacred Harp* and was probably widely sung before that time. More recently it has been used predominantly by Mormons with their hymn "Come, come, ye saints," where the final refrain is "All is well!"

206. Faith of our fathers

Frederick W. Faber's hymn was written in two versions—both appearing in his *Jesus and Mary*, 1849—one for England, the other for Ireland. Both versions make it clear that for Faber the "faith of our fathers" is that of Roman Catholicism. However, with editing the English version is loved by evangelicals the world around, and Roman Catholics are now singing it!

ST. CATHERINE. Written by Henri F. Hemy, the tune was originally set to a Roman Catholic hymn in Part II of his volume, *Crown of Jesus Music*, 1864. The title of the hymn was "St. Catherine, Virgin and Martyr." James G. Walton made a new arrangement and used this adaptation in *Plain Song Music for the Holy Communion*, 1874.

207. Blest be the tie that binds

The hymn's author, John D. Fawcett, having received a call to a church in London, resigned his pastorate in Wainsgate, Yorkshire and was preparing to move, with personal belongings all packed and loaded. His congregation was grief stricken at the thought of his leaving and he and his wife shared the feeling, so they changed their plans and decided to remain. It has been said that this hymn was written as the result of this experience, and it first appeared in Fawcett's *Hymns adapted to the circumstances of Public Worship and Private Devotion,* 1782.

DENNIS. The tune first appeared in Mason and Webb's *The Psaltery,* 1845. Lowell Mason found it among the manuscripts of J. G. Nägeli, a Swiss music publisher. It is thought to be named for a town in Massachusetts.

208. There's a church within us, O Lord

This text was written by Kent Schneider in 1967 in a small dormitory room at Chicago Theological Seminary. He says:

> While in seminary, I began doing jazz worship services throughout the country. Sometimes I met people who were "up tight" about what went on in their church buildings. It may have been part of the "edifice complex" of the late 60's.

> I wrote the song one evening after coming in from a church meeting. At that meeting the board of trustees had just voted not to allow an over-crowded school to use its Sunday school rooms during the week for fear that the little children would "mark up the building." The sad irony of this event is that fifteen years before, when this church was looking for a place to meet, it asked the same school if it could use its rooms on Sunday morning, and the school said "yes." I was very disgusted with people who lost sight of the needs of others, while trying to preserve "religion." I didn't think that that was what Jesus taught. "The Church Within Us" became a simple attempt to make an affirmative statement about something I believed.

The song was copyrighted in 1967 and first appeared in *Songs for Celebration,* 1969, published by Center for Contemporary Celebration, Chicago. Since it has been handled by Hope Publishing Company it has had wide usage, appearing in many folk collections and hymnals.

THE CHURCH WITHIN US. Kent Schneider has written about the music:

> I wanted to write a simple, strong melody that could be used in jazz or folk idioms and one that was easily sung.

Its name is the original title of the song.

209. Glorious things of thee are spoken

This hymn first appeared in Book I of *Olney Hymns,* 1779, edited by

William Cowper and John Newton, where its title was "Zion, or the City of God." It is thought to be one of Newton's greatest hymns and was said to be the "only joyful hymn in the Olney collection."

AUSTRIAN HYMN. See "Praise the Lord! ye heavens, adore Him," No. 17.

210. Here, O my Lord, I see Thee face to face
Horatius Bonar wrote this hymn at the request of his older brother, John J. Bonar, pastor of St. Andrew's Free Church, Greenock, Scotland. It was first printed in a leaflet distributed to the congregation following the observance of the Lord's Supper on the first Sunday in October, 1855. It was later included in Bonar's *Hymns of Faith and Hope,* first series, 1857.

LANGRAN. James Langran wrote this music for "Abide with Me" and it first appeared in leaflet form in 1861. It later was included in John Foster's *Psalms and Hymns Adapted to the Services of the Church of England,* 1863.

211. Bread of the world in mercy broken
This communion hymn by Reginald Heber was first included in his collection, published posthumously, *Hymns Written and Adapted to the weekly Church Services of the Year,* 1827. It was titled "Before the Sacrament."

EUCHARISTIC HYMN. The tune was composed for the text by John S. B. Hodges while he was rector of Grace Episcopal Church, Newark, N.J. It appeared first in his *Book of Common Praise,* 1869, named for the Communion service for which the text was written.

212. According to Thy gracious word
Based on Luke 22:19, these lines were first printed in author James Montgomery's *Christian Psalmist,* 1825. A favorite communion hymn, it reminds us of Christ's command "This do in remembrance of me."

MARTYRDOM. See "Alas! and did my Savior bleed?", No. 156.

213. Let us break bread together
As is true of folk songs, there is no known author or composer for this spiritual. In his book *Negro Slave Songs in the United States,* 1953, Miles Mark Fisher has suggested that after the Civil War it was sung by blacks as a communion hymn. It may be derived from a song they used to convene

secret meetings, when such gatherings were prohibited in the colony of Virginia.

LET US BREAK BREAD. The history of the tune is lost in the traditions of black worship of the 18th and 19th centuries. John W. Work says it was first published by William Lawrence in 1928. Like many spirituals, it has become known through choral arrangements. This harmonization was made by Carlton R. Young for *Methodist Hymnal,* © 1964.

214. We bless the name of Christ the Lord

This baptism hymn was written by Samuel F. Coffman in 1926, and was included in the Mennonite *Church Hymnal,* edited by J. D. Brunk and S. F. Coffman (Scottdale, Pa., Mennonite Publishing Co., 1927).

RETREAT. See "From every stormy wind that blows," No. 430.

215. Come, Holy Spirit, Dove divine

While Adoniram Judson was translating the Bible into Burmese about 1829, he wrote the hymn "Our Savior bowed beneath the wave." "Come, Holy Spirit, Dove Divine" is made up of stanzas taken from Judson's baptism hymn and first appeared in Winchell's *Collection,* 1832.

MARYTON. The tune was written by H. Percy Smith for the hymn "Sun of my Soul, Thou Savior dear," and first appeared in *Church Hymns with Tunes* (London, 1874).

216. See Israel's gentle Shepherd stand

This text was first published in Job Orton's posthumous edition of Philip Doddridge's *Hymns Founded on Various Texts in the Holy Scriptures,* 1755. Based on Mark 10:14, its original title was "Christ's Condescending Regard to Little Children."

SERENITY. See "O Jesus, King most wonderful," No. 73.

217. Savior, who Thy flock art feeding

This is the best known of William Mühlenberg's hymns, and it first appeared in *Prayer Book Collection,* 1826.

BROCKLESBURY. Brocklesbury is a town near Dover, England where the composer Charlotte A. Barnard lived and died. Her tune's date has been given as 1868, but *The Hymnal Companion* locates it first in Tucker's *Hymnal with Tunes Old and New,* 1872.

218. The Bible stands like a rock undaunted

Haldor Lillenas wrote these words and set them to music in 1917, sending the song to the song-evangelist Arthur McKee, who included it in *Tabernacle Hymns No. 2* (Chicago: Tabernacle Publishing Co., 1921).

RIDGE LINE. In preparing the copy for *Hymns for the Living Church* it seemed desirable to include this song about the Bible, but to find a new tune. Editor Donald P. Hustad wrote the new setting in 1973 and named it for the street on which he lives in Louisville, Kentucky. A choral arrangement has become a virtual theme song of the Boyce Bible School, affiliated with Southern Baptist Theological Seminary.

219. O Word of God incarnate

This text by William Walsham How based on Psalm 119:105 first appeared in the 1867 supplement to *Psalms and Hymns,* compiled by How and Thomas Baker Morrell.

MUNICH. See "O Savior, precious Savior," No. 98.

220. Break Thou the bread of life

This hymn (first two stanzas) was written by Mary A. Lathbury in 1877 at the request of Bishop John H. Vincent, one of the founders of the Chautauqua Literary and Scientific Circle. It is based on Christ's feeding the multitude and was intended to be used by groups devoted to Bible study. Tradition requires that it be sung at Sunday evening vespers at the Chautauqua assembly in New York.

It has recently come to light that stanzas three and four were added by Alexander Groves and first appeared in the *Wesleyan Methodist Magazine* (London, September, 1913).

BREAD OF LIFE. The tune (named for part of the first phrase) was composed in 1877 for the text by William F. Sherwin, choral director of the Chautauqua institution. It appeared in Chautauqua publications and then in *The Calvary Selection of Spiritual Songs,* 1878.

221. The heavens declare Thy glory, Lord

This paraphrase of Psalm 19 first appeared in Watts' *Psalms of David Imitated in the Language of the New Testament,* 1719 under the title "The Book of Nature and of Scripture Compared," or "The Glory and Success of the Gospel."

WINCHESTER NEW. See "O Splendor of God's glory bright," No. 16.

222. Sing them over again to me

This song was written by Philip Bliss at the request of the publisher, Fleming H. Revell, for the first issue of *Words of Life,* 1874, a Sunday School paper. Two years later it was introduced in an evangelistic campaign which George Stebbins and Dr. George Pentecost were conducting in New Haven, Connecticut.

WORDS OF LIFE. The tune was written by Bliss at the time he wrote the words; both were published in the magazine, *Words of Life,* 1874.

223. God hath spoken by His prophets

George W. Briggs' words were written in 1952 and published by the Hymn Society of America in a pamphlet, "Ten New Bible Hymns" (1953). In conjunction with the National Christian Council and in celebration of the publication of the Revised Standard Version of the Bible, the Hymn Society had asked for new texts on the values and history of Holy Scripture. The ten were selected from more than 300 entries.

HYMN TO JOY. See "Joyful, joyful, we adore Thee," No. 25.

224. How firm a foundation

These words first appeared in Dr. John Rippon's *A Selection of Hymns from the Best Authors,* 1787 under the title "Exceeding Great and Precious Promises." The authorship was ascribed merely to "K". Later reprints gave "Kn" and "Keen." It is thought that the author was Richard Keen, precentor in the church pastored by Dr. Rippon, and composer of the tune to which the words were originally set.

FOUNDATION. The source of the tune has been as much in question as the authorship of the text. However, it seems to have first appeared in Joseph Funk's *Genuine Church Music,* 1832, and later in *The Sacred Harp,* 1844 where it was called "Bellevue." It is generally agreed that it was one of the most widely sung folk hymn tunes in the South.

225. Standing on the promises

R. Kelso Carter wrote these words and published them in *Songs of Perfect Love,* 1886, which was compiled by John R. Sweney and Carter.

PROMISES. The tune was written by R. Kelso Carter for his own text, and was first named in *Baptist Hymnal,* 1956. In *Music in Evangelism,* Phil Kerr suggests that the martial flavor of the song may be due to Carter's association with the Pennsylvania Military Academy.

226. Holy Bible, book divine

This text was written by John Burton, Sr. and appeared first in his *Youth's Monitor in Verse, a Series of Little Tales, Emblems, Poems and Songs,* 1803. An English Baptist Sunday School teacher, Burton also included the hymn in his *Hymns for Sunday Schools, or Incentives for Early Piety,* 1806.

ALETTA. Composed by William B. Bradbury, the tune first appeared as the setting for "Weary Sinners, Keep Thine Eyes" in *The Jubilee,* 1858.

227. Lord, Thy Word abideth

Henry Baker's text was written for the first edition of *Hymns Ancient and Modern,* 1861, of which he was editor. It bore the caption: "Thy word is a lantern unto my feet, and a light unto my paths" (Psalm 119:105).

RAVENSHAW. The tune accompanied the above text in *Hymns Ancient and Modern,* 1861. It was adapted by William H. Monk from a medieval melody which first appeared in Michael Weisse's *Ein Neu Gesengbüchlen,* 1531, the earliest German hymnbook published by the Bohemian Brethren. Monk called it "Ravenshaw"—a homestead name.

228. I saw the cross of Jesus

This hymn by Frederick Whitfield was included in his *Sacred Poems and Prose,* 1861. Although it had been written and appeared on a single sheet in 1855, its first inclusion in a volume was in Ryle's *Hymns for the Church,* 1860.

WHITFIELD. The anonymous tune was named for the author of the words by the editors of *Baptist Hymnal,* 1956. It is also known as "Calcutta" because it was long attributed to Reginald Heber, Bishop of Calcultta. (A detailed account is given by Maurice Frost in *The Choir,* LI, No. 5, p. 91.) Its earliest known appearance was in *The Sunday-Scholar's Tune Book,* 1869.

229. O the deep, deep love of Jesus

In 1926, the year after his death at the age of 92, this was probably the best-known hymn of S. Trevor Francis; it was then that Pickering and Inglis, Ltd. of London and Glasgow released his collected works in a volume, *O the Deep, Deep Love of Jesus, and other poems.* The Irish *Church Hymnal* dates the hymn 1875. Its first publishing cannot be located, but it was included in *Song Companion to the Scriptures* (1911) compiled and published by G. Campbell Morgan, and in *Alexander's Hymns* (1913).

TON-Y-BOTEL. See "Once to every man and nation," No. 463.

230. There is a fountain filled with blood

Based on Zechariah 13:1 and written in 1770 or 1771 by William Cowper, this hymn first appeared in Conyer's *Collection of Psalms and Hymns,* 1772 and was included in *Olney Hymns,* 1779. Through the years, many have criticized the imagery of the text and have offered revisions. It is gratifying that the original remains in common use. The order of phrases in stanza five was changed by the editors of *Worship and Service Hymnal,* 1957, to achieve a positive climax.

CLEANSING FOUNTAIN. Because its style is reminiscent of early American camp-meeting songs, many scholars feel that the music is incorrectly attributed to Lowell Mason. Mason did write a similar tune called "Cowper" for this text in 1830 and this no doubt caused the confusion.

231. Free from the law, O happy condition

This text was written by Philip P. Bliss, as was the music. George C. Stebbins in his *Memoirs and Reminiscences* says that during Moody and Sankey's first visit to Scotland in 1873, this hymn helped to break down prejudice against gospel songs, because its expression was so scriptural and in perfect agreement with Scottish Reformed teaching.

ONCE FOR ALL. The tune was written by Philip P. Bliss for his words. The complete hymn first appeared in his *Sunshine for Sunday Schools,* 1873 and then in *Gospel Hymns and Sacred Songs,* 1875, in which he collaborated with Ira D. Sankey.

232. I hear the Savior say

This text was written by Elvina M. Hall on the flyleaf of a hymnal one Sunday morning, during a lengthy pastoral prayer. She gave the poem to her pastor and he in turn coupled it with a new tune written by the church organist, John T. Grape.

ALL TO CHRIST. John T. Grape's tune (named after the original title "All to Christ I owe") was written, he says, when his church was undergoing remodeling and the cabinet organ was left in his care. The resulting melody was approved by his wife, but criticized by his choir and other friends. It has achieved wide usage since Grape's pastor, a Rev. Schrick, coupled it with Mrs. Hall's words and it was published in *Sabbath Chords,* 1868.

233. There's a wideness in God's mercy

This text is part of a thirteen-verse poem by Frederick W. Faber entitled "Come to Jesus," and beginning "Souls of men, why will ye scatter," published in his *Hymns,* 1862. Faber included a shorter version in *Oratory Hymns,* 1854.

WELLESLEY. The music was written for her graduation hymn by Lizzie S. Tourjée when she was a high school senior. Her father Dr. Eben Tourjée, founder of the New England Conservatory of Music, named the tune for the newly-established Wellesley College, which his daughter attended for one year. He included it in the *Hymnal of the Methodist Episcopal Church with Tunes,* 1878, of which he was one of the editors.

234. These are the facts

As a member of the *Psalm Praise* team of writers, Michael Saward was given the task to prepare an "Easter canticle" to be an alternative to the traditional Anglican "Christ our Passover is sacrificed for us." It was written on Trinity Sunday, June 6, 1971 at his home in Beckenham, Kent, England, and appeared in *Psalm Praise* (1973, Falcon Books, London).

It is only fair to report that Rev. Saward expressed keen disappointment that the editors of *Hymns for the Living Church* omitted his fifth stanza—a repetition of the first. Users of the hymn are urged to repeat stanza one as the hymn's conclusion, if they so choose. Mr. Saward also regretted the elisions (changing "family" and "victory" to "fam'ly" and "vict'ry") to match syllables with melody notes, and the addition of an "Amen." These are standard American practices that are evidently not the norm in England.

YVONNE. The tune is named for the wife of composer Norman L. Warren. He says he was inspired by these "very good words" and that he wrote the music in Leamington Spa, England where he has been vicar of St. Paul's Church since 1963. It appeared with Michael Saward's development of I Corinthians 15:3, in *Psalm Praise,* 1973.

235. "What must I do?" the trembling jailor cried

In response to our question, Avis B. Christiansen tells about writing this hymn:

> The music, including the words of the chorus "Believe on the Lord Jesus Christ" was sent to me by the publisher . . . with the request that I write the verses. I never met composer Harry Clarke personally.

BELIEVE. The music was written by Harry D. Clarke, and the completed song appeared in *Tabernacle Hymns, No. 2* (Chicago: Tabernacle Publishing Company, 1921).

236. On a hill far away

The text for this hymn came to George Bennard during evangelistic services he was conducting in Michigan, as a result of his meditating on John 3:16 and praying for a full understanding of the cross. After many frustrated attempts to write and several experiences in which he saw the redeeming grace of God at work during those meetings, he was able to complete the poem. The song probably appeared first in leaflet form, and later in *Heart and Life Songs, for the Church, Sunday School, Home and Camp-meeting*, 1915, published by Hope Publishing Company for Chicago Evangelistic Institute, and edited by Iva D. Vennard, Joseph H. Smith and Bennard.

OLD RUGGED CROSS. The tune (bearing the name of the song's traditional title) was written simultaneously with the words by George Bennard. Homer Rodeheaver bought the copyright from the author, published it and made contracts with various recording companies for its reproduction. For many years it was acknowledged to be America's favorite gospel hymn.

237. What can wash away my sin?

Robert Lowry wrote this text and tune, probably while he was pastor of the Park Avenue Baptist Church, Plainfield, N.J. It was first published in *Gospel Music*, compiled by William H. Doane and Lowry in 1876, with the reference "Without the shedding of blood there is no remission of sin" (Heb. 9:22).

PLAINFIELD. Lowry's tune was named "Plainfield" in *Baptist Hymnal*, 1956 after the New Jersey town in which he served as pastor and where he died.

238. Depth of mercy! can there be

This text by Charles Wesley is part of a longer hymn entitled "After a Relapse into Sin." It was originally published in its entirety in *Hymns and Sacred Poems* by John and Charles Wesley, 1740.

SEYMOUR. The tune (also called "Weber") was taken from the opening chorus of *Oberon*, Carl Maria von Weber's last opera. Henry W. Greatorex arranged it as a hymn tune for his *Collection*, 1851 and named it for a Mr. Seymour, a bass singer in his choir at Center Church, Hartford, Connecticut.

239. O happy day that fixed my choice

Originally entitled "Rejoicing in our Covenant engagements to God," this text was written by Philip Doddridge. It appeared posthumously without the refrain in Doddridge's *Hymns, founded on Various Texts in the Holy Scriptures*, 1755. The hymn is said to have been chosen by Prince Albert, consort of Queen Victoria, to be sung on occasions when members of the royal family were confirmed. The refrain is anonymous.

HAPPY DAY. The refrain melody is from a popular song by Edward F. Rimbault entitled "Happy Land." The remainder is probably the work of other anonymous musicians. The full tune appeared in William McDonald's *The Wesleyan Sacred Harp*, 1854 set to another hymn text, but the same refrain, "Happy day, happy day, When Jesus washed my sins away!"

240. Marvelous grace of our loving Lord

These words are by Julia H. Johnston. They appeared in *Hymns Tried and True*, compiled by D. B. Towner and published by Moody Bible Institute, Chicago, 1911.

MOODY. The music was written for these words in 1910 by Daniel B. Towner, for many years head of the Music Department of Moody Bible Institute in Chicago.

241. Jesus, Thy blood and righteousness

Nicolaus Ludwig von Zinzendorf completed this hymn in 1739 on his return from visiting Moravian missionaries in the West Indies. The original German text had 33 stanzas and appeared in appendix no. 8 to *Hernnhut Gesang Buch*. John Wesley's selective translation reduced the verses to 24 and they were first published in *Hymns and Sacred Poems*, 1740 under the title "The Believer's Triumph."

GERMANY. The tune appeared in William Gardiner's *Sacred Melodies*, 1815. Gardiner attributed the tune to the German composer Ludwig van Beethoven, asserting: "It is somewhere in the works of Beethoven, but where I cannot now point out." More likely, it is mostly the work of Gardiner himself.

242. Not what these hands have done

The text written by Horatius Bonar appeared in his *Hymns of Faith and Hope*, 1861 with the heading "Salvation through Christ alone."

ST. ANDREW. Joseph Barnby composed the tune in 1866 while he was organist of St. Andrew's Church, London. It was originally written for John S. B. Monsell's hymn, "Sweet Is Thy Mercy, Lord" and appeared unnamed with that text in Barnby's *Hymn Tunes,* 1869. The tune name appeared with the music in the posthumous edition of *Hymn Tunes,* 1897.

243. He took my feet from the miry clay

This traditional spiritual, obviously based on Psalm 40:1–2, appears in none of the major collections of black music. It is believed to have appeared first in a publication of the Rodeheaver Hall-Mack Company and may have been "collected" by Frederick Hall, who was associated with that organization.

YES, HE DID. The author first heard this music when he began to play accompaniments for George Beverly Shea, the gospel singer, in 1942. It is one of Shea's favorites.

244. Jesus, I will trust Thee

This hymn by Mary Jane Walker appeared first in the 1864 appendix to (her husband) Edwin Walker's *Psalms and Hymns for Public and Social Worship,* 1855.

ST. ALBAN. The source of this tune has been identified as "the slow movement in A of Franz Joseph Haydn's Symphony in D." It appeared with the words "Onward, Christian Soldiers" in *Hymns Ancient and Modern,* 1861. St. Alban was the first English saint and martyr.

245. Wonderful grace of Jesus

While he was pastor of the Church of the Nazarene at Auburn, Illinois, 1916–1919, Haldor Lillenas wrote much music for the historic song evangelist, Charles M. Alexander, including this choir selection. Homer Hammontree first introduced it in 1918 in the Bible Conference at Northfield, Massachusetts founded by D. L. Moody. It was published in *Tabernacle Choir,* 1922, edited by R. J. Oliver and Lance Latham. It is listed as No. 95 in the index of *Conference Hymnal,* 1919, compiled by Charles M. Alexander, but another song appears on those pages—evidently substituted at the last moment.

WONDERFUL GRACE. Haldor Lillenas complained that most people sing this music too fast. "A song should be performed in such a fashion that the words can be comfortably pronounced without undue haste," he said.

Amazingly enough, he received only $5.00 for this composition, which has become popular the world around.

246. Jesus, Lover of my soul

Charles Wesley wrote these lines in 1738 shortly after his conversion, and published them in *Hymns and Sacred Poems,* 1740 with the heading "In Time of Prayer and Temptation." Because of the intensely personal nature of the hymn, John Wesley opposed its use in public worship.

ABERYSTWYTH. The city of Aberystwyth in North Wales gave this tune its name. The melody was composed by Joseph Parry, Professor of Music at University College in that city. It was set with another text in *Ail Tonau ac Emynau* in 1879, and later put with Wesley's hymn in Parry's cantata *Ceridwen.*

247. I lay my sins on Jesus

This text by Horatius Bonar is generally supposed to be his first hymn and it was written for children. He apologized that "it might be good gospel but it is not good poetry." Its first appearance was in his *Songs for the Wilderness,* 1843.

AURELIA. See "The Church's one foundation," No. 200.

248. And can it be that I should gain

Charles Wesley's text was written shortly after his conversion in 1738, and it was published that same year in *Psalms and Hymns.* In his "Journal" for May 23, 1738, Wesley notes that he had difficulty in completing the hymn "because of Satan creating doubts about it . . . and causing him to feel he displeased God with its writing." He realized that it was the "device of the enemy to keep God from receiving the glory due him." It is said that the hymn was quoted to Wesley on his deathbed.

SAGINA. Thomas Campbell's melody was one of 23 original tunes in his publication, *The Bouquet,* 1825. All the tunes were named after botanical terms; "sagina" was a plant that grew profusely on the thin rocky soil of the Roman Campagna. The music is typical of the "somewhat flamboyant" Methodist tunes of the period.

249. There shall be showers of blessing

This gospel song was written by the well-known evangelist Daniel W.

Whittle in the late 19th century. It first appeared in *Gospel Hymns No. 4,* 1883.

SHOWERS OF BLESSING. The tune was written by James McGranahan, who traveled with Major Whittle as music director. It appeared with the above text in its initial printing.

250. Arise, my soul, arise!
The hymn by Charles Wesley first appeared in *Hymns and Sacred Poems,* 1742 under the title "Behold the Man." Ira D. Sankey claimed that it had been the direct instrumentality in the saving of thousands of souls.

TOWNER. The tune may be of early American "shape note" heritage, but its source is unknown. It appeared as an alternate melody "arranged by D. B. Towner" for these words in *The Ideal Song and Hymn Book* (Revell, 1909).

251. My song shall be of Jesus
The original of this song by Fanny J. Crosby was published in Ira D. Sankey's *Sacred Songs and Solos,* 1875. E. Margaret Clarkson revised it in 1973 at the request of the editors of *Hymns for the Living Church.*

ALSTYNE. William Howard Doane wrote this tune for the words of Fanny Crosby, whose married name was Mrs. Alexander Van Alstyne.

252. O soul, are you weary and troubled?
The story of this hymn, sometimes titled "The Heavenly Vision," appeared in a booklet by its author-composer, Helen Howarth Lemmel. In 1918 she saw these words in a pamphlet entitled "Focussed" by a missionary, Lillias Trotter:

> So then, turn your eyes upon HIM. Look full into His face and you will find that the things of earth will acquire a strange, new dimness.

Mrs. Lemmel continued:

> Suddenly, as if commanded to stop and listen, I stood still, and, singing in my soul and spirit was the chorus, with not one conscious moment of putting word to word to make rhyme, or note to note to make melody . . . The verses were written . . . the same week, after the usual manner of composition, but none the less dictated by the Holy Spirit.

The hymn was first published in 1918 in a pamphlet released by C. C. Birchard in London, England. In 1922, the National Sunday School Union of London included it in *Glad Songs,* a collection of 67 numbers by Mrs.

Lemmel. It became popular through its use that same year at the Keswick Convention in northern England. It first appeared in the United States in *Gospel Truth in Song, No. 2,* published by Harry D. Clarke in 1924 in Chicago.

LEMMEL. The tune is named for Helen Howarth Lemmel, author-composer of this song which has been translated into many languages around the world.

253. A ruler once came to Jesus by night

In 1877 George C. Stebbins was assisting Dr. George F. Pentecost in evangelistic meetings and one of the latter's sermons was "The New Birth," based on John 3:3. Stebbins was impressed with the rhythm of the passage and passed the suggestion along to William T. Sleeper, who completed the text. The hymn first appeared in *Gospel Hymns No. 3,* 1878.

BORN AGAIN. George C. Stebbins wrote this music to accompany William Sleeper's words. Text and tune have always appeared together.

254. "Whosoever heareth," shout, shout the sound

This text and tune were written by Philip P. Bliss during the winter of 1869–70. In a series of meetings conducted with Henry Moorhouse, the English evangelist preached on John 3:16 every night for a week. Inspired by this experience and a new, clearer view of the love of God, Bliss wrote the hymn. It was first published in George F. Root's *The Prize,* 1870.

WHOSOEVER. Philip Bliss wrote the tune for his words, which was his usual practice.

255. Would you be free from the burden of sin?

Both words and music were written by Lewis E. Jones while attending a camp meeting at Mountain Lake Park, Maryland. It was first published in *Songs of Praise and Victory,* compiled by William J. Kirkpatrick and H. L. Gilmour in 1899.

POWER IN THE BLOOD. The tune name was given by the editors of *Baptist Hymnal,* 1956.

256. Come to the Savior now

John Murch Wigner, son of an English Baptist minister, wrote this hymn in 1871. It was first published in the Supplement to the English Baptist

Psalms and Hymns, 1880, compiled by the author's father, John Thomas Wigner.

INVITATION. The music was composed by Frederick C. Maker to fit this text, and first appeared in *The Bristol Tune Book,* 1881.

257. The Savior is waiting
This invitation hymn was written by Ralph Carmichael for evangelistic services conducted by Dr. Lester Harnish at Temple Baptist Church in Los Angeles. It was first published in 1958 as a sheet music solo, by Sacred Songs, Inc. The harmonization by Don Hustad was copyrighted by Sacred Songs in 1966 and appeared in *Favorite Hymns of Praise* (Tabernacle Publishing Company, Chicago, 1967).

CARMICHAEL. Ralph Carmichael wrote both words and music of the hymn. The tune name was selected in his honor by the editors of *Hymns for the Living Church.*

258. Come, every soul by sin oppressed
The original gospel song by John H. Stockton had five stanzas and first appeared in his *Salvation Melodies No. 1,* 1874. In its early printings, the refrain repeated the phrase "come to Jesus" three times. On board ship enroute to Britain with D. L. Moody, Ira Sankey altered the hymn to tell "how" to come to Jesus—"only trust Him." It was published in this form in 1875 in *Sacred Songs and Solos* (London) and in *Gospel Hymns and Sacred Songs* (New York).

MINERVA. Since John H. Stockton wrote both words and music, the tune is sometimes called "Stockton." The name "Minerva" has appeared occasionally, but its significance is unknown.

259. Are you weary, heavy laden?
In writing these lines, John Mason Neale is thought to have been inspired by four Greek words which he came across in his extensive reading in that language. The hymn first appeared in his *Hymns of the Eastern Church,* 1862, where the first phrase was "Art Thou Weary, Art Thou Languid?" *Hymns for the Living Church* has taken the lead in modernizing the hymn's full text.

STEPHANOS. In early appearances, John Mason Neale credited the above hymn to St. Stephen the Sabaite, hence the tune name. The melody was written by Henry W. Baker and first appeared with the text in the Appendix to *Hymns Ancient and Modern,* 1868.

260. Just as I am, without one plea

Charlotte Elliott wrote these words as a "simple, candid expression of trust and personal confession." She was ill at home, and the rest of the family was engaged at a bazaar to raise funds to build a college at Brighton, England. Her writings, along with this hymn, appeared in her *Invalid's Hymn Book,* 1836. Miss Elliott received thousands of letters thanking her for this particular hymn, and in recent years it has been recognized as the official invitation song in Billy Graham crusades.

WOODWORTH. The music widely used for this hymn in America was written by William Bradbury. It was originally set to "The God of Love Will Sure Indulge" in *Third Book of Psalmody,* 1849, better known as the "Mendelssohn Collection" by Thomas Hastings and Bradbury. The tune with this text appeared in the collections of *Gospel Hymns and Sacred Songs* (1875–1891) used by Moody and Sankey in their evangelistic campaigns. The coda was heard by the editor of *Hymns for the Living Church* while playing for a Billy Graham crusade in Denmark.

261. The whole world was lost in the darkness of sin

This text and tune were written by Philip P. Bliss in the summer of 1875. In *Memoirs of Philip P. Bliss,* D. W. Whittle says: "It came to him all together, words and music, one morning while passing through the hall to his room, and was at once written out." Based on John 8:12 and 9:5 where Jesus says "I am the light of the world," the hymn first appeared in *The International Lessons Monthly,* 1875, and the same year in *Gospel Hymns and Sacred Songs, No. 1.*

LIGHT OF THE WORLD. The music was written by P. P. Bliss simultaneously with the words.

262. O Jesus, Thou art standing

In writing this text, William W. How was inspired by reading a beautiful poem by Jean Ingelow, entitled "Brothers, and a Sermon." It was first published in the Supplement to *Psalms and Hymns,* 1867, edited by How and Thomas B. Morrell.

ST. HILDA. The first two phrases of the music come from a tune credited to Justin H. Knecht in the *Vollständige Sammlung,* 1799, edited by Johann F. Christmann and Knecht. Edward Husband extended the melody to its present form in 1871. The significance of the tune name is not apparent; St. Hilda was of royal rank and very influential in English church life in the seventh century.

263. Somebody's knocking at your door

The words and music of this traditional spiritual are of unknown origin but they are obviously based on Revelation 3:20, "Behold, I stand at the door and knock. . ."

SOMEBODY'S KNOCKING. This melody and text appear in a slightly different version by John W. Work, Jr. and Frederick J. Work in *Folk Songs of the American Negro*, 1907.

264. Have you any room for Jesus?

In *Gospel Hymns No. 3,* 1878 this song appears with the author credit "Arr. by W.W.D."—obviously Daniel W. Whittle's initials in reverse order. The hymn bears the scripture reference, "Behold I stand at the door and knock" (Revelation 3:20).

ANY ROOM. C. C. Williams' tune has appeared with these words since their first printing.

265. I've a message from the Lord, Hallelujah!

William A. Ogden wrote the words and music of this song. Its first printing was in *Triumphant Songs for Sunday Schools and Gospel Meetings* "used by Rev. Sam P. Jones in his revival work" and published in 1887 by E. O. Excell.

LOOK AND LIVE. The tune name and song's traditional title are derived from an experience of Moses and the Israelites told in Numbers 21, and from Hebrews 12:2 (RSV), "Looking to Jesus, the pioneer and perfecter of our faith."

266. Softly and tenderly Jesus is calling

Will L. Thompson, "The Bard of Ohio," wrote this favorite invitation hymn. When Dwight L. Moody lay on his death-bed, Thompson paid him a visit. Moody feebly took his visitor's hand and said: "Will, I would rather have written 'Softly and tenderly Jesus is calling' than anything I have been able to do in my whole life." Some books list the copyright date as 1880, but its first printing seems to be in J. S. Inskip's *Songs of Triumph,* 1882.

THOMPSON. To honor the author/composer of this gospel song, the editors of *Baptist Hymnal,* 1956 named the tune "Thompson."

267. Out of my bondage, sorrow and night

William T. Sleeper had collaborated with George C. Stebbins in 1877 in writing "Ye Must Be Born Again." Consequently, when he finished the words for this invitation hymn, he sent them to Stebbins, who wrote the tune.

JESUS, I COME. The complete gospel song was first published in *Gospel Hymns No. 5,* 1887 under the Scripture text, "Deliver me, O my God" (Psalm 71:4).

268. If you are tired of the load of your sin

Lelia N. Morris wrote both the words and music for this gospel hymn. George Sanville, in his book *Forty Gospel Hymn Stories,* says the hymn was inspired by an altar service at Mountain Lake Park, Maryland at which Mrs. Morris and Dr. Henry L. Gilmour were leading a woman to faith in Christ. The encouraging phrases they used became the song's refrain. Before the camp meeting closed Mrs. Morris had completed the hymn. It was published in *Pentecostal Praises,* 1898, compiled by William J. Kirkpatrick and Gilmour.

McCONNELSVILLE. The tune is called "McConnelsville" after the town in Ohio where author Lelia N. Morris lived.

269. Come, ye sinners, poor and needy

This text by Joseph Hart, a Congregational minister, originally began "Come, ye sinners, poor and wretched." It was first published in his *Hymns Composed on Various Subjects,* 1759 in seven six-line stanzas, with the heading "Come, and Welcome, to Jesus Christ." The refrain is part of an anonymous "Prodigal Son" hymn appearing in American collections in the nineteenth century, "Far, far away from my loving Father."

ARISE. The tune (named after the refrain text) is an American folk melody of unknown origin. Set to the hymn "Mercy, O Thou Son of David" it appears in William Walker's *Southern Harmony,* 1835.

270. I am coming to the cross

William McDonald wrote this hymn to aid "seekers of heart purity" while at the altar. He wrote: "As I was sitting in my study one day the line of thought came rushing into my mind, and in a few minutes the hymn was on paper." It was first sung at a camp meeting in Hamilton, Massachusetts on June 22, 1870, and published in *American Baptist Praise Book,* 1871.

TRUSTING. The tune was composed by William G. Fischer and was possibly first set to a secular text. It was this melody that inspired McDonald as he wrote these sacred words.

271. Sinners Jesus will receive

The German hymn beginning "Jesus nimmt die Sünder an! Saget doch dies Trostwort allen," by Erdmann Neumeister, was written as a conclusion to a sermon on Luke 15:2. Originally it had eight six-line stanzas, and appeared in the author's *Evangelischer Nachklang*, 1718. The translation by Emma F. Bevan appeared in her *Songs of the Eternal Life*, 1858. This adaptation uses only the first four lines of each stanza, and takes the refrain from stanza six.

NEUMEISTER. James McGranahan composed the music originally for male voices, and it was included in *The Gospel Male Choir No. 2*, 1883. It appeared the same year in this mixed-voice setting in *The Gospel Choir*, compiled by Ira D. Sankey and McGranahan. The tune was called "Neumeister" (after the German author) in the *Mennonite Hymnary*, 1940.

272. Jesus is tenderly calling you home

The text "Jesus is tenderly calling thee home" was written by Fanny Crosby. In *Hymns for the Living Church*, the editors have modernized the four stanzas by changing "thee" and "thy" to "you" and "your."

CALLING TODAY. George C. Stebbins wrote the music for these words in 1883, after returning from an evangelistic tour through Scotland with D. L. Moody. Text and tune first appeared in *Gospel Hymns No. 4*, 1883. In his *Memoirs and Reminiscences*, Stebbins states:

> The music was written with the view of making the song available as an invitation hymn; but that it would meet with instant favor, and in a few years would become generally known, did not enter my mind.

273. "Give Me thy heart," says the Father above

One of the few gospel songs written in a trinitarian outline, Eliza E. Hewitt's text was copyrighted in 1898. With William J. Kirkpatrick's tune, it appeared in *Pentecostal Praises*, 1900, published by Hall-Mack, Philadelphia.

ZERUIAH. In the first printing of this song, the composer is listed as A. F. Bourne; "Annie F. Bourne" is one of William J. Kirkpatrick's pseudonyms (his second wife was Sara Kellogg Bourne). The tune name shown here is after Zeruiah Edmunds Stites, mother of Eliza E. Hewitt, author of these words.

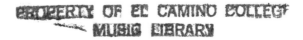

274. I've heard the King!

These words were penned by Grant Colfax Tullar during the Second World War. He had just heard a broadcast message from King George VI of England. Remembering that Christians communicate regularly with the eternal "King of Kings," he wrote these lines.

HIGHLANDS. Editor Donald P. Hustad wrote the music while he was living in La Grange Highlands, Illinois—hence the tune name. When he began work on *Tabernacle Hymns No. 5* in 1950 this text was in the Tabernacle Publishing Company files. At the encouragement of Gordon D. Shorney, president of the company, he set the words to music. The completed song was published in that hymnal in 1953.

275. Come, we that love the Lord

This hymn by Isaac Watts was first published in ten stanzas in his *Hymns and Spiritual Songs, Book II,* 1707 entitled "Heavenly Joy on Earth." During its history, several minor word changes have been made.

MARCHING TO ZION. The tune and the words of the refrain "We're marching to Zion" were written by Robert Lowry in 1867. The complete song first appeared in *Silver Spray,* 1868, a collection of Sunday School songs.

276. In the stars His handiwork I see

The complete song was written by Ralph Carmichael in 1964 for the Billy Graham film, "The Restless Ones." It was first published in 1965 in sheet music form by Lexicon Music, Inc., and since that time it has appeared in many folksong booklets. This is its first appearance in a standard hymnal.

HE'S EVERYTHING TO ME. This tune name—the familiar title of the song—was chosen by the editors of *Hymns for the Living Church.* In *Baptist Hymnal,* 1975 the name is given as "Woodland Hills."

277. Jesus my Lord will love me forever

This favorite gospel song was first published in *Word of Life Melodies (No. 1),* 1943, by Gospel Songs, Inc. (Norman Clayton Publishing Company), Malverne, N.Y. Words and music were written by Norman J. Clayton that same year.

ELLSWORTH. Ellsworth, a town in Connecticut, was a former residence of author-composer Norman Clayton.

278. Jesus is all the world to me

Will L. Thompson wrote both words and music of this hymn, which appeared in the author's *New Century Hymnal*, 1904.

ELIZABETH. Author-composer Will L. Thompson married Miss Elizabeth Johnson in 1891 at East Liverpool, Ohio, and the tune is named for her.

279. Alas! and did my Savior bleed?

This poem of consecration by Isaac Watts first appeared in his *Hymns and Spiritual Songs,* 1707 with the caption "Godly Sorrow Arising from the Sufferings of Christ." The hymn originally had six four-line stanzas, all of which have undergone alteration. Fanny Crosby said her "soul flooded with celestial light" at the time of her conversion, when this hymn was sung.

HUDSON. The complete song appeared in this form in *Songs of Peace, Love and Joy,* 1885, compiled by Ralph E. Hudson. Although he is given credit for composing it, the refrain melody appears with other words and is also credited to other individuals in late 19th century publications. Ira D. Sankey used the music with "I'm not ashamed to own my Lord" in his British-published *Sacred Songs and Solos.* It is a possibility that both words and melody of the refrain were commonly known and used in the campmeeting tradition, and that Hudson simply added them to his own original melody for the Watts stanzas.

280. I have a song I love to sing

Both words and music were written by Edwin O. Excell and were included in *Echoes of Eden for the Sunday School,* which Excell compiled and published in Chicago in 1884. It originally had five stanzas.

OTHELLO. The tune name "Othello" is the author-composer's middle name and was first given in *Baptist Hymnal,* 1956.

281. What a wonderful change in my life has been wrought

Rufus H. McDaniel penned these words as an expression of faith following the death of his son in 1914.

McDANIEL. The tune was composed for McDaniel's words in 1914 by Charles H. Gabriel. It first appeared in pamphlet form and was introduced to the Billy Sunday campaign in Philadelphia in 1915 by Gabriel and

Homer Rodeheaver. Rodeheaver purchased the manuscript and it appeared in his *Songs for Service*, 1915.

282. Nor silver nor gold hath obtained my redemption

James M. Gray's verses, written in 1900, are based on I Peter 1:18, 19, "Ye were not redeemed with corruptible things, like silver and gold . . . but with the precious blood of Christ." They were first published in *Hymns of Faith and Praise* (Lorenz, 1901).

PRICELESS. D. B. Towner wrote the tune for these words and compiled the volume in which they appeared.

283. All my life long I had panted

We are indebted to Keith Clark, founder of the Clark Hymnological Library at Houghton, New York for the information on this hymn and author. George Beverly Shea tells a story of his personal knowledge of the author in *Crusade Hymn Stories*, 1967.

In the manuscript autobiography of Clara Tear Williams in the Houghton College Library, she records:

> About 1875 I was helping in meetings in Troy, Ohio where Prof. R. E. Hudson conducted the singing, when just before retiring one night he asked me to write a song for a book he was preparing to publish. Before sleeping I wrote "Satisfied." In the morning he composed the music.

In the original printing the refrain was "Hallelujah! I have found it— What my soul so long has craved!" The present version was found in the *Wesleyan Methodist Hymnal*, 1910. The second line was originally "For a draught," and was changed to "For a drink" by Hope Publishing Company editors in *Crusader Hymns*, 1966.

SATISFIED. "Satisfied" was the original song title in the first printing in *Gems of Gospel Song*, 1881, compiled by E. A. Hoffman, J. H. Tenney and (composer) Ralph E. Hudson.

284. Yesterday He died for me

In a delightful letter, the layman evangelist Jack Wyrtzen says:

> Actually Don (Jack's composer son) wrote "Yesterday, Today and Tomorrow" from an outline that I had been preaching on, "Three Days in the Life of a Christian." He developed the theme. I don't really know why he put my name on it. I think when we get to heaven, the Lord will give him credit for the entire hymn!"

YESTERDAY, TODAY AND TOMORROW. Whether or not he was largely responsible for the lyrics, the music is Don Wyrtzen's. The song was first printed in 1966 in *Word of Life Camp Songbook*. The tune name is the song's title.

285. Redeemed, how I love to proclaim it

Fanny J. Crosby's popular gospel song first appeared with William J. Kirkpatrick's tune in *Songs of Redeeming Love*, 1882, edited by John R. Sweney, C. C. McCabe, T. C. O'Kane and Kirkpatrick.

ADA. Shortly before *Hymns for the Living Church* went to press, this new tune was substituted for the traditional one by Kirkpatrick. It was written by A. L. Butler for the Singing Churchmen of Oklahoma, who presented it at the 1966 Southern Baptist Convention in Detroit. It was first published in *The Church Musician*, July, 1967. The tune is named for Ada, Oklahoma where Mr. Butler serves as minister of music in the First Baptist Church.

286. Years I spent in vanity and pride

The words were written by William R. Newell while he was associated with the Moody Bible Institute of Chicago. His thoughts took form one day on his way to a lecture, so he stepped into a room and wrote them down. Continuing on to his class he met Daniel B. Towner, director of the Music Department at the Institute, and handed him the words. Dr. Towner completed the tune immediately and it first appeared in *Famous Hymns*, 1895.

CALVARY. The tune name is derived from the traditional title for the hymn, "At Calvary."

287. My faith has found a resting place

Little is known about Lidie H. Edmunds or her hymn, which appeared in *Songs of Joy and Gladness, No. 2* (1891, McDonald, Gill and Company).

LANDÅS. "Landås" is the name of a town in Norway. In the hymnal mentioned above, the music is listed as a Norse melody, arranged by William J. Kirkpatrick.

288. Amazing grace! how sweet the sound

John Newton's lines—probably the best-loved hymn of Southern Baptists—were written while he was curate at Olney, Bucks, England. His early life was one of immorality, debauchery and failure. "Amazing Grace" could well be his own testimony of his conversion and his life as a Christian. The hymn first appeared in *Olney Hymns,* 1779 in six four-line stanzas, and it bore the title "Faith's Review and Expectation." The fourth stanza of the present version is anonymous and appears as the final verse in other hymns (e.g., "Jerusalem, my happy home" and "When I can read my title clear") in many early American collections. E. O. Excell combined Newton's first three stanzas and the anonymous fourth stanza in his *Coronation Hymns,* 1910.

AMAZING GRACE. This early American melody of unknown origin appeared in *Virginia Harmony,* 1831, compiled by James P. Carrell and David S. Clayton, and in most of the other oblong tune books published in the South in the nineteenth century. The present form of the music is credited to E. O. Excell who included it in his *Make His Praise Glorious,* 1900.

289. Down at the cross where my Savior died

There is no information available on the writing of this hymn by Elisha A. Hoffman. It first appeared in *Joy to the World,* 1878, compiled by T. C. O'Kane, C. C. McCabe and John R. Sweney.

GLORY TO HIS NAME. The tune was composed by John H. Stockton, but no other information is available. Its name was the traditional hymn title.

290. I belong to the King

This text by Ida L. (Reed) Smith was inspired by a story she read as a youth. Entitled "A Princess in Calico," it told of a little girl who remained happy although her life was full of misfortune. When asked how she could smile through her troubles, she replied "Oh, it's because I belong to the King!" Ida Smith's life was also one of trials. She was sick, lonely, impoverished, and bed-ridden for years. From a hospital bed she wrote the words of this hymn.

The Rodeheaver Company controlled this copyright for many years and they report that it was first filed in 1900. However, it has been located in *New Songs of the Gospel* (Hall-Mack, 1905) with an 1896 copyright date.

CLIFTON. The name Maurice A. Clifton, often given as composer of this tune, is a pseudonym for J. Lincoln Hall.

291. All my sins have been forgiven

Phillip Hiller's best hymns were contained in two series, each titled *Geistliches Liederkästlein,* and published in Stuttgart in 1762 and 1767. Each volume contained 366 short hymns, one for each day of the year. This hymn ("Schuld und Strafe sind erlassen" in the original form) comes from the second volume (1767).

Esther Bergen's translation was made in 1959 while she was serving with her husband as a missionary in Mexico. She found the German hymn in *Gesangbuch*, 1952, published by the Mennonite Brethren of Canada. Her version was first published in that denomination's *The Hymn Book*, 1960.

GREENVILLE. This melody by Jean Jacques Rousseau was written for a song in his successful opera, *Le Devin du Village* (1752). It has also appeared in a piano setting entitled "Rousseau's Dream." Since 1823 it has been used in American hymnals, usually with Joseph Hart's words "Come, Ye Sinners, Poor and Needy."

292. Out of the depths to the glory above

Avis Burgeson Christiansen wrote the words to fit Haldor Lillenas' melody, at the request of Arthur McKee, for many years a song evangelist and manager of the Winona Lake Bible Conference (Indiana). They appeared in *Tabernacle Praises, No. 1,* edited by McKee for Tabernacle Publishing Company.

LILLENAS. The editors of *Hymns for the Living Church* gave the name of composer Haldor Lillenas to his tune. Mr. Lillenas had sent the music with words titled "Let It Be You and I" (by Alfred Barrett) to Arthur McKee. When McKee's book was published, to Lillenas' amazement Avis B. Christiansen's words were used. At first he was quite unhappy about the switch, but was reconciled to the idea when the song was a success.

293. Naught have I gotten but what I received

James M. Gray wrote the poem while he was dean of Moody Bible Institute. It was first printed in *Revival Hymns,* 1905, released by the Institute's Bible Colportage Association.

ONLY A SINNER. Daniel B. Towner, director of Moody Bible Institute's music course, wrote the music and (with Charles M. Alexander) compiled the volume in which it first appeared. The tune name is the song's traditional title.

294. I stand amazed in the presence

Both text and tune were written by Charles H. Gabriel. They first appeared in *Praises,* 1905, compiled and published by E. O. Excell.

MY SAVIOR'S LOVE. The tune bears the traditional hymn title as its name.

295. I know not why God's wondrous grace

The text by Daniel W. Whittle was based on II Timothy 1:12, and the refrain is a literal repetition of that verse (King James version).

EL NATHAN. The tune was written by James W. McGranahan, song leader in evangelistic campaigns conducted by Major Whittle. Text and tune both appeared for the first time in *Gospel Hymns No. 4*, 1883. "El Nathan" was a pseudonym regularly used by Daniel W. Whittle.

296. I will sing the wondrous story

The text by Francis H. Rowley was written while he was conducting a revival at the First Baptist Church at North Adams, Massachusetts in 1886, the third year of his pastorate there. He was assisted by a young Swiss musician named Peter Bilhorn who suggested that Rowley write a hymn for which he would compose the music. The following night the words came without any particular effort. Ira D. Sankey says that he changed the first line from "Can't you sing the wondrous story" to its present form.

WONDROUS STORY. Peter Bilhorn showed the completed hymn and his tune to Ira D. Sankey who liked it and accepted it as a gift. It appeared in his *Sacred Songs and Solos*, 1887, and also in *Gospel Hymns No. 5* the same year. In the latter volume the author's name is given as "Rawley."

297. O, what a Savior, that He died for me!

James McGranahan's song—words and music—appeared under the scripture John 6:47, "He that believeth on me hath everlasting life" in *Gospel Hymns No. 3*, 1878, edited by Ira D. Sankey, George C. Stebbins and McGranahan.

VERILY. The tune name is an abbreviation of the traditional song title, "Verily, Verily."

298. Saved! saved! saved!

Oswald J. Smith says that he wrote this hymn during the First World War. It was copyrighted in *Tabernacle Praises, No. 1* (1918 edition) and included in the songbook used in the Paul Rader-Arthur McKee evangelistic campaigns of 1919. It was first introduced in their meetings in Toronto's Massey Hall one evening when author Smith was selling songbooks in the aisles. He had just resigned from the pastorate of Dale Presbyterian Church, and his ministry was apparently over. Hearing his hymn sung by 3400 voices, he was inspired to believe that God still had work for him. Smith says: "It is still my testimony, every word of it. It is one of my strongest evangelistic songs."

HICKMAN. Roger M. Hickman wrote the music for Smith's hymn. His name was given to the tune by the editors of *Hymns for the Living Church*. It has also been called "Peoples Church" for the great Toronto congregation founded by Dr. Oswald J. Smith.

299. In loving kindness Jesus came

The complete song was written by Charles H. Gabriel. It first appeared in *Revival Hymns*, 1905, compiled by D. B. Towner and Charles M. Alexander and published by the (Moody) Bible Institute Colportage Association, Chicago.

HE LIFTED ME. The tune name has been traditionally used as the title of the hymn.

300. In tenderness He sought me

These words by W. Spencer Walton appeared in *The Coronation Hymnal*, 1894, edited by Adoniram J. Gordon and Arthur T. Pierson, and published by the American Baptist Publishing Society, Philadelphia.

CLARENDON. Adoniram Judson Gordon wrote this tune and it first appeared with these words in the hymnal mentioned above. It is named for the Clarendon Street Baptist Church, Boston, where Gordon was pastor for many years.

Traditionally the music was in 6/8 meter. Donald P. Hustad first arranged it in the smoother 2/2 meter in *Worship and Service Hymnal* (Hope, 1957).

301. Saved by the blood of the Crucified One

S. J. Henderson wrote these words which appeared in *One Hundred Gospel Hymns for Male Voices*, 1902, compiled by D. B. Towner and E. M. Fuller and published by (Moody) Bible Institute Colportage Assn., Chicago, Illinois.

GLORY, I'M SAVED. It seems apparent that Daniel B. Towner wrote the music to fit these words and included the arrangement in his compilation, *One Hundred Gospel Hymns for Male Voices*, 1902. As a congregational hymn it appeared in *The Gospel Hymn Book*, 1903, edited by Towner for Lorenz Publishing Company.

302. I love to tell the story

This hymn is part of a long poem of fifty stanzas in two parts by Arabella

Catherine Hankey (also called simply Katherine Hankey), and was written during a long period of convalescence following a serious illness. Part I, dated January 29, 1866, is entitled "The Story Wanted" and is the source of the song "Tell me the old, old story." Part II, dated November 18, 1866, is called "The Story Told" and contained these lines, which were published in *The Old, Old Story* that same year.

HANKEY. The tune (named for the text's author) was composed by William G. Fischer for these words. It first appeared in a pamphlet entitled *Joyful Songs, Nos. 1 to 3*, 1869. It was first published in a major volume titled *Music for Camp Meetings* in 1872.

303. Talk about a soul that's been converted

The author first heard this spiritual sung as a solo by the popular Methodist church musician and recording artist, Bill Mann, who said that he learned it from a saintly black woman in his native Alabama. John F. Wilson has adapted the traditional words.

HERE'S ONE. Originally a solo, John F. Wilson saw potential in this tune as a male quartet number, and his arrangement first appeared in *Male Quartet Specials, No. 2* (Hope Publishing Company, Chicago, 1966). This hymnal setting is planned for a congregation in unison, or antiphonally with a soloist.

304. There is a name I love to hear

This hymn by Frederick Whitfield was first published in leaflet form in 1855 and appeared in the author's *Sacred Poems and Prose*, 1861. The refrain is probably anonymous.

O, HOW I LOVE JESUS. The tune (named after the refrain text) is of unknown origin. It is found in many collections published in America in the 19th century.

305. I am not skilled to understand

This text was written by Dorothy Greenwell, commonly called "Dora," and was included in her *Songs of Salvation*, 1873. It also appeared in Sankey's *Sacred Songs and Solos* under the caption "My Refuge, My Savior!" (II Samuel 22:3).

GREENWELL. This tune, named for the text's author, was written by William J. Kirkpatrick and first appeared in *Songs of Joy and Gladness*, 1885, compiled by W. McDonald, Joshua Gill, J. R. Sweney and Kirkpatrick.

The name "Greenwell" is also used for another tune by Ernest B. Leslie which appears with Dora Greenwell's words in *Sunday School Hymnary*, 1905.

306. Once far from God and dead in sin

Under the pseudonym "El Nathan," Daniel W. Whittle's hymn appeared in *Gospel Hymns No. 6*, 1891. The accompanying scripture was Galatians 2:20, "Nevertheless I live; yet not I, but Christ liveth in me."

CHRIST LIVETH. The traditional title of this song was "Christ Liveth in Me"; the tune name is an abbreviation. James McGranahan wrote the music and was no doubt responsible for the hymn's appearance in *Gospel Hymns No. 6*.

307. There's not a friend like the lowly Jesus

Hymns of Our Faith says of Johnson Oatman, Jr.: "Beginning about 1892, he wrote many sacred poems which proved highly successful as texts for gospel songs." This song must have been written in those early years. It appeared in *Heaven's Echo, or Songs of the Golden Land,* published *ca.* 1896 by Ward and Drummond in New York, and by George C. Hugg in Philadelphia.

NO, NOT ONE. The music of George C. Hugg appeared with these words. The tune name is the song's historic title.

308. My hope is in the Lord

Norman J. Clayton wrote both the words and music of this hymn in 1945 in Malverne, New York. He first published it in *Word of Life Melodies, No. 2*, 1945.

WAKEFIELD. The tune was given the family name of composer Norman Clayton's mother, Mary Alice Wakefield.

309. I heard the voice of Jesus say

This text by Horatius Bonar was written while he was pastor at Kelso, Scotland. According to the author, it is based on John 1:16, "Of His fulness have all we received, and grace for grace," and others would suggest Matthew 11:28 and John 8:12. The hymn was originally published under the title "The Voice from Galilee" in Bonar's *Hymns Original and Selected*, 1846.

VOX DILECTI. The tune (whose Latin name means "voice of the beloved") was written for this text by John B. Dykes and first appeared in *Hymns Ancient and Modern,* 1868 edition.

310. Under His wings I am safely abiding
In the 1890's William O. Cushing wrote these words based on Psalm 17:8, "Hide me under the shadow of thy wings."

HINGHAM. Ira D. Sankey wrote the music for these words in their appearance in his last major volume, *Sacred Songs No. 1,* 1896. The tune name was chosen by the editors of *Hymns for the Living Church;* the hymn's author William O. Cushing was born at Hingham Center, Massachusetts.

311. Though the angry surges roll
A hundred years ago, many gospel songs took their imagery from the sea. These words by W. C. Martin are typical and the hymn was a favorite for both mixed and male voices in the early 1900's.

MY ANCHOR HOLDS. Unlike more traditional hymns, gospel songs often had a title. The title of this one has been used as the name of Daniel B. Towner's tune, written for these words. The full song was first published in Towner's *One Hundred Gospel Hymns for Male Voices,* 1902 by The (Moody) Bible Institute Colportage Association, Chicago.

312. 'Tis so sweet to trust in Jesus
This text by Louisa M. R. Stead is believed to have been written out of the experience of sorrow because of the death of her husband.

TRUST IN JESUS. The tune was composed by William J. Kirkpatrick for these words. It appeared first in *Songs of Triumph,* 1882, compiled by John R. Sweney and Kirkpatrick.

313. My hope is built on nothing less
This hymn of faith was written in 1834 as Edward Mote thought about the "Gracious Experience of a Christian." The chorus was conceived one morning as he was walking up Holborn Hill, London and four of the verses were completed the same day. He shared them that day in a visit with a Mrs. King, who was dying. The verses so met her spiritual need that he had a thousand copies printed and sent one to *Spiritual Magazine,* without any

signature. The hymn appeared anonymously in an edition of hymns in 1836 compiled by "a Brother Rees" who was credited with authorship in a later edition introduced in 1837. Edward Mote included it and claimed authorship in his *Hymns of Praise,* 1836 under the title: "The Immutable Basis of a Sinner's Hope."

SOLID ROCK. The tune was composed by William Bradbury for this text in 1863. It first appeared in his compilation, *The Devotional Hymn and Tune Book* (Philadelphia: American Baptist Publication Society, 1864).

314. Dying with Jesus, by death reckoned mine

The song evidently developed from a chance remark of the preacher Henry Varley to the American evangelist, Daniel W. Whittle. Varley expressed his feeling that the song "I Need Thee Every Hour" was not his favorite, because he needed Christ "every moment of the day." As a result, Whittle penned these lines.

WHITTLE. The music for D. W. Whittle's words was written by his daughter, May Whittle (early appearances of the song list her as "Mary"), who married D. L. Moody's son, Will. Words and music were copyrighted in 1893 and first printed in leaflets. The song appeared in *Sacred Songs, No. 1,* edited by Ira D. Sankey, James McGranahan and George C. Stebbins (Biglow and Main, Chicago, 1896).

315. O holy Savior, Friend unseen

This text by Charlotte Elliott was written in 1834 shortly after the death of her father. It appeared the same year in her *Invalid's Hymn Book* under the heading "Clinging to Christ" in the category titled "In severe suffering, mental or bodily."

FLEMMING. See "Praise ye the Father," No. 7.

316. O for a faith that will not shrink

This hymn by William Bathurst was written in six four-line stanzas entitled "The Power of Faith." It first appeared in his *Psalms and Hymns for Public and Private Use,* 1831.

ARLINGTON. The tune is adapted from the minuet in the overture to Thomas A. Arne's opera *Artaxerxes,* produced in London in 1762. Its first appearance as a hymn tune is in Ralph Harrison's *Sacred Harmony, Vol. 1,* 1784.

317. Blessed assurance, Jesus is mine

This text by Fanny Crosby was written after listening to a new melody composed by her friend, Phoebe Palmer (Mrs. Joseph) Knapp. When asked what the melody said to her, Fanny Crosby replied "Blessed assurance, Jesus is mine!" Words began to form and the result was this gospel hymn, which has recently been associated with Billy Graham Crusades. It first appeared in John R. Sweney's *Gems of Praise*, 1873.

ASSURANCE. This is one of the instances in which a tune was the inspiration for a text, evidently a common practice in the 19th century. The two have remained together through the years.

318. When we walk with the Lord

The hymn by John H. Sammis was the result of a suggestion by Daniel B. Towner. Professor Towner was singing in a series of meetings conducted by D. L. Moody in Brockton, Massachusetts. In a testimony service which took place he heard a young man say, "I am not quite sure—but I am going to trust, and I am going to obey." Towner jotted down the words and sent them to his friend Sammis, who wrote the refrain first—it is a capsule version of the entire song—and the verses later.

TRUST AND OBEY. The tune (named after the song's historic title) was written by Daniel B. Towner for the text. The entire hymn first appeared in *Hymns Old and New* (Chicago: Fleming H. Revell Company, 1887).

319. Trust in the Lord with all your heart

In 1937, at the suggestion of William M. Runyan, Thomas O. Chisholm sent several of his poems to Wendell P. Loveless, who set this one to music. Several phrases are taken almost directly from Proverbs 3:5. In *Hymns for the Living Church*, the editors changed the pronouns "thine" and "thou" to "your" and "you" since they do not refer to God.

LOVELESS. Composer Wendell P. Loveless says:

> In a day when so many are putting their trust in material possessions, their own puny efforts, drugs, and false religious beliefs, it is well to focus our thought upon the all-powerful, gracious, loving Savior. Many have written to me of the blessing received through the use of this song.

Mr. Loveless included the hymn in his *Radio Songs and Choruses*, 1937.

320. Simply trusting every day

This text by Edgar Page Stites first appeared in a newspaper which was handed to D. L. Moody. In turn, the evangelist gave the clipping to Ira D.

Sankey, his soloist and songleader, asking him to set it to music. Sankey agreed to do so on the condition that Moody would vouch for the doctrine taught in the verses. The evangelist said he would.

TRUSTING JESUS. The tune (bearing the historic song title) was composed by Ira D. Sankey for the text. Words and music first appeared in *Gospel Hymns No. 2,* 1876.

321. Savior, like a shepherd lead us
The authorship of this text is usually attributed to Dorothy A. Thrupp, although there is no positive proof that she wrote it. As the compiler of *Hymns for the Young,* 1836, and author of many of its verses, she included this unsigned poem. It has sometimes been credited to Henry Francis Lyte.

BRADBURY. The tune was composed by William B. Bradbury for these words. The full hymn first appeared in his Sunday School collection, *Oriola,* 1859.

322. The Lord's our rock, in Him we hide
Vernon J. Charlesworth wrote the original hymn about 1880. Ira D. Sankey altered it (probably added the refrain), copyrighted it in 1885 and printed it in *Sacred Songs and Solos,* London and in *Gospel Hymns, No. 5,* 1887. The scripture heading was Psalm 94:22, "My God is the Rock of my refuge."

SHELTER. In *My Life and the Story of the Gospel Hymns,* Ira D. Sankey says:

> I found this hymn in a small paper published in London, called *The Postman.* It was said to be a favorite song of the fishermen on the north coast of England, and they were often heard singing it as they approached their harbors in the time of storm. As the hymn was set to a wierd minor tune, I decided to compose one that could more easily be sung by the people.

323. My Father is rich in houses and lands
This poem by Harriett E. Buell was inspired by a Sunday morning worship experience, and was composed largely while on her way home. As was her custom, she sent the text to the *Northern Christian Advocate,* published in Syracuse, New York, and it appeared in the February 1, 1877 edition. Later, to her surprise, she received a copy of the hymn set to music by Rev. John B. Sumner. He had found the poem in the *Advocate* and had composed the musical setting.

Incidentally, the original title and refrain-phrase was "The Child of a

King." Hope Publishing Company editors changed this to "A Child of the King"—to suggest the uniqueness of God's kingship, and the size of God's family!

BINGHAMTON. The tune was composed (see account above) by John B. Sumner while he was pastor in Binghamton, New York.

324. Be still, my soul
The German hymn "Stille, mein Wille, dein Jesus hilft siegen" by Katharina von Schlegel originally had six stanzas, and was based on Psalm 46:10 and I Thessalonians 4:17; it appeared in *Neue Sammlung Geistlicher Lieder*, 1752. The translation by Jane L. Borthwick has three of the original stanzas. It was first published in Miss Borthwick's *Hymns from the Land of Luther*, second series, 1855.

FINLANDIA. The tune is from the tone poem "Finlandia" by Jean Sibelius and was arranged in hymn form for the Presbyterian *Hymnal*, 1933. Another version appeared earlier in Scotland's *The Church Hymnary, Revised*, 1927.

325. My Shepherd will supply my need
This paraphrase of Psalm 23 first appeared in Isaac Watts' *The Psalms of David, Imitated in the Language of the New Testament, and Apply'd to the Christian State and Worship*, 1719.

RESIGNATION. The tune is an early American melody, composer unknown, which appeared in *Southern Harmony*, 1854. It became popular in a choral setting by the American composer, Virgil Thomson.

326. God of our life, through all the circling years
This poem by Hugh T. Kerr was written for the 50th anniversary celebration of the Shadyside Presbyterian Church, Pittsburgh, Pennsylvania, in 1916. It was revised for inclusion in *The Church School Hymnal for Youth*, 1928.

SANDON. See "Unto the hills around," No. 44.

327. In heavenly love abiding
This text by Anna Laetitia Waring was first published in *Hymns and Meditations*, 1850 under the title "Safety in God." The hymn bore the caption "I will fear no evil, for thou art with me." (Psalm 23:4)

NYLAND. The tune is a Finnish folk melody. It was arranged by David Evans and named for a province in Finland, appearing in *The Revised Church Hymnary*, 1927.

328. Anywhere with Jesus I can safely go

The original version by Jessie H. (Brown) Pounds had three stanzas, including the first two given here. It was published in *Hymns Old and New, No. 1*, 1887, by the Revell Company. Sometime later (probably between 1910 and 1920) two more stanzas were added by Helen Cadbury Alexander (later Dixon), wife of the famous song evangelist, Charles M. Alexander. One of her stanzas is number three of the present version.

SECURITY. Daniel B. Towner wrote the music for the original hymn and edited the songbook in which it first appeared. Its title reflects the message of the words.

329. Walk in the light!

This text by Bernard Barton presents the characteristic Quaker doctrine of the "Inner Light," based on I John 1:7. The hymn first appeared in the author's *Devotional Verses*, 1826.

MANOAH. The tune appeared in Henry W. Greatorex's *Collection of Church Music*, 1851 and no information is available about its source. Tune names chosen by Greatorex had no special significance, but in scripture "Manoah" was the father of Samson.

330. I am trusting Thee, Lord Jesus

This text by Frances Ridley Havergal was said to be the author's favorite of all her hymns. It was written at Ormont, Dessous, Switzerland in 1874. A copy was found in her Bible after her death.

BULLINGER. The tune was written by Ethelbert W. Bullinger in 1874 and first appeared in *Wesley's Hymns and New Supplement*, 1877.

331. He's got the whole world in His hands

In the wide-ranging research of American folk music, this traditional spiritual has recently come to light. Its source is unknown.

WHOLE WORLD. One printing of this melody says it is taken from the "Marion Kerby Collection of Negro Exaltations."

332. To talk with God

These words are from a traditional Hindi (India) hymn, of unknown origin.

HINDI. The music was composed by John F. Wilson as a solo-choir response for a creative worship service at the Village Church (Baptist) of Western Springs, Illinois. It first appeared with these words in *Now*, a folk hymnal (Hope, 1969). "Martin West" is a pseudonym of Mr. Wilson, and that name appears in the hymnal.

333. O to be like Thee! blessed Redeemer

These words of aspiration by Thomas O. Chisholm appeared in 1897 in the *Young People's Hymnal* of the Methodist Episcopal Church, South, compiled by W. D. Kirkland, James Atkins and W. J. Kirkpatrick.

RONDINELLA. Pasquale Rondinella was one of William J. Kirkpatrick's music teachers. The latter wrote the music for Chisholm's poem.

334. More like Jesus would I be

This text by Fanny Crosby was sent to her friend and composer-associate, William H. Doane for a musical setting.

MORE LIKE JESUS. The tune was written for these words by William Howard Doane and the completed hymn first appeared in *Silver Spray*, 1867, compiled by the composer. Doane donated the profits from the songbook's sale to purchase a pipe organ for the YMCA Hall in Cincinnati. The organ, in use for many years, was also called "Silver Spray."

335. Jesus, my Lord, my God, my All

This was one of two original hymns by Henry Collins which were included in his *Hymns for Schools and Missions*, 1854. Frederick Faber has a similar hymn (for Corpus Christi) with the same first line and a final phrase, "Oh, make us love Thee more and more." Three years after publishing this work, Collins himself joined the Church of Rome.

HOLY FAITH. As the name implies, George C. Martin wrote this tune (1889) for "Faith of our Fathers" and it appeared first in *Additional Hymns*, 1894. It is typical of the unison hymns written in England in this period.

336. I want a principle within

These words by Charles Wesley first appeared in the 1749 edition of

Hymns and Sacred Poems. Originally the hymn had five stanzas of eight lines each, with the title "For a Tender Conscience." John Wesley shortened the hymn to five four-line stanzas for his *Collection of Hymns for the Use of the People Called Methodists,* 1780. However, the earlier version has been preferred by hymnal editors through the years; three of the five stanzas are used here.

LLANGLOFFAN. This typical Welsh tune comes from the hymnal, *Hymnau a Thonau,* 1865. It bears striking resemblance to a melody in W. A. Barrett's *English Folksongs,* 1893.

337. I would be true

This hymn by Howard A. Walter was written in 1906 while he was teaching English at Waseda University in Japan. He sent it (in three stanzas entitled "My Creed") to his mother, Mrs. Henry S. Walter; she sent it to *Harper's Bazaar* and they published it in their May, 1907 issue. The fourth stanza was written about 1928 and sent to his cousin, the Rev. Theodore Ainsworth Greene, minister of the First Church of Christ (Congregational), New Britain, Connecticut.

PEEK. The tune was written especially for this text by Joseph Y. Peek, with the assistance of Grant Colfax Tullar, an organist and composer. Peek had met the author, Howard Walter, during the summer of 1909 and had been given a copy of "My Creed." The words brought a melody to Peek's mind; he whistled the tune to Dr. Tullar, who wrote it down and harmonized it.

338. Lord, I want to be a Christian

The origin of this text is uncertain. Eighteenth century records show that a Presbyterian named William Davies was preaching in Virginia between 1748 and 1756. A slave came to him wanting to learn more about Jesus Christ and his duty to God and said, "Lord (sir), I want to be a Christian." In *Negro Slave Songs in the United States,* Miles Mark Fisher suggests that this spiritual could well have originated there about that time.

I WANT TO BE A CHRISTIAN. The tune first appeared in Frederick J. Work's *Folk Songs of the American Negro* (Nashville, 1907). George Pullen Jackson points out that the refrain is similar to the setting of "Come to me, sweet Marie" which he heard sung in rural Maine in the 1880's.

339. More about Jesus would I know

This hymn's author, Eliza E. Hewitt, suffered for many years from a spinal ailment. In later life she wrote several hymns for children. John R.

Sweney became acquainted with her work and collaborated with her in setting a number of poems to music.

SWENEY. This tune was written for this text by John R. Sweney. The complete hymn appeared in *Glad Hallelujahs,* 1887, edited by W. J. Kirkpatrick and Sweney.

340. I need Thee every hour

This text by Annie S. Hawks was written in April, 1872. Mrs. Hawks said that she was so filled with a sense of nearness to the Master that, wondering how one could live without Him, either in joy or pain, the words "I need Thee every hour" flashed into her mind. She put her thoughts down on paper, resulting in the stanzas of the hymn.

NEED. The tune and the refrain text were written by Mrs. Hawk's pastor, Dr. Robert Lowry. The complete hymn was first sung from a pamphlet at a November, 1872 meeting of the National Baptist Sunday School Association in Cincinnati. Later it was published in Lowry's *Royal Diadem,* 1873.

341. Lord Jesus, think on Me

This is the last of ten odes written by Synesius of Cyrene, presenting the Christian faith as seen by a man of neo-Platonist training. It was written in the early years of the fifth century.

The paraphrase by Allen W. Chatfield first appeared in *Hymns Ancient and Modern,* 1875, and later in his own *Songs and Hymns of Earliest Greek Christian Poets, Bishops, and Others translated into English Verse,* 1876.

DAMON. This tune is often called "Southwell" and first appeared in William Damon's *Psalmes of David,* 1579, set to Psalm 45. The present arrangement varies considerably from the original.

342. There is a place of quiet rest

It had been the custom of Rev. Cleland B. McAfee to write a hymn for each communion service in the Presbyterian church of which he was pastor. This hymn was written in 1901 after a great sorrow had come into his life in the death of two nieces from diphtheria. His church choir sang it on Saturday night outside his brother's quarantined house in Chicago, Illinois, and on Sunday morning at communion in the First Presbyterian Church of that city.

McAFEE. This tune was written by Cleland B. McAfee for his text. The completed hymn first appeared in *The Choir Leader,* 1903, a magazine of the Lorenz Publishing Company, Dayton, Ohio.

343. Earthly pleasures vainly call me

This gospel song, with words by James Rowe, first appeared in 1912 in *Make Christ King,* edited by E. O. Excell and William E. Biederwolf (Glad Tidings Publishing Company, Chicago). Later the copyright was purchased by Hope Publishing Company; the renewal was controlled by the Rodeheaver Company.

SPRING HILL. Spring Hill in Bradford County, Pennsylvania was the birthplace of the music's composer, B. D. Ackley.

344. Be Thou my vision

This eighth-century anonymous Irish poem was translated into English prose by Mary E. Byrne and appeared in the journal, *Erin,* Vol. II, 1905. The prose was put into verse by Eleanor H. Hull and published in her *Poem-Book of the Gael,* 1912.

SLANE. The tune was found in Patrick W. Joyce's *Old Irish Folk Music and Songs,* 1909, set to "With my love on the road." It was used with this hymn text in the *Irish Church Hymnal,* 1919. The present arrangement is by Donald Hustad, the editor of *Hymns for the Living Church.*

Slane is a hill near Tara in County Meath, where St. Patrick is said to have challenged the Druid priests by lighting the Paschal fire.

345. Savior, Thy dying love

This hymn by Sylvanus Dryden Phelps appeared in *The Watchman and Reflector,* 1862, a Baptist journal of which he was editor. It was apparently rewritten and submitted to Robert Lowry (at the latter's request) to be included in a Sunday school songbook, *Pure Gold,* 1871, compiled by Lowry and William H. Doane. On his 70th birthday, Phelps received a note from Lowry saying "It is worth living 70 years if nothing comes of it but one such hymn as 'Savior, Thy dying love.'"

SOMETHING FOR THEE. The tune was written by Robert Lowry for this hymn when it was included in *Pure Gold,* 1871. The song's first title was "Something for Thee."

346. O for a heart to praise my God

Charles Wesley's poem of aspiration first appeared in *Hymns and Sacred Poems,* 1742, compiled by the Wesley brothers. It was based on Psalm 51:10, "Make me a clean heart, O God." Various alterations have been made through the years.

AZMON. See "O for a thousand tongues to sing," No. 90.

347. How I praise Thee, precious Savior

This hymn has been associated with the Inter-Varsity Christian Fellowship and the Keswick Convention movement in England and America. It was written by Mary E. Maxwell, of uncertain identity.

CHANNELS. Named from the first word of the refrain, this music was written by Ada Rose Gibbs and appeared with the text in her *Twenty-Four Gems of Sacred Song,* 1900.

348. Nearer, my God, to Thee

This text by Sarah F. Adams was based on the dream of Jacob at Bethel, told in Genesis 28:10–22. It was first published in *Hymns and Anthems,* 1841, compiled by William J. Fox, minister of the Unitarian Church at South Place, Finsbury, England, of which Sarah Adams was a member.

BETHANY. The tune was written for these words by Lowell Mason in 1856 and they appeared together in *Sabbath Hymn and Tune Book,* 1859. Lowell Mason often chose biblical names for his tunes, and he actually used "Bethany" for several different melodies.

349. May the mind of Christ my Savior

Written by Kate B. Wilkinson, of whom little is known, this devotional hymn was first included in *Golden Bells,* 1925.

ST. LEONARDS. A. Cyril Barham-Gould was living at St. Leonard's-on-Sea, England when he wrote this tune. It appeared with the text in *Golden Bells,* 1925.

350. Open my eyes, that I may see

Both words and music were written by Clara H. Scott. The song first appeared in *Best Hymns No. 2,* 1895, compiled by E. A. Hoffman and H. F. Sayles.

SCOTT. The tune was named for the author-composer Clara H. Scott in *Baptist Hymnal,* 1956.

351. O Love that will not let me go

This text was written by George Matheson on June 6, 1882, while he was pastor of the Innellan Church, Argyllshire, Scotland. The nearly-blind Matheson said that it was a time of severe mental anguish, and that he had the impression of having the words dictated by a small inner voice. The writing of the entire hymn took only about five minutes. It first appeared in the January, 1882 issue of *Life and Work*, a monthly magazine published by the Church of Scotland, and later was included in the *Scottish Hymnal*, 1885.

ST. MARGARET. The tune was written for the text by Albert L. Peace and first appeared in the *Scottish Hymnal*, 1885. Like the words, it was written very quickly. The composer said that "the ink of the first note was hardly dry when I had finished the tune." It has been surmised that the melody may be named for Margaret, Queen of Malcolm III of Scotland, who was canonized in 1251.

352. O for a closer walk with God

William Cowper wrote these lines on Dec. 9, 1769 during the illness of a close friend. In a letter written the next day, Cowper said:

> I began to compose the verses yesterday morning before daybreak, but fell asleep at the end of the first two lines; when I waked again, the third and fourth were whispered to my heart in a way which I have often experienced.

The hymn first appeared in *Collection of Psalms and Hymns*, 1772, compiled by William Cowper. Cowper made a few alterations when it was published in *Olney Hymns*, 1779, where it bore the title "Walking with God. Genesis V, 24."

BEATITUDO. The tune was composed by John B. Dykes for the hymn "How bright these glorious spirits shine," published in *Hymns Ancient and Modern*, 1875. "Beatitudo," a word coined by Cicero, means "the condition of blessedness."

353. Nearer, still nearer

Both text and tune were written by Lelia N. (Mrs. C. H.) Morris. They first appeared in *Pentecostal Praises*, 1898, a collection by William J. Kirkpatrick and H. L. Gilmour.

MORRIS. The tune is named for the author-composer.

354. I am Thine, O Lord

Fanny J. Crosby wrote these words while visiting in the home of her musical collaborator, William H. Doane. They had been discussing the nearness of God. The words were written that same evening and entitled "Draw Me Nearer," based on Hebrews 10:22.

I AM THINE. The tune was written by William H. Doane for the text. It first appeared with the words in *Brightest and Best,* 1875, a Sunday School songbook compiled by Doane and Robert Lowry.

355. I'm pressing on the upward way

The words were written by Johnson Oatman, Jr. in 1898. The song was a favorite in "holiness" campmeetings and secured a lasting place in American hymnody.

HIGHER GROUND. Charles H. Gabriel said that he composed this tune in September, 1892 and sold it for five dollars. It was published with the text in *Songs of Love and Praise No. 5,* 1898, compiled by John R. Sweney, Frank M. Davis and J. Howard Entwisle.

356. Draw Thou my soul, O Christ

Lucy Larcom's hymn first appeared in 1892 in a collection of her poems, *At the Beautiful Gate.*

ST. EDMUND. The tune "St. Edmund" was written by Arthur S. Sullivan and was originally set to "We Are But Strangers Here" by T. R. Taylor. It first appeared in *The Hymnary,* 1872. St. Edmund was an early English King who was captured and slain by invading Danes.

357. "Take up your cross," the Savior said

Charles William Everest's text was written in 1833 and published that year in his *Visions of Death and Other Poems.* It originally had six stanzas which have been reduced and considerably altered in various hymnals through the years. The editors of *Hymns for the Living Church* have changed the pronouns "thou" and "thy" to "you" and "your," etc. Otherwise the text is essentially that which appeared in *Hymns Ancient and Modern,* 1861.

QUEBEC. See "Father of heaven, whose love profound," No. 5.

358. We praise Thee, O God

This hymn by William Paton Mackay was based on Habakkuk 3:2 and Psalm 85:6, written in 1863 and revised in 1867. The original text had five stanzas and refrain, and was included in *Gospel Hymns and Sacred Songs,* 1875, compiled by P. P. Bliss and Ira Sankey, under the title "O Lord, revive Thy work."

REVIVE US AGAIN. This tune was composed by John J. Husband sometime around 1815 and was first used with another text, possibly secular. In *Gospel Hymns and Sacred Songs*, 1875, it is set to Horatius Bonar's "Rejoice and be Glad!" Mackay's text was listed as an alternate. Through the years Bonar's words have dropped out of common use and Mackay's hymn has been wedded to this tune.

359. More love to Thee, O Christ

Elizabeth Prentiss wrote these words in 1856 during a difficult time of physical suffering and mental anguish. It has been called "a more explicitly Christian echo" of "Nearer, my God to Thee." Her husband said:

> Like most of her hymns, it is simply a prayer put into the form of verse. She wrote it so hastily that the last stanza was left incomplete, one line having been added in pencil when it was printed. She did not show it, not even to her husband, until many years after it was written; and she wondered not a little that, when published, it met with so much favor.

The hymn was first printed as a leaflet in 1869.

MORE LOVE TO THEE. William H. Doane wrote this tune for the hymn. Words and music appeared together in his *Songs of Devotion,* 1870.

360. Speak, Lord, in the stillness

An excellent hymn to use just before the sermon in a service of worship, these words were written by E. May Grimes while she was living in Pondoland, South Africa, and first published in her *Unseen Realities,* 1920, where they carried these references: I Samuel 3:9, Psalm 62:1 and Job 4:16. The hymn is a favorite at the Keswick Convention in northern England and appeared in *The Keswick Hymn Book,* 1936 as well as the Inter-Varsity hymnals in England and America.

QUIETUDE. Obviously named after the text's emphasis, this melody was written by Harold Green for Ms. Grimes' words, and has always appeared with them.

361. Jesus, keep me near the cross

As were many of Fanny Crosby's poems, this text was written to fit an existing tune by William H. Doane. The completed hymn first appeared in *Bright Jewels,* 1869, compiled by W. B. Bradbury, W. F. Sherwin, Chester G. Allen and Doane.

NEAR THE CROSS. William H. Doane wrote many tunes for Fanny Crosby's texts; in this instance, she wrote the text to fit his tune.

362. More like the Master

Both words and music were written by Charles H. Gabriel in 1906. The hymn first appeared in his *Praise and Service* (Philadelphia: American Baptist Publication Society, 1907).

HANFORD. The tune was first named in *Baptist Hymnal,* 1956, but it has no apparent connection with the hymn or its author-composer.

363. Lord, I hear of showers of blessing

Elizabeth Codner wrote these words in 1860 at Weston-super-Mare in England. She was interested in the spiritual welfare of a group of young people who had attended a meeting in which the contemporary spiritual awakening in Ireland was discussed, and she urged them to share in the blessings of which they had heard. In a time of prayer these words came to her (prompted by Psalm 72:6 and Ezekiel 34:29) and the hymn took form. The text was published first in leaflet form in 1861.

EVEN ME. William B. Bradbury wrote this tune for these words. It was first released in his *Golden Shower of Sunday School Melodies,* 1862 with no author-composer credits. In its first printing the last line was "Let some droppings fall on me."

364. Jesus, Thy boundless love to me

The original text was written by Paul Gerhardt and consisted of sixteen nine-line stanzas. It was first published in the fifth edition of Johann Crüger's *Praxis Pietatis Melica,* 1653. There have been many translations into English, John Wesley's paraphrase being the most popular. It first appeared in *Hymns and Sacred Poems,* 1739.

ST. CATHERINE. See "Faith of our fathers," No. 206.

365. I am weak, but Thou art strong

This anonymous song has the flavor of a "modern spiritual" and began to appear in gospel songbooks in the late 1940's. It was a favorite in the "all night gospel singing" programs in the South.

CLOSER WALK. The traditional title for the song is "Just a Closer Walk," from the refrain.

366. My faith looks up to Thee

Ray Palmer wrote these words as an expression of deep spiritual devotion shortly after graduating from Yale. Some time later, Lowell Mason met the author and asked him if he had anything to contribute to a book which he was about to publish. This text was given to him. The hymn with Mason's tune first appeared in *Songs for Social Worship*, 1832, edited by Mason and Thomas Hastings.

OLIVET. Lowell Mason wrote the tune specifically for these words. He once told the author:

> Mr. Palmer, you may live many years and do many good things, but I think you will be best known to posterity as the author of "My Faith Looks Up to Thee."

"Olivet" is a variant of "Mount of Olives" and perhaps refers to the hymn's message.

367. Fill all my vision, Savior, I pray

Avis Christiansen evidently handed this poem to composer Homer Hammontree while he was director of the Sacred Music Department of Moody Bible Institute, Chicago. Her husband, E. C. Christiansen, was a vice-president of that institution. She says in a recent letter:

> Mr. Hammontree was always eager to receive hymn lyrics, and I wrote many for him. The song "Fill All My Vision" was truly my own heart's desire. Though it was written many years ago, it is only in recent years that it has been used more extensively.

HAMMONTREE. A booklet of new songs by William M. Runyan, Homer Hammontree and George S. Schuler, published by Moody Press, 1940, marked the first appearance of this tune (by Hammontree) and text. The hymn became popular after it was included in Inter-Varsity's *Hymns*, 1947, compiled by Hammontree's long-time friend and associate, Paul Beckwith.

368. My life, my love I give to Thee

Ralph E. Hudson is best known for his tunes, but he also wrote many texts and added refrains to existing hymns. These words first appeared in *Salvation Echoes*, 1882, compiled and published by the author.

DUNBAR. C. R. Dunbar wrote this tune, and it appeared first with this text as indicated above.

369. I can hear my Savior calling

This hymn was copyrighted in 1890 by J. S. Norris. No information has been found about E. W. Blandy, the author of the words, or the circumstances of the song's writing.

NORRIS. This tune was written by J. S. Norris and it was copyrighted while he pastored the Congregational Church in Webster City, Iowa.

370. Teach me Thy will, O Lord

William M. Runyan included this hymn by Katherine A. Grimes in *The Service Hymnal* (Hope Publishing Company, 1935). Unfortunately he left no information on the author or the origin of the text.

The poem bears a striking resemblance to "Teach Me Thy Way, O Lord" (No. 379), but the words of B. Mansell Ramsey were probably not known to either Ms. Grimes or Mr. Runyan.

TEACH ME. The tune was written for the words by William M. Runyan.

371. Just as I am, Thine own to be

This youth hymn was written by Marianne Hearn who submitted it under the pen-name of "Mary Anne Farningham" to *The Voice of Praise,* a publication of the Sunday School Union of London, in 1887. The original text had six stanzas.

JUST AS I AM. Joseph Barnby composed this tune for Charlotte Elliott's "Just As I Am, Without One Plea." It first appeared in *Home and School Hymnal,* 1892 and is one of 246 tunes composed by Barnby.

372. Have Thine own way, Lord

Adelaide Pollard wrote this hymn in 1902 during a time when she was suffering "great distress of soul." Shortly before, she had tried unsuccessfully to raise funds for a missionary trip to Africa. A prayer meeting had brought peace to her heart and complete abandonment of self in submission to God's will. The text first appeared in *Northfield Hymnal with Alexander's Supplement* compiled by George C. Stebbins in 1907.

ADELAIDE. The tune was written for Adelaide Pollard's text in 1907 by George C. Stebbins, who included it in the hymnal mentioned above.

373. All to Jesus I surrender

This text was written by Judson VanDeVenter while he was conducting a meeting at East Palestine, Ohio, in the home of George Sebring, founder of the Sebring Campmeeting in Sebring, Ohio, and later the town of Sebring, Florida. The words were written in remembrance of the time when, after a long struggle, the author dedicated himself completely to Christian service.

SURRENDER. Winfield S. Weeden composed this melody for the text. It first appeared in *Gospel Songs of Grace and Glory,* 1896, compiled by Weeden, VanDeVenter and Leonard Weaver.

374. Take Thou our minds, dear Lord

William H. Foulkes wrote this text at the request of his friend, Calvin W. Laufer, after meeting by chance on the railway station platform in Stony Brook, Long Island, New York. Dr. Laufer hummed a tune which he had been turning over in his mind, and suggested that it would make a good setting for a young people's hymn. Foulkes penned three stanzas on the back of an envelope while riding on the train. The fourth stanza was written sometime later while he was attending a youth conference in Blairstown, New Jersey.

HALL. The tune by Calvin W. Laufer was first called "Stony Brook" (see story above). It was renamed "Hall" by the author and composer in honor of a mutual friend, William Ralph Hall. The completed hymn first appeared in *Conference Songs,* 1918.

375. God Himself is with us

Gerhard Tersteegen is considered to be one of the great German hymnists and spiritual leaders in the Reformed tradition. He was never ordained but his simple, devout, mystical faith led him to minister to those in spiritual and physical need. His hymn "Gott ist gegenwärtig" appeared in his *Geistliches Blumengärtlein,* 1729 and may be a paraphrase of a work by the French writer Labadie. The composite translation is the work of the editors of the Protestant Episcopal *Hymnal 1940.*

WUNDERBARER KÖNIG. The tune takes its name from the German hymn to which it was first set, "Wunderbarer König, Herrscher von uns allen." It is credited to Joachim Neander, and appeared in his *Bundes-Lieder,* 1680.

376. Make me a captive, Lord

This text by George Matheson was based on the phrase "the prisoner of Jesus Christ" in Ephesians 3:1 and appeared in his *Sacred Songs,* 1890, with the title "Christian Freedom."

DIADEMATA. The tune is discussed with No. 85 where it appears with "Crown Him with many crowns." The author of this handbook wrote an alternate tune for these words which appeared in *Tabernacle Hymns No. 5,*

1953. It was called "Paradoxy," because of the many paradoxes suggested in the text.

377. Jesus, Savior, all I have is Thine

Herman Voss, author-composer of this consecration hymn, has written:

> The song "Jesus, Savior" was written during my days at Moody Bible Institute. Both Dr. Houghton (president of M.B.I.) and Wendell P. Loveless strongly influenced me. I heard them speak of the need for complete surrender to the will of God. The blessed Holy Spirit made me see my own need and these words came from my lips—
> "Jesus, Savior, all I have is Thine,
> Body, soul and will I now resign."
> The other words seemed to follow and simply fall in place.

VOSS. Herman Voss also said:

> Incidentally, the melody came along with the words. To me this is more than a beautiful song of devotion. It is the dedication of my life to God.

The song was published in Wendell Loveless' *New Radio Songs and Choruses, No. 3* (1940).

378. Lord, speak to me, that I may speak

This text was written by Frances Ridley Havergal at Winterdyne, in England on April 28, 1872. It appeared first in a leaflet with the title "A Worker's Prayer" and the scripture reference, Romans 14:7. It was later published in Miss Havergal's *Under the Surface,* 1874.

CANONBURY. The tune is an arrangement of one of Robert Schumann's piano pieces in his *Nachtstücke,* Opus 23, 1839. It is first found as a hymn tune in J. Ireland Tucker's *Hymnal with Tunes, Old and New,* 1872. "Canonbury" is the name of a street and a square in Islington, London.

379. Teach me Thy way, O Lord

Our inquiry to the last copyright holder, Mr. George Taylor of the Cross Printing Works, Stainland, Halifax, England, revealed that he had no information about this song or its author-composer, B. Mansell Ramsey, because "all records were destroyed by fire in 1969." A brief article released in 1974 in *The Life of Faith* (the house organ of Marshall, Morgan & Scott Publications, Ltd., London) solicited information and brought a response that led to material that is included in the biography section. The *Anglican Hymn Book,* 1965 dates the hymn 1919, and it appeared in 1925 in a leaflet published by John T. Park, then in charge of the Cross Printing Works.

This hymn came to be known in the United States through *Hymns* of the Inter-Varsity Christian Fellowship, and is no doubt based on Psalm 27:11.

CAMACHA. The tune was also written by B. Mansell Ramsey and no doubt contributed much to the hymn's popularity. It is named for Ramsey's residence, "Camacha" in Chichester, Sussex, where he lived and died.

380. Living for Jesus a life that is true

Thomas O. Chisholm wrote these words in 1917 at the request of C. Harold Lowden, who had composed the tune for another text and used it in a Children's Day service in 1915. Recognizing that the tune was worthy of stronger words, he sent it to Chisholm, suggesting the title "Living for Jesus." The hymn was published on a single sheet in the spring of 1917, and later that same year it appeared in *Uplifting Songs,* compiled by Lowden and Rufus W. Miller.

LIVING. The tune by C. Harold Lowden led to the writing of the words, "Living for Jesus" (see above). The composer chose the tune name for its appearance in *Baptist Hymnal,* 1956.

381. Not I, but Christ

Another hymn of consecration to Christ and identification with Him, this text by Ada A. Whiddington was a favorite at the interdenominational conference held in the lake district of northern England every July, the Keswick Convention. It probably dates from *ca.* 1880, though *Treasury of Praise* (Taiwan, 1963) says 1891. With another tune, it was included in *Sacred Songs No. 1,* 1896 edited by Ira D. Sankey, James McGranahan and George C. Stebbins, and in the final edition (1903) of *Sacred Songs and Solos.*

EXALTATION. Little is known about C. H. Forrest, or the writing of this tune. It was first published in *Golden Bells,* 1925 and appears in *The Keswick Hymnal,* 1936, with a refrain (omitted here) but no credits. All records of that volume were lost in the fire of London during World War II.

382. Only one life to offer

This poem was written by Avis B. Christiansen in Chicago, Illinois in 1936 or 1937. She handed it to Merrill Dunlop at the close of a service at the Chicago Gospel Tabernacle, for his consideration as a potential hymn. In a letter of February 6, 1976, she says:

> The conviction that I have only one life to offer, is what prompted me to write that song ... All of my songs have come from my own heart

experiences with the Lord through more than sixty years of writing for His glory.

ONLY ONE LIFE. The music was composed by Merrill Dunlop as a setting for the poem Avis Christiansen had given him. Text and tune first appeared in Dunlop's *Songs of a Christian,* published by Chicago Gospel Tabernacle in 1937.

383. "Are ye able," said the Master
Earl Marlatt wrote this hymn in 1925 for a consecration service in the Boston University School of Religious Education. First printed as a leaflet, it was entitled "Challenge" and was inspired by Christ's pointed question to his disciples recorded in Matthew 20:22 which Marlatt had used the previous Sunday in a sermon. Its first hymnbook inclusion was in *American Student Hymnal,* 1928.

BEACON HILL. Harry S. Mason wrote this tune in April, 1924 when he was a graduate student at Boston University School of Religious Education. *Hymns of Our Faith* says that it was originally a setting for a text entered in a school song contest. The song did not win the prize, to the surprise and disappointment of many, including Professor Earl Marlatt. The following spring, Marlatt was asked to write a hymn for the consecration service and the words quickly came to him as he remembered Mason's melody.

The tune name was chosen by the composer; "Beacon Hill" was once the location of the Boston University School of Theology.

384. All for Jesus! All for Jesus!
These words by Mary D. James were coupled with a tune by John R. Sweney in *Redemption Songs,* 1889, edited by Sweney, William J. Kirkpatrick and John J. Lowe.

WYCLIFF. This tune by John Stainer is set to William Sparrow-Simpson's poem with the same title—"All for Jesus"—as the final hymn in the oratorio, *The Crucifixion,* 1887.

385. Take my life and let it be
This text by Frances Ridley Havergal was written on February 4, 1874 and first published that same year in Snepp's *Songs of Grace and Glory* (Appendix), and in 1878 in her own *Loyal Responses* under the heading "Self-consecration to Christ."

According to Miss Havergal's account, the words came to her during a night of personal praise and prayer, following a spiritual victory in her ministry.

HENDON. See "Ask ye what great thing I know," No. 144.

386. Lord Jesus, I long to be perfectly whole

The refrain of this text is taken almost verbatim from Psalm 51:7. The hymn by James L. Nicholson originally contained six stanzas, each beginning with "Dear Jesus" instead of "Lord Jesus." It first appeared in a 16-page pamphlet entitled *Joyful Songs No. 4,* 1872. Further revision was made by the editors of *Hymns for the Living Church.*

FISCHER. William G. Fischer wrote this tune and it appeared with the text in its original publishing. In 1876 Mr. Fischer led the Moody-Sankey choir in the campaign at 13th and Market Streets in Philadelphia; it is quite possible that this hymn was used in that evangelistic crusade.

387. Search me, O God

J. Edwin Orr is known around the world as an evangelist and a student of "revival movements." He reports that he wrote this hymn in 1936 at a time of "inspiration during an intense movement of the Spirit" in Ngaruawahia, New Zealand. It first appeared in *All Your Need,* published by Marshall, Morgan and Scott, London, 1936.

MAORI. J. Edwin Orr says he first heard this melody and used it with these words in Ngaruawahia, New Zealand. He identifies it as a folksong of the Maori aborigines. It does resemble the songs of other Polynesian peoples, such as the Hawaiians. In the United States it has also appeared with the popular ballad "Now Is the Hour."

388. God who touches earth with beauty

Mary S. Edgar wrote this hymn for campers in 1925 and was awarded first prize in a contest conducted by the American Camping Association the following year. It has been translated into many languages. With permission of the copyright owners, the text was revised extensively by the editors of *Hymns for the Living Church.*

GENEVA. During the time C. Harold Lowden was music editor for the Sunday School Board of the Evangelical and Reformed Church (now United Church of Christ), this text was brought to his attention, and he set it to this music. It was first sung from leaflets at an International Sunday School Association meeting in Chicago.

389. Purer in heart, O God

This hymn was written by Fannie E. (Mrs. E. L.) Davison.

PURER IN HEART. The tune was written for this text by James H. Fillmore, and the complete hymn first appeared in *Songs of Gratitude,* 1877, compiled by Fillmore.

390. More holiness give me

Both words and music of this hymn were written by Philip P. Bliss. It first appeared in *Sunshine for Sunday Schools,* 1873, compiled by him.

MY PRAYER. The tune name was the original title given to the hymn by Philip P. Bliss.

391. We are climbing Jacob's ladder

This text was undoubtedly inspired by Jacob's dream at Bethel (Genesis 28). It was included in John W. Work's collection *American Negro Songs and Spirituals,* 1940 and, as is true of all traditional spirituals, no author is named. Miles M. Fisher (in *Negro Slave Songs in the United States,* 1953) reminds us that the "Jacob's ladder" theme was heard in American spirituals beginning about 1825.

JACOB'S LADDER. The tune is a traditional spiritual melody and was probably always associated with these words.

392. Take time to be holy

Ira D. Sankey says that William D. Longstaff wrote this hymn after hearing a sermon at New Brighton, England on I Peter 1:10, "Be ye holy as I am holy." George C. Stebbins says it was written after a service at the Keswick Convention in north England, where the words "Take time to be holy" were quoted. It first appeared in an English publication *ca.* 1882, and later in *Hymns of Consecration,* used at Keswick.

HOLINESS. The tune was written for the text in 1890 by George C. Stebbins while he was in India for meetings and conferences. A friend had given him the poem, clipped from a periodical. Stebbins mailed the tune to Ira D. Sankey in New York, who included it in his *Winnowed Songs for Sunday School,* 1890, and in the 1891 editions of *Gospel Hymns* and *Sacred Songs and Solos.*

393. There's within my heart a melody

It is believed that Luther B. Bridgers wrote these words shortly after a tragedy in his life. While he was conducting a revival, his wife and children were burned to death in a fire at her parent's home in Harrodsburg, Kentucky. The song first appeared in *The Revival No. 6,* 1910 compiled and published by Charlie D. Tillman.

SWEETEST NAME. The tune, composed by Bridgers to accompany the text, is named for the second phrase of the refrain. Ernest K. Emurian, in *Forty True Stories of Famous Gospel Songs* points out that the melody bears a resemblance to Englemann's popular piano solo, "Melody of Love."

394. Jesus, I am resting, resting
This text was written in 1876 by Jean Sophia Pigott. No other information is available.

TRANQUILLITY. The tune, named after this text's emphasis, was composed by James Mountain for these words, and published in his *Hymns of Consecration and Faith,* 1876.

395. Lord of our life, and God of our salvation
Originally entitled "Sapphic Ode, For Spiritual and Temporal Peace," the hymn "Christe, du Beistand deiner Kreuzgemeine" was written by Matthäus Apelles von Löwenstern in 1644, near the close of the Thirty Years' War. Philip Pusey wrote this free paraphrase in 1834 and published it in Reinagle's *Psalm and Hymn Tunes,* 1840. He described his hymn as referring "to the state of the Church—that is to say, the Church of England in 1834—assailed from without, enfeebled and distracted within, but on the eve of a great awakening."

FLEMMING. See "Praise ye the Father," No. 7.

396. Peace, perfect peace
While spending a summer holiday at Harrogate, England in 1875, Edward H. Bickersteth heard the Vicar of Harrogate preach on the text "Thou wilt keep him in perfect peace whose mind is stayed on thee" (Isaiah 26:3). That afternoon, while visiting an aged and dying relative, Dr. Bickersteth wrote this hymn and read it to him. The words have remained substantially as he originally wrote them. The hymn was first released in Bickersteth's *Songs in the House of Pilgrimage,* 1875.

PAX TECUM. The tune (whose name means "Peace be with you") was written for these words by George Thomas Caldbeck. Dr. Charles Vincent revised and harmonized it for its first appearance in *The Hymnal Companion to the Book of Common Prayer,* second edition, 1877.

The story is told that in 1912, Caldbeck was arrested for selling tracts door-to-door in London. The case was dismissed when the magistrate learned that he was the composer of this famous and popular tune.

397. Like a river glorious

This text was written by Frances Ridley Havergal at Leamington, England in 1874. It appeared (without music) in her *Loyal Responses,* 1878.

WYE VALLEY. The tune was written by James Mountain for these words, and they first appeared together in his *Hymns of Consecration and Faith,* 1876.

398. I come to the garden alone

C. Austin Miles wrote this text and tune in March, 1912. The editor of *Hymns for the Living Church* gives the account in *Crusader Hymn Stories,* 1967. The hymn has often been categorized as "sentimental and erotic," but it is better appreciated when it is understood to be based on Mary Magdalene's experience, as she met Jesus in the garden outside the open tomb on Easter morning.

GARDEN. The tune name comes from the traditional title for these words, "In the Garden." This popular gospel song was first published in *The Gospel Message, No. 2* (Philadelphia: Hall-Mack Publishing Company, 1912).

399. There is sunshine in my soul today

Eliza E. Hewitt wrote this hymn when, after a long convalescence, she had been allowed to take a short walk outdoors on a bright spring day. A school teacher, she had been struck across the back with a heavy slate, by a boy who was being disciplined. After six months in a heavy cast she was finally released, and the song expressed her gratitude for recovery.

SUNSHINE. John R. Sweney composed music for this song and, together with William J. Kirkpatrick, released it in *Glad Hallelujahs,* 1887.

400. O safe to the Rock that is higher than I

William O. Cushing wrote these lines in Moravia, New York in 1876 as a result of a call from Ira Sankey for something new to help in his gospel work. Cushing prayed, "Lord, give me something that may glorify Thee," and this hymn is the result. He added: "It must be said of this hymn that it is the outgrowth of many tears, many heart conflicts and soul yearnings, of which the world can know nothing."

HIDING IN THEE. The tune was composed by Ira D. Sankey to accompany these words. It first appeared in *Welcome Tidings,* compiled by Robert Lowry, William H. Doane and Sankey in 1877, and bears the original song title "Hiding in Thee."

401. When peace like a river attendeth my way
These words were written by Horatio G. Spafford following the loss of four daughters in an accident at sea. The family was scheduled to travel to Europe in November, 1873. Being delayed by last minute business developments, Spafford sent his wife and the girls on ahead. In mid-ocean their ship, the French liner Ville du Havre, collided with an English sailing ship and foundered. Mrs. Spafford only was saved and cabled her husband "saved alone." Spafford started immediately for Europe and, while on the high seas near the scene of the tragedy, wrote this hymn.

VILLE DU HAVRE. Philip P. Bliss wrote this tune for the text and it first appeared in *Gospel Hymns No. 2,* 1876, compiled by Ira D. Sankey and Bliss. It is named for the ship mentioned above.

402. A wonderful Savior is Jesus my Lord
According to the *Companion to the Songbook of the Salvation Army* (London, 1970) this text was written by Fanny Crosby to fit William Kirkpatrick's tune, and first appeared in *The Finest of the Wheat, No. 1,* 1890, compiled by George D. Elderkin, R. R. McCabe, John R. Sweney and Kirkpatrick.

KIRKPATRICK. This tune by William J. Kirkpatrick evidently inspired the writing of the text. Fanny J. Crosby followed this procedure in working with several composers.

403. Walking in sunlight all of my journey
Henry J. Zelley, a Methodist minister who supported the holiness camp meetings during his long ministry, wrote this hymn in 1899. It appeared in *Gospel Praises,* published that year by Hall-Mack in Philadelphia, and edited by William J. Kirkpatrick and H. L. Gilmour.

Evangelist Charles E. Fuller of "The Old Fashioned Revival Hour" broadcast paraphrased this refrain, beginning "Heavenly sunshine."

HEAVENLY SUNLIGHT. George H. Cook wrote the music and then asked Henry Zelley for appropriate words. "Heavenly Sunlight" was the result.

404. I have a song that Jesus gave me

In *Crusade Hymn Stories,* there is a complete story of the writing of this hymn by Elton M. Roth. On a hot afternoon in 1923, while he was conducting an evangelistic meeting in a small town in Texas, Roth strolled into a quiet church. Walking up and down the aisle he began humming and singing, "In my heart there rings a melody." In an hour words and music were completed.

HEART MELODY. The tune name is derived from the refrain, and from Ephesians 5:19, "singing and making melody in your heart to the Lord." Elton Roth introduced the song in the open air service the same night it was written. In those days he had an association with the E. O. Excell Company, and the song was first printed in his *Campaign Melodies,* 1924. The following year it appeared in Hope Publishing Company's *Hymns of Praise, No. 2.*

405. Come, come, ye saints

In his diary for April 15, 1846 William Clayton recorded that he wrote a new song—"All is Well"—while traveling with Brigham Young's "Latter Day Saints" from Nauvoo, Illinois toward the Great Salt Lake in the west. Actually the refrain "All is well!" had appeared in a hymn about death and heaven, set to the same tune in *The Sacred Harp,* 1844.

Only the first stanza of the present song is Clayton's, with slight revision. The rest is the work of Avis B. Christiansen, written at the request of Donald P. Hustad for inclusion in *Crusader Hymns* (Chicago: Hope Publishing Company, 1966).

ALL IS WELL. See "Renew Thy church, her ministries restore," No. 205.

406. There's a peace in my heart

Anne S. Murphy wrote both words and music for this hymn. It was copyrighted in 1908, but its first published appearance has not been located. Phil Kerr (in *Music in Evangelism*) says that he visited Mrs. Murphy shortly before her death and found "that in spite of severe testing she maintained unusual serenity and inward peace, actually putting into practice the message of her song."

CONSTANTLY ABIDING. The tune name is the traditional title of this favorite gospel song.

407. Dear Lord and Father of mankind

"The Brewing of Soma," a 17-stanza poem by John Greenleaf Whittier which first appeared in the *Atlantic Monthly,* April, 1872, described the attempts pagan peoples make to worship their gods. "Soma" is an intoxicating drink which produced "a frenzy, a sacred madness, an ecstatic storm of drunken joy." Whittier, a Quaker, concludes his poem with six stanzas beginning "Dear Lord and Father of mankind," in which he extols the quietness of true Christian worship. They were first used as a hymn by W. Garrett Horder, editor of an English Baptist hymnal, and of *Worship Song,* 1884.

REST. The tune was composed for this text by Frederick C. Maker for publication in the *Congregational Church Hymnal* (London, 1887). It is named "Rest" because of the emphasis of the words.

408. I will sing of my Redeemer

This text written by Philip P. Bliss was found in his trunk following the train wreck in which he and his wife lost their lives. (See the biographical sketch in another part of this volume). The words first appeared in *Welcome Tidings, A New Collection for Sunday School,* 1877.

HYFRYDOL. For many years these words were always sung to music written by James McGranahan, who followed P. P. Bliss as songleader for Evangelist D. W. Whittle.

The tune "Hyfrydol" has been used increasingly in recent years and has given these historic words new life and meaning. In *Companion to Baptist Hymnal,* William J. Reynolds points out that it was used with Philip P. Bliss's "I will sing the wondrous story" in the Gipsy Smith Special Supplement to *Hallowed Hymns, New and Old,* compiled and edited by I. Allan Sankey and published by Biglow & Main in 1909. For further information, see "Come, Thou long expected Jesus," No. 102.

409. Loved with everlasting love

George W. Robinson wrote these words which first appeared in *Hymns of Consecration and Faith,* 1876. In commenting on the meaning of the hymn, Dr. Millar Patrick (in the Supplement to the *Handbook to the Church Hymnary*) quotes from Henry Martyn's *Cambridge Diary:*

> Since I have known God in a saving manner, painting, poetry and music have had charms unknown to me before, for Religion has refined my mind and made it susceptible of impressions from the sublime and beautiful.

EVERLASTING LOVE. James Mountain compiled the first edition of *Hymns of Consecration and Faith,* 1876, and wrote the tune for these words for inclusion in that collection.

410. O what a wonderful, wonderful day

The story of the writing of this gospel song of testimony is told by the author-composer, John W. Peterson:

> The place was the Montrose Bible Conference, Montrose, Pennsylvania. The occasion was a morning service. When opportunity was given for personal testimony, an old gentleman rose to his feet to tell of the saving work of God in his heart. As he spoke his face glowed, especially when he rehearsed that night when he came to Jesus Christ. "Heaven came down and glory filled my soul" was the way he expressed it! I was on the platform that morning, in charge of the music. Immediately the words caught fire in my heart and I jotted them down. I realized he had given me a wonderful theme for a song. Later that week I completed it—both words and music.

HEAVEN CAME DOWN. The complete gospel song was written in August, 1961 and appeared the same year in *Miracle Melodies, No. 4* (Singspiration, Grand Rapids, Michigan).

411. Happiness is to know the Savior

Ira Stanphill says that he wrote this text and tune about 1967—for no particular reason other than the truth of the title. It was first published in 1968 in *Ira Stanphill Favorites Vol. I* (Singspiration, Inc.).

HAPPINESS IS THE LORD. The tune name is the traditional title of Ira Stanphill's gospel song.

412. Just when I need Him Jesus is near

This hymn was written by William C. Poole and was one of a number of poems submitted to composer Charles H. Gabriel in 1907. It was Poole's first attempt to write a hymn text.

GABRIEL. The tune was composed for the text by Charles H. Gabriel, and he copyrighted both words and music in 1907. The song was purchased by E. O. Excell and first published in his *Service in Song,* 1909.

413. God is my strong salvation

In this hymn James Montgomery gives a free paraphrase of Psalm 27 (especially verses 1, 3, 14) in two stanzas of eight lines each. It was first published in his *Songs of Zion, Being Imitations of Psalms,* 1882.

WEDLOCK. A traditional American folk melody, this tune appeared in one variant in *The Sacred Harp,* 1844, and with these words in *Methodist*

Hymnal, 1964. George Pullen Jackson included it in his *Down-East Spirituals* (No. 56) and suggests it is related to an Irish chantey.

The harmonization by Donald P. Hustad was made for *Hymns for the Living Church* and has been used in *Baptist Hymnal,* 1975.

414. Mid all the traffic of the ways

John Oxenham wrote the words during World War I and they appeared in a collection of his verse entitled *The Vision Splendid,* 1917. The poem was titled "Sanctuary."

ST. AGNES. See "Jesus, the very thought of Thee," No. 83.

415. There is a balm in Gilead

George Pullen Jackson (in *White and Negro Spirituals*) reminds us that the phrase "sin-sick soul" is found in hymns of both Charles Wesley and John Newton. This traditional spiritual is traced to the Newton words:

> How lost was my condition
> Till Jesus made me whole,
> There is but one Physician
> Can cure a sin-sick soul.

In early American history the Newton text was associated with the Scottish folk tune "Banks of Sweet Dundee" with no refrain, though in black worship the words bore little resemblance to the original. The refrain evidently appeared in revival meetings and was published in the upstate New York *Revivalist* of 1868.

BALM IN GILEAD. The refrain, which gives the tune its name, is based on the words of Jeremiah 8:22: "Is there no balm in Gilead; is there no physician there?"

416. Does Jesus care?

The poem by Frank E. Graeff was written following a time when he had experienced despondency, doubt and physical agony. Known as a "spiritual optimist," Graeff turned his thoughts to Jesus Christ and sought for solace and strength in God's Word. I Peter 5:7 was particularly meaningful during this time of struggle and the words "He careth for you" brought him great comfort.

MY SAVIOR CARES. The music was written by J. Lincoln Hall for this text and he once said that this setting was his "most inspired piece of music." The complete song was copyrighted in 1901 but the first publication is uncertain. It did appear in *New Songs of the Gospel, No. 2* (Hall-Mack, 1905).

417. What a fellowship, what a joy divine

The text was written by Elisha A. Hoffman at the request of A. J. Showalter, composer of its accompanying tune. In an expression of sympathy to two former students, Showalter had quoted Deuteronomy 33:27, "The eternal God is thy refuge, and underneath are the everlasting arms." He was immediately impressed that the words could be the basis of a good song. He wrote the refrain and the music, and asked Hoffman to submit appropriate stanzas.

SHOWALTER. The tune was written by Anthony J. Showalter as described above. The complete hymn first appeared in *The Glad Evangel for Revival, Camp, and Evangelistic Meetings,* 1887, compiled by L. M. Evilsizer, S. J. Perry and Showalter.

418. In the hour of trial

The first manuscript of this hymn by James Montgomery bore the date October 13, 1834 and the title "In Trial and Temptation." It was not published until 1853, when it was included in the author's *Original Hymns for Public, Private, and Social Devotion* under the caption, "Prayers on Pilgrimage." The original text has undergone several revisions.

PENITENCE. Spencer Lane wrote this melody one Sunday in 1875 for use in the evening service at St. James' Episcopal Church, Woonsocket, Rhode Island. The hymn of James Montgomery had been chosen with a tune which did not appeal to Mr. Lane, so he wrote a new setting for it which was included in Charles L. Hutchins' *Church Hymnal,* 1879. Its name reflects the sentiment of the words.

419. Father, whate'er of earthly bliss

With the title "Desiring Resignation and Thankfulness," this hymn of Anne Steele was first published in ten stanzas (beginning "When I survey life's varied scene") in her *Poems on Subjects Chiefly Devotional,* 1760. This hymn setting offers the last three stanzas of her poem in a version largely taken from Augustus Toplady's revision in his *Psalms and Hymns,* 1776.

NAOMI. The tune was first published by Lowell Mason in 1836 in the periodical, *Occasional Psalm and Hymn Tunes,* and also in his *Modern Psalmist,* 1839. The original melody has been attributed to Johann Nägeli, though there is little information to substantiate this. "Naomi" is another of the biblical names used by Mason for hymn tunes.

420. If thou but suffer God to guide thee

Written by Georg Neumark in 1641, this text was captioned "A Song of Comfort: God will care for and help every one in His own time." The hymn was born out of a fortuitous change in Neumark's circumstances—following a time of hardship he was appointed to a tutorship. Catherine Winkworth made two translations of the German original; this version appeared in her *Chorale Book for England*, 1863.

NEUMARK. The tune was written by Georg Neumark and appeared with his words in his *Fortgepflantzer Musikalisch Poetischer Lustwald*, 1657. It has been set to no less than 400 different hymns.

421. Be not dismayed whate'er betide

Civilla D. Martin wrote the words one Sunday afternoon in 1904, while her husband was on a preaching assignment and she remained ill in bed in Lestershire, New York. Mr. Martin wrote the music when he returned that same day, and the hymn was sung in the evening.

GOD CARES. W. Stillman Martin's tune appeared with his wife's words in *Songs of Redemption and Praise*, 1905, compiled by Martin and evangelist John A. Davis, founder and president of the Practical Bible Training School, Lestershire, New York.

422. Give to the winds your fears

Paul Gerhardt's German hymn based on Psalm 37:5 was printed in Johann Crüger's *Praxis Pietatis Melica*, 1653, and has been translated into English more than twenty times. John Wesley's setting, which appeared in *Hymns and Sacred Poems*, 1739, has been "modernized" slightly by the editors of *Hymns for the Living Church*.

DIADEMATA. See "Crown Him with many crowns," No. 85.

423. Come, ye disconsolate, where'er ye languish

Thomas Moore was the author of some 32 hymns, of which this is the only one still in common use. He was better known for such secular favorites as "Believe Me, if All Those Endearing Young Charms" and "The Last Rose of Summer." Two stanzas of this hymn appeared in Moore's

Sacred Songs, 1824. Thomas Hastings added a third stanza and altered the other two somewhat, and his revision was published in *Spiritual Songs for Social Worship,* 1831, compiled by Hastings and Lowell Mason.

CONSOLATOR. Thomas Moore said the tune was a "German air" which inspired him to write the original text. It is unclear whether Samuel Webbe composed it or arranged an already existing melody, but it was first published in his *Collection of Motetts,* 1792. It appeared with these words in *Spiritual Songs for Social Worship,* 1831.

The tune has been called "Consolation," but the name used here distinguishes it from a melody written by Felix Mendelssohn (No. 425).

424. Immortal Love, forever full

"Our Master" was the title of a 38-stanza poem by John Greenleaf Whittier, published in his *Tent on the Beach and Other Poems,* 1867. The typical hymnal version (stanzas 5, 13, 14, 16 of the original) omits the first stanza, given here.

SERENITY. See "O Jesus, King most wonderful!", No. 73.

425. We would see Jesus; for the shadows lengthen

Based on the words found in John 12:21, this hymn of Anna B. Warner first appeared in six stanzas in her collection *Hymns for the Church Militant,* published in 1858. It is believed to have been written some time earlier.

CONSOLATION. This hymn tune is adapted from No. 3 of Felix Mendelssohn's *Songs Without Words,* Opus 30, for piano, entitled "Consolation" in some editions. In various versions, it has been used as a hymn setting since the 1860's.

426. Is your burden heavy?

In 1968 Ralph Carmichael wrote this song for the closing musical theme of a religious radio broadcast. He gave it the title "Reach Out to Jesus." It was first published in March, 1969 in *102 Strings, Vol. 2,* by Lexicon Music, Inc. This is its first appearance in a standard hymnal.

REACH OUT TO JESUS. Ralph Carmichael invariably writes the music for his own poems. The tune gets its name from the song's original title.

427. Jesus, my Savior, look on me

With the title "Christ, All in All," this text by Charlotte Elliott first appeared in her *Thoughts in Verse on Sacred Subjects,* 1869.

SULLIVAN. The music by Arthur Sullivan was composed for these words for their appearance in his *Church Hymns,* 1874. The tune is also called "Hanford" after the locale in Dorsetshire, England where Sullivan wrote it.

428. Lord, I have shut the door

No doubt William M. Runyan, in writing these words, was giving an exposition of Matthew 6:6, "But thou, when thou prayest, enter into thy room, and when thou hast shut thy door, pray to thy Father, which is in secret. . ." The hymn was first printed in Runyan's *Songs of Salvation and Service,* 1923.

SANCTUARY. William Runyan wrote the music for many of his own hymns, including this one. The tune name reflects the imagery of the words.

429. Prayer is the soul's sincere desire

At the request of Edward Bickersteth, James Montgomery wrote this text in 1818 for the former's *Treatise on Prayer,* 1819. The poem originally had eight stanzas, and the 2nd, 6th and 7th have been omitted in this hymnal.

CAMPMEETING. The tune is an American folk melody, well-known in early 19th century camp meetings. It was reharmonized and named by Robert G. McCutchan for the *Methodist Hymnal,* 1935, of which he was editor.

430. From every stormy wind that blows

Hugh Stowell's poem first appeared with the title "Peace at the Mercy-Seat" in his first volume of *Winter's Wreath, a Collection of Original Compositions in Prose and Verse,* an illustrated annual published from 1828 to 1832. In 1831 it was rewritten for his *Selection of Psalms and Hymns Suited to the Services of the Church of England.*

RETREAT. Named for its common association with Stowell's text, the tune was composed by Thomas Hastings and first printed in his *Sacred Songs for Family and Social Worship,* 1842.

431. Come, my soul, your plea prepare

John Newton's hymn was suggested by Solomon's dream recounted in I Kings 3:5–9, and was published in Book I of *Olney Hymns,* 1779. The original first line, "Come, my soul, your suit prepare," suggests that prayer is like a lawyer's argument in court; the present version retains the imagery and may be easier understood.

SEYMOUR. See "Depth of mercy! can there be," No. 238.

432. Talk with us, Lord
This hymn by Charles Wesley, entitled "On a Journey," was first published in six stanzas in *Hymns and Sacred Poems,* 1740. John Wesley altered the words somewhat for his *Collection of Hymns for the Use of the People Called Methodists,* 1780.

GRÄFENBERG. This melody first appeared anonymously in the second edition of *Praxis Pietatis Melica,* 1647. In the 1653 edition the chorale was initialed "J.C." and it is ascribed to Johann Crüger, though it bears resemblance to psalm tunes in the Genevan Psalter, 1562. "Gräfenberg" is a town with a "spa" in Silesia.

433. 'Tis the blessed hour of prayer
The lyrics by Fanny J. Crosby first appeared in *Good as Gold,* 1880, a Sunday School collection compiled by Robert Lowry and William H. Doane and published by Biglow and Main, New York.

BLESSED HOUR. William H. Doane's tune has always appeared with these words of Fanny Crosby.

434. Sweet hour of prayer
The words of this hymn appeared in *The New York Observer* September 13, 1845, a contribution by Rev. Thomas Salmon, who had recently come to the United States from England. He explained that the poem was written by W. W. Walford, a blind fellow-clergyman in Warwickshire.

There is some uncertainty about the identification of "W. W. Walford." William J. Reynolds, in his *Hymns of Our Faith,* gives a detailed account of research which suggests that this may be the work of William Walford of Homerton. It is the similarity between the hymn and Walford's book, *The Manner of Prayer (ca.* 1842), that led to the conclusion. The first inclusion of the text in a hymnal was in the Baptist edition of *Church Melodies,* compiled by Thomas Hastings and Robert Turnbull in 1859.

SWEET HOUR. The earliest publication to contain this tune, composed by William Bradbury for this hymn, is believed to be his compilation, *The Golden Chain* (New York, 1861).

435. What a Friend we have in Jesus

Joseph M. Scriven wrote these words *ca.* 1855 to comfort his mother in a time of sorrow, never intending them to have any wider use. A friend saw the manuscript when sitting with Scriven during the author's last illness. Scriven admitted, "The Lord and I wrote it between us." The hymn evidently appeared first (and anonymously) in Horace L. Hasting's *Social Hymns, Original and Selected,* 1865.

CONVERSE. Composed for these words by Charles Converse in 1868, this melody first appeared in *Silver Wings,* 1870, compiled by "Karl Reden" (Converse's pseudonym). When Philip P. Bliss and Ira D. Sankey were completing the copy for their famous *Gospel Hymns and Sacred Songs,* 1875, this hymn was substituted for another shortly before publication. Sankey later remarked that "the last hymn that went into the book became one of the first in favor."

436. I have a Savior, He's pleading in glory

Ira D. Sankey found this poem by S. O'Malley Clough in Ireland in 1874, during his first visit to the British Isles with evangelist Dwight L. Moody. In the ensuing months the hymn became very popular, though Sankey may never have known who the author was. Clough wrote the words in 1860 and it was first printed on a broadsheet.

INTERCESSION. The tune Sankey wrote for these words was his second attempt at composing, and the full hymn appeared in his *Sacred Songs and Solos* in England, and *Gospel Hymns and Sacred Songs,* 1875 in America.

437. I must tell Jesus all of my trials

Both words and music of this hymn were written by Elisha Hoffman and appeared in *Pentecostal Hymns* (Chicago: Hope Publishing Company, 1894). Hoffman was one of the hymnal's editors and he says that the song was inspired by the response of a parishioner whom he had counseled. "Yes," she exclaimed, echoing his own words, "I must tell Jesus!"

ORWIGSBURG. The tune is named for Orwigsburg, Pennsylvania, where author-composer Elisha Hoffman was born.

438. Teach me to pray, Lord

These words were written by Albert S. Reitz in 1925, following a soul-stirring Day of Prayer conducted by the Evangelical Prayer Union. Reitz was pastor of the Rosehill Baptist Church in Los Angeles, California at the time.

REITZ. Albert Reitz composed this tune shortly after writing the words. The full hymn was first published in *Gospel Solos and Duets No. 2,* 1925, compiled by Herbert G. Tovey.

439. He leadeth me, O blessed thought

While still a young man, Joseph H. Gilmore served as a "pulpit supply" at the First Baptist Church in Philadelphia. He planned to give an exposition of the 23rd Psalm but could get no further than "He leadeth me." He saw in those words significance and beauty he had never before imagined. After the service, Gilmore penciled the hymn while being entertained in the home of one of the church's deacons, and eventually gave it to his wife. Months later she sent it to the *Watchman and Reflector,* a Boston paper, and they published it (Vol. XLIII, No. 49) without Gilmore's knowledge.

HE LEADETH ME. William Bradbury saw Gilmore's hymn in the *Watchman and Reflector* and set it to music. The text was also modified so as to provide a refrain. The tune first appeared with the text in Bradbury's *The Golden Censer,* 1864.

440. All the way my Savior leads me

These words came to Fanny Crosby after she had been the recipient of unexpected good fortune, and as she meditated on God's goodness.

ALL THE WAY. Fanny Crosby sent her poem to Robert Lowry who composed the tune. It appeared first in *Brightest and Best,* 1875, a Sunday School collection compiled by William H. Doane and Lowry, and was headed by the scripture "The Lord alone did lead him" (Deuteronomy 32:12).

441. Lead us, O Father

William H. Burleigh's hymn was originally entitled "Prayer for Guidance," and first appeared in *The New Congregational Hymn Book,* 1859. Another important early appearance was in *Lyra Sacra Americana,* 1868, an English collection of American hymns edited by C. D. Cleveland; because of this collection's popularity, the hymn is almost better known in England than in America.

LANGRAN. See "Here, O my Lord, I see Thee face to face," No. 210.

442. Lead, kindly Light

John H. Newman wrote these words in a time of stress when he was suffering physically, mentally and spiritually. Following a stay in southern Europe and frustrating delays in arranging passage home, he was sailing toward Marseilles on his way back to England, when the ship was becalmed for a week in the straits of Bonifacio in the Mediterranean. During this time, Newman was writing continually and the date given for this text is June 16, 1833. It was first published in the *British Magazine*, March, 1834 under the title "Faith—Heavenly Leadings," and afterwards in *Lyra Apostolica*, 1836.

LUX BENIGNA. The tune (whose name is "kindly light") was written by John B. Dykes. It is said to have come to him one day in 1865 while walking through the busy Strand in London. It was originally called "St. Oswald" and first appeared in Barry's *Psalms and Hymns for the Church, School, and Home* (London, 1867). In 1868 it was revised and set to Cardinal Newman's poem in the Appendix to the first edition of *Hymns Ancient and Modern*. Newman generously credited the popularity of the hymn to Dyke's tune. It has also been pointed out that words written on a calmed sea, wedded to a tune composed in the turmoil of a busy city, have together blessed the hearts of many.

443. Jesus, I my cross have taken

This text by Henry F. Lyte, perhaps his most popular hymn during the 19th century, first appeared in his *Sacred Poetry*, 1824 signed "G." In his *Poems, Chiefly Religious*, 1833, Lyte acknowledged authorship.

Companion to the Songbook of the Salvation Army (London, 1961) suggests that the words "may have been written as a memorial to his wife's courage and fortitude at a time when she had to choose between her home and freedom to serve the Lord in the Methodist communion." Interesting, if true, since she later married Lyte, who was a leading clergyman in the Church of England.

ELLESDIE. In many hymn collections, Wolfgang A. Mozart has been credited as the source of this tune. In *Winnowed Hymns*, 1873 its source is given as "Air, Mozart, Arr. by H.P.M." The tune first appeared (with no credit) in Joshua Leavitt's *The Christian Lyre*, Vol. 11, 1831, and it is assumed that Hubert P. Main simply harmonized the melody he found in that book; he never explained the "Mozart" source. The name "Ellesdie" is thought to be derived from the initials "L.S.D." of an individual unknown.

444. Take Thou my hand, O Father

In the original German text "So nimm denn meine Hände" by Julie von Hausmann (published in her *Maiblumen*, Vol. 1, 1862) the words "God" or "Christ" were not mentioned. This caused many less-than-devout young couples to use the hymn for a wedding song, sung to each other. In the translation by Herman Brückner the meaning is clarified. Traditionally, German-language churches in the United States have sung the hymn effectively at the conclusion of the rite of confirmation on Palm Sunday.

SO NIMM DENN MEINE HÄNDE. The tune first appeared in Friedrich Silcher's *Kinderlieder*, Vol. III, 1842, where it was set to "Wie könnt ich ruhig schlafen" (How could I sleep peacefully?) It was first associated with this text (in German) in *Grosse Missionsharfe* (Gütersloh, 1883).

445. Children of the heavenly King
Perhaps the most popular of John Cennick's hymns, this text first appeared in his *Sacred Hymns for the Children of God in the Days of Their Pilgrimage*, Part III, 1742. It was entitled "Encouragement to Praise."

VIENNA. Justin H. Knecht's tune first appeared in *Vollständige Sammlung*, 1799, edited by J. F. Christmann and Knecht.

446. Jesus, Savior, pilot me
This favorite hymn text appeared anonymously in *Sailor's Magazine*, 1871 and the same year in *The Baptist Praise Book*. Dr. Edward Hopper revealed that he was the author following its appearance in *Spiritual Songs*, 1878. When he wrote these words, Hopper was pastor of the Church of the Sea and Land in New York City, and he was undoubtedly thinking of the experiences of the many sailors who attended services there.

ARFON. The tune has been called "a traditional Welsh melody" in many sources. However, it also appears in two collections of French Christmas carols, suggesting it is of Gallic heritage. Erik Routley (in *Companion to Congregational Praise*) concludes that it seems impossible to determine the tune's origin.

447. Because the Lord is my Shepherd
Ralph Carmichael wrote this paraphrase of Psalm 23 in 1969 for the Billy Graham film about Palestine—"His Land." In the film the song was sung by the young Britisher, Cliff Richard. It was first published in 1970 by Lexicon Music, Inc. in *Now—Cliff Barrows and The Gang*.

THE NEW 23RD. The song has always been known by this name, since it is a paraphrase of the best-loved "Shepherd's Psalm."

448. Guide me, O Thou great Jehovah
William Williams' text first appeared in his collection of Welsh hymns,

Alleluia, 1745, entitled "Strength to pass through the Wilderness." In *Crusade Hymn Stories,* the author of this companion presents a complete analysis of the hymn and its imagery from the journey of the Israelites to the land of Canaan.

In his *Hymns on Various Subjects,* 1771, Peter Williams translated three of the stanzas into English. A year later the original author (or possibly his son John) made another English translation, retaining the first stanza of Peter Williams' version and adding a fourth. This hymn was first printed in 1772 in leaflet form and then included in Lady Huntingdon's *Collection,* 1772 or 1773. The first three stanzas of this second version are offered here.

CWM RHONDDA. The tune (pronounced "coom rawnthuh") was composed by John Hughes in 1907 for the annual Baptist Cymanfau Ganu (Singing Festival) at Capel Rhondda, an industrial area in Pontypridd, Wales. It was first printed in Great Britain in the revised *Fellowship Hymn-Book,* 1933. Interestingly enough, the tune was copyrighted in the United States in 1927 in an arrangement by E. Edwin Young that appeared in *The Voice of Thanksgiving No. 4* (Chicago: The Bible Institute Colportage Association, 1928).

449. I feel the winds of God today

Little is known about the writing of this hymn or its first appearance in print. It is the work of Jessie Adams, an English Quaker lady, and is reported to have been written "after a long period of service as a teacher in which she felt a considerable measure of disappointment and failure."

KINGSFOLD. The history of this traditional melody of England and Ireland is recounted in *Companion to Congregational Praise* (London, 1953) by Erik Routley. Ralph Vaughan Williams composed a fantasia on it for strings and harp entitled "Dives and Lazarus," and the tune was often associated with that ancient carol. Vaughan Williams also arranged it as a hymn tune in *English Hymnal,* 1906.

This harmonization by Ellwood Shermer Wolf was made for *Hymns and Songs of the Spirit,* 1966, where it appeared with Ms. Adams' words.

450. Jesus, still lead on

A cento from two of the hymns of Nikolaus von Zinzendorf, this text first appeared in the *Brüder Gesangbuch,* 1778 and was probably put together by one of its editors, Christian Gregor. Zinzendorf's "Seelenbräutigam, O du Gottes Lamm!" had 11 stanzas and was published in September, 1721; it is also the source of John Wesley's "O Thou, to whose all-searching sight." The other hymn, "Glanz der Ewigkeit," also had 11 stanzas and was published in May, 1721. There have been many English translations of Gregor's adaptation but this one by Jane Laurie Borthwick is preferred today. The setting first appeared in *The Free Church Magazine,* 1846 and later, slightly revised, in Miss Borthwick's *Hymns from the Land of Luther,* 1854.

ROCHELLE. The melody by Adam Drese is also called "Seelenbräutigam" (soul's bridegroom) from the German hymn mentioned above. It was first published in *Geistreiches Gesang-Buch,* 1698.

451. I have decided to follow Jesus

This anonymous song appeared in the United States during the 1960's and was prominently featured in Billy Graham crusade meetings. It may have originated among national Christians in India.

ASSAM. It is reported that the melody has roots in Assam, a state in India where Christian missions have a long history.

452. I want Jesus to walk with me

Though the source of this American folk hymn is unknown, it is probably one of the "white spirituals" which thrived for more than two hundred years in the rural Appalachian culture.

WALK WITH ME. Unlike black spirituals (and similar to "Poor, Wayfaring Stranger," No. 540) this music has no refrain. It may have been adapted from an English folk tune brought to these shores by the early settlers.

453. Encamped along the hills of light

John H. Yates wrote a number of poems and sent them to Ira D. Sankey, who composed appropriate tunes. In *My Life and the Story of the Gospel Hymns,* Sankey states that this hymn was first published in *The Christian Endeavor Hymnbook.* In *Gospel Hymns No. 6,* 1891, it appeared with the copyright registered that year by Biglow and Main. Evidently both hymnals were released that same year.

SANKEY. Ira D. Sankey wrote comparatively few hymn tunes but most of them, including this one named for him, have been strong enough to survive.

454. Awake, my soul, stretch every nerve

"Pressing on in the Christian Race" was the title of this hymn when it appeared in a collection of Philip Doddridge's *Hymns, founded on various texts in the Holy Scriptures,* published posthumously in 1755. The text has many scriptural allusions: Phil. 3:13–14, I Cor. 9:24, Heb. 12:1, II Tim. 4:8, and Rev. 4:10. It was written to be sung after one of Doddridge's sermons.

CHRISTMAS. See "While shepherds watched their flocks," No. 119.

455–456. Stand up, stand up for Jesus

These words by George Duffield were inspired by the dying message of Dudley A. Tyng, a heroic and faithful Episcopalian minister in Philadelphia during the great revival of 1858, usually known as "The Work of God in Philadelphia." The story is told completely in *Crusade Hymn Stories,* pp. 19–20.

Tyng died as the result of an accident on the family farm. In his last moments he said to his father, "Stand up for Jesus; father, stand up for Jesus; and tell my brethren of the ministry wherever you meet them, to stand up for Jesus!" The following Sunday, after Tyng's death, George Duffield preached on Ephesians 6:14 in Temple Presbyterian Church and the verses of the hymn were used as a concluding exhortation. The hymn first appeared as a leaflet for Sunday School children, and was badly garbled in the *Church Psalmist,* 1858. In its present form it first appeared in *Lyra Sacra Americana,* 1868.

GEIBEL. Adam Geibel composed this setting for Duffield's hymn and published it in 1901 in his *Uplift Voices.*

WEBB. This tune was probably first associated with this text in William B. Bradbury's *Golden Chain of Sabbath School Melodies,* 1861. The music was composed by George J. Webb during a voyage from England to America, and was set to the secular words, "'Tis Dawn, the Lark is Singing." The song appeared in *The Odeon: A Collection of Secular Melodies,* 1837, compiled by Webb and Lowell Mason.

457. Lead on, O King Eternal

Ernest Warburton Shurtleff wrote these words on the occasion of his graduation from Andover Theological Seminary in 1887. The hymn met with instant success and was published the same year in his *Hymns of the Faith.*

LANCASHIRE. See "The day of resurrection," No. 168.

458. Soldiers of Christ, arise

Based on Ephesians 6:10–20, these words of Charles Wesley appeared in *Hymns and Sacred Poems,* 1749 with the title "The Whole Armour of God." The hymn originally contained sixteen stanzas of eight lines each.

DIADEMATA. See "Crown Him with many crowns," No. 85.

459. There's a royal banner given for display

The text appears in *Gospel Hymns No. 5,* 1887 credited to "El Nathan," a frequently used pseudonym of Daniel W. Whittle. It was based on Psalm 60:4, "Thou hast given a banner to them that fear thee, that it may be displayed because of the truth."

ROYAL BANNER. The tune was written for Major Whittle's words by James McGranahan, his song leader in evangelism in the late 19th century.

460. Who is on the Lord's side?

Frances Ridley Havergal's hymn was written October 13, 1877 and entitled "Home Missions." It was based on I Chronicles 12:18 and first published in Miss Havergal's *Loyal Responses,* 1878.

ARMAGEDDON. The name is derived from the location of the cataclysmic struggle which is associated prophetically with the end of history and mentioned in Revelation 16:16. The tune is an adaptation of a German melody credited to Luise Reichardt in Part III of Layriz's *Kern des deutschen Kirchengesangs,* 1853. John Goss's adaptation appeared in the present form in *The Church Psalter and Hymn-Book,* 1872 set to "Onward, Christian soldiers."

461. Rise up, O men of God!

William Pierson Merrill wrote these words in 1911 after the editor of *The Continent* requested a hymn appropriate for the "brotherhood movement" of the Presbyterian Church. The author said he "got a start" from an article by Gerald Stanley Lee entitled "The Church of the Strong Men," and that the text was completed on a steamer on Lake Michigan. The hymn first appeared in the February 16, 1911 edition of *The Continent.*

FESTAL SONG. The tune's name is related to its first association with the text "Awake and sing the song" in *The Hymnal Revised and Enlarged,* 1894. William Walter's music was first used with "Rise up, O men of God" in *Pilgrim Hymnal,* 1912.

462. My soul, be on your guard

Under the title "Steadfastness," this hymn by George Heath first appeared in 1781 in his *Hymns and Poetic Essays Sacred to the Public and Private Worship of the Deity.*

LABAN. Bearing another of the Old Testament names chosen by composer Lowell Mason, this melody was written in 1830 and published in his *Spiritual Songs for Social Worship,* 1832. The tune is also called "Conflict" because of its common association with Heath's words.

463. Once to every man and nation

In 1845 James Russell Lowell wrote a poem entitled "The Present Crisis" in protest against the United States' involvement in the war with Mexico, and it was published in his *Poems,* 1849. W. Garrett Horder chose 16 of the original 90 lines for his *Hymns, Supplemental to existing collections,* 1896. His cento appears here in altered form, with one stanza omitted.

TON-Y-BOTEL. Originally associated with his anthem "Goleu yn y Glyn" or "Light in the Valley," Thomas J. Williams' music first appeared as a hymn tune in the Welsh volume *Llwalyfr Moliant,* 1890 under the name commonly used in British hymnals, "Ebenezer." The name "Ton-Y-Botel" was given to it by a young English singer who told the romantic-but-fictional story of the "tune-in-a-bottle" which had been washed ashore on the coast of Wales.

464. We are living, we are dwelling

As a young man in his early twenties, Arthur Cleveland Coxe responded to the challenges of the year 1840 with these words which still seem appropriate today. They first appeared under the title "Watchwords" in Coxe's *Athanasion . . . also miscellaneous poems,* 1842.

AUSTRIAN HYMN. See "Praise the Lord! ye heavens, adore Him," No. 17.

465. Give of your best to the Master

This text was written by Howard B. Grose, presumably for a Christian Endeavor hymnal he was editing. The dates of its writing and publication are unknown.

BARNARD. This is probably one of the melodies written for secular texts by Charlotte A. Barnard under the pen-name "Claribel." It is not known when it was first associated with these words.

466. God of grace and God of glory

Written for the dedication of the Riverside Church in New York City, October 5, 1930, this hymn by Harry E. Fosdick appeared in *Praise and Service,* 1932 set to the tune "Regent Square." Dr. Fosdick was one of the principals in the fundamentalist-modernist struggle of the 1920's and 1930's, but these words can be the prayer of all true Christians.

CWM RHONDDA. See "Guide me, O Thou great Jehovah," No. 448.

467. The Son of God goes forth to war

Reginald Heber wrote these lines for St. Stephen's Day and they were first published posthumously in his *Hymns written and adapted to the Weekly Church Service of the Year,* 1827. A full study of this "Christian martyrs" hymn, by Billy Graham, appears in *Crusade Hymn Stories.*

ALL SAINTS, NEW. Written for this text by Henry S. Cutler, this tune was first published in *The Hymnal with Tunes Old and New,* 1872. "New" was added to the tune name to avoid confusion with the earlier melody called "All Saints" in *Geistreiches Gesang-buch,* Darmstadt, 1698.

468. Soldiers, who are Christ's below

In the original Latin, this hymn ("Pugnate, Christi Milites") was first found in the *Bourges Breviary,* 1734 and later in Newman's *Hymni Ecclesiae,* 1838. John Haldenby Clark made the English translation on Palm Sunday, 1865 and it was included in the 1868 Appendix to the first edition of *Hymns Ancient and Modern.*

CRUCIS MILITES. Myles B. Foster wrote and named this tune for William Walsham How's hymn, "Soldiers of the cross, arise." It was introduced in the 1889 Supplement to the 1875 edition of *Hymns Ancient and Modern.*

469. Fight the good fight with all thy might!

Written for the Anglican service for the 19th Sunday after Trinity, this text by John S. B. Monsell first appeared in his *Hymns of Love and Praise for the Church's Year,* 1863. It was based on I Timothy 6:12, "Fight the good fight of faith."

PENTECOST. In 1864 William Boyd composed this music and named it for the Whitsuntide hymn "Come, Holy Ghost, our souls inspire," at the request of Sabine Baring-Gould, who wanted a simple tune for those words. It was first published in *Thirty-two Hymn Tunes composed by members of the University of Oxford,* 1868. The tune was later bought by Arthur Sullivan who was editing *Church Hymns,* 1874. Boyd was dismayed to see his music wedded to the text "Fight the good fight" in that hymnal, but time has proved it to be a good marriage!

470. Onward, Christian soldiers

This text was written by Sabine Baring-Gould in 1864 for a Children's Festival at Horbury Bridge, Yorkshire. The hymn was sung "in a procession with cross and banners" as the children marched from one village to another, a traditional practice in 19th century England. It was first published in *The Church Times*, October 15, 1864.

ST. GERTRUDE. Arthur S. Sullivan composed this tune for the text, and the full hymn appeared in the *Musical Times* of December, 1871, and in *The Hymnary*, 1872. The tune name is said to be for Mrs. Gertrude Clay-Ker-Seymer, in whose home Sullivan was a visitor when he wrote the music. The composer frequently "canonized" his friends in this way.

471. Give me a passion for souls, dear Lord

These words, expressing concern about soul-winning, were written by Herbert G. Tovey, probably while he was a student at Moody Bible Institute in Chicago. The hymn was copyrighted in 1914 and included in his *Gospel Solos and Duets, No. 1*. Affiliated Music Enterprises, Inc., which handles the copyrights owned by Tovey, issued a new arrangement copyrighted in 1953.

BIOLA. The music was written by Foss L. Fellers, a pianist and teacher at Moody Bible Institute. The tune is named for "Biola"—the Bible Institute of Los Angeles, where author Herbert Tovey taught for many years.

472. From Greenland's icy mountains

In 1819, King George III authorized a missionary service and collection to be taken on Whitsunday (Pentecost) for the missionary work of the "Society for the Propagation of the Gospel in Foreign Parts." On Saturday evening Dr. Shipley, vicar of Wrexham was preparing for the morning service, together with his son-in-law, Reginald Heber, who was to assist. Shipley asked Heber if he could write something suitable to sing. Three stanzas were produced in about fifteen minutes and a fourth soon after! The tune Heber selected for use the next morning was from *The Beggar's Opera*—the selection titled "'Twas when the seas were roaring." The hymn first appeared in the *Evangelical Magazine*, July, 1821 and later in Heber's posthumous *Hymns*, 1827.

MISSIONARY HYMN. Tradition records that a young woman, impressed with the hymn of Heber, invited a young bank clerk named Lowell Mason to write a suitable tune. The melody, like the text, was written in a very short time. It was first published for soprano solo and dedicated to Miss Mary W. Howard of Savannah, Georgia, presumably the person who made the request. It first appeared as a hymn tune in the Boston Handel and Haydn Society's *Collection of Church Music*, 1829, edited by Mason.

473. "Take up thy cross and follow Me"

Billy Graham has given a devotional based on this hymn in *Crusade Hymn Stories* (Hope, 1967).

The words were written by B. B. McKinney while he was attending the state Sunday School Convention in Clanton, Alabama in January, 1936. The speaker was R. S. Jones, a missionary to Brazil, and McKinney was leading the music. Over dinner one evening, Jones told the songleader that he would not be able to return to the mission field because of ill health. When McKinney asked about his future plans Jones replied, "I don't know, but wherever He leads I'll go." The words stayed with McKinney who promptly sat down and wrote both words and music. At the meeting that night, the songleader told this story and sang the hymn as a solo. It first appeared in *Songs of Victory*, 1937, the first collection McKinney prepared for the Sunday School Board of the Southern Baptist Convention.

FALLS CREEK. B. B. McKinney directed the music at the Falls Creek Baptist Assembly in Oklahoma for many years. This hymn was introduced at the assembly in 1936, before its publication the following year.

474. Remember all the people

This missionary hymn by Percy Dearmer was written in 1929 at the request of the Church Missionary Society (Anglican) for their children's magazine, *The Round World*. It was published in *Songs of Praise for Boys and Girls*, 1930.

FAR OFF LANDS. The tune takes its name from the hymn's first line, and is a traditional melody of the Bohemian Brethren. Percy Dearmer evidently found it set to "Hur Ljuvt det är att komma" in the Swedish *Hemmets Koralbok*, 1921.

475. The battle is the Lord's

This hymn was written by E. Margaret Clarkson in 1959 or 1960 as a result of meditating on the scriptures and on the idea of the sovereign will of God regarding missions. It was first published in *Hymns of the Christian Life*, 1962 after she showed it to Dr. A. W. Tozer, author and pastor in the Christian and Missionary Alliance, and he expressed his approval of it.

LEONI. See "The God of Abraham praise," No. 36.

476. O Christian, haste, your mission high fulfilling

Mary Ann Thomson began to write this hymn one night in 1868 as she sat up with one of her children who was ill. Her intention was to produce a missionary text to the tune which was then associated with Faber's hymn "Hark, hark, my soul, angelic songs are swelling," but it remained unfinished because she could not come up with a suitable refrain. Three years later she completed the work and it was first included in the Protestant Episcopal *Hymnal*, 1892. The editors of *Hymns for the Living Church* made several "modernizations" in the text, including the first line, originally "O Zion, haste."

TIDINGS. The tune was composed by James Walch in 1875 as a setting for Faber's "Hark, hark, my soul." He felt that existing tunes (including Mary Thomson's favorite, mentioned above) were not adequate. It first appeared with the above text in *The Church Hymnal*, 1894 and is named for a central word in the refrain.

477. The sending, Lord, springs from Thy yearning heart

The hymn was inspired by the adoption of "The Mission Affirmations" by the Lutheran Church-Missouri Synod in 1965. William J. Danker wrote these words for a mission chapel service at Concordia Theological Seminary in St. Louis. They also won a prize in the hymn contest conducted prior to the Congress on Evangelism in Berlin, 1966. The text was published in *Christianity Today*, sponsor of the contest, that same year. Later it was included in *Worship Supplement*, 1969, released by Concordia Publishing House.

SINE NOMINE. See "For all the saints," No. 533.

478. "Must I go, and empty handed?"

The writing of this text was suggested in 1877 when the author, Charles C. Luther, heard a certain Rev. A. G. Upham tell the story of a young man who was about to die after living only a month as a Christian. Regretting his apparently-fruitless life, he had said, "I am not afraid to die; Jesus saves me now, but must I go empty-handed?"

PROVIDENCE. The music was written for these words in Providence, Rhode Island where composer George C. Stebbins was engaged in meetings with Dr. George F. Pentecost. Stebbins had received the text from author Charles C. Luther. Words and music appeared together in *Gospel Hymns No. 3*, 1878.

479. Christ was born in a distant land

Gene Bartlett began writing this text in December, 1967 and finished it early in 1968. It was commissioned by Claude Rhea, who was then consultant on music ministry with the Foreign Mission Board of the Southern Baptist Convention. It first appeared in *Crusade Hymns,* 1968, published by Broadman Press.

RHEA. The music was composed by Gene Barlett as a setting for his own words, and named for Dr. Claude Rhea, who had commissioned the hymn.

480. Rescue the perishing

In 1869 Fanny Crosby visited a rescue mission in the slums of New York City and was greatly moved by the sad, desperate men around her. The song title "Rescue the Perishing" had been suggested by William H. Doane a few days earlier, and while she sat in the mission the words began to form. Before she retired that night, the hymn was completed.

RESCUE. Fanny Crosby sent these words to William H. Doane, who composed the music. The complete hymn first appeared in Doane's *Songs of Devotion* (New York: Biglow and Main, 1870).

481. So send I you

E. Margaret Clarkson says that she wrote this text when she was twenty-two years old. She had been teaching in northern Canada for three years, where she found almost no Christian fellowship. One night, reading the scriptures, she was reminded that this was her "missionary" obedience—to go where God sent her, regardless. She said that in later years she came to know that there is *joy* in obedience, and regretted the somber tone of the hymn. In fact she wrote another "optimistic" version. However, God has used and blessed the original setting, and it seems to be preferred. It was written at Kirkland Lake, Ontario in 1937 and first appeared in a magazine in 1939.

TORONTO. John W. Peterson's share in this song is told in his own words:

> A hand-copied version of the poem was handed me by a fellow WMBI staff member with the suggestion that I read it on one of my radio programs. (I was responsible for twenty or so programs at the Moody Bible Institute station at the time.) I did use the poem and was so deeply moved by the power of the words that I took them with me on a Kansas vacation the following month. One day while improvising at the piano in my mother's home in Wichita, with the poem spread out before me, the melody came. Again I was deeply moved as I sang through the new song. I called in several members of my family and sang the number for them. Somehow I sensed that God would greatly use it. It was not till much later that I learned that the words had been written by Miss E. Margaret Clarkson.

The tune name is for Toronto, Canada where Miss Clarkson has lived for many years. The completed song was first published in *Melody-Aire Low Voice Songs* (Moody Press, 1954).

482. Lonely voices crying in the city

Having spent considerable time assisting in Billy Graham crusades in large cities throughout the world, Billie Hanks, Jr. wrote this hymn expressing the need of the lonely people he found everywhere. As a Christian, he knew they needed Christ, but they did not realize their need.

LONELY VOICES. The tune name expresses the theme of the hymn. Billie Hanks, Jr. conceived and composed the piece as a solo with guitar accompaniment.

The author of this volume heard Hanks sing an early version in a U. S. Army base chapel in Berlin during the World Congress on Evangelism in 1966; it was completed the same year after Hanks returned home to Texas. The piece achieved popularity as a choral octavo and sacred folk song released by Hope Publishing Company in 1967. This is its first appearance in a standard hymnal.

483. We've a story to tell to the nations

Words and music by H. Ernest Nichol were written in 1896 and published that same year in *The Sunday School Hymnary*.

MESSAGE. H. Ernest Nichol made a practice of writing original tunes to his many Sunday School hymns, signing his correct name, but he used the pseudonym "Colin Sterne" (an anagram on his middle and last names) for the texts.

484. It only takes a spark

One of the most successful sacred youth "musicals" of the past few years was *Tell It Like It Is,* co-authored by Kurt Kaiser and Ralph Carmichael and published by Lexicon Music in 1969. In this popular work Kurt Kaiser wrote the song beginning "It only takes a spark." He gives this report:

> There was a need for an invitation type number, and in keeping with our set guideline that the idiom had to be fresh, the words restated in current terminology an important doctrine, namely "Go ye into all the world and preach the gospel. . ."

The song has appeared in many folk song books, but this is its first inclusion in a major hymnal.

PASS IT ON. In the hymnal, the song's title is the tune name. In other publications, it is sometimes called "Brooks Drive" after the street on which Kaiser lives in Waco, Texas. Kurt says that the song was written by the fireplace in the den of his home—"a peaceful setting and an important retreat for me."

485. The vision of a dying world

These words were written by Anne Ortlund and won first prize in the contest to find a theme hymn for the World Congress on Evangelism, held in Berlin in 1966. It was first published in July, 1966 in *Christianity Today*, sponsor of the Congress and the contest. The hymn bore the title "Macedonia" from Acts 16:9, "Come over into Macedonia and help us." It has appeared in many hymnals and many languages around the world.

ALL SAINTS, NEW. The author of this volume was chairman of the music committee and the hymn contest for the World Congress on Evangelism in Berlin in 1966. He chose this tune for use with the text at that time. See also "The Son of God goes forth to war," No. 467.

486. We have heard the joyful sound

Priscilla J. Owens wrote these words for a missionary service in the Sunday School where she served faithfully for fifty years. They were originally sung to the music of "Vive le Roi" from Meyerbeer's opera *Les Huguenots* and first appeared in *The Revivalist,* 1868.

JESUS SAVES. William Kirkpatrick wrote this tune for Miss Owens' words. It first appeared in *Songs of Redeeming Love,* 1882, edited by John R. Sweney, C. C. McCabe, T. C. O'Kane, and Kirkpatrick.

487. Far, far away, in death and darkness dwelling

James McGranahan is best known as a writer of gospel hymn melodies, but he also wrote five texts, including this one. Until recently the first phrase included the words "in heathen darkness dwelling." The song, copyrighted in 1886 and based on Matthew 28:18 and Mark 16:15, appeared in *Gospel Hymns No. 5,* 1887 with the author credit "G.M.J." (obviously McGranahan). It also appeared in one of the editions of *Sacred Songs and Solos,* published in England.

GO YE. The historic title of the missionary song is "Go Ye Into All the World," of which this tune name is an abbreviation. James McGranahan wrote the music for his own text.

488. Heralds of Christ

At a summer conference at Northfield, Massachusetts in 1894, Mrs. Laura S. Copenhaver was scheduled to be one of the speakers. It became necessary for her to cancel her appearance but she sent this hymn "in her place." In writing it she said she was inspired by "a deep sense of unity with the builders of the King's Highway in far lands, next door to me in America, and even with those great ones I had known as a child, now gone on with the immortals by way of Africa and India." (From a letter to Robert G. McCutchan, quoted in *Our Hymnody*.) The poem was originally titled "The King's Highway" and was published in a leaflet in 1915. It seems to have made its first hymnal appearance in *Hymns for the Living Age*, 1923.

NATIONAL HYMN. See "God of our fathers," No. 526.

489. Jesus shall reign where'er the sun

Isaac Watts first published this paraphrase of Psalm 72 in his *Psalms of David, Imitated in the Language of the New Testament*, 1719. It was entitled "Christ's Kingdom among the Gentiles," and is said to have been translated into more languages and dialects than any of the other hymns Watts has written.

DUKE STREET. John Hatton, composer of this tune, lived on Duke Street in St. Helen's, England. His tune first appeared anonymously in *A Select Collection of Psalm and Hymn Tunes* compiled by Henry Boyd in 1793, under the heading "Addison's 19th Psalm." In 1805 it was included in William Dixon's *Euphonia* and was there attributed to Hatton.

490. Fling out the banner! let it float

The St. Mary's School in Burlington, New Jersey was founded by George Washington Doane, Bishop of New Jersey for the Protestant Episcopal Church. This text was written by Doane in 1848, at the request of the students, for a flag raising at St. Mary's. It was first printed in *Verses for 1851 in Commemoration of the Third Jubilee of the Society for the Propagation of the Gospel*.

WALTHAM. John Baptiste Calkin composed the tune for Bishop Doane's words. It was first published in *The Hymnary*, London, 1872, but has not recently been used in England.

491. I'll tell to all that God is love

Homer Rodeheaver copyrighted this song, with words by Alfred H.

Ackley, in 1923. It appeared that year in Rodeheaver's publications, *Golden Bells* and *Progressive Sunday School Songs*.

TILL THE WHOLE WORLD KNOWS. Bentley D. Ackley, brother of the song's author, composed this music. The tune name was used for many years as the song's title.

492. Through all the world let every nation sing

In 1967 Paul Liljestrand asked Bryan J. Leech to write a new hymn for a missionary conference to be held at Calvary Baptist Church in New York City. It was first published with Liljestrand's music in the July, 1970 issue of *The Hymn*, journal of the Hymn Society of America.

CONRAD. Paul Liljestrand wrote the tune for the above text and named it after his father, Conrad Liljestrand. This is the first printing of text and tune in a hymnal.

493. Hark, the voice of Jesus calling

Daniel March, a Congregational minister, was scheduled to deliver a sermon to the Philadelphia Christian Association meeting at the Clinton Avenue Church on October 18, 1868. His text was "Here am I; send me" (Isaiah 6:8), but he could not find an appropriate closing hymn. Consequently he wrote these words and they were first sung from manuscript. The hymn was first published in *Bright Jewels*, 1869, with the first line "Hark, the voice of Jesus crying."

ELLESDIE. See "Jesus, I my cross have taken," No. 443.

494. Eternal God, whose power upholds

Henry W. Tweedy wrote this text in 1929 and entered it in the Hymn Society of America's competition for the purpose of securing new missionary hymns. With more than one thousand hymns submitted, this one was awarded first place. It was first sung at the Riverdale Presbyterian Church, New York City on May 30, 1930. It has appeared in several American hymnals since that time, including *Methodist Hymnal*, 1935.

PILGRIM. This is another of the traditional American folk melodies of unknown (and possibly secular) origin. It first appeared in *Southern Harmony*, 1835.

495. Must Jesus bear the cross alone

Several authors contributed to this hymn as we know it. Stanza one is said to be an altered quatrain which originally appeared in Thomas Shepherd's *Penitential Cries*, 1693. According to Julian's *Dictionary*, stanza two first appeared in a missionary collection published at Norwich, England *ca.* 1810, author unknown. Stanza three first appeared in *The Oberlin Social and Sabbath School Hymn Book*, compiled by George N. Allen in 1844; in certain references, Allen is given credit for some of these words.

MAITLAND. The tune was composed by George N. Allen and was included with the above text in his *Oberlin Social and Sabbath School Hymn Book*, 1844. The tune is called "Cross and Crown" in Henry Ward Beecher's *Plymouth Collection*, 1855 and is identified as "a western melody." The hymn's popularity is credited to its appearance in this last volume.

496. A charge to keep I have

Charles Wesley's hymn is based on Leviticus 8:35, " . . . keep the charge of the Lord, that ye die not." It first appeared in *Short Hymns on Select Passages of Holy Scripture*, 1762. It has been pointed out that Wesley followed Matthew Henry's commentary on the scripture passage, almost phrase by phrase.

BOYLSTON. First appearing in *The Choir*, 1832, the tune was written by Lowell Mason as a setting for "Our days are as grass." "Boylston" is the name of a town in Massachusetts, Mason's native state, and also of a famous street in Boston.

497. There is joy in serving Jesus

This was the first of nearly one hundred gospel hymns on which author Oswald J. Smith and composer B. D. Ackley collaborated. It was first published by the Hall-Mack Company in *Christian Hymns and Songs*, 1931. The author says the words express the joy that he has experienced in serving the Lord Jesus Christ.

JOY IN SERVING JESUS. The tune name of Bentley D. Ackley's melody is the familiar title of this gospel song.

498. Come, all Christians, be committed

Eva B. Lloyd's hymn was a winning text in the 1966 Southern Baptist hymn writing competition. It was written in 1963 in Maryville, Missouri and first appeared in *Eight New Christian Service Hymns*, published by Broadman Press in 1966. Later it was included in *Worship Hymnal*, 1971, the hymnbook of Mennonite Brethren in the United States.

BEACH SPRING. James H. Wood wrote an anthem based on this early American melody and it was published with the words "Come, ye sinners" in 1958 by Broadman Press; this hymn setting is part of his anthem arrangement. The original tune appeared in duple meter in *The Sacred Harp*, 1844, attributed to B. F. White.

499. The Master has come, and He calls us to follow

This text by Sarah Doudney first appeared in *Songs of Gladness*, published by the Sunday School Union in London in 1871. It was titled "Jesus and Mary of Bethany," and is based on Martha's words, "The Master is come and calleth for thee" (John 11:28).

ASH GROVE. The tune is a traditional Welsh melody. It was originally associated with a secular song about lovers strolling in a grove of ash trees.

500. Go, labor on; spend, and be spent

Horatius Bonar's text was written and published at Kelso, Scotland in 1843 in a small booklet of hymns. The same year it appeared under the heading "Labour for Christ" in *Songs for the Wilderness*. Dr. Bonar had previously written texts for young people. This is said to be his first "adult" hymn, written for the use of workers in his mission district at Leith, Scotland.

TRURO. Appearing anonymously, the tune was included in *Psalmodia Evangelica: A Collection of Psalms and Hymns in Three Parts for Public Worship*, 1789, published by Thomas Williams. "Truro" is the name of an ancient town in the southwestern part of Cornwall, England.

501. Reach out to your neighbor

This text and tune were written by Roger Copeland in 1970 while on a retreat with fellow staff members of Bellevue Baptist Church, Hurst, Texas. He says:

> As we contemplated the ministry of our local church, the idea was presented that we adopt a theme song. Taking a guitar, pen and paper, I sat on the patio overlooking Lake Tenkiller in northeast Oklahoma. After prayer, the Lord provided the song.

REACH OUT. Roger Copeland wrote the tune for his own text, and the song first appeared in 1971 as a choral octavo released by Hope Publishing Company. This is its first appearance in a hymnal.

502. Master, no offering, costly and sweet

Edwin Pond Parker was pastor of Center Church, Hartford, Connecticut

166

for fifty years. He was well known as a poet and musician, as well as a preacher and pastor. He wrote this hymn to be used as the summation and conclusion of one of his sermons, and it was first published in *The Christian Hymnal*, 1889.

LOVE'S OFFERING. The tune was written by Dr. Parker for these words. Its title no doubt refers to the text.

503. Jesus calls us; o'er the tumult

Cecil Frances Alexander wrote this hymn for St. Andrew's Day, 1852 and it is based on Matthew 4:18–20. It first appeared in *Hymns for Public Worship*, 1852. Interestingly enough, these words written by a woman were adopted as the official hymn of the Brotherhood of St. Andrew of the Protestant Episcopal Church in the United States and the Church of England in Canada. The second stanza (referring to Jesus' encounter with Andrew) is omitted in this volume and in most hymnals of non-liturgical churches.

GALILEE. William Jude wrote the tune for these words, and it first appeared in *Congregational Church Hymns*, 1887. It is named for the place—"by the Sea of Galilee"—where Jesus met Peter and Andrew.

504. O Master, let me walk with Thee

This text as originally written by Washington Gladden was a poem of three eight-line stanzas which appeared in a devotional column, "The Still Hour," in *The Sunday Afternoon*, 1879, a magazine edited by Gladden. Charles H. Richards is responsible for turning the poem into a hymn by eliminating the second stanza and spreading the remaining two over four verses of four lines each. It appeared in Richards' *Songs of Christian Praise*, 1880.

MARYTON. See "Come, Holy Spirit, Dove divine," No. 215.

505. Out in the highways and byways of life

According to George S. Schuler, Ira B. Wilson wrote these words *ca.* 1909. Curiously enough, Wilson evidently could not remember having written them, and he is best known as a composer. The song was first published in 1924 as a leaflet (with Schuler's music) and introduced at an International Sunday School Convention in Cleveland, Ohio. Later it appeared in *Songs of Evangelism*, 1925, edited by Schuler, E. O. Excell and W. E. Biederwolf (Glad Tidings Publishing Company, Chicago).

SCHULER. In early printings, this setting is dedicated to the choir of Moody Memorial Church, Chicago. It was probably written during a period when its composer, George Schuler, directed that choir.

506. O Jesus, I have promised

John E. Bode wrote this hymn in 1866 for the confirmation of his daughter and two sons, with the first line "O Jesus, we have promised." It was printed in leaflet form by the Society for the Promotion of Christian Knowledge in 1868 and bore the title, "For the Newly Confirmed." It was also included in the Appendix to *Psalms and Hymns,* 1869, published by the same society.

ANGEL'S STORY. Arthur H. Mann composed this tune as a setting for "I love to hear the story which angel voices tell" by Mrs. E. H. Miller. It first appeared in *The Methodist Sunday School Hymnbook,* 1881.

507. We give Thee but Thine own

An excellent offertory hymn, the words by William How were written in 1858. The hymn was not published until 1864 when it was included in *Psalms and Hymns,* second edition, edited by How and Thomas Baker Morrell.

SCHUMANN. Appearing first in the *Cantica Laudis* published by Lowell Mason and George J. Webb in 1850, this tune was the setting for "Thou shalt, O Lord, descend." The German composer Robert Schumann has been credited with writing it—hence the name. However, the melody cannot be found in any of Schumann's works.

508. I gave my life for thee

As a young girl, Frances Ridley Havergal saw the motto "I did this for thee; what hast thou done for Me?" under a picture of the crucifixion in the study of a prominent German pastor. She quickly penciled these lines on a scrap of paper. On reflection, she thought the poem was unworthy and threw it on the fire, only to have it fall out untouched. Her father encouraged her by writing a melody for it. The hymn appeared in leaflet form in 1859, and then was published in the magazine *Good Words,* February, 1860.

KENOSIS. The tune was written by Philip P. Bliss especially for this text, and was dedicated to the "Railroad Chapel Sunday School, Chicago." It was first published in Bliss's *Sunshine for Sunday Schools,* 1873.

"Kenosis" is a Greek word and refers to Christ's self-humiliation.

509. Is your life a channel of blessing?

Harper G. Smyth wrote these words in 1903. The hymn was published in *Hymns, Psalms, and Gospel Songs,* 1904, compiled by James McGranahan.

EUCLID. The tune was also written by Harper G. Smyth, for these words. The tune name refers to the Euclid Avenue Baptist Church in Cleveland, Ohio, where Smyth was music director.

510. Am I a soldier of the cross?

This text was written by Isaac Watts and appeared at the conclusion of a sermon on "Holy Fortitude," based on I Corinthians 16:13. It was published in Watts' *Sermons,* 1721–24.

ARLINGTON. See "O for a faith that will not shrink," No. 316.

511. Forth in Thy name, O Lord, I go

Under the title "For Believers Before Work," this text by Charles Wesley first appeared in the 1749 edition of the Wesley brothers' *Hymns and Sacred Poems.*

KEBLE. The tune was written by John B. Dykes for John Keble, as a setting for the latter's "Sun of my soul." It appeared first in the 1875 edition of *Hymns Ancient and Modern.* The present arrangement by Austin C. Lovelace appeared in *Methodist Hymnal,* 1964.

512. Lord, whose love through humble service

Albert F. Bayly wrote this poem in response to an invitation by the Hymn Society of America to submit hymns on social welfare. It was named "Conference Hymn" for the second National Conference on the Churches and Social Welfare held in Cleveland, Ohio, October 23–27, 1961. The Hymn Society published it in *Seven New Social Welfare Hymns,* 1961. It first appeared in a major volume in *Methodist Hymnal,* 1964.

HYFRYDOL. See "Come, Thou long expected Jesus," No. 102.

513. In Christ there is no East or West

This text was written by John Oxenham for "The Pageant of Darkness and Light" presented by the London Missionary Society for the missionary exhibition at the Agricultural Hall in London, 1908. It was first published in Oxenham's *Bees in Amber,* 1913.

McKEE. In 1939 Harry T. Burleigh adapted this tune from the spiritual, "I know the angel's done changed my name." It was named to honor the rector of St. George's Church, New York City, where Burleigh was soloist for many years. The spiritual first appeared in print in the 1884 edition of *Jubilee Songs,* published by Fisk University; as a hymn tune it was included in the Protestant Episcopal *Hymnal 1940.*

514. Where cross the crowded ways of life

This "Prayer for the City" was written by Frank Mason North at the request of Caleb T. Winchester for a new missionary text to be included in the *Methodist Hymnal,* 1905. The resulting hymn was based on a sermon Dr. North had preached on Matthew 22:9, "Go, therefore, into the highways..." It was first printed in *The Christian City,* June, 1903, the journal of the Methodist City Missionary Society, of which North was editor.

GERMANY. See "Jesus, Thy blood and righteousness," No. 241.

515. Hope of the world

This text by Georgia Harkness was awarded first prize in a contest sponsored by the Hymn Society of America which attracted more than five hundred entries. It was used as planned at the Second Assembly of the World Council of Churches in Evanston, Illinois, 1954. First printed in the Hymn Society's bulletin, *Eleven Ecumenical Hymns,* 1954, it also appeared in *Baptist Hymnal,* 1956 and *Worship and Service Hymnal,* 1957.

VICAR. The tune was written especially for this text in 1963 by V. Earle Copes, for the *Methodist Hymnal,* 1964. It is named for the composer's father, Vicar Copes.

516. Father eternal, Ruler of creation

The hymn was written by Laurence Housman in 1919 at the request of H. R. L. Sheppard (rector of St. Martin's-in-the-Fields, London) for the Life and Liberty Movement, which was organized after World War I to promote world peace. It was published with Geoffrey Shaw's tune in the original edition of *Songs of Praise,* 1925.

LANGHAM. Geoffrey Shaw wrote this tune for the text, and it was first sung at a meeting of the Life and Liberty Movement in Queen's Hall, London in 1921. It is no doubt named for Langham Place, the location of the British Broadcasting Company studios in London; for many years Shaw was chairman of the educational music committee of the B.B.C.

517. We thank Thee that Thy mandate

In 1968 the Hymn Society of America published a request for hymns on "the ministry," and Ernest K. Emurian wrote this text as an expression of his personal response. He patterned it on the three-fold ministry of Jesus—preaching, teaching and healing. The first and last stanzas speak of all three; the second stanza emphasizes preaching, the third is about teaching, and the fourth, healing. Says Rev. Emurian: "This is my concept of my calling."

The hymn was first published in *Worship Hymnal*, 1971, published by Mennonite Brethren in the United States.

LANCASHIRE. See "The day of resurrection," No. 168.

518. Whatsoever you do to the least of my brothers

Sensing the need for new songs for youth worship at St. Celestine's parish in Elmwood Park, Illinois, Pastor Willard F. Jabusch wrote this text based on Matthew 25:34–40. It was first released in *Songs of Good News*, 1967, published by ACTA, Chicago.

WHATSOEVER YOU DO. Willard F. Jabusch wrote this contemporary folk tune for his words and they have always appeared together.

519. Peace in our time, O Lord

John Oxenham's poem was inspired by the return of Prime Minister Neville Chamberlain from the Munich Conference of September, 1938, where he claimed to secure "peace for our time." It was published in the *Missionary Review of the World*, LXII (December, 1938) and later in the *Hymnal*, 1940. History has proved that both Chamberlain and Oxenham were overly optimistic in 1938, but the hymn remains an appropriate prayer for Christians.

DIADEMATA. See "Crown Him with many crowns," No. 85.

520. O beautiful for spacious skies

Katharine Lee Bates writes that her original poem was inspired by an expedition to the top of Pike's Peak in 1893. The opening lines came to her as she looked out over the "sea-like expanse of fertile country spreading away so far under the ample skies." A visit to the "alabaster city" at the Columbian Exposition in Chicago that same year was responsible for the last stanza. In 1904 Miss Bates rewrote the hymn simplifying the phraseology, and the revised version was first printed in the *Boston Evening Tran-*

script, Nov. 19, 1904. Further revision was made in 1918 to produce the present hymn.

MATERNA. The tune was written by Samuel Augustus Ward in 1882 for the text "O mother, dear Jerusalem," hence the tune name—"motherly." In 1912 the president of the Massachusetts Agricultural College asked permission of Ward's widow to use the tune for Miss Bates' hymn. At least sixty tunes have been used with these words, but "Materna" is now the accepted setting.

521. Not alone for mighty empire

This hymn was written by William P. Merrill in 1909 when he was pastor of the Sixth Avenue Presbyterian Church in Chicago, and was inspired by a prayer offered by Jenkin Lloyd Jones in a union Thanksgiving service. Merrill said he went home "and wrote a rather diffusive hymn about it and later made it over into the present one." It was first printed in a Presbyterian journal, *The Continent,* in 1911, and in 1935 it entered both the Presbyterian *Hymnal* and *The Methodist Hymnal.*

HYFRYDOL. See "Come, Thou long expected Jesus," No. 102.

522. Mine eyes have seen the glory

In December, 1861, six months after the Civil War began, Julia Ward Howe and her husband traveled to Washington with Governor and Mrs. Andrews of Massachusetts. During the journey, she heard troops along the road singing "John Brown's body lies a-mouldering in the grave," and was reminded of this fine tune. James Freeman Clarke, her pastor and a member of the traveling group, suggested she write more fitting words. Mrs. Howe completed them that same night, and showed them to Dr. Clarke a day or so later. *The Atlantic Monthly* issue of February, 1862 printed the poem under the title "The Battle Hymn of the Republic."

BATTLE HYMN. The source of the tune is unknown, though it has occasionally been attributed to William Steffe. It was associated with many different texts, including the camp-meeting song "Say, brothers, will you meet us" and, according to Louis Elson in *National Music of America,* it was known in the South long before the Civil War.

523. Great God of nations

Written by Alfred Woodhull in 1828 when he was only 18 years old, this text (originally "God of the passing year, to Thee") was published in the Presbyterian collection, *Psalms and Hymns* (1829), under the title

"Thanksgiving Hymn." The poem has been altered many times and its authorship was clarified in Hatfield's *Church Hymn Book*, 1872.

ST. PETERSBURG. The tune was written by Dimitri S. Bortniansky, possibly in 1822. It was the setting for Gerhard Tersteegen's hymn "Ich bete an die Macht der Liebe" in Tscherlitsky's *Choralbuch*, 1825.

Tscherlitsky was organist in the city of St. Petersburg (now Leningrad), for which the tune is named. This shortened version of the melody was arranged by the editors of *Hymns for the Living Church*.

524. Lord, while for all mankind we pray

These words were written in 1837 by John R. Wreford, a British Unitarian minister, as a "prayer for our country." They were published about the time of Queen Victoria's accession to the British throne, in J. R. Beard's *Collection of Hymns for Public and Private Worship*, 1837.

HARLECH. The tune (whose full name is "March of the men of Harlech") is taken from *Gorhoffed Gwŷr Harlech*, a collection of Welsh harp music. This music was originally written by "professional bards and harpers" and performed in inns and royal houses in Wales.

525. My country, 'tis of thee

Several different accounts of this hymn's origin are available, more than one traceable to its author. The text was written by Samuel Francis Smith, a Baptist seminarian, and was first sung at the Independence Day exercises of the Boston Sabbath School Union, Park Street Church, July 4, 1831. Evidently Lowell Mason had brought a number of volumes of German songs to Smith requesting that he look them over and translate anything that was particularly appealing. Coming upon the tune "God Save the King," Smith was inspired to write this original patriotic text. The hymn was first published in *The Choir, or Union Collection of Church Music*, compiled by Lowell Mason in 1832.

AMERICA. The music is of unknown origin. Many authorities believe that it came from England, although it was also set to continental patriotic texts. The first printed copy of the tune in present form was found in the *Thesaurus Musicus, ca.* 1745.

526. God of our fathers, whose almighty hand

Produced in 1876 and intended for the 100th anniversary of the Declaration of Independence, this text was later selected as the official hymn for the centennial celebration of the adoption of the Constitution. It was written by Daniel Crane Roberts while he was rector of St. Thomas' Episcopal Church, Brandon, Vermont and originally sung to the tune "Russian Hymn," with which it appeared in the Protestant Episcopal *Hymnal,* 1892.

NATIONAL HYMN. George William Warren, organist of New York City's St. Thomas' Church, composed this tune for this text. It was used at the Columbia celebration in St. Thomas' Church on October 8, 1892 and published in the revised musical edition of the Protestant Episcopal *Hymnal,* 1894.

527. God the Omnipotent!

This text is a composite. Stanzas one, two and four were written for the tune "Russian Hymn" by Henry F. Chorley in 1842, and were published in John Hullah's *Part Music,* 1842 with the title "In Time of War." In Great Britain the first phrase is still sung: "God the All-terrible!"

During the Franco-Prussian War in 1870, John Ellerton wrote a similar hymn beginning "God the Almighty, in wisdom ordaining," which included the third stanza printed here. This hymn was published in Robert Brown-Borthwick's *Select Hymns for Church and Home,* 1871. The hymns appeared in a combined version in *Church Hymns,* 1871 (1874 ed.). Subsequent printings have received textual alterations.

RUSSIAN HYMN. The music was written in 1833 by Alexis F. Lvov at the request of Czar Nicholas for a truly-Russian national hymn tune. Before this, the British melody "God Save the King" had been the setting for the Russian national song.

528. Lord of life and King of glory

This hymn—"A Mother's Prayer"—was written by Christian Burke in December, 1903 and published February, 1904 in *The Treasury,* under the heading "Prize Hymn for Mothers' Union Service." It was also included in *The English Hymnal,* 1906.

SICILIAN MARINER'S HYMN. It seems that J. G. Herder found this tune sometime between 1788 and 1799 in Italy. W. D. Tattersall included it in his *Improved Psalmody,* 1794 and called it "Sicilian Hymn." Herder himself printed it with a Roman Catholic text in his *Stimmen der Völker in Liedern,* 1807 under the heading (translated) "To the Virgin Mary. A Sicilian Boat Song."

529. O perfect Love, all human thought transcending

Members of Dorothy Gurney's family were singing hymns at home in

Ambleside, England one Sunday evening in 1883. Her sister's favorite hymn tune was Dyke's "Strength and Stay" and she was bemoaning the fact that the words associated with it were not appropriate for her forthcoming marriage. Her complaint sent Mrs. Gurney (then Dorothy Blomfield) into the library with pencil and paper. Fifteen minutes later she came back with three stanzas of "O perfect Love." The text was first included in the Supplement to *Hymns Ancient and Modern*, 1889.

Stanza four is the final doxology from John Ellerton's "O Strength and Stay," a paraphrase of the Latin "Rerum Deux tenax vigor." This was the hymn text sung by Mrs. Gurney's family on the occasion mentioned above.

SANDRINGHAM. The tune is arranged from an anthem composed by Joseph Barnby in 1889 (using this text) for the marriage of the Duke and Duchess of Fife. It first appeared as a hymn tune in *The Church Hymnary*, 1898, and soon replaced "Strength and Stay" as a favorite for English weddings. The tune is called "Sandringham" after a residence of the English royal family located in Norfolk.

530. Gracious Savior, who didst honor
No information has been found concerning this hymn by Emily Shirreff.

KOMM, O KOMM. This anonymous melody was included in the *Neuvermehrtes Gesangbuch,* published in Meiningen in 1693, and evidently compiled by Duke Bernhard of Saxony. The tune name indicates that it has at some time been associated with a German hymn which begins "Komm, O Komm."

531. Happy the home when God is there
Entitled "The Happy Home," this hymn by Henry Ware, Jr. (sometimes called "the younger") first appeared in *Selections of Hymns and Poetry for the Use of Infant and Juvenile Schools and Families*, 3rd ed., 1846, compiled by Mrs. Herbert Mayo. The authorship was obscure for some time and was finally clarified in *Methodist Hymnal*, 1935.

ST. AGNES. See "Jesus, the very thought of Thee," No. 83.

532. O happy home, where Thou art loved
The German hymn, "O selig Haus, wo man Dich aufgenommen" by Carl J. P. Spitta, was written in 1826 and first published in his *Psalter und Harfe*, 1833. It was translated by Sarah Borthwick Findlater and included in her *Hymns from the Land of Luther* (3rd series, 1858) under the reference, Luke 19:9, "This day is salvation come to this house." The altered version used here appeared in the Scottish *Church Hymnary*, 1898.

Mrs. Findlater's daughter once said, "That simple little hymn of hers . . . is really an epitome of her home life with my father—they were so single-eyed in their longing to serve God."

HENLEY. See "We would see Jesus; lo! His star is shining," No. 125.

533. For all the saints who from their labors rest

Several of the hymns written by William Walsham How have gained wide popularity in England and America. This memorial hymn first appeared in *Hymns for Saints' Days, and Other Hymns,* 1864, compiled by Earl Nelson, a nephew of England's heroic Admiral Nelson. The hymn originally had eleven stanzas and began "For all thy saints."

SINE NOMINE. Ralph Vaughan Williams composed the tune for this text's appearance in *English Hymnal,* 1906. Erik Routley reports that at first the tune was condemned as "jazz music," but more recently it is judged to be one of the great tunes of the century. The name "Sine Nomine" means "without a name."

534. Face to face with Christ my Savior

Carrie E. Breck sent this poem to Grant C. Tullar in 1898 suggesting that he provide a musical setting for her words. Tullar had just written a tune for his own text "All for me the Savior suffered," while assisting in evangelistic services in the Methodist Episcopal Church in Rutherford, New Jersey. Mrs. Breck's poem fit his tune so perfectly that he discarded his own words and used hers.

FACE TO FACE. Grant C. Tullar wrote the tune as recounted above. It appeared with these words in *Sermons in Song, No. 2,* 1899, published by the Tullar-Meredith Company, New York.

535. The sands of time are sinking

Anne Ross Cousin created her hymn from phrases in the letters of Samuel Rutherford (1600–1661), the famous Scottish preacher. Her daughter once said that Mrs. Cousin "fitted the pattern of her verses line by line" as she sat sewing in the manse at Irvine, where Rev. Cousin was pastor of the Scottish Free Church. The poem was first published in *The Christian Treasury,* 1857, and later separately as *Last Words of Samuel Rutherford.* It was sung at the bedside of the famous British Baptist preacher C. H. Spurgeon on January 17, 1892, shortly before his death, and was the favorite hymn of evangelist D. L. Moody.

RUTHERFORD. The tune, named for its association with these words (see account above), is based on a melody by Chrétien Urhan in *Chants Chrétien*, 1834. This arrangement by Edward F. Rimbault was published in *Psalms and Hymns for Divine Worship*, 1867.

536. Jerusalem the golden

Bernard of Cluny is best known for his poem "De Contemptu Mundi" ("On the Contemptibleness of the World") comprised of some 2,966 lines and written in the difficult pattern of dactylic hexameter. After completing the poem about 1145, Bernard said "Unless the Spirit of wisdom and understanding had flowed in upon me, I could not have put together so long a work in so difficult a meter."

John Mason Neale's first translation of ninety-five lines appeared in his *Mediaeval Hymns and Sequences*, 1851, from which this cento is drawn. The fourth stanza was added in *Hymns Ancient and Modern*, 1861, and was not found in the original Latin.

EWING. Alexander Ewing's tune was written in 1853 for a translation of Part IV of Bernard of Cluny's hymn—"For thee, O dear, dear country." In *Hymns Ancient and Modern*, 1861 it appeared with this text, and they have been coupled ever since.

537. Ten thousand times ten thousand

The magazine *Good Works*, VIII (March, 1867) first carried this text in three stanzas by Henry Alford. That same year these stanzas were published in Alford's *Year of Praise*. The fourth stanza was added in 1870 in the *Lord's Prayer Illustrated*, compiled by F. R. Pickersgill and Alford.

ALFORD. John B. Dykes composed this music for Alford's text and it appeared in the revised edition of *Hymns Ancient and Modern*, 1875.

538. When all my labors and trials are o'er

Ed Card, superintendent of the Sunshine Rescue Mission in St. Louis, Missouri, was known as "Old Glory Face." He was always "bubbling over" with Christian joy, and during a sermon he would frequently explode with the exclamation "Glory!" His prayers generally ended with "And that will be glory for me!"

Card's life of praise inspired Charles Gabriel to write both the words and music of this gospel song. It first appeared in *Make His Praise Glorious*, 1900, published in Chicago by E. O. Excell.

GLORY SONG. In the revival crusades of Billy Sunday in the early twentieth century, this music was consistently known as "The Glory Song."

539. Jerusalem, my happy home

The original old-English version of this text is significant enough hymnologically to receive almost four pages (580–583) in Julian's *Dictionary*. The twenty-six stanzas appear in a British Museum manuscript that dates from about 1600. It has the title "A Song made by F.B.P. to the tune of Diana." The initials are probably those of an unknown Roman Catholic priest, and the text closely resembles a passage in the meditations of St. Augustine, which was popular reading in the sixteenth century. The poem was first published in 1601 (in 19 verses) in *The Song of Mary the Mother of Christ, with a Description of Heavenly Jerusalem*. The present hymnal version is limited to five stanzas.

LAND OF REST. See "Begin, my tongue, some heavenly theme," No. 15.

540. I'm just a poor, wayfaring stranger

The roots of this folk hymn are so deep in American history that it is impossible to trace them. Under the title "Parting Friends" in *Social Harp*, author McCurry gives a similar song beginning "Farewell, my friends, I'm bound for Canaan" which "he learned from Mrs. Catharine Penn" in 1829. There are both black- and white-spiritual variants of this song, and they are much alike.

WAYFARING STRANGER. The first part of the melody appeared in the Georgia *Sacred Harp*, 1844. The last section is quoted in Nathaniel Dett's *Folk Songs of the Negroes, sung at Hampton Institute*, 1827. In both instances, the music is set to other words.

541. Love divine, so great and wondrous

There are conflicting reports about the origin of this hymn. Elsie Ahlwén says that she knew the words of the refrain, "Han skall öppna pärleporten," in her native Sweden and sang them to "her own melody." She also says that, when she was conducting meetings in Chicago in 1930, an individual gave her a copy of Frederick Blom's complete hymn which "Blom had written in prison"—presumably for drunkenness, during a period when he was estranged from God and the church. Ms. Ahlwén says that she selected five of the original nine verses, copyrighted them in Swedish, wrote her own melody and used it widely in her evangelistic meetings. She also secured a translation by "a Rev. Ohlson" of a Swedish Lutheran Church in Duluth, Minnesota.

An article appeared in Sweden's *Stridsropet* (War Cry), No. 52, 1960 written by Brigadier Oscar Blomgren of the Salvation Army. In a translation supplied by hymnologist J. Irving Erickson, Blomgren says:

> In the winter of 1916, when we were stationed at Chicago's 7th Corps,
> Fred Blom made a surprise visit. (They had not seen him for about 14

years.) He was no longer a pastor but worked in the office of a travel agency. This was just before Christmas. Soon after New Year's he visited us again one afternoon. I had a severe cold and was confined to my bed. We noticed that Blom was not himself. He appeared sad and gloomy.. My wife did her best to encourage our friend, cooked coffee and set a festive table.

During the Christmas season we had sung a carol that had become popular. It was a poem to which Alfred Dulin, a young musician from Norway who.. had stayed with us, wrote a simple but beautiful melody. The poem had been taken from the Christmas edition of *From All Lands*, 1906. My wife introduced the song to Blom and sang it several times for him. After a while, Blom picked up a guitar, played a few chords and sang:

> Wonderful, festive, clear
> Star-filled Christmas night!
> Your wonders, every hour,
> Make the sorrowing heart glad.
> (Tr. from the Swedish)

Suddenly Fred Blom took out his pen, asked for a sheet of paper, and after an hour's silence had written five stanzas and a chorus to the song "The Pearly Gates." As a title he wrote "Because of the Blood." Elsie Ahlwén, a singing evangelist from Örebro, who visited America and held evangelistic meetings there in 1929–30, made use of the song and thereby popularized it.. She called it "Pärleporten" and altered somewhat the words of the chorus. Fred Blom had written ".. And surely will let me in," but Elsie Ahlwén used this version ".. so that I may enter in."

Fred Blom wrote the song in my wife's songbook, signed it and added the date, 1917, and she has always kept that book in safekeeping...

It seems impossible to reconcile these two stories at this time. At any rate, it was a translation by Nathaniel Carlson which became accepted by English-speaking Christians and is used in *Hymns for the Living Church*.

PEARLY GATES. In our hymnal, as in every publication of this song, Elsie Ahlwén is given credit for writing the music. In the light of the story given above, this will have to be reconsidered. We are inclined to think that she may have been honestly mistaken. Frederick Blom had returned to Sweden by 1921 and was again in the ministry. No doubt he used his song, whose melody had possibly been written by Alfred Dulin for another text. In those years, Elsie Ahlwén was a young woman in her teens, and she may have heard the melody along with the words—as she says, she knew the refrain in her native Sweden. Later, when the full text was given her, it is possible that a previously-heard melody came to her spontaneously, and she may have honestly thought it was created by her.

542. In heaven above

Laurentius Laurentii Laurinus wrote the original poem in 1622 at the time of his wife's death; it was appended to the funeral sermon. It was adapted by a fellow Swede, Johann Åström, into a lyric hymn almost 200 years later. Soon afterward, William Maccall gave us the English version.

HAUGE. The Norse folk melody was beautifully arranged by Edvard Grieg in one of his last writings, *Psalms* (1906). The tune is named for a coastal town on the southern tip of Norway, about 125 miles from Grieg's home near Bergen.

543. Then I saw a new heaven and earth

A paraphrase of selected passages in Revelation, chapters 21 and 22, Christopher M. Idle wrote this text in 1972 as a part of a contemporary hymn project sponsored by a number of evangelical clergymen of the Church of England. It was first published in *Psalm Praise* (Falcon Press, London, 1973).

The editor of *Hymns for the Living Church* found the hymn in the pews of All Souls', Langham Place, London in late 1972 when he was practicing for examinations of the Royal College of Organists; All Souls' vicar, Michael Baughen, was editor of *Psalm Praise.*

NEW HEAVEN. Norman L. Warren, one of the musical editors of *Psalm Praise,* wrote the tune for this text while he was watching his two children receive a swimming lesson in Leamington Spa, England, where they live. He says he was challenged by these "superb words."

544. When I can read my title clear

This was a favorite hymn in 18th century America, especially in the South. Its author Isaac Watts included it in his *Hymns and Spiritual Songs,* 1707. He titled it "The Hopes of Heaven our Support under Trials on Earth."

PISGAH. Typical of the religious folk tunes sung in the South early in the 19th century, this melody appeared in *Kentucky Harmony,* 1816 credited to J. C. Lowry. Around 1819 it was found in *Tennessee Harmony* credited to Alexander Johnson.

"Pisgah" is a mountain ridge near Mount Nebo, not far from the Dead Sea, from which Moses viewed the land of Canaan.

545. On Jordan's stormy banks I stand

Samuel Stennett, an English Baptist preacher, wrote this hymn which first appeared in John Rippon's *Selection of Hymns* (London, 1787) under the title "Heaven Anticipated."

PROMISED LAND. This is one of the many traditional melodies used in America in the early part of the 19th century. Researchers have pointed out its resemblance to "I'll go and enlist for a sailor" in Sharp's *Morris Dances*. Its first hymnic appearance dates back to William Walker's *Southern Harmony*, 1835, where it is attributed to "Miss M. Durham." Rigdon M. McIntosh altered it (partly by changing the tonality from minor to major), added the refrain and published it in *The Gospel Light*, 1895, edited by H. R. Christie.

546. Sing the wondrous love of Jesus

The author Eliza E. Hewitt was a regular attendant at the Methodist camp meeting at Ocean Grove, New Jersey. There she often met Emily D. Wilson, composer of this music. No doubt it was this mutual interest in the conference center that eventually produced this hymn. *Pentecostal Praises*, 1898, compiled by William J. Kirkpatrick and Henry L. Gilmour, first brought it to public attention and wide use.

HEAVEN. Emily D. Wilson wrote the music for the words of her friend, Eliza E. Hewitt. The tune name first appeared in the *Baptist Hymnal*, 1956.

547. Jesus, we want to meet

This Nigerian hymn was written by A. T. Olajide Olude in 1949 for a monthly service at Abeokuta to popularize the use of Yoruba music in Christian worship. While he was serving at the United Nations in New York City in 1962, Biodun Adebesin translated the text into English at the request of Austin Lovelace and of Carlton R. Young, editor of the *Methodist Hymnal*, 1964. It was put into verse by Austin Lovelace.

JESU A FE PADE. The tune was also written by Mr. Olude, inspired by the indigenous music of his native Lagos and Ibadan. It was arranged by his countryman, M. O. Ajose. The name "Jesu a fe pade" means "Praise" or "Opening of Sunday Worship."

548. Safely through another week

John Newton's text first appeared in Richard Conyers' *A Collection of Psalms and Hymns*, 1774, titled "Saturday Evening." It appeared five years later in *Olney Hymns*, edited by John Newton and William Cowper. Through the years, several changes have been made to adapt the hymn for Sunday morning worship.

SABBATH. Lowell Mason arranged this tune for these words. It appeared in his *Hallelujah*, 1824 under the name of "Olean" and was identified as "a German melody." The tune's name refers to Newton's original lyrics.

549. O day of rest and gladness

This text was No. 1 in Christopher Wordsworth's *Holy Year, or Hymns for Sundays and Holydays,* 1862—a collection of 117 original poems. With slight alteration, it appeared in the 1868 Appendix to the first edition of *Hymns Ancient and Modern.* It is based on Psalm 118:24, "This is the day which the Lord hath made; we will rejoice and be glad in it."

MENDEBRAS. This is a German folk melody arranged by Lowell Mason. It first appeared in his *Modern Psalmist,* 1839 set to "I love Thy kingdom, Lord." Charles Robinson is said to have been the first to unite this text and this tune in his *Songs for the Sanctuary,* 1865.

550. When morning gilds the skies

The anonymous German hymn "Beim frühen Morgenlicht" was found in the Würzburg *Katholisches Gesangbuch,* 1828. It later appeared in other forms leading to the conclusion that this was not the original source. Edward Caswall translated the hymn into English and in 1854 it was published in six stanzas in Formby's *Catholic Hymns.* Other verses were added in 1858, and various centos have been made for hymnal use.

LAUDES DOMINI. The tune (whose name is Latin for "Praises of the Lord") was written by Joseph Barnby for this text and was published in the Appendix to *Hymns Ancient and Modern,* 1868.

551. Awake, my soul, and with the sun

Thomas Ken issued a *Manual of Prayers* for the students at Winchester College in 1674, with instructions to "be sure to sing the Morning and Evening Hymn in your chamber devoutly." This text appeared as the "Morning Hymn" in the 1695 edition. Note that the final stanza is our common "Doxology."

MORNING HYMN. Composed and named for this text by François H. Barthélémon at the request of the chaplain of the Female Orphan Asylum, London, the tune was first published as "New Jerusalem" in the supplement to the *Hymns and Psalms used at the Asylum for Female Orphans,* edited *ca.* 1785 by W. Gawler.

552. Still, still with Thee

Based on Psalm 139:18, "When I awake I am still with Thee," this poem was written by Harriet Beecher Stowe in 1853 as an expression of her consciousness of the overshadowing presence of God. It is said that she often arose at four-thirty in the morning to enjoy the coming of dawn and the singing of the birds. This is one of three hymns by Mrs. Stowe which her distinguished brother Henry Ward Beecher included in his *Plymouth Collection of Hymns and Tunes*, 1855.

CONSOLATION. See "We would see Jesus; for the shadows lengthen," No. 425.

553. Morning has broken

Songs of Praise Discussed (London, 1933) has this note about Eleanor Farjeon's hymn which appeared first in *Songs of Praise* (1931):

> There being no known hymn in this short dactylic meter, and something being also wanted on the theme of thanksgiving for each day as it comes, Miss Farjeon was asked to make a poem to fit the lovely Gaelic tune.

The information below shows that the first part of the comment was incorrect. Nevertheless, the words (with this tune) became very popular in the United States in the 1960's.

BUNESSAN. According to James Moffat's *Handbook to the Church Hymnary* (1927), this tune "was noted down by Alexander Fraser from the singing of a wandering Highland singer. Its bold movements are in keeping with the freedom shown in Gaelic song." It was printed in *Songs and Hymns of the Gael* (1888) and appeared in the *Irish Church Hymnal* (1917) with the words "Child in the manger." David Evans' arrangement is from the *Church Hymnary* (Rev. ed., 1927), with the same Christmas text. The music first appeared with "Morning has broken" in *Songs of Praise* (1931).

554. Abide with me: fast falls the eventide

It was long thought—for a while debated—and recently confirmed that Henry Francis Lyte wrote this hymn in 1847 as he was about to leave his pastorate at Lower Brixham and take a trip to southern France in an unsuccessful effort to regain his health.

The opening words were inspired by Luke 24:29, "Abide with us: for it is toward evening, and the day is far spent." The poem appeared in a leaflet in 1847 and then in the *Remains of Henry Francis Lyte,* 1850.

EVENTIDE. There are conflicting stories about the tune's composing, as well. William H. Monk's widow says it was written at a time of great sorrow—one evening as she and her husband watched the setting sun. Another version says it was created in ten minutes one night, at the end of a meeting of the committee which edited the first edition of *Hymns Ancient and Modern*, 1861. Monk was music editor of that historic hymnal.

555. Now the day is over

This children's hymn was written by Sabine Baring-Gould in 1865 and was based on Proverbs 3:24, "Thou shalt lie down, and thy sleep shall be sweet." It was first published in *The Church Times*, February 16, 1867 and the following year it appeared in the Appendix to *Hymns Ancient and Modern*.

MERRIAL. The tune was written by Joseph Barnby in 1868 and appeared unnamed in his *Original Hymn Tunes*, 1869. The name "Merrial" is an adaptation of "Mary L."—daughter of Charles S. Robinson, who introduced the tune to America in his *Spiritual Songs*.

556. Softly now the light of day

Based on Psalm 141:2, "Let my prayer be set before thee ... as the evening sacrifice," this hymn by George W. Doane was published in his *Songs by the Way*, 1824, under the heading "Evening."

SEYMOUR. See "Depth of mercy! can there be," No. 238.

557. Day is dying in the west

Mary A. Lathbury wrote this hymn in 1877 at the request of Bishop John H. Vincent, founder of the Chautauqua Assembly on Lake Chautauqua, New York. It was included in *The Calvary Selection of Sacred Songs*, 1878, and is still sung at each Sunday vesper service at the Chautauqua Assembly.

CHAUTAUQUA. William F. Sherwin, director of music at the Chautauqua Assembly, composed the music for this text in 1877. The tune is also called "Evening Praise."

558. Savior, breathe an evening blessing

The author, James Edmeston, included this hymn in his *Sacred Lyrics*, 1820, and it appeared in *Christian Psalmody*, 1833, compiled by Edward Bickersteth. The text was inspired by a quotation from Henry Salt's *Voyage to Abyssinia* (London, 1814): "At night their short evening hymn, 'Jesu Mahaxaroo'—'Jesus forgive us'—stole through the camp."

EVENING PRAYER. George Stebbins wrote this tune for a prayer response when he was director of music at Tremont Temple Baptist Church, Boston. His tune was joined to Edmeston's text in *Gospel Hymns No. 3*, 1878, edited by Stebbins, Ira D. Sankey and James McGranahan.

559. Sun of my soul, Thou Savior dear

Written in 1820, John Keble first published his hymn in *The Christian Year*, 1827. The original text had fourteen stanzas and appeared under the heading "Evening."

HURSLEY. The original melody was found in the *Katholisches Gesangbuch* (Vienna, *ca.* 1774) as a setting for the German *Te Deum*, "Grosser Gott, wir loben dich." The present form of the tune was selected by John Keble and his wife as a setting for this text. It first appeared in the *Metrical Psalter*, 1855, compiled by W. J. Irons and Henry Lahee.

"Hursley" is the name of the parish in England where the Rev. Keble was vicar for thirty years.

560. Another year is dawning

In 1874 Frances R. Havergal sent this hymn text to her friends on a New Year's greeting card. The poem was titled "A Happy New Year! Ever Such May It Be," and was later published in her *Under the Surface*, 1874.

AURELIA. See "The Church's one foundation," No. 200.

561. Day by day and with each passing moment

Carolina Sandell Berg, sometimes called "the Swedish Fanny Crosby," wrote this text in 1865. For a number of years she published a "Bible Calendar" of inspirational articles, and this song first appeared in her *Korsblomman* for 1866. Oscar Ahnfelt included it in his *Andeliga Sånger*, 1872 with his musical setting. The English translation by Andrew L. Skoog is the most popular and most accurate of all the versions available, and it was used in *Mission Hymns,* 1921 and *The Covenant Hymnal,* 1931.

BLOTT EN DAG. Named for the first words of the Swedish version, the music was written for the text by Oscar Ahnfelt. It is said that Mrs. Berg lengthened each line of her original poem by one syllable, at Ahnfelt's suggestion, in order to give the song a "softer and more natural rhythm."

562. Praise to God, your praises bring

William C. Gannett wrote this hymn in 1872 for a harvest festival in St. Paul, Minnesota, where he served as minister of a Unitarian church. It was first published in *The Thought of God in Hymns and Poems,* compiled by Frederick L. Hosmer and Gannett in 1885.

SAVANNAH. The melody is of German origin. It seems to have first appeared in England in the *Foundery Collection,* 1742, compiled by John

Wesley for use in the Foundery Chapel. It is named for Savannah, Georgia where John and Charles Wesley served as Anglican missionaries, 1735–1738.

563. Great God, we sing that mighty hand

This is one of the hymns of Philip Doddridge published posthumously by his friend Job Orton in a collection of Doddridge's work, entitled *Hymns Founded on Various Texts in the Holy Scriptures,* 1755. It had the caption "Help obtained from God, Acts XXVI, 22. For the New Year."

WAREHAM. William Knapp wrote this melody and published it in *A Sett of New Psalm Tunes and Anthems in Four Parts,* 1738. In that book it was a setting for Psalm 36:5–10, with the heading "For ye Holy Sacrament." "The tune is named for the birthplace of the composer—Wareham, Dorsetshire, England.

564. Now thank we all our God

Beginning "Nun danket alle Gott," the first two stanzas of this hymn were written by Martin Rinkart as a table grace for his family during the time of the Thirty Years' War in 17th century Germany. The hymn was first published in Rinkart's *Jesu Hertz-Büchlein,* 1636, and was sung at the conclusion of the Peace of Westphalia, ending that devastating war. The translation by Catherine Winkworth appeared in her *Lyra Germanica,* 1858.

NUN DANKET ALLE GOTT. The tune, with title from the German text, has been associated with this hymn since they appeared together in Johann Crüger's *Praxis Pietatis Melica,* 1647. While it bore no credits, it is believed that Crüger himself wrote the music.

565. Come, ye thankful people, come

Henry Alford's hymn appears to be written for the Harvest and Thanksgiving season, but it has a strong eschatological reference to the consummation of history as Jesus taught it in Matthew 13:36–43. Several alterations were made after the hymn first appeared in Alford's *Psalms and Hymns,* 1844.

ST. GEORGE'S, WINDSOR. The tune was written by George J. Elvey for James Montgomery's text "Hark! the song of jubilee" and was first published in E. H. Thorne's *Selection of Psalm and Hymn-Tunes,* 1858. In *Hymns Ancient and Modern,* 1861, it appeared with Alford's words. The tune is named for the historic royal chapel at Windsor Castle, where Elvey served as organist and choirmaster for 47 years.

566. We plow the fields, and scatter

"Wir pflügen und wir streuen," a hymn by Matthias Claudius, was first published in 1782 as a part of *Paul Erdmann's Fest,* a sketch portraying a harvest festival in a farm home in north Germany. Jane Campbell translated the "Peasants' Song" into English and it appeared in Charles S. Bere's *Garland of Songs,* 1861.

WIR PFLÜGEN. This tune appeared anonymously with Claudius' text in the second edition of *Lieder für Volksschulen,* 1800, compiled by A. L. Hoppenstedt. In Lindner's *Jügenfreund,* 1812, it is credited to Johann Abraham Peter Schulz.

567. God, who made the earth

Sarah Betts Rhodes wrote this hymn in 1870 for the Whitsuntide (Pentecost) Festival of the Sheffield Sunday School Union. It was first published in 1879 in the *Methodist Sunday School Hymn Book.*

CALDWELL CHURCH. David W. Smart wrote this tune for these words in a children's collection, *Learning As We Sing* (Hope, 1967). It is named after a beautiful white country church in the community of Caldwell, near Mr. Smart's boyhood home in the mountains of central Pennsylvania.

568. For all the blessings of the year

No conclusive information has been found relating to the origin of this hymn by Albert H. Hutchinson. It has been published successively in *Songs of Worship* (Canada), *Hymns for the Widening Kingdom,* and *Methodist Hymnal,* 1935. *The Beacon Hymnal,* 1924 gives 1909 as the date of writing; no other information is available.

OLDBRIDGE. Robert N. Quaile wrote the tune in 1903 and it was published in *English Hymnal,* 1906. The tune name suggests there may be some connection between this melody and "Athlone"—another tune credited to Quaile. Athlone is a town in central Ireland which boasts a historic old bridge.

569. When upon life's billows you are tempest-tossed

Johnson Oatman, a Methodist minister, is the author of this text which first appeared in *Songs for Young People,* compiled and published by E. O. Excell (Chicago, 1897).

BLESSINGS. Edwin O. Excell wrote the music for the text's first publication in 1897. The tune name was given in *Baptist Hymnal,* 1956.

570. We gather together to ask the Lord's blessing

This "national hymn" was written by an unknown author at the end of the 16th century in celebration of the Netherlands' freedom from Spanish rule. It was first published in Adrian Valerius' *Nederlandtsche Gedenckclanck*, 1626. The English translation was made by Theodore Baker and appeared in *Dutch Folk Songs*, 1917 compiled by Coenraad V. Bos.

KREMSER. Named for the arranger, Edward Kremser, this was one of six tunes taken from Valerius' collection (above) and published in Kremser's *Sechs altniederländische Volkslieder*, 1877. Kremser had discovered and revised the music after 250 years of neglect.

571. Thanks to God for my Redeemer

This is one of the favorite thanksgiving songs of Swedish heritage. It was written by August Ludvig Storm, a Salvation Army officer, and first published in *Stridsropet* ("The War Cry"), December 5, 1891 and later in the Swedish Salvation Army songbook. The English translation by Carl E. Backstrom was made for *The Covenant Hymnal* (Chicago, 1931).

In his hymn commentary, *Sing with Understanding*, James P. Davies notes that author Storm gives thanks for many of the negative aspects of life—tears, storms and pain—and that he had himself experienced a partial paralysis from the age of thirty-seven.

TACK, O GUD. The tune's name is the beginning of the original Swedish text. It was composed by John Alfred Hultman and published with the Swedish words in *Solskenssånger*, 1910. After that, the song quickly became popular in both Sweden and America.

572–573. Praise God from whom all blessings flow

The traditional Doxology is the closing stanza of Thomas Ken's "Morning and Evening Hymns" (See No. 551). Ken revised the hymns to their present form in 1709.

OLD HUNDREDTH. See "All people that on earth do dwell," No. 20.

PORT JERVIS. Richard Avery and Donald Marsh say they "felt the need for a merry, lively tune" for these classic words, to be sung when "events in history or in our personal and corporate life inspire light-hearted and over-flowing joy. The calypso style of Spanish cultures seems a good style for expression of these feelings." The music was written in 1963 and first published in *Hymns Hot and Carols Cool*, 1967.

According to the composers, the tune name (not used in this hymnal) "gives credit to the city where we worship, live, write, travel from and return to!"

188

574. Glory be to God the Father

This paraphrase of the historic Gloria Patri by Carlton Young was written, he says, "in response to the innovative work of Avery and Marsh, and dedicated to them."

Unnamed Tune. Composer Carlton Young says of this tune: "The musical style is Broadway musical ballad, one of several styles which serve as the base of Avery and Marsh's music and appeals to white middle-class American Protestants." Words and music were written in Dallas, Texas in 1972 and first appeared in *14 Canticles and Responses,* 1973, published by Agape, a division of Hope Publishing Company.

575–576. Glory be to the Father

The "Gloria Patri" is known as the Lesser Doxology in contrast to "Gloria in excelsis," the Greater Doxology. The ascription of praise to the Holy Trinity based on Matthew 28:19 may have been used in the days of the Apostles, certainly by the second century. The second half of the text, however, did not come into being until after the Arian controversy in the fourth century. Since that time, in liturgical worship it has been sung after each psalm and canticle.

GREATOREX. The tune is from Henry W. Greatorex's *Collection of Psalm and Hymn Tunes,* 1851. It was published when he was organist and director of music at Calvary Episcopal Church in New York City.

MEINEKE. Christoph Meineke published this tune to "Evening Prayer" in his *Music for the Church,* 1844, composed for use in St. Paul's Church, Baltimore, Maryland.

577. Jesus, stand among us

These lines were written by William Pennefather for the conferences which he began at Barnet and continued at Mildmay Park, London. It was published posthumously in *Original Hymns and Thoughts in Verse,* 1873.

BEMERTON. Friedrich Filitz's tune first appeared in his *Choralbuch,* 1847, set to the German hymn "Wem in Leidenstagen."

"Bemerton" was George Herbert's parish; there is no apparent significance to its use here.

578. The Lord is in His holy temple

The "Call to Worship" is quoted from Habbakuk 2:20, which follows a passage that condemns the worship of idols.

QUAM DILECTA. George F. Root is credited with writing this music. "Quam dilecta" are the opening words in Latin of Psalm 84:1, "How lovely are thy tabernacles, O Lord of hosts."

579. Holy, holy, holy, Lord God of hosts
This text is the Anglican form of the "Sanctus" (Isaiah 6:3b), with the "Gloria tibi" added ("Glory be to Thee," etc.)

Unnamed Tune. This tune is credited to Samuel Sebastian Wesley, who was probably the finest musician in that gifted family.

580. Now to the King of heaven
According to James Moffatt (*Handbook to the Church Hymnary,* 1927) this doxology is made up of lines from Isaac Watts' paraphrase of Psalm 148 and a hymn by Philip Doddridge.

ST. JOHN. The tune was found in *The Parish Choir,* 1851, where it appeared anonymously.

581. There's a sweet, sweet Spirit
The song was first published as sheet music in 1963 by Manna Music, Inc., Burbank, California. Doris Akers says that she wrote the words and music in Los Angeles, California in 1960:

> After a very inspiring prayer service with the Sky Pilot Choir, where the Holy Spirit had made manifest His wonderful power, I said within myself, "There's a sweet, sweet spirit in this place"—from whence words seemed to flow.

SWEET, SWEET SPIRIT. The editors of *Hymns for the Living Church* chose to use the song's commonly-used title as the tune name.

582. All things are Thine
This is the first stanza of a hymn written in 1872 by John Greenleaf Whittier for the dedication of Plymouth Congregational Church in St. Paul, Minnesota. It was included in Whittier's *Complete Poetical Works,* 1876 and in *Congregational Hymns,* 1884, compiled by W. Garrett Horder.

HERR JESU CHRIST. This is one of eighty melodies which appeared in *Pensum Sacrum,* 1648, a collection of Latin odes written by University of

Prague professors. In 1651 the tune was set to "Herr Jesu Christ, dich zu uns wend" in *Cantionale Sacrum.*

583. We give Thee but Thine own

This is the first strophe of an offertory hymn (No. 507) written by William Walsham How in 1858. It was first published in *Psalms and Hymns,* 1864, jointly edited by How and Thomas Baker Morrell.

SCHUMANN. See "We give Thee but Thine own," No. 507.

584. All things come of Thee, O Lord

These words are quoted verbatim from I Chronicles 29:14 (KJV), and are part of David's last great prayer of thanksgiving shortly before his death and the enthronement of Solomon.

Unnamed Tune. This musical setting was written by John F. Wilson in 1967 as a choral response for the choir of the First Methodist Church, La Grange, Illinois. It was published in *Choir Praise* (Hope Publishing Company, Chicago, 1967).

585. Hear our prayer, O Lord

These words are derived from Psalm 143:1a, "Hear my prayer, O Lord, give ear to my supplications." The final phrase echoes the traditional "Dona nobis pacem" which closes the Agnus Dei—"grant us Thy peace."

Unnamed Tune. This melody by George Whelpton was written in 1897. It was published in leaflet form and later in H. Augustine Smith's *Hymns for American Youth,* 1924.

586. Hear our prayer, O heavenly Father

The words of the prayer response are very similar to those which frequently conclude a spoken petition in public worship.

Unnamed Tune. The brief musical setting is attributed to Frederic Chopin, but it cannot be positively traced to one of his compositions.

587. Let the words of my mouth

The text is taken verbatim from the King James version of Psalm 19:14. The response is used in both Jewish and Christian worship.

Unnamed Tune. The music is credited to Adolph Baumbach, and is dated 1862.

588. Amens
The word "Amen" has been used for possibly 3000 years in both Hebrew and Christian worship, usually as a congregational response to prayer. It is said to mean, "So be it!" (See I Cor. 14:16.)

DRESDEN is sometimes attributed to Johann Gottlieb Naumann (1741–1801), and was presumably written for use in the royal chapel at Dresden. It appeared in the Zittau choir book, and the motive is heard in Mendelssohn's *Reformation Symphony* and Wagner's *Parsifal.*

THREEFOLD (Danish) is of unknown origin, but widely used in Denmark's churches.

THREEFOLD (Traditional) is also of unknown origin.

FOURFOLD is credited to John Stainer, though its first appearance cannot be documented.

SEVENFOLD by John Stainer was written to be sung after the consecration prayer in the Eucharist. It was published in Stainer's *Choir-Book for the Office of Holy Communion,* 1873.

589. May the grace of Christ our Savior
John Newton wrote this short paraphrase of II Corinthians 13:14 and it was first published in *Olney Hymns,* 1779. Written to be sung at the close of the service, it was originally a single stanza of eight lines. In 1878 it was divided into two stanzas.

OMNI DEI. "Omni Dei" were the opening words of the Latin text with which this tune appeared in Corner's *Grosscatholisch Gesangbuch,* Nürnberg, 1631.

590. Thou wilt keep him in perfect peace
These words are taken verbatim from Isaiah 26:3, omitting only the last phrase.

DUKE'S TUNE. This is an abbreviated version of the tune "Duke's Street," using the beginning and final phrases. The original melody was found in *The Scottish Psalter,* 1615.

591. Lord, let us now depart in peace

Based on the Song of Simeon in Luke 2 ("Nunc Dimittis"), these words may have been written by the music's composer, George Whelpton.

DISMISSAL. George Whelpton probably included this setting in a four-page leaflet of responses he published about 1900.

DICTIONARY OF AUTHORS AND COMPOSERS

Abelard, Peter (b. 1079, Le Pallet, Fr.; d. Apr. 21, 1142, St. Martel, near Chalon), born of nobility, was a lecturer at Notre Dame Cathedral, Paris at the age of 22; has been called "the first of the modernists" for his critical approach to the scriptures and the writings of the church fathers; fled to Brittany with Heloise, niece of Canon Fulbert, because of their storied love affair—they were married and a son was born; returning to Paris, was emasculated by thugs, at the instigation of Fulbert; became a monk, and Heloise entered a convent; resumed his teaching and in time was convicted of heresy after a trial instituted by Bernard of Clairvaux; was on his way to Rome to appeal his case, when he died; is buried beside Heloise in the cemetery of Père-la-Chaise, Paris; wrote a hymnal for Heloise's convent, and the hymns have been collected and re-edited in Dreves' *Hymnarius Paraclitensis,* 1891.

Alone Thou goest forth, O Lord (133)

Ackley, Alfred Henry (b. Jan. 21, 1887, Spring Hill, Pa.; d. July 3, 1960, Whittier, Calif.), a capable cellist, received his early musical training from his father, and later studied at the Royal Academy of Music, London and with Hans Kronold in New York City; graduated from Westminster Theological Seminary, Maryland, and served Presbyterian churches in Pennsylvania and California, including a period as assistant to Dr. Hugh Thompson Kerr (*q.v.,* editor of the Presbyterian *Hymnal,* 1933) at Shadyside Presbyterian Church of Pittsburgh, Pa.; in collaboration with his elder brother Bentley (*q.v.*), wrote words and/or music of perhaps 1000 hymns and gospel songs, and helped compile hymnals and songbooks for the Rodeheaver Publishing Company; received the honorary D.Sac.Mus. degree from John Brown University.

I serve a risen Savior (158); I'll tell to all that God is love (491)

ACKLEY (158)

Ackley, Bentley DeForest (b. Sept. 27, 1872, Spring Hill, Pa.; d. Sept. 3, 1958, Winona Lake, Ind.) as a boy learned to play the melodeon, piano, cornet, clarinet and piccolo, accompanying his father on music-teaching trips, and playing in his 14-piece band; in 1888 went to New York to study stenography, and served as organist in churches of New York City and Brooklyn; in 1907 joined the Billy Sunday-Homer Rodeheaver evangelistic team as secretary-pianist and traveled with them for eight years, supplying new songs for congregation, solo and choir; as composer and editor for the Rodeheaver Company, wrote more than 3000 hymn tunes; received the honorary D.Sac.Mus. degree from Bob Jones University.

SPRING HILL (343); TILL THE WHOLE WORLD KNOWS (491); JOY IN SERVING JESUS (497)

Adams, Jessie (b. Sept. 9, 1863, Ipswich, Suffolk, Eng.; d. July 15, 1954, York, Eng.) preferred to remain anonymous; was a member of the Society of Friends, a progressive teacher and a leader of the local adult school in Frimley, England.

I feel the winds of God today (449)

Adams, Sarah Flower (b. Feb. 22, 1805, Harlow, Essex, Eng.; d. Aug. 14, 1848, London, Eng.) was the second daughter of Benjamin Flower, a political journalist, and married William Bridges Adams, a civil engineer, in 1834; frequently released both poetry and prose in *The Repository*, a periodical edited by her minister, William Johnson Fox, a Unitarian; contributed 13 hymns to Fox's compilation, *Hymns and Anthems*, 1841, for use in his church; published two major works: *Vivia Perpetua* (1841), a religious dramatic poem in five acts, and *The Flock at the Fountain* (1845), a catechism for children, with hymns.

Nearer, my God, to Thee (348)

Addison, Joseph (b. May 1, 1672, Milston, Wilts, Eng.; d. June 17, 1719, London, Eng.), the son of an Anglican clergyman, was educated at Charterhouse and at Magdalen College, Oxford; abandoned his preparation for the ministry and turned his interest to literature and politics; joined the Whig Party and held several important offices, including Chief Secretary for Ireland; is remembered for literary contributions to the *Tatler*, the *Guardian*, the *Freeholder*, and the *Spectator;* published poems (which later became hymns) in the *Spectator*, a daily paper founded by him in 1711.

When all Thy mercies, O my God (38); The spacious firmament on high (54)

Adebesin, Biodun Akinremi Olvsoji (b. Jan. 1, 1928, Lagos, Nigeria) began playing piano at an early age and continued his musical training in school and college in his native Nigeria; has a certificate from Cambridge University and is an Associate of the Royal College of Music; is also gifted in popular music, and has played in jazz, theater, and club bands and orchestras; has been a teacher, civil servant, banker, and a member of the Nigerian diplomatic service; wrote *Okanlawon* and *Ale Wa Adara*.

Jesus, we want to meet (trans.) (547)

Ahlwén, Elsie R. (b. 1905, Örebro, Sweden) came to the United States as a young woman and studied at Moody Bible Institute, Chicago, Ill.; became an evangelist and worked among the Swedish-speaking people in Chicago and later, across the United States, preaching and singing; later married

Daniel A. Sundeen, a business man, and they continued their ministry together while raising their family; retired to live in Manchester, N. H.

    PEARLY GATES (541)

Ahnfelt, Oscar (b. May 31, 1813, Gullarp, Skåne, Sweden; d. Oct. 22, 1882, Karishamn, Sweden) grew up in a parsonage and shared good music and literature from his earliest years; received elementary education from his older brothers, then enrolled in the University at Lund; in 1840 began to study music in Stockholm and came under the influence of the religious revival led by Carl Rosenius; joined the movement and began traveling on a full-time basis, singing, playing and preaching; was harassed in his activity because of the Conventicles Edict, but was vindicated in his ministry after a command performance before King Karl XV; met and married Clara Strömberg, who wrote many songs of her own; through the financial help of Jenny Lind, "the Swedish Nightingale," published his musical settings of words by Lina Sandell and others, beginning in 1850 and continuing through 12 editions by 1877, the volumes usually known as Ahnfelt's *Andeliga Sånger.*

    BLOTT EN DAG (561)

Ajose, Michael Olatunji (b. Sept. 16, 1912, Lagos, Nigeria) attended King's School and Methodist Boys' High School in Lagos, Nigeria, with private study in piano and organ; was assistant organist at Wesley Church in Olowogbowo, Lagos and in 1957 became full-time organist; has been the official synod organist of the Methodist Conference since 1963; was appointed General Secretary of the Association of Church Musicians in Nigeria, Lagos branch, and says: "The aim of that association is to collect, compose, edit, and publish indigenous musical compositions suitable for divine worship."

    JESU A FE PADE (arr.) (547)

Akers, Doris Mae (b. May 21, 1922, Brookfield, Mo.) attended high school and business college; has had no special training in music, but wrote her first gospel song at age 10, and has won many awards for singing, song writing and choir directing; is affiliated with the Full Gospel church in Columbus, Ohio and has served as choir director, making outstanding recordings; has written over 300 gospel songs.

    There's a sweet, sweet Spirit (581)

    SWEET, SWEET SPIRIT (581)

Alexander, Cecil Frances Humphreys (b. 1818, Co. Tyrone, Ire.; d. Oct. 12, 1895, Londonderry, Ire.) specialized in writing hymns for children; the daughter of a major in the Royal Marines, was born at Miltown House in County Tyrone, Ireland; in 1850, married the Rev. William Alexander, rector of the parish of Termonmongan who was appointed Bishop of Derry and Raphoe in 1867, and became (Anglican) Primate of all Ireland in 1893; before her marriage, published *Verses for Holy Seasons,* 1846 and

Hymns for Little Children, 1848, her most famous collection which was printed in more than 100 editions; also produced: *Narrative Hymns for Village Schools* (1853), *Poems on Subjects in the Old Testament* (1854 and 1857), and *Hymns Descriptive and Devotional* (1858); contributed hymns to *Lyra Anglicana, Psalms and Hymns*, and *Hymns Ancient and Modern*.

All things bright and beautiful (53); Jesus calls us; o'er the tumult (503)

Alford, Henry (b. Oct. 7, 1810, London, Eng.; d. Jan. 12, 1871, Canterbury, Eng.) was born into a family which boasted five consecutive generations of clergymen, and was educated at Ilminster Grammar School and Trinity College, Cambridge; in 1833 was ordained in the Church of England, and served as curate to his father at Winkfield, Wiltshire and then at Ampton; became vicar of Wymeswold, Leicestershire in 1835, where he served for 18 years; was appointed dean of Canterbury Cathedral, 1857; is best remembered for his 4-volume commentary on the Greek New Testament; wrote many original hymns and translations which are found in *Psalms and Hymns* (1844), *Poetical Works* (1853), and *The Year of Praise* (1867).

Ten thousand times ten thousand (537); Come, ye thankful people, come (565)

Alington, Cyril Argentine (b. Oct. 22, 1872, Ipswich, Eng.; d. May 16, 1955, St. Leonards, Herts, Eng.), the son of an Anglican minister, was educated at Marlborough School and Trinity College, Oxford, and ordained a priest in 1901; was a teacher at Shrewsbury School and then at Eton (1908–33) and finally, Dean of Durham (1933–51); wrote and published many hymns, essays, novels and theological works.

Good Christian men, rejoice and sing (170)

Allen, Blaine Hamilton (b. Jan. 30, 1943, Independence, Kan.), the son of a minister-author-lecturer-teacher, attended the Pentecostal Bible College in Sacramento, Calif. and had many years of formal training in both piano and organ; for three years served as associate pastor of Vancouver (Wash.) Foursquare Church; presently is organist at Lighthouse Mission Church in Portland, Ore. and a member of MASADA, a professional mixed quartet; has written approximately 50 hymn texts and tunes.

Little Baby Jesus, born in Bethlehem (123)
YULE SPIRITUAL (123)

Allen, Chester G. (b. 1838; d. 1878), despite the popularity of his tune "Joyful Song," remains basically unknown; contributed to several compilations of Sunday School songs, such as *Bright Jewels*, 1869, collaborating with William Bradbury, W. H. Doane, W. F. Sherwin and others.

JOYFUL SONG (96)

Allen, George Nelson (b. Sept. 7, 1812, Mansfield, Ohio; d. Dec. 9, 1877, Cincinnati, Ohio) graduated from Oberlin College in 1838 and stayed on as a member of the faculty, teaching music and geology until his retirement in 1865; initiated the choral and instrumental programs of music education which later developed into the famed Oberlin Conservatory of Music; contributed to several music collections and compiled *The Oberlin Social and Sabbath School Hymn Book*, 1844.

MAITLAND (495)

Ambrose of Milan (b. *ca.* 340, Treves, Ger.; d. Apr. 4, 397, Milan, It.) has been called the "Father of Church Song" because he wrote simple and expressive hymns which congregations could sing; the son of a Roman nobleman, was educated in preparation for a civil career; became governor of northern Italy and lived in Milan; at the death of the Arian bishop, was elected to the post by public acclamation at the age of 34, even though he had not yet been baptized; gave his fortune to the poor and to the church and became a staunch supporter of the Nicene (trinitarian) faith.

O Splendor of God's glory bright (16)

Antes, John (b. Mar. 24, 1740, Frederick, Pa.; d. Dec. 17, 1811, Bristol, Eng.) was a Moravian minister and missionary, a watchmaker by profession, and a musician by avocation; was one of 11 children, the son of Heinrich Antes, who was active in buying land in Pennsylvania and North Carolina for Moravian settlements; received early training, academically and musically, in his own home, where his father had established a school for boys; in 1764 was "called for service" to the international headquarters of the Moravians in Herrnhut, Saxony; was ordained a Moravian minister in 1769 and spent the following twelve years in Egypt, the first American missionary to serve in that country; in 1781 left Egypt, spent two years in Germany and settled in Fulneck, Eng.; composed a number of choral works for four voices and instruments, and some chorales, and is acclaimed as one of the finest early American composers of sacred music.

MONKLAND (50)

Arne, Thomas Augustine (b. Mar. 12, 1710, London, Eng.; d. Mar. 5, 1778, London, Eng.) was educated at Eton for a career in law, but chose music instead for his profession; won recognition as a composer when he wrote the music for Joseph Addison's (*q.v.*) *Rosamond*, 1733; wrote operas (*e.g., Comus*, 1738, and *Alfred*, 1740) and oratorios (*Abel*, 1744, and *Judith*, 1733); is remembered mostly for the song, "Rule, Brittania!" (the finale from *Alfred*); was among the first to introduce women's voices into choral writing.

ARLINGTON (316, 510)

Åström, Johan (b. Nov. 30, 1767, Gävle, Sweden; d. Feb. 29, 1844) lived during the "golden age of Swedish hymnody"; left fatherless at age 13, received early training from his mother, attended Uppsala University and was ordained in 1793; was briefly pastor of the German church in Norrköping, then appointed rector (1805) at Tuna and Stavby and (1821) at Sigtuna and Altuna; assisted Archbishop Johan Olof Wallin in preparing

the *Psalmbok* (1816–18), and the 1819 edition contained 11 of his hymns and several translations.
  In heaven above (adapt.) (542)

Atkins, George. No information can be found on this author.
  Brethren, we have met to worship (199)

Atkinson, Frederick Cook (b. Aug. 21, 1841, Norwich, Eng.; d. 1896, East Dereham, Eng.) was a boy chorister at Norwich Cathedral and later was assistant to Dr. Zechariah Buck, organist and choirmaster; received his Mus.B. degree at Cambridge in 1867; served as organist-choirmaster at St. Luke's Church in Manningham, Bradford, at Norwich Cathedral (1881–85) and St. Mary's Parish Church in Lewisham (after 1886); composed a number of (Anglican) services, anthems, hymn tunes and instrumental pieces.
  MORECAMBE (198)

Avery, Richard Kinsey (b. Aug. 26, 1934, Visalia, Calif.) is one-half of the "Avery and Marsh team" of contemporary worship specialists; was educated at the University of Redlands (B.A.) and Union Theological Seminary (M.Div.) and has had special training in piano and choral music; in 1960 became pastor of the First Presbyterian Church in Port Jervis, N.Y. and still serves there; has written over 100 hymns and contributed articles to *Presbyterian Life, Colloquy,* and other magazines; is co-founder with Donald Marsh (*q.v.*) of Proclamation Productions, Inc., and says of their creative activity: "We work together in producing our hymns, both writing words and music and exchanging ideas and self-criticism throughout the process."
  PORT JERVIS (573) (not named in the hymnal)

Babcock, Maltbie Davenport (b. Aug. 3, 1858, Syracuse, N.Y.; d. May 18, 1901, Naples, It.), a member of a socially prominent family, was educated at Syracuse University and Auburn Theological Seminary, where he excelled as a student, as an athlete and also as a musician; was ordained a minister in the Presbyterian Church and served briefly in Lockport, N.Y., for 14 years in Baltimore, Md., and in 1899 was called to the Brick Presbyterian Church of New York City; died in 1901 while on a trip to the Holy Land, so his pastorate at the Brick Church was cut short after 18 months; left a literary heritage which was collected and published shortly after his death—*Thoughts for Every-day Living,* 1901.
  This is my Father's world (58)

Bach, Johann Sebastian (b. Mar. 21, 1685, Eisenach, Ger.; d. July 28, 1750, Leipzig, Ger.) was undoubtedly the greatest musical genius to give his principal attention to music for the church; was born into an extremely gifted musical family, trained at Ohrdruf and Lüneburg and served for a short time as organist at Arnstadt and Mühlhausen; spent his professional and creative life in three cities: Weimar (1708–17), Anhalt-Cöthen (1718–

23), and in Leipzig (1723–50), where he was cantor of St. Thomas' Church; wrote almost 300 church cantatas, and a great quantity of music for organ; provided settings for the Lutheran chorales which have been presented as models of four-part harmonization in music theory classes; was a devout Christian and felt himself divinely called to provide the best music for the worship of God.

PASSION CHORALE (arr.) (136)

Backstrom, Carl Ernest (b. May 2, 1901, Stockholm, Sweden) emigrated to the United States in 1907 with his parents and the family became active in the Swedish Pilgrim Church (Covenant), Brooklyn, N.Y.; after completing high school, worked at the Chase National Bank for four years; attended the University of Pennsylvania and North Park Theological Seminary in Chicago, graduating in 1926; took graduate work at the University of Chicago and was ordained in 1928; served Mission Covenant churches in Lincoln, Neb., Lanyon, Ia., and Youngstown, Ohio; in 1948 transferred his membership to the Presbyterian church; retired to live in Chautauqua, N.Y.

Thanks to God for my Redeemer (trans.) (571)

Baker, Henry (b. 1835, Nuneham, Oxford, Eng.; d. Apr. 15, 1910, Wimbledon, London, Eng.), the son of an Anglican clergyman, studied civil engineering at Winchester and Cooper's Hill, and spent many years in India, building railroads; at the encouragement of John B. Dykes (*q.v.*), completed a degree in music at Exeter College, Oxford (1867); released many of his tunes in W. Garrett Horder's *Worship Song*, 1905.

QUEBEC (5, 91, 357)

Baker, Henry Williams (b. May 27, 1821, London, Eng.; d. Feb. 12, 1877, Monkland, Herts, Eng.) has a secure place in hymn history as the "editor-in-chief" of the historic *Hymns Ancient and Modern*, 1861; was educated at Trinity College, Cambridge, ordained in 1844 and appointed vicar at Monkland, near Leominster, and remained there until his death in 1877; served for almost 20 years as chairman of the committee which compiled *Hymns Ancient and Modern;* although criticized as "authoritarian and ruthless" in his editing decisions, no doubt profoundly influenced the hymn singing of the Anglican communion, and thus all of Christendom, for the past 100 years and more.

The King of love my Shepherd is (46); Of the Father's love begotten (trans.) (122); Lord, Thy Word abideth (227)

STEPHANOS (259)

Baker, Theodore (b. June 3, 1851, New York, N.Y.; d. Oct. 13, 1934, Dresden, Ger.) first prepared for a career in business, but turned to music; studied at the University of Leipzig, where his doctoral dissertation (1881) was the first serious study of the music of the American Indian; returned to America in 1891 and served as literary editor and translator for G.

Schirmer, Inc.; published *A Dictionary of Musical Terms* (1895) and *Baker's Biographical Dictionary of Musicians* (1900 and 1905); retired in 1926 and lived in Germany until his death.

We gather together (trans.) (570)

Bakewell, John (b. 1721, Brailsford, Derby, Eng.; d. Mar. 18, 1819, Lewisham, Eng.) as a young man came to faith in God through study of Thomas Boston's *Fourfold State;* was an ardent evangelist who became involved in the Wesleyan movement in 1749, and was encouraged to begin writing hymns; directed the Greenwich Royal Park Academy for many years and is said to have brought Methodism to the city of Greenwich; died at the age of 98 and was buried behind City Road Chapel in London, not far from John Wesley's (*q.v.*) grave.

Hail, Thou once despised Jesus (95)

Barham-Gould, Arthur Cyril (b. 1891, England; d. Feb. 14, 1953, Tunbridge, Kent, Eng.) was educated at Ridley Hall, Cambridge and ordained in the Church of England in 1927; served as curate at All Souls', Langham Place (1927–29) and Holy Trinity, Brompton (1932–36); was vicar of St. Paul's, Onslow Square (1936–53).

ST. LEONARDS (349)

Baring-Gould, Sabine (b. Jan. 28, 1834, Exeter, Eng.; d. Jan. 2, 1924, Lew-Trenchard, Devon, Eng.) was the oldest son of the squire of a large estate, and spent much of his early life in France and Germany; received degrees at Clare College, Cambridge and was active in choir schools; was ordained in the Church of England in 1865 and served as curate of Horbury, writing many hymns for the children of the Horbury Bridge Mission; in 1881 inherited the family estate and was appointed rector of Lew-Trenchard, serving as country squire and parson for the rest of his life; published a great variety of books on travel, mythology, poetry, fiction, history, and theology; was a pioneer collector of English folk-songs and collaborated in publishing *Songs and Ballads of the West* (1889–91), *A Garland of Country Song* (1894), and *English Folk-songs for Schools.*

Onward, Christian soldiers (470); Now the day is over (555)

Barnard, Charlotte Alington (b. Dec. 23, 1830, Eng.; d. Jan. 30, 1869, Dover, Eng.) studied music theory and composition under William Henry Holmes, professor of piano at the Royal Academy of Music; published over 100 ballads under the pseudonym "Claribel," the best-known of which is "Come Back to Erin"; also wrote and published two volumes of poetry.

BROCKLESBURY (217); BARNARD (465)

Barnby, Joseph (b. Aug. 12, 1838, York, Eng.; d. Jan. 28, 1896, London, Eng.) as a boy was a precocious chorister at York Minster, becoming an organist at 12 and a choirmaster at 14; received the Fellowship degree at the Royal Academy of Music; was organist and choirmaster at St. Andrew's

Church, Wells St., London and then at St. Anne's, Soho, where the singing of the Bach passion music became an annual event; was appointed musical advisor to Novello and Company, 1861; served as precentor of Eton College (1875–92), resigning to become principal of the Guildhall School of Music; composed an oratorio, many anthems and liturgical services; edited five hymnbooks: *The Hymnary* (1872), *The Congregational Mission Hymnal* (1890), *The Congregational Sunday School Hymnal* (1891), *The Home and School Hymnal* (1893), and co-edited *The Cathedral Psalter* (1873); had his 246 hymn tunes published in one volume in 1897, after his death.

ST. ANDREW (242); JUST AS I AM (371); SANDRINGHAM (529); LAUDES DOMINI (550); MERRIAL (555)

Barraclough, Henry (b. Dec. 14, 1891, Windhill, York, Eng.) wrote "Ivory Palaces," one of the best known gospel songs controlled by Hope Publishing Company; received his education in Bradford Grammar School in England and studied piano and organ, beginning at age five; remained in Bradford as claims adjuster for the Car and General Insurance Company; from 1911 to 1913 was secretary to Sir George Scott Robertson, a member of Parliament; in 1914 joined the Chapman-Alexander evangelistic team as pianist when the preacher and song leader came to England, and returned with them to the United States; during World War I, served with the A.E.F. in France; from 1919 to 1961 served the General Assembly of the Presbyterian Church, U.S.A., first as secretary, and then as manager of the Department of Administration; received the honorary LL.D. degree from Bloomfield College and Seminary (N.J.); has written some 20 hymn texts and 120 hymn tunes; lives in retirement in Elkins Park, Pa.

My Lord has garments so wondrous fine (150)
MONTREAT (150)

Barthélémon, François Hippolyte (b. July 27, 1741, Bordeaux, Fr.; d. July 23, 1808, London, Eng.) was born in the home of an official of the French government, but his mother was from a wealthy Irish family; served briefly in the Irish brigade, but left the army to study music on the continent; in 1765 went to England as a professional violinist and later conducted orchestras at Vauxhall and Marylebone Gardens; was closely associated with Franz Joseph Haydn during the composer's stay in London; wrote five operas, one oratorio, six symphonies, violin sonatas, concertos, etc.; was a member of the Swedenborgian Church, and suffered misfortune and ill health in his later life.

MORNING HYMN (551)

Bartlett, Eugene Monroe, Jr. (b. May 4, 1918, Greenwood, Ark.) is the son of a music teacher and publisher, receiving his first training in his father's "singing normals"; received his formal education at John Brown University (B.A.) and Oklahoma Baptist University (B.M., honorary D.Mus.); served as minister of music in three Arkansas Baptist churches; from 1947 to 1954 was minister of music at Trinity Baptist Church, Oklahoma City; since 1954 has been Director of Church Music for The Baptist General Convention of

Oklahoma; has written approximately 50 hymn texts and tunes, as well as many anthems.

Christ was born in a distant land (479)

RHEA (479)

Barton, Bernard (b. Jan. 31, 1784, London, Eng.; d. Feb. 19, 1849, Woodbridge, Eng.), remembered as England's "Quaker Poet," received training at a Quaker school in Ipswich; as a youth, was apprenticed to a shopkeeper at Halstead, Essex and later joined his brother in the corn and coal business in Woodbridge, Suffolk; spent a year in Liverpool engaged in tutoring, and then returned permanently to Woodbridge, working as a bank clerk for some 40 years; enjoyed the friendship of famous authors, including Charles Lamb, Lord Byron, Walter Scott and Robert Southey; published several volumes of poetry and prose between 1812 and 1845, including *Devotional Verses*, 1826, and *Household Verses*, 1849; is credited with 20 hymns, which come from these and similar collections.

Walk in the light! (329)

Bateman, Christian Henry (b. Aug. 9, 1813, Wyke, York, Eng.; d. July 27, 1889, Carlisle, Eng.) studied for the Moravian ministry and briefly pastored in that fellowship; served three Congregational churches in Scotland and England and then was ordained in the Church of England; from 1869 to 1894 was curate of St. Luke's, Jersey, vicar of All Saints', Childshill, and finally curate of St. John's, Penymyndd; edited *Sacred Melodies for Sabbath Schools and Families*, 1843 (which had wide use in the Sunday Schools of Scotland) and *The Children's Hymnal and Christian Year*, 1872.

Come, Christians, join to sing (60)

Bates, Katharine Lee (b. Aug. 12, 1859, Falmouth, Mass.; d. Mar. 28, 1929, Wellesley, Mass.) wrote one of our best-known national hymns, "America the Beautiful"; was educated at Wellesley College, graduating in 1880; taught high school for six years, then joined the faculty at Wellesley and eventually became head of the English department; was the author or editor of approximately two dozen works and compilations, including a textbook, *History of American Literature* (1908), and volumes of poetry: *America the Beautiful* (1911), *Fairy Gold* (1916), and *The Pilgrim Ship* (1926).

O beautiful for spacious skies (520)

Bathurst, William Hiley (b. Aug. 28, 1796, Clevedale, near Bristol, Eng.; d. Nov. 25, 1877, Lydney Park, Gloucester, Eng.), the son of Charles Bragge, one-time member of Parliament for Bristol, was educated at Winchester and Christ Church, Oxford; after graduating (1818), assumed the rectorship of the parish church on his uncle's estate at Barwick-in-Elmet and changed his name to "Bathurst," after his uncle; in 1852 resigned as rector and returned to the family estate at Lydney Park, because he took exception to certain doctrinal teachings of the church relating to baptism and burial services; wrote or edited: *Psalms and Hymns for Public and Private*

Use (1831), *Metrical Musings, or Thoughts on Sacred Subjects in Verse* (1849), and *The Georgics of Virgil* (1849).

O for a faith that will not shrink (316)

Baumbach, Adolph (b. 1830, Germany; d. Apr. 3, 1880, Chicago, Ill.) received his musical education in his native Germany; emigrated to the United States in his mid-20's and taught piano and organ in Boston, and later in Chicago; published a collection of sacred music for quartet choirs.

Unnamed tune (587)

Baxter, Lydia (b. Sept. 8, 1809, Petersburg, N.Y.; d. June 22, 1874, New York, N.Y.) wrote her one lasting hymn at the age of 61, four years before her death; with her sister was converted under the ministry of Rev. Eben Tucker, a Baptist missionary, and they were largely responsible for forming a Baptist church in their home town; married and moved to New York City, where she continued her Christian activity; was a bedridden invalid for many years, but her home was a common meeting place for many religious leaders; published a book of devotional poems, *Gems by the Wayside*, 1855, and wrote a number of gospel songs.

Take the name of Jesus with you (66)

Bayly, Albert Frederick (b. Sept. 6, 1901, Bexhill on Sea, Sussex, Eng.) for a brief period trained to be a ship builder at the Royal Dockyard School at Portsmouth, then received the B.A. degree from London University and studied for the ministry at Mansfield College, Oxford; beginning in 1928, served four Congregational churches in Northumberland, Lancashire and East Yorks; has been a pastor at Thaxted, Essex since 1962; has published several books of verse, among them *Again I Say Rejoice*, 1967; has also written several missionary pageants and librettos for W. L. Lloyd Webber's cantatas.

Lord, whose love through humble service (512)

Beethoven, Ludwig van (b. Dec. 16, 1770, Bonn, Ger.; d. Mar. 26, 1827, Vienna, Aust.) brought "sonata form" music (symphonies, quartets, concerti and sonatas) to full maturity; was born into a musical family and showed talent at a very early age; at the age of 12, studied with Neefe, the court organist, and became acquainted with the works of J. S. Bach (*q.v.*); visited Vienna at age 17 and met Mozart (*q.v.*), and later studied briefly with Haydn (*q.v.*); from the age of 28 suffered deafness, which was total when he was 45; during his mature years, wrote his most outstanding sacred works: *Christ on the Mount of Olives* (*ca.*1803), *Mass in C* (1807), and *Missa Solemnis* (1818–23); is credited with several hymn tunes that are adapted from his larger works.

HYMN TO JOY (25, 223)

Bennard, George (b. Feb. 4, 1873, Youngstown, Ohio; d. Oct. 10, 1958, Reed City, Mich.) wrote "The Old Rugged Cross," for many years acknowledged to be America's favorite gospel song; as a child, was converted while attending a Salvation Army meeting in Lucas, Iowa; at age 16, became the sole support of his mother and four sisters, when his father died; moved his family to Illinois, later married and he and his wife became workers in the Salvation Army; after several years, resigned to become a Methodist evangelist, preaching mostly in the north-central part of the United States and in Canada; in later years lived at Reed City, Michigan, where a twelve-foot wooden cross memorializes his contribution to hymnody.

On a hill far away (236)

OLD RUGGED CROSS (236)

Berg, Carolina V. Sandell (b. Oct. 3, 1832, Fröderyd, Swed.; d. July 27, 1903, Stockholm, Swed.), who signed her hymns "L.S." (Lina Sandell), has been called "the Fanny Crosby of Sweden"; was very frail as a girl and spent a great deal of time with her father, who was a Lutheran minister; after her father's tragic death (see No. 41), found comfort in writing hymns and produced 650 during her lifetime; married C. O. Berg in 1867; credited much of the popularity of her hymns to the music written for them by Oscar Ahnfelt (*q.v.*), a "spiritual troubadour" of his day; with the financial help of the famous Swedish soprano, Jenny Lind, published many of her songs in Ahnfelt's *Andeliga Sånger,* 1850.

Children of the heavenly Father (41); Day by day and with each passing moment (561)

Bergen, Esther Cathryn (b. June 18, 1921, Morden, Manitoba), the daughter of a Mennonite minister, received her education at The Mennonite Collegiate Institute, Gretna, Man., and the Normal School and Mennonite Brethren Bible College in Winnipeg, with special training in music composition; taught in the public schools of Manitoba for four years, and later taught music at the Mennonite Brethren Bible College, and was Dean/Registrar at the Canadian Mennonite Bible College; with her husband, Menno Bergen, was a missionary in Mexico, 1956–68, and they presently serve the Herbert Mennonite Church, Herbert, Sask.; has translated some 150 hymn texts, written considerable poetry and composed several hymn tunes.

All my sins have been forgiven (trans.) (291)

Bernard of Clairvaux (b. *ca.* 1090, Les Fontaines, near Dijon, Fr.; d. Aug. 20, 1153, Clairvaux, Fr.) was born of noble parents, and became one of the religious and political leaders of the 12th century; inherited his deeply religious nature from his mother, who died when he was 14; was educated at Chatillon, but rejected the life of worldly success; *ca.* 1112, entered the Cistercian monastery at Citeaux, bringing about 29 companions with him; in 1115 founded the monastery of Clairvaux, and remained as abbot until his death; was a very effective preacher, a brilliant theologian and wise counselor of both popes and kings; was canonized in 1174.

O Jesus, King most wonderful (73); Jesus, the very thought of Thee (83); Jesus, Thou Joy of loving hearts (91); O sacred Head, now wounded (136)

Bernard of Cluny (b. 12th century, Murles or Morlas, Fr.) has often been confused with Bernard of Clairvaux; is believed to have been born of English parents, and to have lived as a monk at the abbey of Cluny during the time when Peter the Venerable was abbot, 1122–56; in the cloistered setting, wrote *De Contemptu Mundi*, a satire of some 3000 lines condemning the follies and vices of his day, and extolling the joys of the life immortal, and dedicated the work to Peter the Venerable.

Jerusalem the golden (536)

Bethune, George Washington (b. Mar. 18, 1805, New York City, N.Y.; d. Apr. 27, 1862, Florence, Italy) received his education at Dickinson College (Pa.) and Princeton Seminary and was ordained to the Dutch Reformed ministry; served churches in Rinebeck, N.Y. (1827–30), Utica, N.Y. (1830–34), Philadelphia, Pa. (1834–50), and Brooklyn Heights, N.Y. (1850–59); was invited to be chancellor of New York University and later, provost of the University of Pennsylvania, but declined both opportunities because he was "called to the ministry"; wrote many hymns and published many books, including *The Fruits of the Spirit* (1839), *Sermons* (1847), *Lays of Love and Faith* (1847) and *The British Female Poets* (1848); in 1861–62 traveled to Italy for his health, and died suddenly in Florence shortly after preaching at the Scottish Kirk there.

There is no name so sweet on earth (97)

Bevan, Emma Frances (b. Sept. 25, 1827, Oxford, Eng.; d. 1909, Cannes, Fr.) was the daughter of the Rev. Philip Nicholas Shuttleworth, warden of New College, Oxford, who later became Bishop of Chichester; in 1856 married R. C. L. Bevan, of the Lombard Street banking firm in London; is known for her contribution in translating German verse into English, with her hymn versions published in *Songs of Eternal Life*, 1858, and *Songs of Praise for Christian Pilgrims*, 1859.

Sinners Jesus will receive (271)

Bickersteth, Edward Henry (b. Jan. 25, 1825, Islington, Eng.; d. May 16, 1906, London, Eng.), the son of a clergyman, was educated at Trinity College, Cambridge and ordained in the Church of England in 1848; was curate and rector of several small parishes, and (1855–85) vicar of Christ Church, Hampstead; was briefly Dean of Gloucester, and finally Bishop of Exeter, 1885–1900; authored 12 books, including *Psalms and Hymns* (1858), based on his father's *Christian Psalmody* (1833 and 1841); made a significant contribution to hymn singing in the *Hymnal Companion to the Book of Common Prayer* (1870, rev. 1877), which was adopted by most evangelical Anglican churches; wrote mostly subjective poems and John Julian says that his best works were his hymns for private devotion.

Peace, perfect peace (396)

Bilhorn, Peter Philip (b. July 22, 1865, Mendota, Ill.; d. Dec. 13, 1936, Los Angeles, Calif.) was the son of a carriage maker who was killed in the Civil

War three months before Peter's birth—the Bavarian family name of Pulhorn had been changed to Bilhorn by Abraham Lincoln when he was a judge in Ottawa, Ill.; moved with the family to Chicago, and with his older brother established the Eureka Wagon and Carriage Works; had a fine voice and was a popular singer in concert halls and beer gardens in the Chicago area; was converted in a revival (1883) conducted by George F. Pentecost and George C. Stebbins (*q.v.*), after which he concentrated on his music education, studying with Frederick W. Root and George C. Stebbins; traveled widely in evangelistic work, and developed a small portable reed organ for his own use, that became very popular and was manufactured by the Bilhorn Folding Organ Company; composed a large number of gospel songs and was highly respected as a successful publisher in the Chicago area; was the first song leader for Evangelist Billy Sunday; published *Crowning Glory, No. 1* (1888), *Crowning Glory, No. 2, Soul-Winning Songs, Choice Songs, Sunshine Songs, Songs for Male Choruses* (2 Vols.), three anthem books, and many others.

WONDROUS STORY (296)

Blandy, E. W. Nothing is known concerning this author.

I can hear my Savior calling (369)

Bliss, Philip Paul (b. July 9, 1838, Clearfield Co., Pa.; d. Dec. 29, 1876, near Ashtabula, Ohio) as a boy worked on a farm and in lumber camps, and received his earliest musical training under J. G. Towner (father of D. B. Towner, *q.v.*) and W. B. Bradbury (*q.v.*); became an itinerant music teacher during the winter months and attended the Normal Academy of Music in Geneseo, N.Y. for several summers; in 1864 sold his first song to Root and Cady, music publishers in Chicago, and was associated with them as a writer for four years; encouraged by D. L. Moody to become a singing evangelist, was associated with Major D. W. Whittle (*q.v.*) in revival meetings beginning in March, 1874, traveling extensively throughout the midwest and south; on his way to an engagement in Moody's Tabernacle in Chicago, was killed trying to rescue his wife from the fire following a train wreck near Ashtabula, Ohio; wrote many successful gospel songs for George F. Root's (*q.v.*) collections; helped to compile: *The Charm, a Collection of Sunday School Music* (1871), *Sunshine for Sunday Schools* (1873), *Gospel Songs, a Choice Collection of Hymns and Tunes, New and Old, for Gospel Meetings, Sunday Schools, Etc.* (1874), and (with Ira D. Sankey, *q.v.*) *Gospel Hymns and Sacred Songs* (1875) and *Gospel Hymns No. 2* (1876).

"Man of Sorrows," what a name (155); Sing them over again to me (222); Free from the law, O happy condition (231); "Whosoever heareth," shout, shout the sound! (254); The whole world was lost in the darkness of sin (261); More holiness give me (390); I will sing of my Redeemer (408)

HALLELUJAH! WHAT A SAVIOR! (155); WORDS OF LIFE (222); ONCE FOR ALL (231); WHOSOEVER (254); LIGHT OF THE WORLD (261); MY PRAYER (390); VILLE DU HAVRE (401); KENOSIS (508)

Blom, Fredrik Arvid (b. May 21, 1867, near Enköping, Sweden; d. May 24, 1927, Uddevalla, Sweden) as a young man received his certificate as a "chief mate" sailor; came to America in the 1890's and became an officer in the Salvation Army in Chicago; studied at North Park College and Seminary (1901–1904) and pastored a Mission Covenant Church; resigned his church in 1915, and later explained: "I drifted from God . . . and became embittered with myself, the world, and not the least with ministers who looked on me with suspicion because I was a member of the Socialist party"; was renewed in his faith at a Salvation Army meeting and appointed pastor of the Swedish Congregational Church, Titusville, Pa.; returned to Sweden in 1921 and served churches in the Swedish Covenant in Säter, Dalarna, and Rättvik; in 1926 became pastor of the Baptist church in Uddevalla; evidently wrote a number of hymns but only this one is commonly known in America.

This information was supplied by J. Irving Erickson, author of *Twice-Born Hymns* (Chicago: Covenant Press, 1976) and chairman of the commission which prepared *The Covenant Hymnal*, 1973.

Love divine, so great and wondrous (541)

Boberg, Carl Gustaf (b. Aug. 16, 1859, Mönsterås, Sweden; d. Jan. 7, 1940, Kalmar, Sweden), the son of a shipyard carpenter, was a sailor for several years; was converted at the age of 19, attended a Bible school in Kristinehamn and was a lay preacher in his hometown for two years; was editor of the weekly *Sanningsvittnet* (Witness of the Truth) from 1890–1916; represented his district as a member of the Swedish parliament for 13 years between 1912 and 1931; published several books of poetry and many hymns, and was a member of the committees which compiled the first two hymnals of the Swedish Covenant.

How great Thou art (32)

Bode, John Ernest (b. Feb. 23, 1816, St. Pancras, London, Eng.; d. Oct. 6, 1874, Castle Camps, Cambridge, Eng.) was educated at Eton, Charterhouse and Christ Church, Oxford, where he was the first to receive the Hertford Scholarship (1835); served seven years as tutor in his college; was ordained in 1843 and became rector at Westwell, Oxfordshire in 1847; in 1860 was appointed rector at Castle Camps, Cambridgeshire and remained there until his death; delivered the Bampton Lectures at Oxford in 1855; was a gifted poet whose published works include: *Ballads from Herodotus* (1853), *Short Occasional Poems* (1858), and *Hymns for the Gospel of the Day, for Each Sunday and the Festivals of Our Lord* (1860).

O Jesus, I have promised (506)

Bonar, Horatius (b. Dec. 19, 1808, Edinburgh, Scot.; d. July 31, 1889, Edinburgh, Scot.) is considered to be the most eminent of the Scottish hymn-writers, and was a preacher of reknown; received his education at the University of Edinburgh and at the age of 30 was ordained at Kelso and put in charge of the North Parish; in the ecclesiastical struggle of 1843, was actively involved in organizing the Free Church of Scotland; pastored the

Free Church in Kelso, Chalmers Memorial Church, Edinburgh (1866–83) and was moderator of the General Assembly, 1883; was keenly interested in the Second Coming of Christ and edited the *Journal of Prophecy* for many years; was also one of the editors of *The Border Watch*, the official publication of the Free Church; wrote many hymns, of which 100 are used in English-language hymnals today; wrote and/or published: *Songs for the Wilderness* (1843), *The Bible Hymn Book* (1845), *Hymns, Original and Selected* (1846), *Hymns of Faith and Hope* (1857), *The Song of the New Creation* (1872), and *Communion Hymns* (1881).

Glory be to God the Father (8); Here, O my Lord, I see Thee (210); Not what these hands have done (242); I lay my sins on Jesus (247); I heard the voice of Jesus say (309); Go, labor on; spend, and be spent (500)

Borthwick, Jane Laurie (b. Apr. 9, 1813, Edinburgh, Scot.; d. Sept. 7, 1897, Edinburgh, Scot.) was the eldest daughter of James Borthwick, manager of the North British Insurance Office, Edinburgh; traveled widely on the Continent and was encouraged by her father to use her linguistic gifts in translating; with her sister Sarah (Mrs. Eric) Findlater (*q.v.*), translated German hymns into English and published *Hymns from the Land of Luther* (four eds., 1854–62); signed most of her hymns "H.L.L." (from the above collections); has been rated as second only to Catherine Winkworth in her German-English translations.

Be still my soul (trans.) (324); Jesus, still lead on (trans.) (450)

Bortniansky, Dimitri Stepanovich (b. Oct. 28, 1751, Glukhov, Ukraine; d. Oct. 10, 1825, St. Petersburg, Russia) studied under Baldassare Galuppi, an Italian composer who was musician to the Russian court; with the financial support of Empress Catherine the Great, spent several years in Italy, studying in Bologna, Rome and Naples; returned to St. Petersburg in 1779 to become director of the Imperial Chapel Choir; composed five operas and many liturgical works for choir, and the latter were edited and published by Tschaikowsky in ten volumes, *ca.* 1884.

ST. PETERSBURG (523)

Bottome, Frank (b. May 26, 1823, Belper, Derby, Eng.; d. 1894, Tavistock, Devon, Eng.) entered the ministry of the Methodist Episcopal church in America in 1850; in 1872 received the honorary D.D. degree from Dickinson College, Carlisle, Pa.; wrote a number of hymns and published *Centenary Singer*, 1869 and *Round Lake*, 1872.

O spread the tidings 'round (189)

Bourgeois, Louis (b. *ca.* 1510, Paris, Fr.; d. *ca.* 1561, Paris, Fr.), a follower of John Calvin (*q.v.*), left France and moved to Geneva in 1541, where he was cantor and choirmaster at St. Peter's Church; in 1542 was appointed by Calvin to be musical editor of the Geneva Psalter; in the successive editions (until 1557), provided suitable melodies for the psalms, some adapted from German and French secular sources, and some undoubtedly original tunes; wrote a book of music instruction, *La Droit Chemin de Musique*, 1550; returned to Paris in 1557 and his last known activity was the publishing of a collection of harmonized psalm tunes in 1561.

OLD HUNDREDTH (20)

Bowring, John (b. Oct. 17, 1792, Exeter, Eng.; d. Nov. 23, 1872, Exeter, Eng.) was born of Puritan stock and was affiliated with the branch of Unitarianism which believes that "Christ is all we know of God"; left school at the age of 14 to assist his father in the manufacture of woolen goods; traveled a great deal, and gained proficiency in German, Dutch, Spanish, Portuguese and Italian before he was 16; became one of the world's great linguists, able to converse in 100 languages, and to read some 200; had a keen interest in politics and became editor of the radical *Westminster Review*, 1825; was a member of Parliament and held several posts in foreign service, including the governorship of Hong Kong; was knighted by Queen Victoria in 1854; wrote many original poems and hymns and published *Matins and Vespers, with Hymns and Devotional Pieces*, 1823, and a second collection, *Hymns as a Sequel to the Matins*, 1825.

God is love; His mercy brightens (39); In the cross of Christ I glory (140)

Boyd, William (b. 1847, Montego Bay, Jamaica; d. Feb. 16, 1928, London, Eng.) received early training from Sabine Baring-Gould (*q.v.*) at Hurstpierpoint in England; attended St. Edmund Hall, Oxford and was a choral scholar at Worcester College; became a priest in the Church of England in 1882, was rector of a church in Sussex and became vicar of All Saints, Norfolk Square, London in 1893, where he served until his retirement in 1918; harmonized Baring-Gould's collection of folk music from Iceland, and was one of 14 individuals who contributed to *Thirty-Two Hymn-Tunes composed by Members of the University of Oxford*, 1868.

Fight the good fight with all thy might (469)

Bradbury, William Batchelder (b. Oct. 6, 1816, York, Me.; d. Jan. 7, 1868, Montclair, N.J.) was a pioneer in music for children—in the church and in the public school; as a young man, moved with his family to Boston, where he attended the Boston Academy of Music and sang in the Bowdoin Street Church choir under the direction of Lowell Mason (*q.v.*); served as organist in the First Baptist Church, Brooklyn, and in 1841 became organist at the First Baptist Church, New York City; organized free singing classes, similar to those conducted by Mason in Boston, which resulted in the teaching of music in the New York City public schools; spent two years with his family in Europe (1847–49), studying in Leipzig with Ignaz Moscheles and Moritz Hauptmann; returning to the United States, devoted his time to teaching, conducting musical conventions, composing and editing; in 1854, with his brother founded the Bradbury Piano Company, later united with Knabe; from 1841 to 1867 published 59 music collections, including *The Young Choir* (1841), *The Psalmodist* (1844), *The Choralist* (1847), *The Mendelssohn Collection* (1849), *Psalmista* (1851), *The Shawm* (1853) and *The Jubilee* (1858).

THE SWEETEST NAME (97); OLIVE'S BROW (139); ALETTA

(226); WOODWORTH (260); SOLID ROCK (313); BRADBURY (321); EVEN ME (363); SWEET HOUR (434); HE LEADETH ME (439)

Breck, Carrie E. (b. Jan. 22, 1855, Walden, Vt.; d. Mar. 27, 1934, Portland, Ore.) spent her youth in Vermont, lived briefly in New Jersey and then moved to Portland, Oregon where she remained for the rest of her life; was devoted to her family—a husband, Frank A. Breck, and five daughters—a deeply committed Christian and life-long Presbyterian; according to Phil Kerr (*Music in Evangelism*), wrote more than 2000 poems, many while performing her household duties, though "she could not carry a tune and had no natural sense of pitch, but . . . had a keen sense of rhythm and loved music."

Face to face with Christ my Savior (534)

Bridgers, Luther Burgess (b. Feb. 14, 1884, Margaretsville, N.C.; d. May 27, 1948, Atlanta, Ga.) began preaching when he was 17 years of age, and later was a student at Asbury College in Wilmore, Ky.; pastored Methodist churches for some 12 years and was known for his evangelistic zeal; lost his wife and three sons in 1910 in a fire which destroyed his father-in-law's home in Harrodsburg, Ky.; in 1914, married Miss Aline Winburn, music teacher at Shorter College, Rome, Ga., and for eighteen years engaged in evangelistic work for the Methodist Episcopal Church, South, with the exception of the period following World War I, when he was active in mission work in Belgium, Czechoslovakia, and Russia; after 1932, served churches in Georgia and North Carolina as pastor, and then (1945) retired in Gainesville, Ga.

There's within my heart a melody (393)
SWEETEST NAME (393)

Bridges, Matthew (b. July 14, 1800, Malden, Essex, Eng.; d. Oct. 6, 1894, Sidmouth, Devon, Eng.) grew up in the Church of England, but came under the influence of the Oxford Movement, and like John Henry Newman (*q.v.*) and others, became a Roman Catholic in 1848; lived a number of years in Canada, but returned to England and died while at the Convent of the Assumption in Devon; besides his historical and political contributions, published *Hymns of the Heart,* 1847 and *The Passion of Jesus,* 1852; was introduced as a hymnist to American congregations by Henry Ward Beecher in the latter's *Plymouth Collection,* 1855.

Crown Him with many crowns (st. 1, 4) (85)

Bridges, Robert Seymour (b. Oct. 23, 1844, Walmer, Kent, Eng.; d. Apr. 21, 1930, Boar's Hill, Berks, Eng.), poet laureate of England, was a scholar, musician and physician; was educated at Eton and Corpus Christi College, Oxford, and studied medicine at St. Bartholomew's Hospital in London; gave up medical practice in 1882 because of ill health, and devoted his time to literature and hymnody; published many works, including *Shorter Poems* (1873), *Yattendon Hymnal* (1895–99), *A Practical Discourse on Some Principles* *of Hymn-Singing* (1899), *About Hymns* (1911), *Collected Essays* (1927–36), *Testament of Beauty* (1929) and *Poetical Works* (1929–30); received an honorary LL.D. degree from the University of Michigan in 1924 and was awarded the Order of Merit in 1929.

Ah, holy Jesus, how hast Thou offended (trans.) (152)

Briggs, George Wallace (b. Dec. 14, 1875, Nottingham, Eng.; d. Dec. 30, 1959, Hindhead, Surrey, Eng.), according to Erik Routley (*Companion to Congregational Praise*) was the most prolific of this century's successful hymn writers; was educated at Emmanuel College, Cambridge, served as curate for a brief time in Wakefield, York, and then was a chaplain in the Royal Navy, 1902–09; was appointed vicar of St. Andrew's, Norwich, and in 1918, rector of Loughborough; from 1927–34, was canon of Leicester Cathedral, and from 1934 until his retirement in 1956, canon of Worcester; was one of the founders of the Hymn Society of Great Britain and Ireland; wrote many hymns and prayers for use in English schools and they appeared in *Songs of Praise* (1925), *Prayers and Hymns for Use in Schools* (1927), *Little Bible* (1931), *Prayers and Hymns for Junior Schools* (1933), and *Songs of Faith* (1945).

God hath spoken by His prophets (223)

Brooke, Stopford Augustus (b. Nov. 14, 1832, Glendoen, Donegal, Ire.; d. Mar. 18, 1916, Four Winds, Surrey, Eng.) refused to copyright any of his hymns, saying "they are free, as I think all hymns ought to be, for the use of anyone who may care for them"; was educated at Kingstown, Kidderminster and at Trinity College, Dublin, where he was awarded the Downs Prize and the Vice-Chancellor's Prize for English verse; took holy orders in London in 1857, and was appointed curate at St. Matthew's, Marylebone and later at St. Mary Abbotts, Kensington, after which he became chaplain to the British embassy in Berlin; returned to London after two years, and resumed his ministry at the Chapel of St. James, York St.; in 1867 became chaplain to Queen Victoria, but in 1880 resigned from the Anglican Church to become an independent; published a volume of sermons and many books on English literature, besides *Riquet of the Tuft* (1880), *Poems* (1888), and *Christian Hymns* (*ca.* 1878), edited for his own congregation.

Let the whole creation cry (27)

Brooks, Phillips (b. Dec. 13, 1835, Boston, Mass.; d. Jan. 23, 1893, Boston, Mass.) was one of America's greatest preachers in the last half of the 19th century, gifted in appearance and in personality; attended the Boston Latin School, and in 1855 received his A.B. degree from Harvard; studied for the ministry at the Episcopal Theological Seminary in Alexandria, Va. and was ordained in 1859; served the Church of the Advent in Philadelphia and three years later became rector of Holy Trinity Church; in 1869 became rector of Trinity Church, Boston, where he served for 22 memorable years; had many of his sermons published, and they are still read widely; in 1885 received the D.D. degree from Oxford; had memorized 200 hymns as a child, and frequently quoted them in his sermons; in 1891 was consecrated Bishop of Massachusetts, but served for only two years when death took him.

O little town of Bethlehem (121)

Brownlie, John (b. Aug. 3, 1857, Glasgow, Scot.; d. Nov. 18, 1925, Crieff, Perth, Scot.) received his schooling at the University of Glasgow and the Free Church College in the same city; served as assistant and later (1890) became minister in charge of the Free Church in Portpatrick, Wigtownshire; was active in the community's educational institutions and in 1901 became chairman of the governors of Stanrear High School; wrote many hymns and translations from Latin and Greek, which are found in *Hymns of Our Pilgrimage* (1889), *Zionward and Hymns of the Pilgrim life* (1890), *Pilgrim Songs* (1892), *Hymns from East and West* (1898), *Hymns of the Greek Church* (4 series, 1900–06), and *Hymns from the East* (1907); also wrote the handbook, *Hymns and Hymn-Writers of the Church Hymnary*, 1899.

The King shall come (trans.) (181)

Brückner, Herman H. M. (b. Mar. 11, 1866, Grundy County, Ia.; d. Jan. 25, 1942, Beatrice, Neb.), the son of a Lutheran pastor, was raised in an atmosphere of deep devotion and showed early potential for teaching; completed his theological education at Wartburg Seminary in 1888 and was ordained to the ministry by his father, whom he assisted for a time in the parish work in Derinda, Ill.; served Lutheran congregations in Michigan, Illinois, Kentucky, Wisconsin and Iowa; earned the M.A. degree at the University of Iowa (1917) and served at the Wartburg Seminary during World War I, teaching German-speaking pastors to preach in English; in 1926 began teaching at Hebron College and Academy, remaining until 1941; received the honorary D.D. degree from Wartburg Seminary in 1938; translated many hymns from German and French into English, 72 of which were included in the American Lutheran *Hymnal,* 1930, along with five of his original hymns.

Take Thou my hand, O Father (trans.) (444)

Buchanan, Annabel Morris (b. Oct. 22, 1888, Groesbeck, Tex.) was a graduate of the Landon Conservatory of Music, Dallas, and studied privately with Emil Liebling, William C. Carl, Cornelius Rybner and others; taught music in Texas and Oklahoma and at Stonewall Jackson College in Abingdon, Va.; did extensive research in the folk music of Appalachia, and helped organize the annual White-Top Folk Festivals in Virginia; edited *Folk-Hymns of America,* published in 1938.

LAND OF REST (arr.) (15, 539)

Budry, Edmond Louis (b. Aug. 30, 1854; d. Nov. 12, 1932) studied theology with the "Faculte libre" in Lausanne, Switzerland; for eight years was pastor at Cully and in 1881 went to the Free Church in Vevey, Switzerland, remaining for 35 years; wrote the words of over 60 chorales and many have appeared in French hymnals; was active in translating German, Latin, and English hymns and in writing poetry, to the end of his life.

Thine is the glory, Risen, conquering Son (171)

Buell, Harriett Eugenia Peck (b. Nov. 2, 1834, Cazenovia, N.Y.; d. Feb. 6, 1910, Washington, D. C.) lived in Manlius, N.Y. until 1898, a member of the Methodist Episcopal Church; for 50 years contributed poetry regularly to the *Northern Christian Advocate*, Syracuse, N.Y.; moved to Washington, D.C. where she lived until her death in 1910.

My Father is rich in houses and lands (323)

Bullinger, Ethelbert William (b. Dec. 15, 1837, Canterbury, Eng.; d. June 6, 1913, London, Eng.) was a choirboy at Canterbury Cathedral and studied music with John Pyke Hullah and William H. Monk; was trained for the ministry at King's College, London and became an accomplished Greek and Hebrew scholar, receiving an honorary D.D. degree from the Archbishop of Canterbury in 1881; composed several hymn tunes, but "Bullinger" is one of the few that is still in use.

BULLINGER (330)

Burke, Christian Caroline Anna (b. Sept. 18, 1857, Camberwell, London, Eng.; d. Mar. 4, 1944, Saffron Walden, Essex, Eng.) released her poems periodically in many different journals; published a book of collected verse, *The Flowering of the Almond Tree and Other Poems*, 1896 and 1901.

Lord of life and King of glory (528)

Burleigh, Harry Thacker (b. Dec. 2, 1866, Erie, Pa.; d. Sept. 11, 1949, Stamford, Conn.) was one of the first black musicians to achieve professional success in "serious music" in America; as a boy, sold papers, ran errands, worked as a houseboy, and in the summers was a deck steward on a Great Lakes passenger boat; sang in the choir in St. Paul's Cathedral, Erie, Pa.; won a scholarship at the National Conservatory of Music, New York City, where he later taught for several years; was selected from some 60 applicants to be baritone soloist in the choir of St. George's Church (Episcopal), and remained for 52 years; received an honorary M.A. (Atlanta University) and D.Mus. (Harvard University); was a charter member of the American Society of Composers, Authors, and Publishers; composed many songs and anthems, and arranged negro spirituals.

McKEE (arr.) (513)

Burleigh, William Henry (b. Feb. 2, 1812, Woodstock, Conn.; d. Mar. 18, 1871, Brooklyn, N.Y.) was an American Unitarian, but his hymns are more often sung in Great Britain and in churches of other denominations; was educated in the public schools of Plainfield, Conn., and worked as a printer and journalist, contributing to many periodicals; in 1837 published the *Christian Witness* and the *Temperance Banner* in Pittsburgh, and later moved to Hartford, Conn. to become editor of the anti-slavery paper, *Christian*

Freedom (later called *Charter Oak*); for several years (1849–55) acted as secretary of the New York Temperance Society, and finally moved to New York City to be harbor master; wrote a book of *Poems* which was published in 1841, and reprinted in 1871 with a biographical sketch written by his wife.

Lead us, O Father (441)

Burnap, Uzziah Christopher (b. June 17, 1834, Brooklyn, N.Y.; d. Dec. 8, 1900, Brooklyn, N.Y.) as a young man studied music in Paris; was a prominent Brooklyn dry goods merchant who served as organist for the Reformed Church in Brooklyn Heights for some 37 years; composed and arranged many hymn tunes and was music editor of the Reformed Church hymnal, *Hymns of the Church with Tunes*, 1869; collaborated with John K. Paine of Harvard in compiling *Hymns and Songs of Praise*, 1874.

SERENITY (arr.) (73)

Burton, John, Sr. (b. Feb. 26, 1773, Nottingham, Eng.; d. June 24, 1822, Leicester, Eng.) resided in Nottingham until 1813, and then in Leicester until his death; was a dedicated Baptist layman who wrote his first hymns for the children in his Sunday School; in 1802 published *The Youth's Monitor in Verse, in a Series of Little Tales, Emblems, Poems and Songs;* assisted in compiling the Nottingham *Sunday School Union Hymn Book*, 1810, which had twenty editions by 1861.

Holy Bible, book divine (226)

Butler, Aubrey Lee (b. June 29, 1933, Noble, Okla.), called "Pete" by his friends, received his B.Mus. degree at Oklahoma Baptist University and the M.S.M. at Southern Baptist Theological Seminary, Louisville, Ky.; has served Southern Baptist churches as minister of music, in Oklahoma City (1952–55), Middletown, Ky. (1955–57), Madill, Okla. (1957–60), and since 1960 at Ada, Okla.; a member of ASCAP, has written several hymn tunes, 14 anthems, and a cantata, *Something Wonderful*.

ADA (285)

Byrne, Mary Elizabeth (b. July 1, 1880, Dublin, Ire.; d. Jan. 19, 1931, Dublin, Ire.) received her education at the Dominican Convent in Dublin and the University of Ireland; was an expert in the historic Gaelic language, and employed by her country's Board of Intermediate Education as a researcher; contributed to the *Old and Mid-Irish Dictionary* and *Dictionary of the Irish Language,* and assisted in compiling the *Catalogue* of the Royal Irish Academy.

Be Thou my vision (trans.) (344)

Caird, George Bradford (b. July 19, 1917, Dundee, Scot.) was educated at King Edward School, Birmingham and Peterhouse, Cambridge, studying for the Congregational ministry at Mansfield College, Oxford; served as minister of Highgate Congregational Church, London; in 1946 became professor of Old Testament at St. Stephens' College in Alberta, Canada; in 1950 was named professor of Biblical Studies at McGill University, Montreal; returned to Oxford in 1959 and became Senior Tutor at Mansfield College.

Shepherds came, their praises bringing (trans.) (118)

Caldbeck, George Thomas (b. 1852, Waterford, Ire.; d. Jan. 29, 1918, Epsom, Surrey, Eng.) received training in England at the National Model School in Waterford and at Islington Theological College; wanted to be a missionary but ill health prevented him from being accepted, so he returned to Ireland to become a schoolmaster and evangelist; in 1888 went back to London and became an independent itinerant preacher.

PAX TECUM (396)

Caldwell, William is identifiable only as the publisher of *Union Harmony* (Maryville, Tenn., 1837), which contained forty-two tunes credited to him.

LOVINGKINDNESS (77)

Calkin, John Baptiste (b. Mar. 16, 1827, London, Eng.; d. Apr. 15, 1905, London, Eng.) received his first musical training from his father, James Calkin, a well-known music teacher; at 20, was appointed organist, precentor, and choirmaster of St. Columba College, near Dublin; in 1853 returned to London and served as organist at many different places, including Woburn Chapel, Camden Road Chapel, and St. Thomas' Church; in 1883 was appointed to the faculty of the Guildhall School of Music; was a Fellow of the Royal College of Organists and served on the council of Trinity College, London; is best known for his choral settings of Matins and Vespers services and Holy Communion, in Anglican worship.

WALTHAM (490)

Calvin, John (b. July 10, 1509, Noyon, Picardy, Fr.; d. May 27, 1564, Geneva, Switz.) was the leader of the "Calvinistic" aspect of the Reformation in the 16th century, and initiated the tradition of "psalm singing" in Protestant worship; was educated at College Montaigu and the University of Paris, had a very keen mind and an iron will, but was weak physically; in his early 20's was converted from Roman Catholicism to a personal, evangelical faith; a consummate scholar and theologian, published the first edition of *The Institutes of the Christian Religion* in 1536; wrote many metrical versions of the psalms, and enlisted the aid of Clément Marot, Théodore de Bèze and Louis Bourgeois for the purpose of compiling books of congregational song; published many French psalters, beginning with the Strassburg edition (1539) and culminating in the complete Genevan Psalter, 1562. A more complete story of his life and accomplishments may be found in Haeussler, *The Story of Our Hymns*, 580–583.

I greet Thee, who my sure Redeemer art (80)

Camp, Mabel Johnston (b. Nov. 25, 1871, Chanute, Kan.; d. May 25, 1937, Chicago, Ill.), the daughter of a banker, attended a girl's school in Steubenville, Ohio; had a beautiful contralto voice and was an accomplished pianist; married Norman H. Camp, a promising young lawyer who attended the Union Bible Class taught by William R. Newell (*q.v.*), found Christ as Savior and witnessed to his wife, who also was converted; supported her husband in his evangelistic-teaching ministry, while she was active raising money on Chicago's Gold Coast for the "Fresh Air Camp" for under-privileged children; had many physical problems which caused her to be bedridden for months at a time; wrote a number of hymns which first appeared in books published by the leaders of the Moody Memorial Church, of which she and Mr. Camp were members.

Lift up your heads, pilgrims a-weary (184)

THAT BEAUTIFUL NAME (92); CAMP (184)

Campbell, Jane Montgomery (b. 1817, Paddington, London, Eng.; d. Nov. 15, 1878, Bovey Tracey, Devon, Eng.), a minister's daughter, was very gifted in both music and language; taught music in her father's parish school at St. James', Paddington and translated a number of German hymns into English; helped to compile *Garland of Songs, or an English Liederkranz,* 1861; published *A Handbook for Singers* as a textbook for her classes in the parish school.

We plow the fields, and scatter (trans.) (566)

Campbell, John Douglas Sutherland (b. Aug. 6, 1845, St. James, Westminster, Eng.; d. May 2, 1914, East Cowes, Isle of Wight) was chief of the clan of Campbell and the 9th Duke of Argyle; was educated at Eton, St. Andrews, and Trinity College, Cambridge; married Princess Louise, daughter of Queen Victoria; was Governor-General of Canada (1878–83), and also served as a member of Parliament for South Manchester for a total of 12 years; was well known as a writer of both prose and verse, an earnest Christian and a strong churchman.

Unto the hills around (44)

Campbell, Thomas was evidently a native of Sheffield, England, who compiled a collection of his original tunes called *The Bouquet,* published in 1825. In certain hymnals his birth-death dates are given as 1777–1844, the same as those for a "Thomas Campbell" whom Grove's *Dictionary* (p. 202) identifies as "the Poet, (who) has little in common with hymnody," though he wrote several hymn texts. It is possible these individuals are one and the same.

SAGINA (248)

Carlson, Nathaniel (b. Apr. 17, 1879, Gothenberg, Swed.; d. Aug. 2, 1957, Minneapolis, Minn.) attended the Free Church Bible School, Chicago, and Northwest Bible College, Storm Lake, Ia.; a pastor in the Evangelical Free Church, was editor of *Chicagobladet* for several years; wrote many original hymns, both words and music, and translated many songs from Swedish into English; compiled three editions of *Songs of Trust and Triumph* (1929–32).

Love divine, so great and wondrous (trans.) (541)

Carmichael, Ralph Richard (b. May 27, 1927, Quincy, Ill.), born in a minister's home, began to study violin at age four; graduated from high school and attended Southern California College, Costa Mesa, but, according to his own report, "failed college"; served as minister of music at Calvary Assembly, Inglewood, Calif. beginning in 1946, and at Temple Baptist Church, Los Angeles, 1954; long active in professional music in Hollywood, wrote the musical scores for Billy Graham films: *Mr. Texas, For Pete's Sake, The Restless Ones* and *His Land;* is founder (1964) and President of Lexicon Music, Inc., producer of sacred music and recordings; has written some 200 songs in many styles and co-authored several religious folk musicals, including *Tell It Like It Is, Natural High* and *New Wine;* published *The New Church Hymnal,* 1976.

> The Savior is waiting (257); In the stars His handiwork I see (276); Is your burden heavy? (426); Because the Lord is my Shepherd (447)
> CARMICHAEL (257); HE'S EVERYTHING TO ME (276); REACH OUT TO JESUS (426); THE NEW 23RD (447)

Carter, Russell Kelso (b. Nov. 18, 1849, Baltimore, Md.; d. Aug. 23, 1928, Catonsville, Md.) during his lifetime was successively a professor, a sheep rancher, a minister, an author and publisher, and a physician; as a student was an excellent athlete; graduated in the first class of the Pennsylvania Military Academy in 1867, and returned as professor (chemistry, natural science, civil engineering and mathematics) for a number of years; 1873–76, raised sheep in California; in 1887 was ordained into the Methodist ministry and became very active in the Holiness camp meetings; published a great deal in the areas of mathematics, science and religion, as well as several novels; assisted A. B. Simpson in compiling *Hymns of the Christian Life,* 1891, for use in churches of the Christian and Missionary Alliance (contributed some 68 original tunes and 52 poems to this hymnal); later in life, studied medicine and became a practicing physician in Baltimore.

> Standing on the promises (225)
> PROMISES (225)

Caswall, Edward (b. July 15, 1814, Yately, Hants, Eng.; d. Jan. 2, 1878, Edgbaston, Birmingham, Eng.), born in the vicarage at Yately, was educated at Marlborough and Brasenose College, Oxford; was ordained (Anglican Church) in 1839, and appointed curate of Stratford-sub-Castle, near Salisbury; during the Oxford movement, developed great interest in the Roman ritual and in 1847, resigned his pastorate and was received into the Roman Catholic Church; after his wife's death in 1849, became a priest and entered the Oratory of St. Philip Neri at Edgbaston, under Cardinal Newman; a prolific writer, is best known for *Lyra Catholica* (1849) which contained 197 translations of Latin hymns from the *Roman Breviary* and other sources.

> O Jesus, King most wonderful! (trans.) (73); Jesus, the very thought of Thee (trans.) (83); Glory be to Jesus (trans.) (143); When morning gilds the skies (trans.) (550)

Cennick, John (b. Dec. 12, 1718, Reading, Berks, Eng.; d. July 4, 1755, London, Eng.), the son of Quaker parents, grew up in the Church of England; came under the influence of John Wesley (*q.v.*), and gave up his profession of surveyor to join the Methodist movement; was appointed teacher at Kingswood School, Bristol and became a lay preacher; because of doctrinal differences, left the Wesleys and was associated with George Whitefield, but later joined the Moravian Brethren and was ordained by them in 1749; as a Moravian preacher, traveled widely in Germany and Ireland; published *Sacred Hymns for the Children of God* (1741–42) and *Hymns to the Honor of Jesus Christ* (1754), and other works.

Lo, He comes with clouds descending (185); Children of the heavenly King (445)

Chapman, J. Wilbur (b. June 17, 1859, Richmond, Ind.; d. Dec. 25, 1918, Jamaica, L.I., N.Y.) was educated at Lake Forest (Ill.) University and Lane Theological Seminary; was ordained to the Presbyterian ministry and served as a pastor (Albany, N.Y., Philadelphia, and New York City) for almost twenty years; in 1905 became an evangelist, and for more than ten years traveled extensively throughout the world, assisted by Charles M. Alexander, well-known evangelistic singer and choir director; was the first director of the Winona Lake (Ind.) Bible and Chautauqua Conference and was instrumental in starting similar conferences at Montreat, N.C. and Stony Brook, L.I., N.Y.; in 1917 was elected moderator of the General Assembly of the Presbyterian Church, U.S.A.; published eight books, and wrote a number of hymn texts.

Jesus! what a Friend for sinners! (99); One day when heaven was filled with His praises (128)

Charles, Elizabeth Rundle (b. Jan. 2, 1828, Tavistock, Devon, Eng.; d. Mar. 28, 1896, Hampstead Heath, London, Eng.) was the daughter of a member of Parliament and the wife of a lawyer; as a poet, translator, musician, author and painter, became one of the best-known women in England; left numerous writings in many fields, especially church history, which overshadowed somewhat her contribution to hymnody; published *Voice of Christian Life in Song*, 1864, and included some original hymns and translations in *The Chronicles of the Schoenberg-Cotta Family*, 1863.

Praise ye the Father (7)

Charlesworth, Vernon J. (b. Apr. 28, 1839, Barking, Essex, Eng.; d. Jan. 5, 1915, London, Eng.), educated at Homerton College, became co-pastor with Rev. Newman Hall of the old Surrey Chapel in 1864; in 1869 became headmaster of Charles Spurgeon's Stockwell Orphanage; published *The Life of Rowland Hill* (1876), and collaborated with J. Manton Smith in producing *Flowers and Fruits of Sacred Song and Evangelistic Hymns*.

The Lord's our rock, in Him we hide (322)

Chatfield, Allen William (b. Oct. 2, 1808, Chatteris, Cambridge, Eng.; d. Jan. 10, 1896, Much-Marcle, Herts, Eng.) received training at Charterhouse School and Trinity College, Cambridge, where he achieved top class honors; ordained in 1832, was vicar at Stotfold, Bedford and later at Much-Marcle, Herts until his death; translated into Greek some hymns, the litany, the Te Deum, and other parts of the English Church offices; published *Songs and Hymns of the Earliest Greek Christian Poets, Bishops and Others, translated into English Verse,* 1876.

Lord Jesus, think on me (trans.) (341)

Chisholm, Thomas Obediah (b. July 29, 1866, Franklin, Ky.; d. Feb. 29, 1960, Ocean Grove, N.J.), educated in a small country school, became the teacher of that school at age 16; at 21, became associate editor of the weekly newspaper, *The Franklin Favorite;* in 1893 was converted under the ministry of Dr. Henry Clay Morrison (founder of Asbury College and Theological Seminary, Wilmore, Ky.); moved to Louisville at the persuasion of Morrison, and became editor of the *Pentecostal Herald;* was ordained a Methodist minister in 1903 and served a brief pastorate at Scottsville, Ky.; in poor health, moved his family to a farm near Winona Lake, Ind.; became an insurance salesman, moving to Vineland, N.Y. in 1916; retired in 1953 to the Methodist Home for the Aged, Ocean Grove, N.J.; wrote over 1200 poems, of which 800 were published, and many set to music.

Great is Thy faithfulness (37); He was wounded for our transgressions (135); Trust in the Lord with all your heart (319); O to be like Thee! (333); Living for Jesus a life that is true (380)

Chopin, Frederic François (b. Feb. 22, 1810, Zelazowa Wola, Pol.; d. Oct. 17, 1849, Paris, Fr.), a brilliant pianist and a master composer, is remembered for his piano works in many forms; was the son of a Polish mother and a French father; exhibited great talent at a very early age, and studied (with Joseph Elsner) at the Warsaw Conservatorium; in 1832 made his Paris debut, and remained in that city until his death; wrote many compositions which are listed in Grove's *Dictionary of Music and Musicians,* and in other reference works.

Unnamed Tune (586)

Chorley, Henry Fothergill (b. Dec. 15, 1808, Blackley, Lancs, Eng.; d. Feb. 16, 1872, London, Eng.), born of Quaker stock, was largely self-taught; started in a commercial career, but soon discovered that his real interests and gifts lay in music and literature; began to write for the *Athenaeum* and later became its musical editor, as well as music critic for *The Times;* produced many literary works, including *Music and Manners in France and Germany* (1841), *Pomfret* (1845), *Roccabella* (1859), and *The Prodigy* (1866); left a manuscript autobiography, *Memoir and Letters,* which was published posthumously in 1873.

God the Omnipotent! (527)

Christiansen, Avis Marguerite Burgeson (b. Oct. 11, 1895, Chicago, Ill.) collaborated with D. B. Towner (*q.v.*) in her first two songs, included in *Tabernacle Praises,* 1916, the first release of Tabernacle Publishing Company; has lived her entire life in Chicago, and for more than 60 years has written sacred texts which have been set to music by many different composers; is represented in *Hymns for the Living Church* by one hymn published as early as 1920 and another as recently as 1966; was married to the late Ernest C. Christiansen, a vice president of Moody Bible Institute; a longtime member of Moody Church, has written hundreds of gospel hymns and two volumes of poetry.

"What must I do?" (235); Out of the depths to the glory above (292); Fill all my vision, Savior, I pray (367); Only one life to offer (382); Come, come, ye saints (adapt.) (405)

Clark, Jeremiah (b. *ca.* 1669, Eng.; d. Dec. 1, 1707, London, Eng.) studied under John Blow as a chorister in the king's Chapel Royal; served as organist at Winchester College and later at St. Paul's Cathedral; in 1700, with William Croft (*q.v.*), was appointed co-organist of the Chapel Royal; a versatile musician, published a great variety of music for church, concert and stage; took his own life in his house on the grounds of St. Paul's, because of despondency over a thwarted love affair.

ST. MAGNUS (176)

Clark, John Haldenby (b. Jan. 28, 1839, Chesterfield, Derby, Eng.; d. Apr. 14, 1888, Norfolk, Eng.) received his training in Chesterfield and later at St. John's College, Cambridge, graduating in 1861; took Holy Orders and was curate of Barmby Moor and Fangfoss and in 1870, became vicar of West Dereham, Norfolk; published *The Marriage of Cana, and Other Verses,* 1880, containing original poems and translations from the Latin.

Soldiers, who are Christ's below (trans.) (468)

Clark, William H. No information about this individual can be found.

All praise to Him who reigns above (81)

Clarke, Harry D. (b. Jan. 28, 1888, Cardiff, Wales; d. Oct. 14, 1957) was left an orphan at an early age, and had a very hard life as a youth; with the help of a brother, got to London, then Canada, and finally the United States, where he was converted; was a student at the Moody Bible Institute, Chicago in the early 1920's and was active in composing and music publishing; for a number of years was songleader for evangelist Harry Vom Bruch, and also for Billy Sunday in the last years of that evangelist's ministry; later founded the Billy Sunday Memorial Chapel in Sioux City, Ia., and was pastor until 1945; in later life was active in evangelistic work and conferences, with headquarters in Garard's Fort, Pa. and finally in South Milford, Ind.; wrote many songs and choruses, both words and music, which appeared in his *Gospel Truth in Song* (3 vols.), *Fishers of Men, Choruses for Fishers of Men* (2 vols.) and *Songs of Glory;* eventually sold his copyrights to Hope Publishing Company.

BELIEVE (235)

Clarkson, Edith Margaret (b. June 8, 1915, Melville, Sask., Can.) received her schooling at Riverdale Collegiate Institute, Toronto Teachers' College, and University of Toronto; taught elementary school for 38 years (mostly in Toronto), retiring in 1973; has been a member of Presbyterian churches in Toronto, and is active in Inter-Varsity Christian Fellowship, who have published several of her hymns; a prolific and talented writer, has produced textbooks (*Let's Listen to Music*, 1944 and *The Creative Classroom*, 1958), devotional prose (*The Wondrous Cross*, 1966; *God's Hedge*, 1968; *Grace Grows Best in Winter*, 1972), and poetry (*Clear Shining After Rain*, 1962; *Rivers Among the Rocks*, 1968; and *Conversations with a Barred Owl*, 1975); collaborated with the author of this volume in producing lyrics for the cantata, *Celebration of Discipleship*, 1975; has written at least 20 hymns and gospel songs (including the official hymn for the Congress on World Evangelization, Lausanne, Switz., 1974) and has composed music for some of her own texts.

> Come, Thou Fount of every blessing (adapt.) (28); We come, O Christ, to Thee (79); The battle is the Lord's (475); So send I you (481)

Claudius, Matthias (b. Aug. 15, 1740, near Lübeck, Holstein, Ger.; d. Jan. 21, 1815, Hamburg, Ger.), the son of a Lutheran pastor, was educated at the University of Jena; studied for the ministry, but because of poor health and the influence of the rationalism of his day, turned to journalism; was appointed Commissioner of Agriculture and Manufacture of Hesse-Darmstadt, and later became editor of the Hesse-Darmstadt newspaper; came under the influence of Goethe and his associates and began to question his faith, but was restored through a serious illness; was appointed auditor of the Schleswig-Holstein Bank at Altona, 1788; retired at his daughter's home in Hamburg, where he died in 1815; wrote (or translated) and published a large amount of poetry and prose in eight volumes, *Asmus omnia sua secum portans*, 1775–1812.

> We plow the fields, and scatter (566)

Clayton, Norman John (b. Jan. 22, 1903, Brooklyn, N.Y.) first worked on a dairy farm, then spent a number of years in a New York City office, later participated with his father in the construction business; during the depression, worked with a commercial bakery; in the early 1940's, was invited by Jack Wyrtzen (*q.v.*) to be organist for the Word of Life rallies in New York City and remained on Wyrtzen's staff for 15 years; published his own song books, 1945–59, and then merged with the Rodeheaver Company, joining them as a writer-editor; is a Baptist and has been a church organist for 50 years.

> Jesus my Lord will love me forever (277); My hope is in the Lord (308)
> ELLSWORTH (277); WAKEFIELD (308)

Clayton, William (b. July 17, 1814, Penwortham, Lancs, Eng.; d. Dec. 4, 1879, Salt Lake City, Utah) was converted to Mormonism in 1837 and spent three years in missionary work in his native England; emigrated to the United States in 1840 and settled in Nauvoo, Ill., serving as city treasurer and clerk of the Nauvoo Temple; was Joseph Smith's private secretary until the Mormon leader's death in 1844; was one of the group of pioneers who traveled to Utah with Brigham Young, reaching the site of Salt Lake City in 1847; was a member of the Nauvoo Brass Band, and later played second violin in the Salt Lake Theatre orchestra.

Come, come, ye saints (405)

Clement of Alexandria (b. *ca.* 170; d. *ca.* 220), whose full name is given as Titus Flavius Clemens, is thought to have been a native of Athens; probably became a Christian under the teaching of Pantaenus, founder of the Catechetical School (for new believers) in Alexandria; later became the head of this seminary, and the mentor of early Christian theologians, including Origen; authored at least ten works, of which three are considered most important: *Exhortation to the Heathen, Instructor,* and *Stomata, or Miscellanies;* fled from Alexandria during the persecution of Christians by Emperor Severus, and little is known of his later life.

Shepherd of eager youth (74)

Clephane, Elizabeth Cecilia (b. June 18, 1830, Edinburgh, Scot.; d. Feb. 19, 1869, Melrose, Scot.) was author of "The Ninety and Nine," spontaneously set to music by Ira D. Sankey (*q.v.*) in one of D. L. Moody's services in Britain, 1874; was a daughter of the sheriff of Fife, and grew up in the Free Church of Scotland; was affectionately called "Sunbeam" because of her humanitarian concerns; wrote at least eight hymns, printed posthumously (1872–74) in *The Family Treasury,* a Free Church magazine.

Beneath the cross of Jesus (151)

Clough, Samuel O'Malley (b. 1837, Dublin, Ire.; d. 1910, Timahoe, Queens' Co., Ire.), whose family name is sometimes spelled "Cluff," was educated at Trinity College, and ordained a minister in the Church of Ireland (Anglican); in 1874 left the established church and united with the Plymouth Brethren, and later is said to have joined a "holiness" sect; published a group of songs under the title *Timogue Leaflets.*

I have a Savior, He's pleading in glory (436)

Cober, Kenneth L. (b. July 12, 1902, Dayton, Ohio), the son of missionary parents, grew up in Porto Rico; received his education at Bucknell University and Colgate Rochester Divinity School; was pastor of First Baptist Church, Canandaigua, N.Y. and Lafayette Ave. Baptist Church, Buffalo, N. Y.; has served the state conventions of American Baptists in New York, Rhode Island and Connecticut, and was executive director of the Division of Christian Education, American Baptist Convention, 1953–70; in retirement lives at Penney Farms, Florida; has written many books on Christian education, including *The Church's Teaching Ministry,* 1964; was a member of the joint committee for the *Hymnbook for Christian Worship,* 1970.

Renew Thy church, her ministries restore (205)

Codner, Elizabeth (b. 1824, Dartmouth, Devon, Eng.; d. Mar. 28, 1919, Croydon, Surrey, Eng.) was the wife of Rev. Daniel Codner, curate of Peterborough; was associated with Rev. W. and Mrs. Pennefather in their work at Mildmay Protestant Mission, North London, editing their monthly missionary magazine, *Women's Work.*

Lord, I hear of showers of blessing (363)

Coffman, Samuel Frederick (b. June 11, 1872, near Dale Enterprise, Rockingham Co., Va.; d. June 28, 1954, Vineland, Ont., Can.) spent his early years in Elkhart, Ind., graduated from Elkhart High School and attended Moody Bible Institute, Chicago in 1894–95 and 1897–98; was ordained to the ministry in Chicago in April, 1895 and moved to Vineland, Ontario (1896) to serve the Moyer Mennonite Church; in 1903 was ordained to the office of bishop and served Mennonite congregations in the Niagara district; in 1907 organized the Ontario Mennonite Bible School and served as principal until retiring in 1952; was appointed to the music committee of the Mennonite General Conference in 1911 and served the publishing division as hymn editor until 1947; assisted in publishing *Church and Sunday School Hymnal Supplement* (1911), *Life Songs* (1916), *Songs of Cheer for Children* (1928) and *Life Songs No. 2* (1938); wrote a number of hymns and four were included in the Mennonite *Church Hymnal,* 1927, for which he edited the hymns and assisted in editing the music.

We bless the name of Christ the Lord (214)

Collins, Henry (b. 1827, Barningham, Darlington, Eng.; d. Jan. 29, 1919, Coalville, No. Leicester, Eng.) received an M.A. at Oxford and was ordained an Anglican priest in 1853; became a Roman Catholic in 1857 and was admitted to the Cistercian Order in 1860; 1882–1913, served as chaplain to the Cistercian nuns at Staplehill Priory, Wimborne, Dorset; spent his last years at St. Bernard's Abbey (Trappist), Coalville, No. Leicester; contributed two hymns to his collection, *Hymns for Schools and Missions,* 1854.

Jesus, my Lord, my God, my All (335)

Conkey, Ithamar (b. May 5, 1815, Shutesbury, Mass.; d. Apr. 30, 1867, Elizabeth, N.J.) first served as organist and choir director at Central Baptist Church, Norwich, Conn.; in 1850 moved to New York City, where he had a brilliant career as bass soloist in Calvary Episcopal Church and also took part in many oratorio presentations; was soloist and conductor of the quartet-choir at Madison Avenue Baptist Church in New York City for six years preceding his death.

RATHBUN (140)

Converse, Charles Crozat (b. Oct. 7, 1832, Warren, Mass.; d. Oct. 18, 1918, Highwood, N.J.) received his general education at Elmira Academy (N.Y.) and in early life was associated with William B. Bradbury (*q.v.*) and Ira D. Sankey (*q.v.*) in compiling and editing Sunday School songbooks, using the pseudonym "Karl Reden"; later turned to "serious" music and studied in Europe at the Leipzig Conservatory, where he became well acquainted with Franz Liszt and Louis Spohr; returned to America in 1859 and studied law at Albany University; along with his successful law practice in Erie, Pa., was active as a musician and writer, with interests that included philosophy and philology; wrote string quartets, cantatas, chorales, hymn tunes, etc., under many pen names.

CONVERSE (435)

Cook, George Harrison (b. date unknown; d. 1948), according to Phil Kerr in *Music in Evangelism,* was converted at the age of fourteen and had a life-long ministry which included preaching, singing, playing, writing music, directing choirs, organizing bands and orchestras, and training gospel singers; in retirement lived in Ocean Grove, New Jersey.

HEAVENLY SUNLIGHT (403)

Cook, Joseph Simpson (b. Dec. 4, 1859, Durham Co., Eng.; d. May 27, 1933, Toronto, Can.), after early education in England, attended Wesleyan College of McGill University in Montreal, Canada; was ordained to the Methodist ministry and later served the United Church of Canada.

Gentle Mary laid her Child (107)

Cooper, Edward (b. 1770; d. 1833) received schooling at Queen's College and was a fellow of All Souls' College, Oxford; served as rector of the parishes of Hamstall-Ridware and Yoxall, Staffordshire between 1799 and 1833; was one of the ouststanding preachers of the Church of England, and published *Practical and Familiar Sermons* (7 vols.); assisted Jonathan Stubbs in compiling one of the "Staffordshire hymnbooks," *Selection of Psalms and Hymns for Public and Private Use* (1805); in 1811 published *Selection of Psalms and Hymns* for use by his own congregation, with a second edition in 1823.

Father of heaven, whose love profound (5)

Copeland, Roger Alan (b. Mar. 16, 1942, Maud, Okla.) studied piano for 12 years as a youth and received his general education in Maud, Okla.; attended Oklahoma Baptist University (B.A.) and Southwestern Baptist Theological Seminary (M.R.E.); has served several Southern Baptist churches in Oklahoma and Texas as minister of music and youth, and since 1970, the Bellevue Baptist Church, Hurst, Tex.; has written 50 hymn texts and tunes, as well as other contemporary works.

Reach out to your neighbor (501)

REACH OUT (501)

Copenhaver, Laura Scherer (b. Aug. 29, 1868, Marion, Va.; d. Dec. 18, 1940, Marion, Va.) devoted her life to education, church work, and writing, and is credited with beginning the missionary effort of the United Lutheran Church to the Appalachian mountain folk; for 30 years taught English literature at Marion College, a school which her father founded in 1873; wrote a number of pageants and magazine articles that have attracted wide attention.

Heralds of Christ (488)

Copes, Vicar Earle (b. Aug. 12, 1921, Norfolk, Va.) received his B.A. degree at Davidson College (N.C.), his M.S.M. and B.D. at Union Theological Seminary (N.Y.C.), and did further study at the University of Texas; has served as a minister of music in Texas, and as a professor of organ and church music at Hendrix College (Ark.) and Cornell College (Ia.); 1958–67, was music editor for the Methodist General Board of Education in Nashville, Tenn.; since 1967 has been head of the department of organ and church music at Birmingham Southern College (Ala.) and minister of music at Canterbury Methodist Church in Birmingham; has published some 25 anthems, contributed many articles to professional journals, and was the founder and editor of *Music Ministry,* a monthly periodical for Methodist church musicians; was special consultant to the committee which compiled *Methodist Hymnal,* 1966.

> VICAR (515)

Cosin, John (b. Nov. 30, 1594, Norwich, Eng.; d. Jan. 15, 1672, Westminster, Eng.) was trained at Caius College, Cambridge, took Holy Orders and became chaplain to the Bishop of Durham in 1624; served as archdeacon of East Riding, Yorkshire (1625–35), master of Peterhouse, Cambridge (1635–39), and vice-chancellor of Cambridge University (1639–40); was deposed by the "Long Parliament," and served as chaplain to the exiled royal family in France; following the Restoration, was made bishop of Durham and supervised extensive renovation of the cathedral and its library; a liturgical scholar, compiled *Collection of Private Devotions in the Practice of the Ancient Church called the Hours of Prayer,* 1627; assisted in the revision of *The Book of Common Prayer,* 1662, which contains his translation of "Veni, Creator Spiritus."

> Come, Holy Ghost, our souls inspire (trans.) (188)

Cousin, Anne Ross (b. Apr. 27, 1824, Hull, York, Eng.; d. Dec. 6, 1906, Edinburgh, Scot.), an accomplished musician, author and linguist, was the only child of David Ross Cundell, a physician of Leith, Eng.; grew up in the Church of England but later became a Presbyterian and married William Cousin, a Scottish Free Church minister who served successively in Duns, Chelsea, Irvine and Melrose; contributed hymns anonymously to *The Christian Treasury* which were collected and published in *Immanuel's Land and Other Poems,* 1876; has been called "a Scottish Christina Rossetti, with a more pronounced theology."

> The sands of time are sinking (535)

Cowper, William (b. Nov. 15, 1731, Berkhampstead, Herts, Eng.; d. Apr. 25, 1800, East Dereham, Norfolk, Eng.) was regarded by many as the leading English poet of his day, especially for his translation of Homer in 1791; was the son of John C. Cowper, who was chaplain to George II; studied law at Westminster School and was admitted to the bar in 1754, but never practiced; suffered periods of depression throughout his life and had great dread of public appearances; lived mostly under the guardianship of Rev. and Mrs. Morley Unwin; spent his 19 most productive years at Olney, where he collaborated with John Newton in compiling the historic *Olney Hymns,* 1779, with 67 of his texts in the collection.

God moves in a mysterious way (47); There is a fountain filled with blood (230); O for a closer walk with God (352)

Cox, Frances Elizabeth (b. May 10, 1812, Oxford, Eng.; d. Sept. 23, 1897, Headington, Eng.) is known chiefly for her hymns translated from the German; was assisted in her choice of hymns by Baron Bunsen, ambassador of Prussia to England, 1841–54; published *Sacred Hymns from the German,* 1841 and *Hymns from the German,* 1864.

Sing praise to God who reigns above (trans.) (13)

Coxe, Arthur Cleveland (b. May 10, 1818, Mendham, N.J.; d. July 20, 1896, Clifton Springs, N.Y.), son of a prominent Presbyterian minister, Samuel Cox, was educated at New York University; differed with his father on theological issues, attended General Theological Seminary (N.Y.C.) and was ordained an Episcopal priest, changing his name from Cox to Coxe; served as rector of churches in Connecticut, Maryland and New York City and in 1865 was elected Bishop of Western New York; early in life wrote poetry which appeared in his *Advent* (1837), *Christian Ballads* (1840), and *Athanasion* (1842); was a member of the hymnal commission of his own church, but refused to allow his own poems to be included in the Episcopal *Hymnal,* 1871.

We are living, we are dwelling (464)

Croft, William (baptized Dec. 30, 1678, Nether Eatington, Warwick, Eng.; d. Aug. 14, 1727, Bath, Eng.) in early life wrote secular music, but later became one of England's most significant composers of church music; was a boy chorister in St. James' Chapel Royal and studied organ under John Blow; was organist of St. Anne's, Soho for 11 years; served (first with Jeremiah Clark and later alone) as organist of the Chapel Royal; in 1708 followed John Blow as organist of Westminster Abbey and composer to the Chapel Royal; contributed many tunes to *The Divine Companion,* 1707 and the *Supplement to the New Version,* 1708, which mark the transition from the older "Genevan" to the newer style of English psalmody.

HANOVER (19); ST. ANNE (48)

Croly, George (b. Aug. 17, 1780, Dublin, Ire.; d. Nov. 24, 1860, Holborn, Eng.), a graduate of Trinity College, Dublin, took Anglican Holy Orders in 1804 and served in Ireland for six years; at age 30, moved to London and devoted himself with great success to literary work, writing novels, historical and theological works, dramas, poetry, and satires; was editor of *The Universal Review,* and contributed frequently to such publications as *Blackwood's Magazine* and *Britannia;* in 1835 became rector at St. Stephen's and St. Bene't Sherehog, Walbrook, and during his ministry there, published *Psalms and Hymns for Public Worship,* 1854.

Spirit of God, descend upon my heart (198)

Crosby, Fanny Jane (b. Mar. 24, 1820, Putnam Co., N.Y.; d. Feb. 12, 1915, Bridgeport, Conn.) was the most prolific and significant writer of gospel songs in American history, and also a concert singer, organist and harpist; at the age of six weeks, was blinded for life because of improper treatment of an eye infection; began writing verse at the age of eight; studied at the New York City School for the Blind and later taught there, attracting the attention of prominent individuals, including U.S. presidents, because of her poetic gift; married Alexander Van Alstyne, a blind musician, who also taught at the New York school; wrote texts for the minstrel songs and cantatas of George F. Root (*q.v.*) and others, publishing several books of secular verse: *A Blind Girl, and Other Poems* (1844), *Monterey, and Other Poems* (1849), and *A Wreath of Columbia's Flowers* (1858); at age 44 began to write hymns, producing perhaps 8500 texts, many set to music by the day's leading gospel song composers and published, mostly by the Biglow and Main Company; was also active as a devotional speaker and a counselor until she was past 90 years of age; has a recent biographical study, *Fanny Crosby,* by Bernard Ruffin (United Church Press, 1976).

> To God be the glory (40); Praise Him! praise Him! (96); Tell me the story of Jesus (130); My song shall be of Jesus (251); Jesus is tenderly calling you home (272); Redeemed, how I love to proclaim it (285); Blessed assurance, Jesus is mine (317); More like Jesus would I be (334); I am Thine, O Lord (354); Jesus, keep me near the cross (361); A wonderful Savior is Jesus my Lord (402); 'Tis the blessed hour of prayer (433); All the way my Savior leads me (440); Rescue the perishing (480)

Crotch, William (b. July 5, 1775, Green's Lane, Norwich, Eng.; d. Dec. 29, 1847, Taunton, Eng.), a musical prodigy, gave a series of public recitals at the age of four; at age 11, studied at Cambridge with John Randall, and assisted him as organist at both Trinity College and King's College; began theological study at age 13 but decided to follow a musical career, accepting the position of organist at Christ Church, Oxford, while continuing musical studies; received the Mus.B. and Mus.D. degrees at Christ Church and served there (1797–1807) as professor of music; became the first principal of the Royal Academy of Music in 1822; wrote two oratorios, works for organ and piano, 10 anthems, and a number of books on the theory of music, but is remembered primarily for his 74 chants written for Anglican worship.

> ST. MICHAEL (arr.) (22)

Crüger, Johann (b. Apr. 9, 1598, Grossbreesen, Prussia; d. Feb. 23, 1662, Berlin), beginning in 1644, edited the first editions of *Praxis Pietatis Melica* ("the practice of piety through melody")—the most important contribution of the 17th century to hymnody; was educated at the Jesuit College of Olmütz, at the University of Regensburg (studied music under Paul Homberger) and completed his theological work at the University of Wittenberg; from 1622, served as cantor at St. Nicholas Cathedral in Berlin, where he organized and directed the choir; also taught at the *Gymnasium zum Grauen Kloster,* and remained in Berlin until his death; in the above-mentioned volumes, collected chorales and *magnificats* which are a prime source of Lutheran hymnody.

HERZLIEBSTER JESU (152); ZUVERSICHT (159); GRÄFENBERG (432); NUN DANKET ALLE GOTT (564)

Crum, John Macleod Campbell (b. Oct. 12, 1872, Mere Old Hall, Cheshire, Eng.; d. Dec. 19, 1958, Farnham, Surrey, Eng.) was educated at Eton and New College, Oxford; during his long ministry in the Church of England, served as Domestic Chaplain to the Bishop of Oxford, vicar of Mentmore with Ledburn, rector of Farnham, and canon of Canterbury; published theological works, like *Road Mending on the Sacred Way* (1924), *The Original Jerusalem Gospel* (1927) and *St. Mark's Gospel, Two Stages of Its Making* (1936); wrote hymns, principally for children or for special occasions.

Now the green blade riseth (162)

Cummings, William Hayman (b. Aug. 22, 1831, Sidbury, Devon, Eng.; d. June 6, 1915, London, Eng.) at the age of seven sang in the choir at St. Paul's Cathedral and later at Temple Church; at 16, sang in the premiere performance of Mendelssohn's *Elijah* with the composer conducting; as an adult, was highly acclaimed as a tenor soloist in Great Britain and America, particularly for his performances of the Bach Passion music; served as organist at Waltham Abbey, professor of singing (1879–96) at the Royal Academy of Music, and subsequently followed Joseph Barnby (*q.v.*) as principal of the Guildhall School of Music; was renowned as a musicologist (an authority on Purcell!), lecturer and composer.

MENDELSSOHN (arr.) (106)

Cushing, William Orcutt (b. Dec. 31, 1823, Hingham Center, Mass.; d. Oct. 19, 1902, Lisbon, N.Y.), a minister of the Christian Church (Disciples of Christ), served many pastorates in the state of New York; retired from active ministry in 1870 because of ill health which deprived him of his power of speech, and became interested in hymn writing; wrote more than 300 hymns which have been set to music by Ira D. Sankey (*q.v.*), George F. Root (*q.v.*), Robert Lowry (*q.v.*), and others.

Under His wings I am safely abiding (310); O safe to the Rock that is higher than I (400)

Cutler, Henry Stephen (b. Oct. 13, 1824, Boston, Mass.; d. Dec. 5, 1902, Boston, Mass.) is said to be the first church musician to introduce robed choirs to America; received much of his musical training in England, where he became interested in cathedral choirs; returning to Boston, was organist at Grace Episcopal Church, and later at the Church of the Advent, where his choir of men and boys was the first to wear robes in this country; beginning in 1858, served as organist at Trinity Church, New York City for seven years, and then in several other churches in the East; retired in 1885 and returned to Boston; composed anthems, service music and hymn tunes, and published the *Trinity Psalter,* 1864 and *Trinity Anthems,* 1865.

ALL SAINTS, NEW (467, 485)

Danker, William John (b. June 19, 1914, Willow Creek, Minn.) received his schooling at Concordia College (Milwaukee, Wis.), Concordia Seminary (St. Louis, Mo.), Wheaton College (B.A.), University of Chicago (M.A.), and the University of Heidelberg (D.Theol., *magna cum laude*); was ordained and served at St. Paul's Lutheran Church, Harvard, Ill. (1937–42) and Trinity Lutheran Church, West Chicago, Ill. (1942–48); was the first missionary to Japan for the Lutheran Church—Missouri Synod, 1948–55, and then professor at Concordia Seminary and director of the World Mission Institute; since 1974 has been Professor of World Mission at Concordia Seminary in Exile, Director of the Center for World Christian Interaction, and project coordinator for the World Hunger Appeal of the Lutheran Church—Missouri Synod; has published *Two Worlds or None; Rediscovering Missions* (1964), *Profit for the Lord* (1971), *More Than Healing: The Story of Kiyoko Matsuda* (1973), and numerous articles in various publications.

The sending, Lord, springs (477)

Darwall, John (b. 1731, Haughton, Staffs, Eng.; d. Dec. 18, 1789, Walsall, Eng.) received his education at Manchester Grammar School and Brasenose College, Oxford; in 1757 became curate and later, vicar of St. Matthew's Church in Walsall, where he spent the rest of his life; composed two volumes of sonatas for the piano, and tunes for all of the 150 psalms (Tate and Brady's *New Version*) in three manuscript volumes, a few of which were published in various psalters.

DARWALL (70, 79, 177)

Davison, Fannie Estelle (b. 1851, Cuyahoga Falls, Ohio; d. Mar. 10, 1887, Chicago, Ill.), born in Ohio, lost her father in an accident when she was 10; with her mother and new step-father, Henry C. Warner, moved to Carthage, Mo.; married Asa Lee Davison, a court reporter); and they settled in Chicago, Ill., later moving to Madison, Wis.; wrote a number of hymns which appeared in publications of Fillmore Bros., Cincinnati, including *Joy and Gladness* (1880), and *The Voice of Joy* (1882).

Purer in heart, O God (389)

Dearmer, Percy (b. Feb. 27, 1867, Kilburn, Middlesex, Eng.; d. May 29, 1936, Westminster, London, Eng.) attended Westminster School and Christ Church, Oxford; was ordained an Anglican priest in 1892 and served several curacies before becoming vicar of St. Mary's, Primrose Hill, London; a dedicated Christian socialist, served the London Christian Social Union as its secretary, and was chaplain to the British Red Cross in Serbia during World War I; was appointed professor of ecclesiastical art, King's College, London (1919), and in 1931 was made a canon of Westminster; had many intellectual interests, but made his greatest literary contribution as a hymnodist; collaborated with Ralph Vaughan Williams (*q.v.*) in editing the *English Hymnal* (1906), and with both Vaughan Williams and Martin Shaw (*q.v.*) in *Songs of Praise* (1925), *Oxford Book of Carols* (1928), and *Songs of Praise Enlarged* (1931); authored *Songs of Praise Discussed* (1933), a hymnal companion.

Remember all the people (474)

Decius, Nicolaus (b. *ca.*1490, Hof, Franconia, Bavaria; d. Mar. 21, 1541, Stettin) received his training in a Latin school in Hof and the University of Leipzig; became a monk, and served as the provost of the Benedictine nunnery at Steterburg; later, was involved in the Reformation movement and entered the University of Wittenberg to study theology under Martin Luther (*q.v.*) in 1523; served as pastor in Stettin and Leibstadt and finally settled in Mühlhausen; became sympathetic to the cause of the many Calvinists in Mühlhausen and this is thought to be the reason Luther never recognized his work; wrote a number of the earliest Lutheran hymns, two of which are found in almost all Lutheran hymnals, as well as in many others; died suddenly, possibly at the hands of his Roman Catholic enemies.

  All glory be to God on High (10)

  ALLEIN GOTT IN DER HÖH (10)

Dexter, Henry Martyn (b. Aug. 13, 1821, Plympton, Mass.; d. Nov. 13, 1890, Boston, Mass.) graduated from Yale (1840) and Andover Theological Seminary (1844) and was ordained to the Congregational ministry; served as pastor at Manchester, N.H., and was also editor of *The Congregationalist* and *The Congregational Quarterly;* eventually resigned from the pastorate to serve full time as editor of *The Congregationalist and Recorder;* was a careful scholar who was particularly interested in the early roots of Congregationalism in England and Holland; is remembered in hymnology for this one paraphrase, which has been used for over 125 years.

  Shepherd of eager youth (trans.) (74)

Dix, William Chatterton (b. June 14, 1837, Bristol, Eng.; d. Sept. 9, 1898, Cheddar, Somerset, Eng.) was the son of a surgeon who wrote *Life of Chatterton* (the poet); trained at Bristol for a mercantile career and became manager of a marine insurance company in Glasgow; wrote a number of hymns, and versified many translations from the Greek, publishing *Hymns of Love and Joy* (1861), *Altar Songs, Verses on the Holy Eucharist* (1867), *A Vision of All Saints* (1871), and *Seekers of a City* (1878).

  What Child is this, who, laid to rest (adapt.) (105); As with gladness men of old (114); Alleluia! sing to Jesus (174)

Dixon, Helen Cadbury Alexander (b. 1877, Birmingham, Eng.; d. Mar. 1, 1969, Birmingham, Eng.) was the daughter of Richard Cadbury, a prominent British industrialist and philanthropist who was a member of the Quaker fellowship and keenly interested in evangelical mission work; attended the university and spent some time in Germany, studying music and language; in 1904 married Charles M. Alexander, songleader with evangelist R. A. Torrey; traveled with her husband and assisted him in his worldwide ministry with both Torrey and J. Wilbur Chapman (*q.v.*), until his death in 1920; assisted J. Kennedy Maclean in writing the biography, *Charles M. Alexander: A Romance of Song and Soul-Winning,* 1921; in 1924 married Amsji C. Dixon.

  Anywhere with Jesus I can safely go (st. 3) (328)

Doane, George Washington (b. May 27, 1799, Trenton, N.J.; d. Apr. 27, 1859, Burlington, N.J.) was among the first Americans in the Episcopal tradition to support hymn singing apart from psalmody; studied at Union College, Schenectady, N.Y., preparing for a career in law but later turned to theology and was one of the first students at General Theological Seminary, N.Y.C.; was ordained in 1823, and served as assistant priest at Trinity Church, New York; was named professor of rhetoric and *belles-lettres* at Trinity College (Hartford, Conn.) and later became rector of Boston's Trinity Church; was consecrated Bishop of New Jersey at the age of 33, and became one of the leaders of the missionary movement in the Episcopal church; founded St. Mary's Hall, a girl's school, and Burlington College for men; published an American edition of John Keble's (*q.v.*) *Christian Year* in 1834; wrote many hymns, a number of which were included in *Songs by the Way, Chiefly Devotional,* 1824, with reprints in 1859 and 1875.

Fling out the banner! let it float (490); Softly now the light of day (556)

Doane, William Howard (b. Feb. 3, 1832, Preston, Conn.; d. Dec. 24, 1915, South Orange, N.J.) was Fanny Crosby's principal collaborator in writing gospel songs; received schooling at Woodstock Academy, where he conducted the school choir at age 14; as a youth, worked in a cloth manufacturing business with his father; later became the head of a large woodworking machinery plant in Cincinnati, and was a respected civic leader in that city; as an avocation, wrote songs, cantatas, and ballads, both secular and sacred; worked with Moody and Sankey in the cause of evangelism, and was superintendent of the Mt. Auburn Baptist Sunday School at Auburn, Ohio for some 25 years; wrote more than 2200 gospel song tunes and edited over 40 song books, of which *Silver Spray* (1867) was probably the most famous and had the largest sale; left a fortune in trust which has been used in many philanthropic causes, including the construction of Doane Memorial Music Building at Moody Bible Institute, a facility which this book's author had a part in designing.

TO GOD BE THE GLORY (40); PRECIOUS NAME (66); ALSTYNE (251); MORE LIKE JESUS (334); I AM THINE (354); MORE LOVE TO THEE (359); NEAR THE CROSS (361); BLESSED HOUR (433); RESCUE (480)

Doddridge, Philip (b. June 26, 1702, London, Eng.; d. Oct. 26, 1751, Lisbon, Port.) was the youngest of 20 children, only two of whom survived infancy—born into the family of a London merchant who suffered a great deal of religious persecution; orphaned at the age of 13, was offered the opportunity to study for the priesthood in the Church of England by the Duchess of Bedford, but chose instead to attend the nonconformist academy at Kibworth in Leicestershire; in 1729 became a minister at Northampton and for 22 years was head of an academy there; a man of great learning, wrote many theological books, of which *The Rise and Progress of Religion in the Soul* (1745) was the most notable, published in many editions and translated into many different languages; authored almost 400 hymns which showed unusual social and missionary concern for their time, all of them published in 1755, after his death.

See Israel's gentle Shepherd stand (216); O happy day that fixed my choice (239); Awake, my soul, stretch every nerve (454); Great God, we sing that mighty hand (563); Now to the King of heaven (580)

Doudney, Sarah (b. Jan. 15, 1841, Portsea, Eng.; d. Dec. 15, 1926, Headington, Eng.) showed literary ability at a very early age; lived a quiet life in the small village of Cobham in Hampshire, and continued to write throughout her lifetime; wrote many novels, and was a regular contributor to the *Sunday Magazine,* which published many of her poems; is represented by seven hymns in the Sunday School Union's *Songs of Gladness,* 1871, and published her own *Psalms of Life* the same year.

The Master has come, and He calls us to follow (499)

Douglas, Charles Winfred (b. Feb. 15, 1867, Oswego, N.Y.; d. Jan. 18, 1944, Santa Rosa, Calif.) was one of America's foremost authorities on Gregorian chant; the son of a schoolteacher, first served as organist at the local Presbyterian church at the age of 16; received his higher education at Syracuse University and St. Andrew's Divinity School, Syracuse; was ordained an Episcopal priest in 1899 and did further study in England, France and Germany, preparing him for the 40 years of work in which he dominated the liturgical, linguistic, and musical life of the Protestant Episcopal Church; founded the annual summer school of church music at Evergreen, Colo., and served as director of music at the Community of St. Mary, Peekskill, N.Y. (from 1906) and chaplain of the Community of St. Mary, Kenosha, Wis. (from 1934); espoused the revival of plainsong in worship and was in great demand as a lecturer and writer on a variety of subjects; was musical editor of the Episcopal Church's *New Hymnal,* 1916 and 1918, and its successor, *Hymnal 1940;* wrote *Church Music in History and Practice,* 1937, which was revised in 1962 by Leonard Ellinwood.

DIVINUM MYSTERIUM (arr.) (122)

Doving, Carl (b. Mar. 21, 1867, Norddalen, Norway; d. Oct. 2, 1937, Chicago, Ill.) emigrated to the United States at the age of 23, and attended Luther College, Decorah, Ia., and Luther Seminary, St. Paul, Minn.; pastored Norwegian Lutheran congregations in Montevideo and Red Wing, Minn., and Brooklyn, N.Y.; was a gifted linguist, which served him well in his final work as a city missionary in Chicago, visiting in the hospitals of various ethnic neighborhoods; was a member of a committee appointed by three Norwegian synods to compile the English-language *Lutheran Hymnary,* 1913, which included 32 of his translations of German and Scandinavian hymns.

Built on the Rock the church doth stand (trans.) (201)

Draper, William Henry (b. Dec. 19, 1855, Kenilworth, Warwick, Eng.; d. Aug. 9, 1933, Clifton, Bristol, Eng.), after schooling at Cheltenham College and Keble College, Oxford, was ordained in 1880, serving various Anglican churches as curate, vicar and rector; made significant literary contributions in the field of hymnology, specializing in translating hymns from Latin and Greek; published *Hymns for Holy Week* (1897)—translations from the Greek church, *The Victoria Book of Hymns* (1897), *Hymns for Tunes by Orlando Gibbons* (1925), etc.; edited *Seven Spiritual Songs by Thomas Campion* (1919).

All creatures of our God and King (trans.) (59)

Drese, Adam (b. Dec., 1620, Darmstadt, Thüringia; d. Feb. 15, 1701, Arnstadt, Thüringia) was court musician for Duke Wilhelm of Weimar, and under his patronage was sent to Warsaw to study under Marco Sacchi; served as the Duke's *kapellmeister* until Wilhelm's death, when his son Bernhard took Drese with him to Jena; eventually became Mayor of Jena, 1672; was appointed *kapellmeister* at Arnstadt, 1683, and served until his death; became interested in the work of the Pietists, worshipped with them and wrote many tunes for their hymns; because of his new religious convictions, destroyed his operas; wrote a treatise on music theory (remains undiscovered), a collection of instrumental music, and many hymn tunes, 14 of which are in Georg Neumark's *Musikalisches Lustwäldlein,* 1652.

ROCHELLE (450)

Duffield, George, Jr. (b. Sept. 12, 1818, Carlisle, Pa.; d. July 6, 1888, Bloomfield, N.J.) had a long Presbyterian heritage, studied at Yale University and Union Theological Seminary, and was ordained into the Presbyterian ministry in 1840; was dedicated to building up small congregations, so served many different pastorates in New York, New Jersey, Pennsylvania, Illinois and Michigan; for seven years served as a regent of the University of Michigan and for a time was editor of the *Christian Observer,* a Presbyterian family newspaper; in retirement lived in Bloomfield, N.J. with his son, the Rev. Samuel W. Duffield, author of *English Hymns, Their Authors and History,* 1886.

Stand up, stand up for Jesus (455, 456)

Dunbar, C. R. No information has been found on this composer, but he is thought to have lived in America in the late 19th century.

DUNBAR (368)

Dunlop, Merrill Everett (b. May 9, 1905, Chicago, Ill.) in the 1930's was considered an *avant garde* composer of gospel songs; has had many years of specialized study in piano, organ, music theory and composition; received his B.A. degree from Central YMCA College, Chicago and graduated in the class of 1926 at Moody Bible Institute; served as pianist-organist of Moody Church (1921–24) and Director of Music for the Chicago Gospel Tabernacle (1926–53), working with Paul Rader and Clarence Erickson; since 1953 has been involved in musical evangelism with headquarters at his home in Oak Park, Ill.; has written over 700 hymns and gospel songs and published 10 volumes, the most significant of which are *Songs of a Christian,* 1937, and *New Songs of a Christian,* 1941.

OAK PARK (135); ONLY ONE LIFE (382)

Dwight, Timothy (b. May 14, 1752, Northampton, Mass.; d. Jan. 11, 1817, Philadelphia, Pa.), a grandson of the historic preacher Jonathan Edwards, entered Yale University at the age of 13 and graduated with highest honors; so injured his eyesight with long hours of study by candlelight, that as an adult he could read for only 15 minutes a day; served as chaplain in the Revolutionary Army and was a Congregational minister in Greenfield, Conn.; became President of Yale at the age of 43, was loved by the students, and held in high esteem as an educator, teacher, preacher and writer; revised Isaac Watts' (*q.v.*) *Psalms and Hymns*, adding 33 of his own texts to the completed work which was published in 1801 and known as "Dwight's Watts," the most popular hymnal in Presbyterian and Congregational churches in Connecticut in the early 19th century.

I love Thy kingdom, Lord (203)

Dyer, Samuel (b. Nov. 4, 1785, Wellshire, Eng.; d. July 20, 1835, Hoboken, N.J.) was educated in his native England and came to America in 1811, teaching music and directing choirs in New York City and Philadelphia; after a brief return visit to England for further study and research, settled in Baltimore and seriously engaged in writing; was in much demand as a conductor of singing schools in the south and east and at one time was conductor of the New York Sacred Music Society; published church music materials under the titles: *New Selection of Sacred Music* (1817), *The Philadelphia Collection of Sacred Music,* (N.Y., 1828) and *Anthems* (1822 and 1834), all with several editions that are considered important contributions to hymnody.

MENDON (arr.) (30, 188)

Dykes, John Bacchus (b. Mar. 10, 1823, Kingston-upon-Hull, Eng.; d. Jan. 22, 1876, Ticehurst, Sussex, Eng.) at ten years of age played the organ in Hull, where his grandfather was minister; was trained at Wakefield and St. Catherine's College, Cambridge, and later in life received an honorary D.Mus. degree from Durham University; after a brief pastorate, became a minor canon and precentor at Durham Cathedral; in 1862 became vicar of St. Oswald, Durham, and remained until his death; is credited with having written 300 hymn tunes, most of which first appeared in one of the editions of *Hymns Ancient and Modern* or Chope's *Congregational Hymn and Tune Book,* 1857.

NICAEA (1); MELITA (2); DOMINUS REGIT ME (46); ST. AGNES (83, 197, 414, 531); LITANY OF THE PASSION (202); VOX DILECTI (309); BEATITUDO (352); LUX BENIGNA (442); KEBLE (511); ALFORD (537)

Edgar, Mary Susanne (b. May 23, 1889, Sundridge, Ontario, Can.), educated at Havergal College and the University of Toronto, was also a graduate of the National Training School of the Y.W.C.A. in New York City; a member of the Anglican church, was for many years associated with the Y.W.C.A. of Canada, and established Camp Glen Bernard for Girls in northern Ontario; traveled widely, then retired in Toronto in 1955; published collections of poems and essays, *Woodfire and Candlelight* (1945), *Under Open Skies* (1955), and *A Christmas Wreath of Verse* (1965), and wrote a number of hymns, mostly for outdoor or ecumenical use.

God who touches earth with beauty (388)

Edmeston, James (b. Sept. 10, 1791, London, Eng.; d. Jan. 7, 1867, Homerton, Middlesex, Eng.) was born into a family of Congregationalists, but later joined the Church of England; a prominent London architect, surveyor and teacher, was greatly interested in the work of the London Orphan Asylum; wrote some 2000 hymns, many for use in his family's devotional time and many for the children of the orphans' home; published *Sacred Lyrics*, 1820 and *Infant Breathings, Being Hymns for the Young*, 1846.

Savior, breathe an evening blessing (558)

Edmunds, Lidie H. Positive information about this author is not available. However, research by Andrew J. Hayden of Tonbridge, Kent, England recently uncovered the recorded death of a "Lydia Hornsby Edmonds" (*sic*) in 1889 at the age of 40, in Bristol. Not all births before 1875 were recorded in England and her birthdate could not be traced. It is quite possible that this is the same individual.

My faith has found a resting place (287)

Ellerton, John (b. Dec. 16, 1826, London, Eng.; d. June 15, 1893, Torquay, Devon, Eng.) received his schooling at King William's College on the Isle of Man and Trinity College, Cambridge; was ordained in 1850 and served as curate of Eastbourne and of Brighton, vicar of Crewe Greene, and rector of Hinstock, of Barnes, and of White Roding; first wrote hymns for children in his parish at Brighton; became recognized as an authoritative hymnologist of his day; assisted in compiling the 1875 and 1889 editions of *Hymns Ancient and Modern, Church Hymns* (1871), and the *London Mission Hymn Book* (1884); wrote 68 hymns for special days and observances, and translated a large number which are still in use; published *Hymns for Schools and Bible Classes* (1859) and *Hymns, Original and Translated* (1888).

"Welcome, happy morning!" (trans.) (169); God the Omnipotent! (st. 3) (527); O perfect Love, all human thought transcending (st. 4) (529)

Elliott, Charlotte (b. Mar. 18, 1789, London, Eng.; d. Sept. 22, 1871, Brighton, Eng.), though an invalid for the last 50 years of her life, was one of Britain's outstanding women-hymnists in the 19th century; through a long friendship with the Geneva evangelist, H. A. César Malan, was strongly influenced to devote her life to religious and humanitarian writing; wrote 150 hymns which appeared in *The Invalid's Hymn-Book* (1834), *Hours of Sorrow* (1836), *Hymns for a Week* (1839), *Psalms and Hymns for Public, Private and Social Worship* (1838–48), and *Thoughts in Verse on Sacred Subjects* (1869).

Just as I am, without one plea (260); O holy Savior, Friend unseen (315); Jesus, my Savior, look on me (427)

Elliott, Emily Elizabeth Steele (b. July 22, 1836, Brighton, Eng.; d. Aug. 3, 1897, London, Eng.) was the niece of Charlotte Elliott (*q.v.*) and the daughter of an Anglican clergyman; wrote a large number of hymns for use in their parish church in Brighton and also in hospitals and infirmaries; was editor for many years of *The Church Missionary Juvenile Instructor,* in which her hymns frequently appeared; published *Chimes of Consecration* (1873) and *Chimes for Daily Service* (1880).

Thou didst leave Thy throne (124)

Ellor, James (b. 1819, Droylsden, Lancs, Eng.; d. Sept. 27, 1899, Newburgh, N.Y.) learned the hat making trade as a youth in his home town; also had musical gifts and directed the choir in the Wesleyan Chapel at the age of 18; came to the United States in 1843 and resumed the hat making trade; in later life was blind.

DIADEM (62)

Elvey, George Job (b. Mar. 27, 1816, Canterbury, Eng.; d. Dec. 9, 1893, Windlesham, Surrey, Eng.), born into a musical family, was a boy chorister at Canterbury Cathedral, and studied with his brother Stephen at the Royal Academy of Music; was a capable organist at age 17, and at 19 was appointed "master of the boys" and organist at St. George's Chapel, Windsor, serving the royal family there for almost 50 years; was knighted by Queen Victoria in 1871; composed two oratorios, *The Resurrection and Ascension* (1840) and *Mount Carmel* (1886), as well as anthems and service music.

DIADEMATA (85, 376, 422, 458, 519); ST. GEORGE'S, WINDSOR (565)

Emurian, Ernest Krikor (b. Feb. 20, 1912, Philadelphia, Pa.) is a fourth generation preacher and the son of a composer, hymn writer and publisher; received his B.A. degree at Davidson College (N.C.), B.D. from Union Theological Seminary (Va.), and Th.M. from Princeton Theological Seminary (N.J.); was awarded the honorary D.D. degree in 1971 from Randolph-Macon College in Virginia; a Methodist, has served various churches in the Virginia Conference and, since 1962 has been pastor of Cherrydale United Methodist Church in Arlington; is the author of 19 books (mostly popular studies in hymnology) and 60 hymns; has composed hymn tunes, anthems and semi-popular songs and was a pioneer in religious drama, with 120 plays to his credit; is a popular lecturer on hymnology and religious drama, and a "philosophical humorist," appearing at conventions and conferences in many states.

We thank Thee that Thy mandate (517)

Evans, David (b. Feb. 6, 1874, Resolven, Glamorgan, Wales; d. May 17, 1948, Rhosllan-nerchrugog, near Wrexham, Wales) received his education at Arnold College in Swansea, University College in Cardiff, and Oxford University (Mus.D.); was organist at the Jewin Street Welsh Presbyterian Church in London; 1903-39, served as professor of music at the University College, Cardiff; edited the Welsh musical periodical *Y Cerddor,* and was a leader in the Welsh singing festivals; composed *Alcestis* for chorus and string orchestra, and many cantatas and anthems; was musical editor of the *Church Hymnary* (rev. 1927), used in many English-speaking Presbyterian churches around the world.

MADRID (arr.) (60); NYLAND (arr.) (327); BUNESSAN (arr.) (553)

Everest, Charles William (b. May 27, 1814, East Windsor, Conn.; d. Jan. 11, 1877, Waterbury, Conn.) graduated from Trinity College, Hartford and was ordained in 1842; served as rector of the Episcopal church in Hampden, Conn. for 31 years; at the age of 19, published *Visions of Death and Other Poems,* 1833; contributed texts to *Hymns Ancient and Modern,* 1861.

"Take up your cross," the Savior said (357)

Ewing, Alexander (b. Jan. 3, 1830, Old Machar, Aberdeen, Scot.; d. July 11, 1895, Taunton, Somerset, Eng.) is remembered in hymnology for this one world-renowned hymn tune; an accomplished musician, studied the art in Heidelberg, but never pursued it professionally; studied law briefly at Marischal College, Aberdeen and became a member of the Haydn Society and Harmonic Choir while there; served during the Crimean War (1855) and rose to the rank of Lieutenant-Colonel; a skilled linguist, served his government's foreign service in Australia and China.

EWING (536)

Excell, Edwin Othello (b. Dec. 13, 1851, Stark Co., Ohio; d. June 10, 1921, Louisville, Ky.), the son of a German Reformed pastor, worked as a plasterer and bricklayer as a young man; also had musical gifts, and became popular as a singing school teacher; was converted while leading the music in a revival in a Methodist Episcopal Church; turned his interest to sacred music, studied under George F. (*q.v.*) and Frederick Root and published gospel songbooks after moving to Chicago in 1883; was well-known as a congregational song leader, working with Evangelist Sam Jones; died while assisting Gipsy Smith in a citywide revival in Louisville, Ky.; composed music for over 2000 gospel songs and published some 90 songbooks; left a large number of copyrights, which were purchased by Hope Publishing Company in 1931 and combined with their affiliate, Biglow and Main, to become the Biglow-Main-Excell Company.

I have a song I love to sing (280)

EXCELL (146); OTHELLO (280); AMAZING GRACE (arr.) (288); BLESSINGS (569)

Faber, Frederick William (b. June 28, 1814, Calverly, York, Eng.; d. Sept. 26, 1863, London, Eng.) was trained at Shrewsbury and Harrow and received higher education at Balliol and University Colleges, Oxford; in 1842 was ordained in the Church of England and served the parish of Elton, Hunts as rector; in 1845, became a Roman Catholic and was eventually appointed superior of the Brompton Oratory in London; desired to produce hymns for Roman Catholics with the same appeal as Newton and Cowper's *Olney Hymns;* wrote 150 hymns, published in his *Hymns* (1849 and 1862), *Jesus and Mary—Catholic Hymns for Singing and Reading* (1849 and 1852), *All for Jesus, or the Easy Ways of Divine Love* (1853), and *Oratory Hymns* (1854).

My God, how wonderful Thou art (33); Faith of our fathers (206); There's a wideness in God's mercy (233)

Fallersleben, Heinrich August Hoffmann von (see Hoffmann, Heinrich August)

Farjeon, Eleanor (b. Feb. 13, 1881, Westminster, London, Eng.; d. June 5, 1965, Hampstead, London, Eng.) was born into a family that included a renowned English novelist and a famous actor; was educated privately, published her first book, *Nursery Rhymes of London Town* in 1916, and went on to write approximately 80 other works—novels, plays, poems, music and books for children; received several awards, including the Carnegie Medal, Hans Anderson International Medal, and Regina Medal; published many books, including *A Nursery in the Nineties* (1935), *Martin Pippin in the Daisyfield* (1937), *The Glass Slipper* (1944), *Silversand and Snow* (1951), and *The Last Four Years* (1958); became a Roman Catholic at the age of 70, and is the subject of biographies by Eileen H. Colwell (1961) and Denys M. Blakelock (1966).
    Morning has broken (553)

Fawcett, John (b. Jan. 6, 1740, Lidget Green, York, Eng.; d. July 25, 1817, Hebden Bridge, York, Eng.) was converted when he was 16 under the preaching of George Whitefield; joined the Methodist movement in the Church of England for a time; later united with the Baptists, was ordained in 1763, and served churches at Wainsgate and at Hebden Bridge as pastor; at Hebden Bridge, turned a part of his home into a school for neighborhood children; declined the presidency of the Baptist academy in Bristol, but founded the Northern Education Society (now Rawdon College); wrote essays and sermons, and *Devotional Commentary on the Holy Scriptures*, 1811; published *Hymns adapted to the Circumstances of Public Worship and Private Devotion*, 1782, whose 166 hymns were written to be sung at the conclusion of his sermons.
    Blest be the tie that binds (207)

Featherstone, William Ralph (b. July 23, 1846, Montreal, Que.; d. May 20, 1873, Montreal, Que.) is also listed as "William Rolf Featherston" and seems not to have left much historical record; evidently was a member, with his parents, of the Wesleyan Methodist Church (now St. James United Church) in Montreal, spending his life in that city.
    My Jesus, I love Thee (72)

Fecamp, Jean de (see Jean de Fecamp)

Fellers, Foss Luke (b. 1887; d. 1924) was a teacher of music at Moody Bible Institute about 1910–1924; wrote and published one of the early books of piano arrangements of hymns. No other information can be found.
    BIOLA (471)

Ferguson, Manie Payne (b. 1850, Carlow, Ireland; d. date unknown) with her husband, T. P. Ferguson, founded a number of "Peniel" missions on the west coast, and branches have been established in other parts of the world; was committed to a Wesleyan ("holiness") theological emphasis; wrote a number of hymns and published them in *Echoes from Beulah.*

Joys are flowing like a river (192)

Filitz, Friedrich (b. Mar. 16, 1804, Arnstadt, Thüringia; d. Dec. 8, 1876, Munich, Ger.) earned a doctorate in philosophy; lived in Berlin, 1843–47, and spent the rest of his life in Munich; assisted in publishing a collection of 16th and 17th century chorales in 1845; edited *Vierstimmiges Choralbuch* (1847), and *Allgemeine Gesang und Gebetbuch* (1846)—a book of four-part settings for texts of his poet-friend, von Bunsen.

WEM IN LEIDENSTAGEN (143); BREMERTON (577)

Fillmore, James Henry (b. June 1, 1849, Cincinnati, Ohio; d. Feb. 8, 1936, Cincinnati, Ohio) was the son of A. D. Fillmore, an ordained minister (Christian Church) who was also a composer, publisher and singing school teacher; at 16, when his father died, took over the music classes to support the family; with his brothers, founded the Fillmore Bros. Music House of Cincinnati; issued a periodical monthly, *The Musical Messenger,* and his hymns appeared in this publication as well as in many collections, of which *Songs of Glory* (1874) was first; wrote and published many anthems, cantatas, and hymn tunes.

HANNAH (157); PURER IN HEART (389)

Findlater, Sarah Laurie Borthwick (b. Nov. 26, 1823, Edinburgh, Scot.; d. Dec. 25, 1907, Torquay, Devon, Eng.) was the youngest daughter of James Borthwick, manager of the North British Insurance Office, Edinburgh; with her sister Jane Borthwick·(*q.v.*), translated hymns from the German, 53 of which were published in *Hymns from the Land of Luther* (1854–62); married Eric John Findlater, a Scottish Free Church minister at Lochearnhead, Perthshire.

O happy home, where Thou art loved (trans.) (532)

Fischer, William Gustavus (b. Oct. 14, 1835, Baltimore, Md.; d. Aug. 12, 1912, Philadelphia, Pa.) became interested in music as a youth, through attending a singing class in a German-speaking church in Philadelphia; while learning the bookbinding trade, devoted his evenings to musical study; became a famous teacher and choral conductor, taught music at Girard College, Philadelphia (1858–68) and then went into partnership with John E. Gould in a retail piano business; wrote over 200 gospel songs and was much in demand as a conductor and song leader for revivals, including the Moody-Sankey campaign of 1876.

TRUSTING (270); HANKEY (302); FISCHER (386)

Flemming, Friedrich Ferdinand (b. Feb. 28, 1778, Neuhausen, Saxony; d. May 27, 1813, Berlin, Ger.), a physician by profession and musician by avocation, studied at Wittenberg, Jena, Vienna and Trieste; practiced medicine in Berlin and continued to be active as a composer until he died at the age of 35; is largely known today for his male-voice setting of "Integer Vitae," one of Horace's odes, which is adapted as a hymn tune for many different texts.

FLEMMING (7, 315, 395)

Forrest, C. H. No information can be found.

EXALTATION (381)

Fortunatus, Venantius Honorius (b. *ca.* 530 near Treviso, It.; d. *ca.* 609, Poitiers, Fr.) was the chief Latin poet of the age in which he lived, who eventually turned his gifts to the service of God; studied oratory and poetry at Ravenna; made a pilgrimage in 565 to the tomb of St. Martin of Tours, and met Queen Rhadegonda who persuaded him to settle at Poitiers; was admitted to the priesthood and in 599 became Bishop of Poitiers; wrote many hymns, including a volume, *Hymns for all the Festivals of the Christian Year*, which is lost.

"Welcome, happy morning!" (169)

Fosdick, Harry Emerson (b. May 24, 1878, Buffalo, N.Y.; d. Oct. 5, 1969, Bronxville, N.Y.) is remembered as "a fighting liberal" in the fundamentalist-modernist controversy of the 1920's, but has produced some helpful devotional studies and a fine hymn; was educated at Colgate University, Union Theological Seminary, and Columbia University, and was ordained to the Baptist ministry in 1903; served First Baptist Church, Montclair, N.J. (1904–15); taught homiletics (1908–15) and occupied the chair of practical theology at Union (1915–46); was pastor of First Presbyterian Church, New York City (1919–26); in 1926 became pastor of Park Avenue Baptist Church, which later became Riverside Church; wrote 32 books, including the popular volume, *The Meaning of Prayer* (1915), an autobiography, *The Living of These Days* (1956), and several hymns.

God of grace and God of glory (466)

Foster, Myles Birket (b. Nov. 29, 1851, London, Eng.; d. Dec. 18, 1922, London, Eng.), the son of an artist, was educated at Brighton and Guildford Grammar School and entered the stock exchange; subsequently enrolled at the Royal Academy of Music and held organist's posts at St. James' Church, Marylebone and St. George's, Campden Hill; from 1880–92 was organist at the Foundling Hospital and at Her Majesty's Theatre, and choirmaster of St. Alban's, Holborn; composed children's cantatas and much church music; co-edited *Methodist Free Church Hymns*, 1889, and authored *History of the Philharmonic Society* (London, 1913).

CRUCIS MILITES (468)

Foulkes, William Hiram (b. June 26, 1877, Quincy, Mich.; d. Jan., 1962, Smithtown, L.I., N. Y.) came from a long line of Presbyterian ministers, and was himself a leader of his denomination, being elected Moderator of the General Assembly of the Presbyterian Church in the U. S. A. in 1937;

was educated at Emporia College (Kan.), Kansas Wesleyan University and McCormick Theological Seminary (Chicago, Ill.), with graduate study at New College, Edinburgh, Scotland; served Presbyterian churches in Illinois, Iowa, Oregon, Ohio, New York City and New Jersey, retiring in 1941 to live at Stony Brook, L.I., N.Y.; wrote poetry (especially sonnets), beginning with his student days, and published many volumes, including *Sunset by the Wayside* (1917), *Living Bread from the Fourth Gospel* (1914) and *Homespun, Along Friendly Roads* (1936); assisted in writing the *Handbook to the Presbyterian Hymnal* (1935).

Take Thou our minds, dear Lord (374)

Francis of Assisi (b. *ca.* 1182, Assisi, It.; d. Oct. 4, 1226, Assisi, It.), the son of a prosperous cloth merchant, was a self-indulgent youth; because of a serious physical illness in his early 20's, turned his back on his wealth to devote his life to prayer, poverty and caring for the needy; with his little band of followers, became a wandering preacher throughout all Italy; loved all living things and is known as "the patron saint of animals"; adapted Italian secular song to suit his spiritual purposes, creating the historic, folkish *laudi spirituali,* which endured in history to the 17th century; founded the Franciscan order of the Roman Catholic Church.

All creatures of our God and King (59)

Francis, Samuel Trevor (b. Nov. 19, 1834, Cheshunt, Herts, Eng.; d. Dec. 28, 1925, Worthing, Sussex, Eng.) early in life moved with his family to Hull where he received his basic education from his grandmother and aunt, with whom he lived for two years; was a member of the surpliced choir in the parish church of Hull, and began to write poetry at an early age; later affiliated with the "Plymouth Brethren" and a biography appears in H. Pickering's *Chief Men Among the Brethren,* 1931; became a merchant in London, and wrote numerous hymns which appeared in various periodicals and religious newspapers, as well as the *Enlarged London Hymn Book,* 1873; acted as assistant to Ira Sankey (*q.v.*) during the Moody-Sankey meetings, 1873–75; became known as an effective devotional speaker, in Britain and around the world; authored *Gems from the Revised Version, with Poems* (1891), and *Whence-Whither, and Other Poems* (1898); had his collected verse published by Pickering and Inglis in 1926, *O the Deep, Deep Love of Jesus, and Other Poems;* died at Groombridge Nursing Home in Worthing, Sussex.

O the deep, deep love of Jesus (229)

Franz, Ignace (b. October 12, 1719, Protzau, Silesia; d. 1790) was a recognized German-Catholic hymnologist and compiler; studied in Glaz and Breslau; as an ordained priest, was appointed chaplain at Gross-Glogau, 1753, and archpriest at Schlawa; in 1766 became assessor in the apostolic vicar's office in Breslau, probably holding that position until his death; published ten books, of which the most significant is *Katholisches Gesangbuch, ca.* 1774 (containing 47 of his own hymns), and a tunebook (1778).

Holy God, we praise Thy name (9)

Frazer, George West (b. 1830, Bally, near Sligo, Ire.; d. Jan. 24, 1896, Cheltenham, Gloucs, Eng.), of Scottish ancestry, was born in the family of a police inspector in Ireland; was converted at the age of 20 in a revival meeting in Dublin, and throughout life associated with Plymouth Brethren assemblies; was employed in a Dublin bank, and gave a great deal of his time to evangelistic work; later resigned his position to give full time to the ministry, visiting many assemblies throughout England; wrote many hymns which were published in three separate volumes: *Midnight Praises, Day-Dawn Praises,* and *The Day-Spring.*

God, our Father, we adore Thee (3)

Gabriel, Charles Hutchinson (b. Aug. 18, 1856, Wilton, Ia.; d. Sept. 15, 1932, Los Angeles, Calif.) was the most popular gospel song composer during the Billy Sunday-Homer Rodeheaver evangelistic crusades, 1910–20; grew up on an Iowa farm, where he taught himself to play the family's reed organ; at 16, taught in singing schools and soon became a recognized teacher and composer; was briefly music director of a Methodist church in San Francisco; in 1895 settled in Chicago and was active in composing and publishing, becoming associated with the Rodeheaver Hall-Mack Co. in 1912; wrote both words and music for a great number of songs, often using the pseudonym "Charlotte G. Homer"; edited many compilations for different voicings and uses.

I stand amazed in the presence (294); In loving kindness Jesus came (299); More like the Master (362); When all my labors and trials are o'er (538)

McDANIEL (281); MY SAVIOR'S LOVE (294); HE LIFTED ME (299); HIGHER GROUND (355); HANFORD (362); GABRIEL (412); GLORY SONG (538)

Gannett, William Channing (b. Mar. 13, 1840, Boston, Mass.; d. Dec. 15, 1923, Rochester, N.Y.) was educated at Harvard University, Harvard Divinity School and Cambridge University; ministered to freed slaves following the Civil War; became a Unitarian minister and served several pastorates, including First Unitarian Church in Rochester, N.Y.; worked with Frederick Lucian Hosmer in compiling *The Thought of God in Hymns and Poems* (1885); also published *A Year of Miracle* (1882), *The Childhood of Jesus* (1890), and *Frances David* (1914).

Praise to God, your praises bring (562)

Gardiner, William (b. Mar. 15, 1770, Leicester, Eng.; d. Nov. 16, 1853, Leicester, Eng.) inherited a hosiery manufacturing business, and successfully combined his business career with an unusual talent for music; was interested in musicians and took every opportunity to meet them and hear their performances; claimed to be the first to present Beethoven's music in England; introduced the concept of adapting classic works for use as hymn tunes; published *Sacred Melodies from Haydn, Mozart, and Beethoven, Adapted to the Best English Poets and Appropriated to the Use of the British Church* (2 vols., 1812 and 1815).

LYONS (21); BELMONT (38); GERMANY (241, 514)

Gastoldi, Giovanni Giacomo (b. *ca.* 1556, Caravaggio, Italy; d. 1622), an Italian composer, was *maestro di cappella* at the Santa Barbara church, Mantua (1581–1622); authored *Balletti a 5 per cantare, suonare, e ballare* (1591–95), *Balletti a 3 voci* (1594) and *Canzonette a 3 voci;* wrote two tunes which were adapted by Johann Lindemann (*q.v.*) and set to the hymns "Jesu, wollst uns weisen" and "In dir ist Freude."

    IN DIR IST FREUDE (64)

Gauntlett, Henry John (b. July 9, 1805, Wellington, Shrops, Eng.; d. Feb. 21, 1876, London, Eng.) became organist in his father's church at Olney when he was nine, and later served as choirmaster; trained in law and was admitted to practice, but gave it up by 1844; served as organist and choirmaster for several leading congregations in the greater London area through the years; was one of Britain's leading musicians in the mid-19th century—interested in reform in organ design and the use of plainsong in liturgy; wrote much organ music, anthems, and perhaps 10,000 hymn tunes; compiled and published: *Hymnal for Matins and Evensong* (1844), *The Church Hymnal and Tune-book* (1844–51), *Cantus Melodici* (1845), *The Congregationalist Psalmist* (1851), and *Tunes, New and Old* (1868); was granted a doctorate in music in 1843 by the Archbishop of Canterbury because of the high quality of his work.

    STUTTGART (arr.) (34); IRBY (109)

Geibel, Adam (b. Sept. 15, 1855, Baden, Ger.; d. Aug. 3, 1933, Philadelphia, Pa.) came to America as a young child; like Fanny Crosby, lost his sight when he was very young through improper medical attention to an eye infection; gifted in music, became a skillful organist, conductor and composer; formed the Adam Geibel Publishing Company, which later became the Hall-Mack Company, and eventually was joined with the Rodeheaver Company; composed both sacred and secular music in many forms, and was especially successful in writing for men's voices ("Kentucky Babe" was one of his most popular songs).

    GEIBEL (455)

Gellert, Christian Fürchtegott (b. July 4, 1715, Hainichen, Saxony; d. Dec. 13, 1769, Leipzig, Ger.), the son of a Lutheran clergyman-poet, entered the University of Leipzig to study theology; after graduation, served as assistant to his father, but physical and emotional weakness caused him to leave the ministry and become a private tutor; returned to the University to study and took a minor post on the faculty, lecturing in poetry and rhetoric and later, was professor of philosophy; was revered and loved by his students, among whom were Goethe and Lessing; wrote a book of popular *Tales and Fables* (1746–48) which had many printings and translations; published *Spiritual Odes and Songs* (1757), containing 54 of his own hymns, which was immediately successful.

    Jesus lives and so shall I (159)

Gerhardt, Paul (b. Mar. 12, 1607, Gräfenhainichen, Saxony; d. May 27, 1676, Lübben, Saxe Merseburg) is one of the best-loved hymn writers in the German tradition; was trained in the Elector's school at Grimma and the University of Wittenberg, where he was helped by Paul Röber and Jacob Martini to learn the purpose and use of hymnody; in 1642 became a tutor in the home of Andreas Barthold, an attorney in Berlin, and eventually married Barthold's daughter; knew Johann Crüger (*q.v.*) and published hymns in his *Geistliche Kirchenmelodien,* 1649 and *Praxis Pietatis Melica,* 1656; was ordained in 1651 and later served at Mittenwalde, Berlin (where Johann Crüger was choirmaster) and Lübben; in early life, suffered the terrors of the Thirty Years' War, and much of his life was marked with tragedy—four of his children died in infancy, his wife died after 13 years of marriage, and he was the center of theological and political controversy under Frederick William I, Elector of Saxony; still reflects spiritual serenity in his "Cross and Comfort" hymns, of which translator Catherine Winkworth said: "The religious song of Saxony finds its purest and sweetest expression in his writing."

O sacred Head, now wounded (136); Jesus, Thy boundless love to me (364); Give to the winds your fears (422)

Giardini, Felice de (b. Apr. 12, 1716, Turin, Italy; d. June 8, 1796, Moscow, Russia) was a chorister at the Cathedral of Milan; played violin in opera orchestras in Rome and Naples and then gave concerts in Italy, in Germany (1748), and in London (1750); lived in England (1752–84), teaching, performing and conducting, and became impresario of the Italian Opera in London; a friend of nobility, including the Countess of Huntingdon, was commissioned to write hymn tunes for Martin Madan's (*q.v.*) *The Collection of Psalm and Hymn Tunes,* 1769 (provided four tunes, but only this one has remained in use); suffered several reverses in his operas and went to Moscow in 1796, where he died less than three months after his arrival.

ITALIAN HYMN (4, 74)

Gibbs, Ada Rose (b. 1865; d. 1905) spent her life in England and was evidently active in the Keswick Convention movement; was married to William James Gibbs, sometime superintendent of the Central Hall (Methodist), Bromley, Kent, and was the mother of one of the former directors of Marshall, Morgan and Scott, Ltd., who owned this song's copyright; published *Twenty-Four Gems of Sacred Song,* whose preface is dated July 1, 1900.

CHANNELS (347)

Gilmore, Joseph Henry (b. Apr. 29, 1834, Boston, Mass.; d. July 23, 1918, Rochester, N.Y.) served as private secretary to his father, Joseph A. Gilmore, governor of New Hampshire during the Civil War; was educated at Phillips Academy, Brown University and Newton Theological Seminary, ordained to the Baptist ministry in 1862, and served churches in Fisherville, N.H. and Rochester, N.Y.; for a short time, while serving his father, was also editor of the *Daily Monitor* in Concord, N.H.; was appointed professor of logic and English literature at the University of Rochester, 1868–1911; wrote and published in his academic discipline: *The Art of Expression,*

1876 and *Outlines of English and American Literature*, 1905; also published *He Leadeth Me, and Other Religious Poems*, 1877.

He leadeth me, O blessed thought (439)

Gladden, Washington (b. Feb. 11, 1836, Pottsgrove, Pa.; d. July 2, 1918, Columbus, Ohio), educated at Owego Academy and Williams College, was ordained into the Congregational ministry in 1860; served churches in New York and Massachusetts, and in 1882 began a pastorate at First Congregational Church, Columbus, Ohio which lasted 32 years; was moderator of the National Council of Congregational Churches, 1904–07, and an early proponent of the social implications of the gospel; was the author of some 32 works, including: *The Christian Way* (1877), *Things New and Old* (1884), *Applied Christianity* (1887), *Who Wrote the Bible?* (1891), *Art and Morality* (1897), *Christianity in Socialism* (1905), and *Recollections* (1909).

O Master, let me walk with Thee (504)

Gläser, Carl Gotthelf (b. May 4, 1784, Weissenfels, Ger.; d. Apr. 16, 1829, Barmen, Ger.) received his first musical training from his father and later attended the *Thomasschule* in Leipzig where Johann A. Hiller was director; both studied and taught piano and violin in Leipzig, and then settled in Barmen where he added voice and choral music to his expertise, and was involved in composing and publishing.

AZMON (90, 346)

Gordon, Adoniram Judson (b. Apr. 19, 1836, New Hampton, N.H.; d. Feb. 2, 1895, Boston, Mass.) was named for the pioneer Baptist missionary to India-Burma, and in turn is memorialized in the naming of Gordon College and Seminary, near Boston; received his training at Brown University and Newton Theological Seminary, was ordained to the Baptist ministry (1863) and served the church at Jamaica Plain, Mass., and beginning in 1869, the Clarendon Street Baptist Church, Boston; was a close friend and supporter of D. L. Moody; edited *The Service of Song for Baptist Churches,* 1871 and *The Vestry Hymn and Tune Book,* 1872; was editor of the monthly, *The Watchword,* and author of a series of books called *Quiet Talks.*

GORDON (72); CLARENDON (300)

Goss, John (b. Dec. 27, 1800, Fareham, Eng.; d. May 10, 1880, London, Eng.) was a leader of English church music in the early 19th century, who was overshadowed only by Samuel Sebastian Wesley (*q.v.*) in effecting reforms in cathedral music and congregational song; began his career as a chorister in the Chapel Royal where he studied under Thomas Atwood; served as organist of Stockwell Chapel, St. Luke's in Chelsea, and then at St. Paul's Cathedral in London, succeeding Atwood; in 1827 became professor of harmony at the Royal Academy of Music and held this position for some 47 years; was appointed composer to the Chapel Royal, 1856, knighted by Queen Victoria when he retired in 1872, and received an honorary Mus.D. degree (Cambridge) in 1876; wrote anthems, service music and hymn

tunes, released in *Parochial Psalmody* (1826), *An Introduction to Harmony and Thorough Bass* (1833), *257 Chants, Ancient and Modern* (1841), etc.
LAUDA ANIMA (26); ARMAGEDDON (arr.) (460)

Gottschalk, Louis Moreau (b. May 8, 1829, New Orleans, La.; d. Dec. 18, 1869, Rio de Janeiro, Brazil) was America's first concert pianist and world-recognized composer; born to an English father and a French mother, was a child prodigy, sent to Paris to study at the age of 13; was predicted by Chopin, who attended his debut, to become a "king of pianists," and did win acclaim from music lovers throughout Europe, Latin America and the United States; wrote many popular piano pieces, such as "The Dying Poet" and "The Last Hope" and included them in his recitals; died of yellow fever in Rio de Janeiro, while performing at a festival of his music; composed several larger works: a symphony, *La Nuit des Tropiques,* an overture, a cantata and two operas.
MERCY (194)

Graeff, Frank E. (b. Dec. 19, 1860, Tamaqua, Pa.; d. July 29, 1919, Ocean Grove, N.J.) was widely known as "The Sunshine Minister," though he experienced very difficult times in his life; was reared and educated in "Pennsylvania Dutch" country, and felt called to the ministry early in life; was admitted to the Philadelphia Conference of the Methodist Church in 1890, and served many different churches in the years that followed; was devoted to the little children in his parishes, and became well known for the stories he wrote for them; authored more than 200 hymns and a successful novel, *The Minister's Twins.*
Does Jesus care? (416)

Grant, David (b. Sept. 19, 1833, Aberdeen, Scot.; d. July 30, 1893, Lewisham, London, Eng.) was a tobacconist in Union Street, Aberdeen, Scotland, and an amateur musician who scored music for bands and arranged tunes for the *Northern Psalter;* was a member of the Footdee church and choir; is known today for his hymn tune "Raleigh," and also for his harmonization of Jessie S. Irvine's "Crimond."
CRIMOND (arr.) (45)

Grant, Robert (b. 1779, Bengal, India; d. July 9, 1838, Dalpoorie, India) was the son of Charles Grant, a director of the East India Company; was educated at Magdalene College, Cambridge and began to practice law in 1807; was elected to Parliament as representative from Inverness, Elgin, Norwich, and Finsbury, which had previously been represented by his father; was sympathetic to the Jews and (1833) introduced a bill granting them civil liberties; was made Judge Advocate General in 1832, later (1834) was knighted and sent back to India as Governor of Bombay; was the author of 12 hymns which appeared in the *Christian Observer* and H. V. Elliott's *Psalms and Hymns,* 1835, and were published posthumously by his brother in a volume entitled *Sacred Poems,* 1839.
O worship the King, all glorious above (adapt.) (21)

Grape, John Thomas (b. May 6, 1835, Baltimore, Md.; d. Nov. 2, 1915, Baltimore, Md.) was a successful coal merchant in Baltimore, who, as he said, "dabbled in music for his own amusement"; directed the choir in the Monument Street Methodist Church, and later in the Harford Avenue Methodist Church; wrote a number of hymn tunes, but only this one lives on.

ALL TO CHRIST (232)

Gray, James Martin (b. May 11, 1851, New York, N. Y.; d. Sept. 21, 1935, Chicago, Ill.) was converted while reading William Arnot's *Laws from Heaven for Life on Earth*, and became a rector in the Reformed Episcopal Church, and a lecturer in English Bible at his denomination's seminary in Philadelphia; began to teach at the Bible Institute for Home and Foreign Missions, Chicago in 1893, at the invitation of D. L. Moody; after Moody's death, was named dean and the school was called Moody Bible Institute; became president of Moody Bible Institute in 1925 and remained until he retired in 1934; died in Passavant Hospital, Chicago and was buried in Woodlawn Cemetery, New York City (his birth date is set by the cemetery's response to our phone call, that at his death Dr. Gray was "84 years, 4 months and 10 days old"); authored many books and was responsible for the publication of the *Voice of Thanksgiving* (Nos. 1 to 4, 1913–28), official hymnals of the Moody Bible Institute.

Nor silver nor gold hath obtained my redemption (282); Naught have I gotten but what I received (293)

Greatorex, Henry Wellington (b. Dec. 24, 1813, Burton-on-Trent, Derby, Eng.; d. Sept. 10, 1858, Charleston, S.C.) received early musical training from his father, Thomas Greatorex, a well-known teacher, composer, and organist at Carlisle Cathedral and Westminster Abbey during the reign of King George IV; in 1839 came to America and was organist of Center Church, Hartford, Conn., and later at St. Paul's Church and Calvary Church in New York City; died of yellow fever in Charlestown, S.C., where he had gone to take another position; published a *Collection of Sacred Music*, 1851, whose tunes were marked A.G., T.G. and H.W.G., signifying Anthony Greatorex (Henry's grandfather), Thomas Greatorex (his father), and himself.

MANOAH (329); GREATOREX (575)

Green, Harold (b. Oct. 23, 1871, Helme, York, Eng.; d. Dec. 20, 1930, Malenge Farm, Umzimkalu, Cape Province, South Africa), the son of a minister, was born in the vicarage at Helme, near Huddersfield in Yorkshire; became a missionary to Pondoland in South Africa, serving with the South Africa General Mission; died on the mission field.

QUIETUDE (360)

Greenwell, Dora (b. Dec. 6, 1821, Greenwell Ford, Lanchester, Durham, Eng.; d. Mar. 29, 1882, Clifton, Bristol, Eng.) was born into a well-to-do family, but circumstances made it necessary for her father to sell the family estate; went to live with her two brothers, both clergymen, and then with her widowed mother in Durham, and finally alone in London, Torquay and Clifton; had fragile health, but a keen mind and a loving heart and was especially interested in helping retarded children and outlawing vivisection; published many volumes of verse and devotional books, which have been compared to the writings of Thomas à Kempis, Fénelon and Woolman, including *The Patience of Hope* (1860), *Carmina Crucis* (1869), and *Songs of Salvation* (1873).

I am not skilled to understand (305)

Grimes, Emily May (b. May 10, 1864, Lambeth, Surrey, Eng.; d. July 9, 1927, Folkestone, Kent, Eng.) went as a missionary to Pondoland in South Africa in 1893; in 1904 married Dr. T. W. W. Crawford, a missionary of the Anglican church.

Speak, Lord, in the stillness (360)

Grimes, Katherine A. (b. 1877). No other information is available.

Teach me Thy will, O Lord (370)

Griswold, Alexander Viets (b. Apr. 22, 1766, Simsbury, Conn.; d. Feb. 15, 1843, Boston, Mass.) at the age of ten went to live with his uncle, who was rector of Simsbury (Conn.) parish; studied law, but later prepared for Holy Orders and advanced to the Episcopal priesthood in 1795; in 1811 was elected the first and only bishop of the Eastern Diocese, comprising all of New England except Connecticut, and was Presiding Bishop of the Protestant Episcopal Church, 1836–43; received the D.D. degree from both Princeton and Brown Universities; published *Prayers Adapted to Various Occasions*, 1835, and *The Reformation*, 1843.

Holy Father, great Creator (6)

Grose, Howard Benjamin (b. Sept. 5, 1851, Millerton, N.Y.; d. May 19, 1939) received his education at the University of Chicago and the University of Rochester; in 1883 was ordained to the Baptist ministry and served First Baptist Church in Poughkeepsie, N.Y. (1883–87) and First Baptist Church, Pittsburgh, Pa. (1888–90); was president of the University of South Dakota, and later taught history at the University of Chicago; served as editorial secretary of the American Baptist Home Mission Society (1904–10); was editor of the journal *Missions* for 23 years and wrote a number of books: *Aliens or Americans* (1906), *The Incoming Millions* (1906), *Advance to the Antilles* (1910), and *Never Man So Spake* (1924); in later years, lived in Mount Vernon, N.Y.

Give of your best to the Master (465)

Grüber, Franz Xaver (b. Nov. 25, 1787, Unterweizberg, near Hochburg, Aust.; d. June 7, 1863, Hallein, near Salzburg, Aust.) learned the linen weaving trade at his father's insistence, but his interest in music led him to study the violin and organ without his father's knowledge, and eventually to devote his life to the art; became a schoolmaster in a Roman Catholic

school at Ansdorf and also organist at nearby Oberndorf, where Joseph Mohr (*q.v.*), the author of "Silent Night," was priest; for approximately 30 years was organist and choral director at Hallein, where he died; wrote many compositions, but is best known for this simple hymn tune.
STILLE NACHT (117)

Grundtvig, Nicolai Frederik Severin (b. Sept. 8, 1783, Udby, Seeland; d. Sept. 2, 1872, Vartov, Denmark) was one of Denmark's greatest hymnists, preachers and educators; experienced a period of doubt during his "rationalistic" theological studies at the University of Copenhagen, but his faith was rekindled when he perceived the spiritual poverty of his people; became a teacher and then an assistant to his father, an Evangelical Lutheran pastor; was ordained in 1811 and installed at Udby, but his controversial preaching caused him to be suspended for a period of 13 years; was fully reinstated in 1839 and appointed chaplain to the Vartov hospital, where he remained until his death; led in bringing reforms to Denmark's educational system, and has been called "the father of the public school in Scandinavia"; received the honorary title of Bishop from King Frederik VII in 1863; left five volumes of poems and hymns which were published after his death with the title (translated) *Hymns and Spiritual Songs.*
Built on the Rock the church doth stand (201)

Gurney, Dorothy Frances (b. Oct. 4, 1858, London, Eng.; d. June 15, 1932, London, Eng.) had a long Anglican heritage—her father was rector of St. Andrew Undershaft, London and her grandfather was Bishop Blomfield of Chester and London; married Gerald Gurney, a former actor who was ordained in the Church of England and was also the son of an Anglican clergyman and hymn writer; with her husband, became a Roman Catholic in 1919; wrote two volumes of *Poems,* and *A Little Book of Quiet.*
O perfect Love, all human thought transcending (529)

Hall, Elvina Mabel (b. June 4, 1820, Alexandria, Va.; d. July 18, 1889, Ocean Grove, N.J.), with her husband Richard Hall, was a member of the Monument Street Methodist Church in Baltimore for more than forty years; after Mr. Hall's death, married Rev. Thomas Myers of the Baltimore Conference of the Methodist Church, in 1885.
I hear the Savior say (232)

Hall, J. Lincoln (b. Nov. 4, 1866, Philadelphia, Pa.; d. Nov. 29, 1930, Philadelphia, Pa.) was a prominent song leader, composer and music publisher, who lived and worked in Philadelphia; graduated with high honors from the University of Pennsylvania and later received the honorary Doctor of Music degree from Harriman University; wrote music for many cantatas, oratorios, anthems and hundreds of gospel songs; was associated with the Hall-Mack Publishing Company in Philadelphia (which later joined the Rodeheaver Company), and assisted in compiling many collections of songs.
CLIFTON (290); MY SAVIOR CARES (416)

Hammond, Mary Jane (b. 1878, England; d. Jan. 23, 1964, St. Albans, Herts, Eng.) died at Hilligdon Nursing Home on Hillside Road in St. Albans, Herefordshire. No other information is available.

SPIRITUS VITAE (196)

Hammontree, Homer Alexander (b. Mar. 3, 1884, Greenback, Tenn.; d. Feb. 2, 1965, Maryville, Tenn.) grew up on a farm in Tennessee where his parents were active in the local Presbyterian church; received his early education in Greenback and then attended Maryville (Tenn.) College (B.A. and later, honorary D.D.) and Moody Bible Institute, Chicago; first taught high school, and went on to teach at Murphy College, now disbanded; during World War I, ministered with Rev. Mel Trotter in army camps, and later traveled in evangelism with Trotter, Homer Rodeheaver and Billy Sunday; 1936–42, was director of the music department, Moody Bible Institute; in World War II, again ministered in army installations, and afterward in church conferences and revivals in association with Rev. Paul Beckwith; wrote a number of gospel songs and assisted in the publication of collections.

HAMMONTREE (367)

Hanby, Benjamin Russell (b. 1833; d. 1867), the son of Bishop William Hanby of the United Brethren Church, was himself a minister in that church with a musical avocation that eventually became his life work; was associated with George F. Root (*q.v.*) in music publishing in Chicago, co-editing *Chapel Gems*, 1866; wrote a number of Sunday School songs as well as secular lyrics (including the famous "Darling Nellie Gray," for which his sister wrote the music); died at the early age of 34, just as his career was beginning.

Who is He in yonder stall? (127)

LOWLINESS (127)

Handel, George Frederick (b. Feb. 23, 1685, Halle, Ger.; d. Apr. 14, 1759, London, Eng.) is sometimes described as "a German musician who wrote Italian operas for English audiences"; showed unusual musical gifts at an early age; because of his father's desire that he become a lawyer, entered the University of Halle to study law, but quickly turned to music; studied organ, harpsichord and music theory with Zachau, organist at the Halle Cathedral, and became his assistant; was violinist in the German opera for four years, then traveled through Italy, where he was inspired to write a number of his first operas; in 1713 settled in England (became a British subject in 1727) and enjoyed some 35 years of success in writing and producing "Italian" operas; later turned to the composition of oratorios which have won him lasting fame; also wrote instrumental and organ music in abundance, and three hymn tunes (for the Wesleys), but those commonly used are adapted from other vocal works; was buried in the Poet's Corner of Westminster Abbey.

CHRISTMAS (119, 454); ANTIOCH (120); MACCABEUS (171)

Hankey, Arabella Catherine (b. 1834, Clapham, Eng.; d. 1911, London, Eng.), usually known as "Kate," was born into the family of a banker who belonged to the evangelical "Clapham Sect" associated with William Wilberforce; throughout her life was interested and active in religious work—conducting Bible classes for shop girls, giving money from her writings to foreign missions, and visiting the sick in hospitals; published one important book, *The Old, Old Story and Other Verses*, 1879.

I love to tell the story (302)

Hanks, Billie, Jr. (b. May 24, 1944, San Angelo, Tex.) received his education at Baylor University (B.A.) and Southwestern Baptist Theological Seminary (M.Div.); has been active in evangelism since college days, and at seminary, received the Stella Ross award for evangelism; founded and is president of the International Evangelism Assn. of Fort Worth, Tex., which conducts crusades and publishes a monthly journal; has written *My Spiritual Note Book*, 1974, designed for use in "personal growth in discipleship"; has written words and music for some 40 contemporary songs, many released by Hope Publishing Company.

Lonely voices crying in the city (482)
LONELY VOICES (482)

Hansen, Fred C. M. (b. June 25, 1888, Vejle, Denmark; d. Apr. 4, 1965, Blair, Neb.) came to America with his parents at the age of two; received his higher education at Dana College, the University of Nebraska, and Trinity Seminary; in 1914 was ordained in the United Evangelical Lutheran Church and served churches in Iowa, Wisconsin and Illinois; has served his denomination as a translator and member of hymnal committees; was one of the translators for the *Hymnal for Church and Home*, 1927 and *Service Book and Hymnal*, 1958, and a member of the hymnal commission for the latter.

Built on the Rock the church doth stand (adapt.) (201)

Harkness, Georgia Elma (b. Apr. 21, 1891, Harkness, N.Y.; d. Aug. 30, 1974, Claremont, Calif.) is remembered as one of the leading women theologians of the last generation; was educated at Cornell University (B.A.) and Boston University (M.A., M.R.E., Ph.D.), Harvard University, Yale Divinity School and Union Theological Seminary; an ordained Methodist minister, lectured in theology and philosophy of religion at Elmira College, Mount Holyoke College, Garrett Biblical Institute, Pacific School of Religion and Japanese International Christian University; authored 28 books, three of which are collections of her prayers and poems.

Hope of the world (515)

Harkness, Robert (b. Mar. 2, 1880, Bendigo, Australia; d. May 8, 1961, London, Eng.) was the son of a minister but evidently not a confessing Christian when he was asked to join the Torrey-Alexander team as pianist, during their meetings in June, 1903 in his home town in Australia; was led to Christ by song leader Charles M. Alexander, a life-long specialist in "personal soul winning"; accompanied the singer and Dr. R. A. Torrey in round-the-world evangelistic tours, later working with Dr. J. Wilbur Chapman (*q.v.*) as well; after 1920, appeared in solo programs, entitled "The Music of the Cross"; wrote music for hundreds of gospel songs in his own harmonic style—they were introduced in their campaigns and later published; distributed a correspondence course in "Evangelistic Piano Playing" for many years, which has been published in one volume by Lillenas Publishing Company.

HYFRYDOL (arr.) (99)

Harrison, Ralph (b. Sept. 10, 1748, Chinley, Derby, Eng.; d. Nov. 4, 1810, Manchester, Lancs, Eng.), the son of a free church minister, was educated at Warrington Academy; served as organist and later pastored Cross Street Chapel (Independent), Manchester; helped establish a boys' school and later, Manchester Academy, where he taught the classics; published an English grammar and some manuals of geography, and was editor of *Sacred Harmony* (2 vols., 1784 and 1791) which contained several of his own psalm tunes.

WARRINGTON (29)

Hart, Joseph (b. 1712, London, Eng.; d. May 24, 1768, London, Eng.), well educated and the product of a Christian home, was a school teacher in London; lapsed into dissolute ways and agnostic thought, but was converted at the Moravian Chapel in London, 1757; became pastor of Jewin Street Chapel (Independent) in London, and was a popular preacher and ardent Calvinist; published *Hymns Composed on Various Subjects, with the Author's Experience,* 1759, for use in the Jewin Street Chapel.

Come, ye sinners, poor and needy (269)

Hassler, Hans Leo (b. Oct. 25, 1564, Nuremberg, Ger.; d. June 8, 1612, Frankfurt, Ger.) learned the basics of music from his father and later studied organ and composition with Andrea Gabrieli at St. Mark's in Venice; returning to his homeland in 1585, was organist to Count Octavian Fugger of Augsburg, and then at the Frauenkirche in Nuremberg; later served Emperor Rudolph II and Prince Christian II of Saxony; composed both sacred and secular music, vocal and instrumental, and published: *Cantiones Sacrae* (1591), *Psalmen und christliche Gesang* (1607), and *Kirchengesänge, Psalmen und geistliche Lieder* (1608).

PASSION CHORALE (136)

Hastings, Thomas (b. Oct. 15, 1784, Washington, Conn.; d. May 15, 1872, New York, N.Y.), the son of a physician, attended country school and taught himself the fundamentals of music; began directing choirs at age 18 and compiled sacred music collections; an albino, extremely near-sighted and not attractive of appearance, he was nevertheless an outstanding choral conductor; 1823–32, edited *The Western Recorder,* a religious journal in which he published articles on the improving of church music; in 1832 moved to New York City to work with Lowell Mason (*q.v.*) and a number of churches in the development of the music of worship; assisted Lowell

Mason in publishing *Spiritual Songs for Social Worship, ca.* 1832; edited 50 collections, including *Church Melodies* and *Devotional Hymns and Poems,* and wrote 600 hymns and 1000 hymn tunes.

Come, ye disconsolate (st. 3) (423)

ORTONVILLE (89); TOPLADY (149); RETREAT (214, 430)

Hatch, Edwin (b. Sept. 4, 1835, Derby, Eng.; d. Nov. 10, 1889, Oxford, Eng.), educated at King Edward's School, Birmingham and Pembroke College, Oxford, was confirmed in the Church of England and ordained in 1859; served as a parish priest for a short time before moving to Toronto, Canada where he became professor of classics at Trinity College; in 1867 returned to England as vice-principal of St. Mary's Hall, Oxford, and in 1884 became university reader in church history; was widely acclaimed for his Bampton Lectures (1880) and Hibbert Lectures (1888) on the history of the early church.

Breathe on me, Breath of God (187)

Hatton, John (b. *ca.* 1710, Warrington, Eng.; d. Dec., 1793, St. Helen's, Eng.) has only a few lines in hymn history; was referred to as "John of Warrington" which gives the presumption of his birthplace; lived on Duke Street in St. Helen's in the township of Windle, and was buried from the Presbyterian Chapel there on December 13, 1793.

DUKE STREET (489)

Hausmann, Julie Katharina von (b. 1825, Mitau, Kurland (Latvia); d. 1901, near Wösso, Estonia) was next to the youngest of six daughters of a Gymnasium (preparatory school) teacher, a shy, retiring young woman, never strong physically, but intellectually keen; acted as governess in private homes for brief periods, but eventually devoted herself to caring for her aged father who had become blind; after her father's death in 1864, lived with her sisters in Germany, France and Switzerland, and then with other relatives in Estonia, until her death in 1901; published a devotional book, *Hausbrot* and a three-volume set of poems, entitled *Maiblumen, Lieder einer Stillen im Lande.*

Take Thou my hand, O Father (444)

Havergal, Frances Ridley (b. Dec. 14, 1836, Astley, Eng.; d. June 3, 1879, Caswall Bay, near Swansea, Wales) was, for her 43 years, contemporary with America's Fanny Crosby (*q.v.*) and their two lives had many things in common; was the youngest child of William Henry Havergal (*q.v.*), vicar of Astley, Worcestershire; could read at the age of three, and wrote poetry when she was seven; because of frail health, had limited formal education, but developed great linguistic ability, being fluent in six or seven modern languages, as well as Hebrew and Greek; from the age of 14, was dedicated completely to the service of Christ; lived with her father until his death (1873) and then in Caswall Bay; was an incessant writer, whose collected poems appeared in *Poetical Works,* 1884, after her death.

O Savior, precious Savior (98); I am trusting Thee, Lord Jesus (330); Lord, speak to me, that I may speak (378); Take my life and let it be (385); Like a river glorious (397); Who is on the Lord's side? (460); I gave My life for thee (508); Another year is dawning (560)
HERMAS (169)

Havergal, William Henry (b. Jan. 18, 1793, High Wycombe, Bucks, Eng.; d. Apr. 19, 1870, Leamington, Warwick, Eng.) was trained at Merchant Taylor's School and at St. Edmund's Hall, Oxford, took Anglican Holy Orders and became rector of Astley in Worcestershire; was seriously injured in an accident, so resigned his pastoral duties and turned to writing and publishing church music; returned to active ministry in 1842 as rector of St. Nicholas, Worcester, and from 1845 was honorary canon of Worcester Cathedral; wrote many hymns that were printed in leaflet form for special services in his church; in 1844, for the improving of psalm singing in the church, reprinted Ravenscroft's *Psalter* of 1611 and published *Old Church Psalmody*, 1849 and *A Hundred Psalm and Hymn Tunes*, 1859; wrote *History of the Old 100th Psalm Tune*, 1854.
WINCHESTER NEW (16, 132, 221)

Hawks, Annie Sherwood (b. May 28, 1835, Hoosick, N.Y.; d. Jan. 3, 1918, Bennington, Vt.) resided in Brooklyn, N.Y. and was a member of the Hanson Place Baptist Church for many years; was encouraged to write hymns by her pastor, Robert Lowry (*q.v.*); after the death of her husband, Charles H. Hawks, moved to Bennington, Vt. where she lived with her daughter and son-in-law; wrote over 400 hymns, which were included in such compilations as *Bright Jewels, Pure Gold,* and *Royal Diadem.*
I need Thee every hour (340)

Haydn, Franz Joseph (b. Mar. 31, 1732, Rohrau, Aust.; d. May 31, 1809, Vienna, Aust.) shared with Mozart the leadership of the western musical world in the late 18th century; received early training in the Roman Catholic choir school of St. Stephen's, Vienna; as music director to the court of the Esterhazys for most of his life, had financial security and musical resources to perform his vast output of timeless music; wrote over 100 symphonies, 22 operas, 4 oratorios, and much chamber music; in 1797 visited England and received many honors; an intensely pious man, ended all his music manuscripts with the words "Laus Deo" or "Soli Deo Gloria"; wrote no hymn tunes as such—those that exist are adapted from larger works.
AUSTRIAN HYMN (17, 209, 464); CREATION (54); ST. ALBAN (244)

Haydn, Johann Michael (b. Sept. 14, 1737, Rohrau, Austria; d. Aug. 10, 1806, Salzburg, Austria), the younger brother of Franz Joseph Haydn (*q.v.*), was also a choirboy at St. Stephen's, Vienna; in 1757 became *kappelmeister* at Grosswardein; was musical director to Archbishop Sigismund at the cathedral of Salzburg from 1762 until his death; wrote more than 400 compositions for the church, including oratorios and music for organ with orchestra, few of which have been published.

LYONS (21)

Head, Elizabeth Ann Porter (b. Jan. 1, 1850, probably in Norfolk, Eng.; d. June 28, 1936, Wimbledon, Surrey, Eng.), often listed as "Bessie Porter Head," was the wife of Albert Alfred Head, insurance broker of Henry Head Co., London, and Chairman of the Keswick Convention for several years; a member of the Church of England, wrote many hymn texts, several of which appeared in the *Keswick Hymn Book, ca.* 1937.

O Breath of Life (196)

Hearn, Marianne (b. Dec. 17, 1834, Farningham, Kent, Eng.; d. Mar. 16, 1909, Barmouth, Merioneth, Wales), at the time of her death, was one of the most loved women in British Baptist life; lived many years in Northampton, where she was a member of the College Street Baptist Church; wrote under the pen name "Marianne Farningham"; served on the editorial staff of the *Christian World* and was an editor of *The Sunday School Times;* had a vast literary output which is collected and published in 20 volumes, including *Morning and Evening Hymns for the Week,* 1870, and *Songs of Sunshine,* 1878.

Just as I am, Thine own to be (371)

Heath, George (b. 1750; d. 1822) received his education at the Dissenting Academy in Exeter, England; served as pastor of the Presbyterian church in Honiton, Devonshire, was "proven unworthy" and dismissed, and later entered the Unitarian ministry; published *Hymns and Poetic Essays Sacred to the Public and Private Worship of the Deity,* 1781 and *A History of Bristol,* 1797.

My soul, be on your guard (462)

Heber, Reginald (b. Apr. 21, 1783, Malpas, Cheshire, Eng.; d. Apr. 3, 1826, Trichinopoly, India) is remembered for the impetus he gave to the cause of hymn (vs. psalm) singing in the Church of England, and for the new lyric quality he brought to hymn poetry; studied at the grammar school at Whitchurch, Bristow's select school at Neasdon, Brasenose College, Oxford, and was named a Fellow of All Souls' College, Oxford in 1805; served as rector of his family's parish at Hodnet, Shropshire, 1807-23; in 1823 was appointed Bishop of Calcutta and served there for a short three years when he suddenly died at age 42; wrote many hymns during his Hodnet ministry, which were released from time to time in the *Christian Observer* and which were published posthumously in *Hymns Written and Adapted to the Weekly Service of the Church Year,* 1827.

Holy, holy, holy! (1); Bread of the world in mercy broken (211); The Son of God goes forth to war (467); From Greenland's icy mountains (472)

Hedge, Frederick Henry (b. Dec. 12, 1805, Cambridge, Mass.; d. Aug. 21, 1890, Cambridge, Mass.) was sent to Germany to study at age 13, and graduated from Harvard Divinity School at 20; became a Unitarian minister and served churches in Maine, Rhode Island and Massachusetts; also taught church history and German at Harvard, and shows his scholarly acumen in the monumental *Prose Writers of Germany;* published *Hymns for the Church of Christ,* 1853; has been the subject of two recent biographical studies: *Frederick Henry Hedge, A Cosmopolitan Scholar,* by Orie William Long, 1940, and *Three Christian Transcendentalists,* by Ronald Vale Wells, 1943.

A mighty fortress is our God (11)

Heermann, Johann (b. Oct. 11, 1585, Raudten, Silesia; d. Feb. 17, 1647, Lissa, Posen), the fifth and only surviving child of his parents, was educated at the St. Elisabeth Gymnasium at Breslau and the Gymnasium at Brieg, and for a short time at the University of Strassburg; became a pastor at Koeben in 1611 and remained during the terrors and hardship of the Thirty Years' War, though throat trouble forced him to give up preaching in 1634; wrote many hymns which show his spiritual serenity in spite of personal loss and danger; has had 16 of his hymns translated into English.

Ah, holy Jesus, how hast Thou offended (152)

Helmore, Thomas (b. May 7, 1811, Kidderminster, Worcester, Eng.; d. July 6, 1890, Westminster, London, Eng.), educated at Magdalen Hall, Oxford, was ordained an Anglican priest and served as curate, then vicar in Lichfield Cathedral; for 35 years was vice-principal and precentor of St. Mark's College in Chelsea; in 1846 was made master of the choristers in the Chapel Royal at St. James, where he pioneered in the restoring of plainsong to liturgy; was musical editor of hymnals containing John Mason Neale's (*q.v.*) translations of Latin hymns, and translated Fetis' *Treatise on Choir and Chorus Singing,* 1885; was one of the editors of *The Hymnal Noted,* 1851–54.

VENI EMMANUEL (100)

Hemy, Henri Frederick (b. Nov. 12, 1818, Newcastle-on-Tyne, Eng.; d. 1888, Hartlepool, Durham, Eng.), born of German parents, was organist at St. Andrew's Roman Catholic Church in Newcastle, later taught music in Tynemouth and became professor of music at St. Cuthbert's College in Ushaw, Durham; left the publications: *Crown of Jesus Music,* 1864, a popular volume among Roman Catholics, and *Royal Modern Tutor for the Pianoforte,* 1858, a piano study book which went through many editions.

ST. CATHERINE (206, 364)

Henderson, S. J. No information is available.

Saved by the blood of the Crucified One! (301)

Herbert, George (b. Apr. 3, 1593, Montgomery Castle, Eng.; d. Feb. 1632, Bemerton, Wilts, Eng.) as a young man was a favorite in the court of James I; received his education at Westminster School and Trinity College, Cambridge, took Holy Orders and served for three notable years as rector of

Bemerton, near Salisbury; left a major literary work, *The Temple*, a collection of poems which was published posthumously in 1633; was not known as a hymn composer during his lifetime (because of the psalm tradition), but 100 years later some 40 of his poems were included by the Wesleys in their *Hymns and Sacred Poetry*, 1739.

Let all the world in every corner sing (24)

Hewitt, Eliza Edmunds (b. June 28, 1851, Philadelphia, Pa.; d. Apr. 24, 1920, Philadelphia, Pa.) was educated in the public schools and named valedictorian of her class at the Girls' Normal School in the city of Philadelphia, where she spent her entire life; taught school a number of years; was intensely devoted to the Sunday School movement and gave much time to youth in the Northern Home for Friendless Children, and later in the Calvin Presbyterian Church, where she served as Sunday School superintendent; wrote many poems which were first set to music by John R. Sweney (*q.v.*) and William J. Kirkpatrick (*q.v.*), and later by B. D. Ackley (*q.v.*), C. H. Gabriel (*q.v.*), E. S. Lorenz and Homer Rodeheaver.

"Give Me thy heart," says the Father above (273); More about Jesus would I know (339); There is sunshine in my soul today (399); Sing the wondrous love of Jesus (546)

Hickman, Roger M. (b. Nov. 28, 1888, southwest Missouri; d. Feb. 25, 1968, Lakeland, Fla.) was born, as he said, "in the foothills of the Ozark mountains in southwest Missouri"; at the age of 16 moved to Independence, Mo. and began to study music with private teachers in Kansas City, preparing for a career as a band and orchestra leader; at 20, was converted and felt called to Christian service as a gospel singer; studied at Moody Bible Institute, Chicago, met his wife there, and they served together in evangelistic music until she died in 1942; later served churches in Louisiana and Florida as director of music and Christian education; was Director of the Music Department of Baptist Bible Institute in Lakeland, Fla., 1949–53; wrote over 100 gospel songs, some anthems and cantatas, and collaborated with Arthur McKee in compiling the first volume of *Tabernacle Hymns*, 1916.

HICKMAN (298)

Hiller, Philipp Friedrich (b. Jan. 6, 1699, Mühlhausen, Ger.; d. Apr. 24, 1769, Steinheim, Ger.), son of Johann Jakob Hiller, pastor at Mühlhausen, was educated at the theological schools at Denkendorf and Maulbronn and the University of Tübingen (M.A., 1720); after various appointments as assistant pastor, became pastor of Mühlhausen in 1736, and later of Steinheim (1748); lost his voice in 1751 and had to employ an assistant to preach; wrote many hymns which appeared in *Arndt's Paradies-Gartlein . . . in teutsche Lieder* (*ca.* 1730), *Geistliches Liederkästlein* (1762), and J. J. Rambach's *Haus GesangBuch* (1735), and some five are in common use in English translations.

All my sins have been forgiven (291)

Hine, Stuart Wesley Keene (b. July 25, 1899, London, Eng.) will long be remembered for his translation-paraphrase "How Great Thou Art"; was educated at Cooper's Company School, London and served in the British Army in France during World War I; an ordained Methodist minister, served as a missionary to Poland, Czechoslovakia, Romania and Russia, 1923-39; during World War II, worked with displaced persons in Britain; is now retired in Somerset, and still active in producing evangelical literature.

    How Great Thou Art (trans.) (32)

    O STORE GUD (arr.) (32)

Hodges, John Sebastian Bach (b. 1830, Bristol, Eng.; d. May 1, 1915, Baltimore, Md.) came to America in 1845, and received his education at Columbia University and General Theological Seminary, New York City; was ordained in 1854 and served Episcopal churches in Pennsylvania, Illinois and New Jersey; was rector of St. Paul's, Baltimore for 35 years, where he developed an excellent choir of men and boys; wrote about 100 hymn tunes and anthems and compiled *The Book of Common Praise,* 1869 and the revised edition of *Hymn Tunes,* 1903.

    EUCHARISTIC HYMN (211)

Hoffman, Elisha Albright (b. May 7, 1839, Orwigsburg, Pa.; d. 1929) attended Union Seminary (of the Evangelical Association) and became a minister of the Evangelical Church; was connected with the Evangelical Association publishing house in Cleveland, Ohio for 11 years, and later was pastor of Evangelical and Presbyterian churches; served as editor of many music publications and was a gifted writer of both words and music of gospel songs.

    Christ has for sin atonement made (86); Down at the cross where my Savior died (289); What a fellowship, what a joy divine (417); I must tell Jesus all of my trials (437)

    BENTON HARBOR (86); ORWIGSBURG (437)

Hoffmann, Heinrich August (b. Apr. 2, 1798, Fallersleben, Hanover, Ger.; d. Jan. 29, 1874, Corvey, Westphalia, Ger.) is described in *Grove's Dictionary* as a "German philologist, poet, hymn-writer and amateur composer"; received his education at Helmstedt, Brunswick and at the University of Göttingen, and later studied Dutch literature in Holland; in 1835 was appointed a professor at Breslau and later was librarian to Prince Lippe at Corvey; edited a significant history of German hymns, *Geschichte des deutschen Kirchenliedes* (Hanover, 1832 and 1854) and the famous *Schlesische Volkslieder mit Melodien* (1842).

    CRUSADER'S HYMN (67)

Holden, Oliver (b. Sept. 18, 1765, Shirley, Mass.; d. Sept. 4, 1844, Charlestown, Mass.), a carpenter by trade, moved to Charlestown, Mass. in 1786 and helped to rebuild the city the British had burned; prospered financially, acquired large real estate holdings and opened a general store; was elected to the state legislature for six terms and served as pastor of the Puritan church; taught music and published several tunebooks, including *The American Harmony* (1792), *Union Harmony* (1793), *The Massachusetts Compiler* (1795), *Sacred Dirges, Hymns and Anthems* (1800), *The Modern Collection of Sacred Music* (1800), *Plain Psalmody* (1800), and *The Charlestown Collection of Sacred Songs* (1803); edited the 6th, 7th and 8th editions of *The Worcester Collection* (1797, 1800, and 1803).

CORONATION (63)

Holmes, Oliver Wendell (b. Aug. 29, 1809, Cambridge, Mass.; d. Oct. 7, 1894, Boston, Mass.) is recognized as one of America's leading literary figures; graduated from Harvard and later returned as professor of anatomy and physiology, a position he held for 35 years; was a brilliant lecturer and teacher, and is best remembered for his writings; in 1857 founded the *Atlantic Monthly* and contributed many delightful articles under the captions "The Autocrat of the Breakfast Table," "The Professor at the Breakfast Table," and "Over the Teacups."

Lord of all being, throned afar (30)

Hopper, Edward (b. Feb. 17, 1816, New York, N.Y.; d. Apr. 23, 1888, New York, N.Y.), a graduate of New York University and Union Theological Seminary, New York City, was pastor of Presbyterian churches in Greenville, N.Y., and Sag Harbor, Long Island, N.Y.; for most of his life, was pastor of the Church of the Sea and Land in New York City's harbor area, ministering to seamen from around the world.

Jesus, Savior, pilot me (446)

Housman, Laurence (b. July 18, 1865, Bromsgrove, Worcester, Eng.; d. Feb. 20, 1959, Glastonbury, Somerset, Eng.), trained at Bromsgrove School and South Kensington, was a writer, art critic, poet and playwright; was confirmed in the Church of England, once was drawn to Roman Catholicism, and in later years was sympathetic to the Quakers; published several works, including *Gods and Their Makers, All-Fellows, The Sheepfold, The Preparation of Peace, Palestine Plays, Little Plays of St. Francis,* and *Victoria Regina.*

Father eternal, Ruler of creation (516)

How, William Walsham (b. Dec. 13, 1823, Shrewsbury, Shrops, Eng.; d. Aug. 10, 1897, Leenane, Co. Mayo, Ire.) was known as the "Poor Man's Bishop" for the humanitarian work he did in the slums of East London; was educated at Wadham College, Oxford, and Durham University, ordained an Anglican priest and served in Kidderminster, Shrewsbury, Whittington, and Oswestry; in 1865 was appointed canon of the Anglican church in Rome; in 1879 became Suffragan Bishop of East London, and in 1888, the first bishop of Wakefield; published *Daily Prayers for Churchmen,* 1852, and *Psalms and Hymns,* 1854; was co-editor (with Arthur Sullivan, *q.v.*) of *Church Hymns,* 1871; wrote more than 50 hymns, many of which are still in use.

O Word of God incarnate (219); O Jesus, Thou art standing (262); We give Thee but Thine own (507; 583, response); For all the saints (533)

Howe, Julia Ward (b. May 27, 1819, New York, N.Y.; d. Oct. 17, 1910, Newport, R. I.) followed the lead of her husband, Dr. Samuel Gridley Howe, in support of humanitarian causes; was a pioneer in women's suffrage, an ardent abolitionist, a pacifist and social worker; frequently preached in the Unitarian fellowship, of which she was a member; wrote three volumes of poetry: *Passion Flowers* (1854), *Words of the Hour* (1856), and *Later Lyrics* (1866).

Mine eyes have seen the glory (522)

Hoyle, Richard Birch (b. Mar. 8, 1875, Cloughfold, Lancs, Eng.; d. Dec. 14, 1939, London, Eng.), a Baptist minister and scholar, served several pastorates in England, and in 1934 moved to the United States to take a teaching assignment at Western Theological Seminary; wrote the article on "The Holy Spirit" for the *Encyclopedia of Religion and Ethics;* was a close friend of Suzanne Bidgrain, who edited *Cantate Domino,* the hymnbook adopted by the World Student Christian Federation.

Thine is the glory, risen, conquering Son (trans.) (171)

Hudson, Ralph E. (b. July 9, 1843, Napoleon, Ohio; d. June 14, 1901, Cleveland, Ohio) joined the Union Army and served as a nurse at the General Hospital, Annapolis, Md. during the Civil War; after discharge taught music at Mount Vernon College, Alliance, Ohio, 1864–69; a licensed preacher in the Methodist Episcopal Church, was active in evangelistic work; was a singer, song writer and compiler, who established his own publishing company at Alliance, Ohio; compiled: *Salvation Echoes* (1882), *Gems of Gospel Song* (1884), *Songs of Peace, Love and Joy* (1885), and *Songs of the Ransomed* (1887), all of which were later combined in one volume titled *Quartette;* frequently set standard hymns to gospel song tunes, sometimes adding a refrain of his own.

All praise to Him who reigns above (ref.) (81); Alas, and did my Savior bleed? (ref.) (279); My life, my love I give to Thee (368)
BLESSED NAME (arr.) (81); HUDSON (279); SATISFIED (283)

Hugg, George C. (b. May 23, 1848, near Haddonfield, N.J.; d. Oct. 13, 1907, Philadelphia, Pa.) as a child showed unusual musical gifts, and became choir director of the Presbyterian church in Berlin, N.J. at the age of 12; moved to Philadelphia and served Tabernacle Presbyterian Church and the Broad and Arch Methodist Episcopal Church as choirmaster, and later was active for many years as an elder, assistant Sunday school superintendent and trustee in the Harper Memorial Presbyterian Church; composed church music and published many collections of songs for Sunday school.

NO, NOT ONE (307)

Hughes, John (b. 1873, Dowlais, Wales; d. May 14, 1932, Llantwit Fardre, Pontypridd, Wales) lived in Llantwit Fardre most of his life; at age 12, went to work as a "door boy" at a local mine, Glyn Colliery; later became an official in the traffic department of the Great Western Railway; an active member of the Salem Baptist Church, followed his father as deacon and precentor (music leader); wrote a large number of hymn tunes, Sunday school marches, and anthems.

CWM RHONDDA (448, 466)

Hull, Eleanor Henrietta (b. Jan. 15, 1860, Manchester, Eng.; d. Jan. 13, 1935, London, Eng.), founder and secretary of the Irish Text Society, served as president of the Irish Literary Society of London; authored several volumes on Irish literature and history.

Be Thou my Vision (versified) (344)

Hultman, John Alfred (b. July 6, 1861, Hjärtlanda, Småland, Sweden; d. Aug. 7, 1942, Glendale, Calif.) showed an interest in music very early in his life; came to America with his family at the age of eight and settled on a farm in Essex, Ia.; taught school and directed the church choir in Fridhem, Neb., and later became pastor of the church; 1879–81, studied at the Chicago Atheneum and served as choir director at the Douglas Park Covenant Church, then became an itinerant preacher and musician and traveled through the midwest; in 1896–97 was on the music staff at North Park College and maintained an interest in this school throughout his life; while pastor of the Salem Square Church in Worcester, Mass., continued giving concerts with his son Paul and founded the Hultman Conservatory of Music; moved to Sweden in 1909 and continued to concertize there and in the United States, becoming known as "The Sunshine Singer"; was also a writer and composer of hymns who published *Cymbalen* in 1885 and collaborated with A. L. Skoog (*q.v.*) in producing *Jubelklangen* (1895); helped to compile *Sions Basun*, the first official hymnal of the Evangelical Mission Covenant Church.

TACK, O GUD (571)

Hunter, William (b. May 26, 1811, near Ballymena, Co. Antrim, Ire.; d. Oct. 18, 1877, Cleveland, Ohio) emigrated to America at age six, and the family settled at York, Pa.; studied at Madison College, was ordained to the Methodist ministry and served in the Pittsburgh Conference; edited the Pittsburgh *Conference Journal* (1836–40) and its successor, *Christian Advocate* (1844–52, 1872–76); was appointed Professor of Hebrew at Allegheny College (1855–70); wrote more than 100 hymns, which appeared in his *Select Melodies* (1838–51), *The Minstrel of Zion* (1845), and *Songs of Devotion* (1859).

The great Physician now is near (71)

Husband, Edward (b. 1843; d. 1908) trained at St. Aidan's College, Birkenhead, and was ordained in the Church of England in 1866; served churches in Atherton and Folkestone and was an organ recitalist who frequently lectured on church music; edited and published: *The Mission Hym-*

nal (1874), *Supplemental Tunes to Popular Hymns* (1882), and an *Appendix for Use at the Church of St. Michael and All Angels, Folkestone* (1885).

ST. HILDA (262)

Husband, John Jenkins (b. 1760, Plymouth, Eng.; d. May 19, 1825, Philadelphia, Pa.) was a clerk at Surrey Chapel in his early years in Plymouth, England; came to America in 1809 and settled in Philadelphia, where he conducted "singing schools" and served St. Paul's Protestant Episcopal Church as clerk; composed a number of hymn tunes and anthems, and supplied "an improved mode of teaching music" as a part of Andrew Adgate's *Philadelphia Harmony,* 1790.

REVIVE US AGAIN (358)

Hussey, Jennie Evelyn (b. Feb. 8, 1874, Henniker, N.H.; d. 1958, Concord, N.H.) began writing poetry when she was very young; spent most of her life on the farm where four generations of her Quaker ancestors had lived before her; according to Phil Kerr (*Music in Evangelism*), spent her last years in the Home for the Aged in Concord, N.H.

King of my life, I crown Thee now (154)

Hustad, Donald Paul (b. Oct. 2, 1918, near Echo, Yellow Medicine Co., Minn.) lost his father in a hunting accident at age one, and grew up with his mother and brother at the Boone Biblical College, Boone, Ia.; began to study piano at age four and continued his education at John Fletcher College (B.A., 1940) and Northwestern University (M.Mus., 1945; D.Mus., 1963); Associate of the American Guild of Organists (1969), Fellow of the Royal College of Organists, London (1974), and studied organ in France with Jean Langlais (1972); staff musician, WMBI, Chicago (1942–45) and musical director, "Club Time," ABC Radio (1945–53); Associate Professor of Music, Olivet Nazarene College, Kankakee, Ill., (1946–50); director, Sacred Music Department, Moody Bible Institute, Chicago (1950–63) and conductor of the Moody Chorale with concerts in the United States, Canada and Europe; organist for Billy Graham crusades on five continents (1961–67) and director of "Crusader Men" for the "Hour of Decision" broadcast; since 1966, Professor of Church Music, Southern Baptist Theological Seminary, Louisville, Ky. and designated "V. V. Cooke Professor of Organ" (1975); an editor for Hope Publishing Company, Chicago and Carol Stream, Ill., since 1950; composer of much church music for choir, organ and piano, including the cantata, *Celebration of Discipleship* (1975); assisted in compiling *Tabernacle Hymns, No. 5* (1953), *Worship and Service Hymnal* (1957), *Youth Worship and Sing* (1959), and *Favorite Hymns of Praise* (1967); co-editor with Cliff Barrows of *Crusader Hymns* (1966) and principal editor of *Hymns for the Living Church* (1974); research writer (for members of the Billy Graham team) of *Crusade Hymn Stories* (1967); member of the consulting committee, *Book of Worship for United States Forces* (1974) and member of the executive committee, *Baptist Hymnal* (1975); active as recitalist, recording artist, clinician, lecturer and writer; author of this dictionary-handbook.

RIDGE LINE (218); HIGHLANDS (274); SLANE (arr.) (344); WEDLOCK (arr.) (413)

Hutchinson, Albert H. No information has been found concerning this author.

For all the blessings of the year (568)

Idle, Christopher Martin (b. Sept. 11, 1938, Bromley, Kent, Eng.) received his education at Elthan College, St. Peter's College, Oxford (B.A., 1962) and Clifton Theological College, Bristol; ordained in the Church of England, has served as curate in churches in Lancashire and London, and since 1971 has been priest-in-charge of St. Matthias' Church, Poplar, London; is a prolific writer for magazines and newspapers on such subjects as "Christian communication, the Gospel, and peace," and was once jailed (1960) for participation in non-violent civil disobedience against nuclear weapons; has written and published 23 hymn texts.

Then I saw a new heaven and earth (543)

Ingalls, Jeremiah (b. Mar. 1, 1764, Andover, Mass.; d. Apr. 6, 1828, Hancock, Vt.) during his lifetime was a farmer, cooper, tavern keeper, and singing teacher; settled in Newbury, Vt. where he served as deacon and choir director of the Congregational church for a time; compiled *The Christian Harmony*, 1805, an important collection of folk hymns.

I LOVE THEE (publ.) (87)

Irvine, Jessie Seymour (b. 1836, Dunottar, Scot.; d. 1887, Crimond, Scot.), the daughter of a minister, lived with her father in the manses at Dunottar, in Peterhead and finally, in Crimond; composed the famous tune "Crimond" in the latter town.

CRIMOND (45)

Jabusch, Willard Francis (b. Mar. 12, 1930, Chicago, Ill.) received his education at Quigley Preparatory School, St. Mary of the Lake Seminary (B.A., S.T.B., M.A.) and Northwestern University (Ph.D. 1968), with special training (in music) at the Chicago Conservatory of Music and (in English) at the University of London; served as parish priest, St. James Catholic Church, Chicago, 1956–61; was a teacher, Quigley Preparatory School, 1961–63, and at Niles College (Loyola University), 1963–66; has been a professor at St. Mary of the Lake Seminary since 1968; has written 80 hymn texts and 40 hymn tunes, besides many magazine articles; published the collection, *Sing of Christ Jesus.*

Whatsoever you do to the least (518)
WHATSOEVER YOU DO (518)

Jackson, Robert (b. 1842, Oldham, Lancs, Eng.; d. 1914, Oldham, Lancs, Eng.) was a teacher, composer, conductor, and organist; studied at the

Royal Academy of Music; served as organist and choirmaster at St. Mark's, Grosvenor Square, London; in 1868 succeeded his father as organist and choirmaster at St. Peter's Church, Oldham, remaining 46 years until his death (his father had been there 48 years!).

TRENTHAM (187)

James, Mary D. (b. 1810; d. 1883). No additional information is available.

All for Jesus! All for Jesus! (384)

Jean de Fecamp (b. *ca.* 1000 near Ravenna; d. Feb. 22, 1079, Fecamp, Normandy) studied at Dijon under William, Abbott of St. Benignus; accompanied his mentor to Fecamp (a seaport town near the present Le Havre) in Normandy to reform the Abbey there and establish a Benedictine colony; succeeded William as head of the abbey, 1028–1078; in later life took a trip to the Holy Land and was thrown into prison by the Turks; returned to France in 1076 and retired to Fecamp; wrote a number of ascetic works, many for the use of the widow of Emperor Henry III.

Ah, holy Jesus, how hast Thou offended? (152)

John of Damascus (b. *ca.* 696, Damascus; d. *ca.* 754), a theologian and hymnist who lived and worked at the St. Sabas monastery near Jerusalem, was educated principally by an Italian monk named Cosmos; was an iconolator, defending the use of icons and images in the church; organized the liturgical chants for the Eastern (Orthodox) Church, and is remembered for his hymns (canons) written for office worship on the festival days of the Christian Year; wrote the treatise, *The Fountains of Knowledge.*

Come, ye faithful, raise the strain (164); The day of resurrection (168)

Johnson, William (b. Mar. 28, 1906, near Center City, Minn.) spent his early years on a farm near Lindstrom, Minn. and finished only eight years of schooling; was an avid reader of the Bible and of great literary works; wrote many poems which appeared in such periodicals as *The Lutheran Companion,* and published *Wild Flowers,* 1948; married late in life and was active in farming near Chisago City, Minn.

Deep were His wounds, and red (142)

Johnston, Julia Harriette (b. Jan. 21, 1849, Salineville, Ohio; d. Mar. 6, 1919, Peoria, Ill.) at age six moved to Peoria, Ill., where her father was pastor of the First Presbyterian Church until his death in 1864; remained in Peoria for the rest of her life, and was a leader in the First Presbyterian Sunday School for over 40 years; wrote lesson material for primary grades which was distributed by David C. Cook Publishing Co.; published several books: *School of the Master* (1880), *Bright Threads* (1897), *Indian and Spanish Neighbors* (1905), and *Fifty Missionary Heroes* (1913); wrote approximately 500 hymn poems which were set to music by various composers.

Marvelous grace of our loving Lord (240)

Jones, Joseph David (b. 1827, Bryngrugog, Wales; d. Sept. 17, 1870, Rhuthyn, Wales), a Welsh amateur musician, wrote hymn and psalm tunes; went to London to study music with the money made on the sale of his first collection of psalm tunes, *Y Perganiedydd*, 1847; later taught music in the British School at Rhuthyn, and eventually opened a private school there; published a popular cantata (*The Court of Arthur*), a book for singers, several collections of Welsh melodies, and (with E. Stephen) a collection of hymns and tunes, *Llyfr Tonau ac Emynau*, 1868.

GWALCHMAI (12)

Jones, Lewis Edgar (b. Feb. 8, 1865, Yates City, Ill.; d. Sept. 1, 1936, Santa Barbara, Calif.) was a classmate of Billy Sunday and a graduate of Moody Bible Institute in Chicago; spent his life in YMCA work, serving in different capacities in Davenport, Ia. and Fort Worth, Tex., finally becoming general secretary in Santa Barbara, Calif., a position he held until his retirement in 1925; had the hobby of writing hymns (both words and music), which appeared under various pseudonyms (e.g., Lewis Edgar, Mary Slater, and Edgar Lewis).

Would you be free from the burden of sin? (255)
POWER IN THE BLOOD (255)

Jones, Richard Granville (b. July 26, 1926, Dursley, Gloucs, Eng.) received his training at Truro School in Cornwall, St. John's College, Cambridge (B.A.), and Hartley Victoria Methodist College, Manchester (B.D.); served as staff secretary for the Student Christian Movement in Nottingham for two years, as minister in Methodist churches in Sheffield and Birkenhead, and since 1969 has been Senior Tutor at Hartley Victoria Methodist College; has lectured in Social and Pastoral Theology at Manchester University; has written approximately 12 hymn texts, and published *Worship for Today*, 1967 and *Towards a Radical Church*, 1969.

God of concrete, God of steel (52)

Jude, William Herbert (b. Sept., 1851, Westleton, Suffolk, Eng.; d. Aug. 7, 1922, London, Eng.) began his career as organist of the Blue Coat Hospital, a charitable institution in Liverpool; in 1889 was appointed organist, Stretford Town Hall, near Manchester; was one of the first to travel to Australia from England to play recitals and lecture on musical subjects; was editor of *Monthly Hymnal, Ministry of Music* and *Music and the Higher Life* (1904), *Mission Hymns* (1911), and *Festival Hymns* (1916); composed a number of anthems and songs, and an operetta, *Innocents Abroad*.

GALILEE (503)

Judson, Adoniram (b. Aug. 9, 1788, Malden, Mass.; d. Apr. 12, 1850, at sea, Bay of Bengal), one of the first missionaries from America, was educated at Brown University and Andover Theological Seminary; with his wife, sailed for India in 1812 under the Congregational foreign missions board; from study of the New Testament enroute, was convinced of the validity of Baptist practice, and was baptized by immersion after arriving in

Calcutta; in 1813 was compelled by the British to leave India, settled in Burma and was imprisoned there for many months due to conflict between the Burmese and the British; in 1834 completed a translation of the Bible into Burmese, and in later years compiled a Burmese-English dictionary.

Come, Holy Spirit, Dove divine (215)

Kaiser, Kurt Frederic (b. Dec. 17, 1934, Chicago, Ill.) was born into a hymnic home—his father, Otto Kaiser, was chairman of a hymnbook compilation committee of the Plymouth Brethren; received musical training at Northwestern University (B.Mus., M.Mus.) and is a brilliant pianist, arranger, composer and conductor; since 1959 has been associated with Word, Inc., Waco, Texas and is presently serving as Vice President and Director of Music, in charge of all recording; directs the "Singing Men of Texas," a group of Baptist ministers of music; a deacon in the Baptist church, also serves as pianist for Sunday evening services; has written approximately 60 hymn texts and tunes in contemporary styles; collaborated in several musicals, including *Tell It Like It Is* (1969) and *God's People;* edited *Sing and Celebrate* (I and II); in 1973 received the honorary Doctor of Sacred Music degree from Trinity College, Deerfield, Illinois.

It only takes a spark (484)
PASS IT ON (484)

Keble, John (b. Apr. 25, 1792, Fairford, Gloucs, Eng.; d. Mar. 29, 1866, Bournemouth, Eng.) was first tutored at home by his father, entered Corpus Christi College, Oxford at the age of 14 and graduated with "double first class honors"; was ordained a priest in the Church of England (1816) and served several rural churches; published a hymnal, *The Christian Year,* 1827, of which not less than 96 editions were released during his lifetime; was appointed Professor of Poetry at Oxford in 1831; was a leader in the Oxford Movement, and in 1836 was named Vicar of Hursley, which post he kept until his death.

Sun of my soul, Thou Savior dear (559)

Kelly, Thomas (b. July 13, 1769, Kellyville, Co. Queens, Ire.; d. May 14, 1855, Dublin, Ire.) received his education at Trinity College, Dublin; first studied for the bar, but felt called to the ministry and took Anglican Holy Orders in 1792; because of his evangelical preaching, came into disfavor with the archbishop, left the established church and became an independent minister; a brillant scholar and wealthy, built a number of churches of his sect; published *A Collection of Psalms and Hymns* (1802), *Hymns on Various Passages of Scripture* (1804), and *Hymns by Thomas Kelly, Not Before Published* (1815); wrote at least 765 hymns, and in 1815 published a companion volume of tunes he had written in a variety of meters.

Praise the Savior, ye who know Him! (78); Hark! ten thousand harps and voices (172); Look, ye saints! the sight is glorious (175); The head that once was crowned with thorns (176)

Ken, Thomas (b. July, 1637, Berkhampstead, Herts, Eng.; d. Mar. 19, 1710, Longleat, Wilts, Eng.) was trained at Winchester College and New

College, Oxford, ordained an Anglican priest in 1662 and served several small churches in England; 1669–79, served at Winchester Cathedral and College; published *Manual of Prayers for the Use of the Scholars of Winchester College,* 1674; was briefly chaplain to Princess Mary and later, to the British fleet; in 1685 was made Bishop of Bath and Wells; was one of seven bishops imprisoned in the Tower of London for refusing to subscribe to James II's Declaration of Indulgence, was tried and acquitted; wrote much poetry, published in four volumes in 1721, after his death.

> Awake, my soul, and with the sun (551); Praise God from whom all blessings flow (572, 573)

Kennedy, Benjamin Hall (b. Nov. 4, 1804, Summer Hill, near Birmingham, Eng.; d. Apr. 6, 1889, near Torquay, Devon, Eng.) was trained at King Edward's School (Birmingham), Shrewsbury School, and St. John's, Cambridge; was a fellow at St. John's (1828–36) and headmaster of Shrewsbury School (1836–66); ordained in the Church of England, served as prebendary of Lichfield Cathedral, rector of West Felton, Salop and canon at Ely; was very active in writing, compiling, adapting and translating hymns (mostly from German); published a *Psalter, or the Psalms of David, in English Verse,* 1860, and *Hymnologia Christiana, or Psalms and Hymns Selected and Arranged in the Order of the Christian Seasons,* 1863.

> Ask ye what great thing I know (trans.) (144)

Kerr, Hugh Thompson (b. Feb. 11, 1872, Elora, Can.; d. June 27, 1950, Pittsburgh, Pa.) received his schooling at the University of Toronto and Western Theological Seminary, Pittsburgh; was ordained into the Presbyterian ministry and served churches in Kansas and Illinois, with a long tenure (1913–46) at Shadyside Presbyterian Church, Pittsburgh, where he pioneered in religious broadcasting; was elected Moderator of the General Assembly of the Presbyterian Church in the U.S.A. in 1930; served as chairman of the committees for the Presbyterian *Hymnal,* 1933 and the Presbyterian *Book of Common Worship.*

> God of our life, through all the circling years (326)

Ketchum, Albert Allen (b. Feb. 12, 1894) was a student at Moody Bible Institute about 1920; in 1922–23 wrote 12 to 15 songs which were sold to Harry D. Clarke (*q.v.*) for publication; in the 1940's was associated in business with Delco Products Co. in Los Angeles, and lived in Long Beach, Calif. No other information is available.

> Deep in my heart there's a gladness (93)
> KETCHUM (93)

Kethe, William (d. ca. 1600) is believed to have been a native of Scotland, but no record of his early life is available; was in exile on the Continent during the persecution under "Bloody Mary," spending time in Frankfurt and Geneva; may have been one of the scholars who worked on the English-language Geneva ("Breeches") Bible, 1560; served as chaplain to the British troops under the Earl of Warwick, at Havre; returning to England, was vicar of Childe Oxford, Dorsetshire, 1561–93; contributed 25 metrical psalms to the Anglo-Genevan Psalter, 1561, which later appeared in the Scottish Psalter, 1564–65.

All people that on earth do dwell (20); O worship the King, all glorious above (21)

Kirk, James M. (b. June 18, 1854, Flushing, Ohio; d. July 11, 1945) grew up in a Methodist home and accepted Christ at an early age; became associated with the Christian and Missionary Alliance in 1887, soon after its founding by A. B. Simpson; with his wife, organized the Gospel Mission (affiliated with the Alliance) in Flushing, Ohio in 1907; wrote numerous gospel song texts and tunes, and traveled with a group called "The Ohio Quartet," singing at conventions and gatherings of The Christian and Missionary Alliance.

BLESSED QUIETNESS (arr.) (192)

Kirkpatrick, William James (b. Feb. 27, 1838, Duncannon, Pa.; d. Sept. 20, 1921, Philadelphia, Pa.) received early musical training from his father and later studied with several recognized music teachers; was a fife major during the Civil War, and later a furniture dealer in Philadelphia, 1862–78; edited his first music collection at age 21 (*Devotional Melodies*, 1859), and thereafter compiled some 100 books, collaborating mostly with John R. Sweney (*q.v.*), but also with H. L. Gilmour and John H. Stockton (*q.v.*), and publishing with the John J. Hood Company, Philadelphia; wrote many favorite gospel song melodies for his publications; was a life-long Methodist, associated first with Wharton Street M. E. Church and later director of music for 11 years at Grace M. E. Church.

BLESSED NAME (81); CRADLE SONG (112); DUNCANNON (154); COMFORTER (189); ZERUIAH (273); LANDÅS (287); GREEN-WELL (305); TRUST IN JESUS (312); RONDINELLA (333); KIRKPATRICK (402); JESUS SAVES (486)

Kitchin, George William (b. Dec. 7, 1827, Suffolk, Eng.; d. Oct. 13, 1912, Durham, Eng.), the son of a minister, was educated at Ipswich Grammar School, King's College School and College, and Christ Church, Oxford, where he later served as Censor and Tutor; from 1883–94 was Dean of Winchester, in 1894 became Dean of Durham and in 1909, Chancellor of Durham University; published many books in the areas of archaeology, biography and history.

Lift high the Cross (141)

Knapp, Phoebe Palmer (b. Mar. 9, 1839, New York, N.Y.; d. July 10, 1908, Poland Springs, Me.), daughter of a Methodist evangelist, showed unusual musical talent as a young girl; at age 16 married John Fairfield Knapp, a successful business man and founder of the Metropolitan Life Insurance Company; was a close friend of Fanny Crosby (*q.v.*) and a generous leader in promoting evangelical and humanitarian causes; was mother of Joseph Palmer Knapp (d. 1951), president of Crowell-Collier Publishing Company; published over 500 gospel song tunes; is remembered as composer of the tune "Assurance" and the music for "Open the Gates of the Temple," for both of which Fanny Crosby wrote the words.

ASSURANCE (317)

Knapp, William (b. 1698, Wareham, Dorset, Eng.; d. Sept. 26, 1768, Poole, Dorset, Eng.) was an organist and composer of German descent; served as parish clerk of St. James' Church, Poole for 39 years, announcing the hymns and leading the responses; published *A Sett of New Psalms and Anthems in Four Parts*, 1738 and *New Church Melody*, 1753.

WAREHAM (563)

Knecht, Justin Heinrich (b. Sept. 30, 1752, Biberach, Württemberg, Ger.; d. Dec. 1, 1817, Biberach, Ger.) received his schooling at the convent of Esslingen and learned to play the flute, oboe, trumpet, violin and organ; became professor of literature and directed the musical activities in his home town; for two years (1807–09) was director of the opera and the court orchestra in Stuttgart, then returned to Biberach; collaborating with J. F. Christmann, published *Vollständige Sammlung.....Vierstimmige Choralmelodien für das neue Würtemburgisches Landgesangbuch,* 1799, which included 97 of his own tunes.

ST. HILDA (262); VIENNA (445)

Kocher, Conrad (b. Dec. 16, 1786, Dietzingen, Württemberg, Ger.; d. Mar. 12, 1872, Stuttgart, Ger.) studied piano and composition in St. Petersburg (Leningrad), and later spent a year in Italy, becoming greatly interested in *a cappella* singing and the music of Palestrina (*q.v.*); founded the School of Sacred Song in Stuttgart, 1821, and became the director of music in the collegiate church there, setting a standard for needed reforms in German church music; author of *Die Tonkunst in der Kirche,* 1823, and compiler of *Zionsharfe,* 1855, also wrote two operas, an oratorio, and numerous smaller works.

DIX (55, 114)

Kremser, Edward (b. Apr. 10, 1838, Vienna, Aust.; d. Nov. 26, 1914, Vienna, Aust.) was chorusmaster of the Vienna Männergesangverein and a leader in choral singing in his day; composed many works for voices and instruments, and published the popular *Sechs Altniederländische Volkslieder,* 1877; edited *Wiener Lieder und Tänze* (2 vols.), 1912 and 1913.

KREMSER (arr.) (570)

Lane, Spencer (b. Apr. 7, 1843, Tilton, N.H.; d. Aug. 10, 1903, Readville, Va.) served for three years with the Union Army during the Civil War; studied at the New England Conservatory of Music and became a teacher of voice and instruments in New York City; moving to Woonsocket, R.I., established a music store and was organist and choirmaster at St. James' Protestant Episcopal Church; later worked with a music firm in Baltimore, and was organist and choirmaster at All Saints' Church; wrote some anthems and hymn tunes, mostly during his stay in Rhode Island.

PENITENCE (418)

Langran, James (b. Nov. 10, 1835, St. Pancras, London, Eng.; d. June 8, 1909, Tottenham, London, Eng.) studied with John Baptiste Calkin (*q.v.*), and was organist at St. Paul's, Tottenham (1870–1909) and instructor in music at St. Katherine's Training College from 1878; wrote several services (Anglican) and hymn tunes, and was musical editor of the *New Mitre Hymnal*, 1875; is the subject of a biographical sketch in *Musical Times*, Feb., 1907.

LANGRAN (210, 441)

Larcom, Lucy (b. Mar. 5, 1826, Beverly, Mass.; d. Apr. 17, 1893, Boston, Mass.) interrupted her education to work in the mills at Lowell, Mass. from age 11 to 19; taught "country school" in Illinois, while attending Monticello Female Seminary at Alton; returned to Massachusetts where she continued to teach while studying at Wheaton Seminary at Norton; was a close friend of John Greenleaf Whittier (*q.v.*), who encouraged her in her writing; published several volumes of poetry, including *Wild Roses of Cape Ann* (1881), *Poetical Works* (1885), *At the Beautiful Gate* (1892), *Beckonings* (1886), and *As It Is in Heaven* (1891).

Draw Thou my soul, O Christ (356)

Lathbury, Mary Artemisia (b. Aug. 10, 1841, Manchester, N.Y.; d. Oct. 20, 1913, East Orange, N.J.), the daughter of a Methodist minister, was a professional artist, as well as a writer and poet; served as general editor of youth publications for the Methodist Sunday School Union and much of her poetry first appeared in those journals; founded the youth movement known as the "Look-Up Legion"; was known as the "Poet Laureate of Lake Chautauqua" because of her close association with that New York conference.

Break Thou the bread of life (220); Day is dying in the west (557)

Laufer, Calvin Weiss (b. Apr. 6, 1874, Brodheadsville, Pa.; d. Sept. 20, 1938, Philadelphia, Pa.), educated at Franklin and Marshall College and Union Theological Seminary, was ordained a Presbyterian minister and served churches in New York and New Jersey; was interested in religious education and music, and in 1914 became a field representative of the Presbyterian Board of Publication and Sunday School Work, and later (1925) served as assistant editor of music publications; was a capable author who published: *Keynotes of Optimism* (1911), *The Incomparable Christ* (1914), *The Bible-Story and Content* (1924), *Junior Church School Hymnal* (1927), *The Church School Hymnal for Youth* (1928), *Primary Worship and Music* (1930), *Hymn Lore* (1932), and *When the Little Child Wants to Sing* (1935); was one of the editors of the Presbyterian *Hymnal*, 1933 and associate editor of the *Handbook to the Hymnal*, 1935.

HALL (374)

Laurinus, Laurentius Laurentii (b. 1573, Söderköping, Sweden; d. Nov. 29, 1655) studied at the University of Uppsala and received the master's degree at Wittenberg in 1603; became headmaster of a school in Söderköping; was ordained, and later served as parish priest in Häradshammar and Jonsberg for 46 years, though he was blind for the last part of his life; wrote books in Swedish, German and Latin, and in 1622 published *Musica rudimenta,* Sweden's first textbook on singing; published *Haffenrefferi Compendium Locorum Theologicorum,* and included several songs in an appendix, including the popular "I himmelen."

In heaven above (542)

Leddy, Stephen Dale (b. Sept. 15, 1944, San Angelo, Tex.) was born of musical parents and received early training in piano and violin; attended San Angelo Central High School, Baylor University and the University of Texas (B.S., 1970); has served as Youth and Music Minister in the Trinity Methodist Church in San Angelo, Tex. and the Woodlawn Baptist Church in Austin, Tex.; since 1971 has been Music Director for the International Evangelism Association in Fort Worth, Tex., working in revival crusades in the south and southwest; a Southern Baptist, has written approximately 20 contemporary hymn texts and tunes, several of which have been released by Hope Publishing Company.

Worthy is the Lamb (94)
WORTHY LAMB (94)

Leech, Bryan Jeffery (b. May 14, 1931, Buckhurst Hill, Essex, Eng.) in 1973 won first prize for the hymn "Let God Be God," used in the ecumenical evangelistic movement "Key 73"; was educated at London (England) Bible College, Barrington (Mass.) College (B.A.), and North Park Seminary, Chicago, Illinois and has studied music theory at Westmont (Calif.) College; affiliated with the Evangelical Covenant denomination since coming to the United States in 1955, has served churches in Boston, Montclair (N.J.), and San Francisco, and is presently serving the Montecito Covenant Church in Santa Barbara, Calif.; has written ten hymn texts and five hymn tunes (several have been included in contemporary hymnals), two ballads, a musical play *Ebenezer,* and a musical adaptation of Dickens' "A Christmas Carol"; co-authored the novel *It Must Have Been McNutt;* was a member of the commission which prepared *The Covenant Hymnal,* 1973; assisted in the preparation of *Hymns for the Family of God* (Paragon, 1976).

Thro' all the world let every nation sing (492)

Lemmel, Helen Howarth (b. Nov. 14, 1864, Wardle, Eng.; d. Nov. 1, 1961, Seattle, Wash.), daughter of a Wesleyan Methodist pastor in England, was brought to America in 1873, lived briefly in Mississippi and settled in Wisconsin; a brilliant singer, studied under various teachers here and (for almost four years) in Germany, and sang in concerts and in churches, traveling widely; participated in Chautauqua groups in Illinois and Wisconsin in the early 1900's; taught voice privately in studios in Milwaukee and Madison, Wis., and later at Moody Bible Institute and the Bible Institute of Los Angeles; finally made her home in Seattle, Wash., and was a member of Ballard Baptist Church; wrote about 500 hymns and much music for children.

O soul, are you weary and troubled? (252)
LEMMEL (252)

Liljestrand, Paul Frederick (b. May 15, 1931, Montclair, N.J.) is a professional concert artist under Columbia Artists Management—accompanist for other soloists, organist, and member of the duo-piano team Krellwitz and Liljestrand; received musical training at Juilliard School of Music (B.S., M.S.), and Union Theological Seminary's School of Sacred Music (S.M.M.); was Chairman of the Sacred Music Department of Northeastern Collegiate Bible Institute and Minister of Music at Brookdale (N.J.) Baptist Church; since 1966 has been minister of music, Calvary Baptist Church, New York City, and since 1972, Chairman of the Department of Music, Nyack College, Nyack, N.Y.; has written and published three hymn tunes, three cantatas, and five anthems.

CONRAD (492)

Lillenas, Haldor (b. Nov. 19, 1885 on the island Stord, near Bergen, Norway; d. Aug. 18, 1959, Aspen, Colorado) came to America as an infant, lived with his family in South Dakota for two years and then settled in Astoria, Oregon; was confirmed in the Lutheran Church at the age of 15; through the ministry of the Peniel Mission in Portland, was converted and called to preach; attended Deets Pacific Bible College in Los Angeles (later known as Pasadena College); married Bertha Mae Wilson, a song writer in her own right, and they were both elders in the Church of the Nazarene; completed three-year courses in harmony, counterpoint and composition under Daniel Protheroe and Adolph Rosenbecker at the Siegel-Myers School of Music in Chicago; 1914–24, traveled as an evangelist, and then pastored churches in California, Illinois, Texas and Indiana; during his early years, supplied songs and choir music for many song evangelists, *e.g.* Homer Hammontree, Arthur McKee and Charles M. Alexander; in 1924 founded Lillenas Music Company in Indianapolis, Ind., which was purchased by the Nazarene Publishing Company in 1930, with the founder staying on as music editor for 20 years; wrote some 4,000 texts and tunes; received the honorary D.Mus. degree, Olivet Nazarene College, Kankakee, Ill.

The Bible stands like a rock undaunted (218); Wonderful grace of Jesus (245)
WONDERFUL GRACE (245); LILLENAS (292)

Lindeman, Ludvig Mathias (b. Nov. 28, 1812, Trondheim, Norway; d. May 23, 1887, Oslo, Norway) was acknowledged at his funeral as the man who "taught the Norwegian people to sing"; was born into a prominent Norwegian musical family, possibly of German descent; began to study theology, but gravitated to music and was organist for Our Savior's Church, Oslo from 1839 until his death; is chiefly remembered as a collector of

Norse folk melodies, which activity was subsidized by the national government; prepared musical settings for the Norwegian Lutheran *Salmebog* (1869) which were released in 1877 as *Koralbog for den Norske Kirke.*
KIRKEN DEN ER ET (201)

Lindemann, Johann (b. *ca.* 1550, Gotha, Ger.; d. *ca.* 1634) was a son of the burgess of Gotha and attended the Gymnasium there and the University of Jena; became a cantor in Gotha *ca.* 1571 and remained in that post until 1631; wrote both words and music of sacred songs, and published three volumes of Christmas and New Year's songs in 1598.
In Thee is gladness (64)

Lloyd, Eva Brown (b. Mar. 9, 1912, Jameson, Mo.) received her higher education at Northwest Missouri State University (B.S.), and University of Missouri at Kansas City (M.A.); taught in elementary and secondary schools in Missouri, and for 15 years taught English literature at Northwest Missouri University (Maryville); a Baptist wife and mother, is involved in Christian education in the church, and has served as director of the Women's Missionary Union; has written five hymn texts and published both poetry and prose.
Come, all Christians, be committed (498)

Loes, Harry Dixon (b. Oct. 20, 1892, Kalamazoo, Mich.; d. Feb. 9, 1965, Chicago, Ill.) taught music at Moody Bible Institute when the author of this volume was director of the Sacred Music Department there; born "Harold Loes," was called "Harry" as a child and was known by that name throughout life, choosing his own middle name after Dr. A. C. Dixon, pastor of Moody Church; studied at Moody Bible Institute under D. B. Towner (*q.v.*) and later at the American Conservatory of Music, the Metropolitan School of Music and Chicago Musical College; for twelve years traveled in evangelistic work throughout North America and then (1927–39) was director of music and religious education at Baptist churches in Okmulgee and Muskogee, Okla.; in 1939 joined the music faculty of Moody Bible Institute where he served until his retirement; wrote some 1500 hymn texts and 3000 hymn tunes.
Friends all around us are trying to find (82)
BOUNDLESS PRAISE (76); OKMULGEE (82)

Loizeaux, Alfred Samuel (b. Feb. 12, 1877, Vinton, Ia.; d. May 7, 1962, Towson, Md.) was a director of Loizeaux Brothers, Inc., a publishing firm founded by his forebears as "Bible Truth Depot"; for many years was an executive with the Baltimore Consolidated Light, Heat, and Power Company; a member of a Plymouth Brethren assembly, was one of the founders of the Baltimore School of the Bible, and active in evangelism and missions; after developing a speech difficulty, gave his time largely to writing; edited a monthly devotional magazine, *Help and Food,* for 17 years.
God, our Father, we adore Thee! (st. 3) (3)

Longstaff, William Dunn (b. Jan. 28, 1822, Sunderland, Eng.; d. Apr. 2, 1894, Sunderland, Eng.), the son of a wealthy shipowner, gave generously to philanthropic causes; was associated with the Bethesda Free Chapel, serving as its treasurer; was a close friend of Moody and Sankey (*q.v.*), and also William Booth, and may possibly have been a member of the Salvation Army for a time.

    Take time to be holy (392)

Lovelace, Austin Cole (b. Mar. 26, 1919, Rutherfordton, N.C.) is one of America's leading church musicians today—a teacher, author, composer and organist-director; received his training at High Point College in North Carolina (A.B.) and Union Theological Seminary School of Sacred Music (S.M.M., S.M.D.); has served as minister of music in leading Methodist and Presbyterian churches in North Carolina, Nebraska, Illinois and Colorado; was associate professor of church music at Garrett Theological Seminary, a lecturer in hymnology at Union Theological Seminary, adjunct faculty member at Iliff School of Theology and professor of organ at Temple Buell College, Denver; is at present minister of music, Lovers' Lane Methodist Church, Dallas, Tex.; has published *The Organist and Hymn Playing*, 1962, and *The Anatomy of Hymnody*, 1965; co-authored *Music and Worship in the Church*, 1960 and rev. 1976 (with William G. Rice), and wrote the material on hymn tunes in *Companion to the Hymnal*, 1970; has written a great deal of sacred choral music and many hymn tunes.

    Jesus, we want to meet (versified) (547)

    KEBLE (arr.) (511)

Loveless, Wendell Phillips (b. Feb. 2, 1892, Wheaton, Illinois) was the first employer of this book's author, at radio station WMBI, Chicago; born and raised in Wheaton, Illinois, was engaged in business in Chicago; in 1914 was chosen as a member of an entertainment group that toured the United States for six seasons, giving him experience and training in voice, piano, dramatics and master-of-ceremonies duties, which he used later in Christian ministry; was an officer in the Marine Corps during World War I; was converted as a result of reading the Bible at home; was director of the radio department at Moody Bible Institute, Chicago, 1926–47; later pastored churches in Wheaton, Ill., Boca Raton, Fla., and Honolulu, Hawaii, continuing radio ministry in the last two locations; now retired, still teaches a Bible class at the First Chinese Christian Church in Honolulu; has written several Bible study volumes, a manual on gospel broadcasting, and many gospel songs and choruses, most of which appeared in his *Radio Songs and Choruses of the Gospel* (5 vols.)

    LOVELESS (319)

Lowden, Carl Harold (b. Oct. 12, 1883, Burlington, N. J.; d. Feb. 27, 1963, Collingswood, N. J.), usually listed as "C. Harold Lowden," learned to play the violin as a boy and began writing songs at 12 years of age; was affiliated briefly with the Hall-Mack Company, and for 12 years served as musical editor for the Evangelical and Reformed Church Board; later established his own business in Camden, N. J.; for eight years taught music at the Bible Institute of Pennsylvania (now Philadelphia College of Bible) and served as minister of music for the Linden Baptist Church in Camden, N. J. for 28 years; wrote a large number of hymn tunes and edited many collections.

> LIVING (380); GENEVA (388)

Lowell, James Russell (b. Feb. 22, 1819, Cambridge, Mass.; d. Aug. 12, 1891, Cambridge, Mass.) still lives in history as an outstanding American author of the 19th century, who spoke out on such social issues as slavery and war; graduated from Harvard in 1838 and practiced law for a time; became Professor of Modern Languages at Harvard, 1855; served as United States minister to Spain, 1877–80 and ambassador to England, 1880–85; edited *Atlantic Monthly*, 1857–62 and *North American Review*, 1863–72; retired from Harvard as "professor emeritus," 1886; authored *The Vision of Sir Launfal* (1848), *The Biglow Papers* (1848 and 1862), *Among My Books* (1870 and 1876), and *Political Essays* (1888); is credited with several published hymns which have been adapted from his longer poetic writings.

> Once to every man and nation (463)

Lowry, Robert (b. Mar. 12, 1826, Philadelphia, Pa.; d. Nov. 25, 1899, Plainfield, N. J.), a popular preacher and orator, is perhaps best remembered for his contribution in writing gospel hymns and tunes; was educated at Bucknell University and served Baptist pastorates in Pennsylvania, New York and New Jersey; was also professor of literature at Bucknell University (1869–75) and received his D.D. degree there in 1875; succeeded William Bradbury (*q.v.*) as editor of Sunday School song collections, and collaborated with William H. Doane (*q.v.*) and others in many publications for Biglow and Main, New York City; compiled: *Happy Voices* (1865), *Bright Jewels* (1869), *Royal Diadem* (1873), *Welcome Tidings* (1877), *Gospel Hymn and Tune Book* (1879), *Glad Refrain* (1886), and many others.

> Low in the grave He lay (165); What can wash away my sin? (237); Come, we that love the Lord (ref.) (275)

> CHRIST AROSE (165); PLAINFIELD (237); MARCHING TO ZION (275); NEED (340); SOMETHING FOR THEE (345); ALL THE WAY (440)

Luther, Charles Carroll (b. May 17, 1847, Worcester, Mass.; d. Nov. 4, 1924, Farmingdale, L.I., N.Y.) received his higher education at Brown University and was a journalist and lay evangelist before his ordination to the Baptist ministry (1886); continued in evangelistic work for a while, pastored the First Baptist Church in Bridgeport, Conn. (1891–93) and then returned to evangelism; wrote about 25 texts and compiled *Temple Chimes*, a book of hymns and gospel songs.

> Must I go, and empty handed? (478)

Luther, Martin (b. Nov. 10, 1483, Eisleben, Saxony, Ger.; d. Feb. 18, 1546, Eisleben, Ger.) was the leader of the 16th century Reformation in the tradition we know as "Lutheran" and is credited with the restoration of congregational participation in worship; was educated at Magdeburg, Eisenach, and Erfurt; entered the Augustinian convent at Erfurt and was ordained a priest (1507); taught at the University in Wittenberg, where (1517) he posted his 95 theses against papal abuses and corruption in the church; after a long open struggle, defending his preaching and writings, denied the supremacy of the Pope and broke with Rome; translated the Bible into German and developed liturgies for evangelical worship: *Formula missae,* 1523 and *Deutscher messe,* 1526; wrote 37 hymns and paraphrases, and composed tunes or adapted them from folksong sources; is the subject of an article by Walter Buszin, summing up his contributions to church music, *Musical Quarterly,* XXXII, 1946.

A mighty fortress is our God (11); From heaven above to earth I come (111)
EIN' FESTE BURG (11)

Lvov, Alexis Feodorovitch (b. June 6, 1799, Reval, Estonia; d. Dec. 16, 1870, Romanovo, near Kovno, Lithuania) studied music under his father, who was an authority on church music and folksong, and conductor of the Russian Imperial Chapel choir; served in the Russian army and reached the rank of major-general; followed his father as Director of the Imperial Chapel, editing and publishing chants of the Russian church; was an excellent violinist and wrote music for the violin, as well as three operas, and a great variety of church music.
RUSSIAN HYMN (527)

Lynch, Thomas Toke (b. July 5, 1818, Donmow, Essex, Eng.; d. May 9, 1871, London, Eng.) was a most gifted and influential minister who served several independent congregations in London, Eng., though he was not particularly attractive in appearance nor strong of body; was a musician as well as poet, and composed the tunes for at least 25 of his poems; in 1855 published a collection called *The Rivulet: Hymns for Heart and Voice,* which triggered a violent controversy among Congregationalists because of the "personal" quality of its contents; added 67 hymns in the edition of 1868.
Gracious Spirit, dwell with me (193)

Lyon, Meyer (b. 1751; d. 1797, Kingston, Jamaica), also listed as "Meier Leoni," was cantor in various synagogues in London, including the Great Synagogue (1768–72); entered the opera field but was not successful, due to his lack of acting ability and his unwillingness to sing on Friday nights or Jewish festival days; in 1787 accepted the position of cantor with the Ashkenazic congregation at Kingston, Jamaica and served there until his death.
LEONI (arr.) (36, 475)

Lyte, Henry Francis (b. June 1, 1793, Ednam, near Kelso, Scot.; d. Nov. 20, 1847, Nice, Fr.), orphaned as a child and never strong physically, struggled to acquire an education, and graduated from Trinity College, Dublin in 1814; abandoned plans for a medical career in 1815, took Holy Orders in the Church of England and served parishes in Wexford, Marazion and Lymington; was appointed "perpetual curate" at Lower Brixham, Devonshire, and ministered to that fishing village for 23 years; wrote more than 80 hymns and paraphrases of psalms, which were published in *Poems, Chiefly Religious,* 1833 and *The Spirit of the Psalms,* 1834.

> Praise the Lord, His glories show (12); Praise, my soul, the King of heaven (26); Jesus, I my cross have taken (443); Abide with me: fast falls the eventide (554)

Macaulay, Joseph Cordner (b. July 4, 1900, Belfast, N. Ire.) was trained at Glasgow University (Scotland) and Wheaton College (Ill.), where he earned his B.A. degree with honors and later received the honorary D.D. degree; an ordained Baptist minister, served the Baptist church in Sault Ste. Marie, Ont., and Wheaton (Ill.) Bible Church; was a member of the faculty, Moody Bible Institute, Chicago, and later, president of London College of Bible and Missions (now Ontario Bible College); has served as dean of the New York School of the Bible since 1971, and was interim pastor at Calvary Baptist Church, New York City, 1973–76; has written some 25 hymn texts, and 20 hymn tunes, as well as seven expository volumes, including devotional commentaries on John, Acts and Hebrews.

> We sing the boundless praise (76)

Macduff, John Ross (b. May 23, 1818, Bonhard, Perthshire, Scot.; d. Apr. 30, 1895, Chislehurst, Kent, Eng.) received high school and university training in Edinburgh (later, Universities of Edinburgh, Glasgow and New York all awarded him honorary D.D. degrees); was ordained in the Church of Scotland (1842), served churches in Forfarshire, Perthshire, and Glasgow, and declined an offer by the crown to be appointed to the Cathedral Church of Glasgow; in 1871 resigned the pastorate to devote himself to writing; taking up residence at Chislehurst, Kent, produced many devotional books (e.g., *The Faithful Promise, Morning and Night Watches*) which had enormous sales; was a member of the hymnal committee of the Church of Scotland, and wrote 31 hymns which appeared in *Altar Stones,* 1853, and *The Gates of Praise,* 1876.

> Christ is coming! let creation (183)

Mackay, William Paton (b. May 13, 1839, Montrose, Scot.; d. Aug. 22, 1885, Portree, Scot.), educated at the University of Edinburgh, practiced medicine for a number of years; feeling called to the ministry, was ordained and became pastor of the Prospect St. Presbyterian Church, Hull, 1868; wrote a number of hymns, 17 of which appeared in W. Reid's *Praise Book,* 1872.

> We praise Thee, O God (358)

Macmillan, Ernest Campbell (b. Aug. 18, 1893, Mimico, Ontario; d. May 6, 1973, Toronto, Canada) was the son of Dr. Alexander Macmillan, a Presbyterian minister and editor of the *Hymnary of The United Church of Canada,* 1930; was a child prodigy who played the organ in public at age ten, and studied later at the University of Toronto, University of Edinburgh, and Oxford University; attended the Wagner Festival in Bayreuth at the outbreak of World War I in 1914, and was interned at Ruhleben prison camp for four years; during imprisonment, completed a major work based on Swinburne's ode—*England,* which earned him the Mus.D. degree from Oxford University; after the war, returned to Canada and became conductor of the Toronto Symphony Orchestra, 1931–56, and conductor of the Mendelssohn Choir, 1942–57; was principal of the Music Conservatory, 1926–42, and Dean of the Music Faculty, Toronto University, 1927–52; was knighted by George V in recognition of his service to Canada as composer, teacher, conductor, and organist; has published several music textbooks, and volumes relating to Canada's indigenous Indian and French-Canadian music.

TEMPUS ADEST FLORIDUM (arr.) (107)

Macomber, Winfield (b. Sept. 15, 1865, Bucksport, Me.; d. Oct. 19, 1896, Lisbon, Port.), sometimes identified wrongly as "William," spent his early years in Maine; after his conversion at age 16, was engaged in colportage work under the American Bible Society; in 1890 entered the New York Missionary Training Institute (now Nyack College), and in 1892 sailed as a missionary to Congo under the International Missionary Alliance (now Christian and Missionary Alliance); after one year's service, had to return home for reasons of health; in 1894 was appointed to his *alma mater* as instructor in the Congo language; compiled an English-Fioti grammar and dictionary for missionary candidates; in 1896 returned to Africa and undertook pioneer work on the south bank of the Congo, but after two months, began to deteriorate physically and was compelled to leave for America; got as far as Lisbon, Portugal, where he was hospitalized and died at age 31.

In the glow of early morning (186)
MACOMBER (186)

Madan, Martin (b. 1726, Hertingfordbury, Eng.; d. May 2, 1790, Epsom, Surrey, Eng.), educated at Westminster School and Christ Church, Oxford, was admitted to the bar in 1748; was converted after hearing John Wesley (*q.v.*) preach, gave up law and was ordained to the Anglican ministry; served as chaplain at Lock Hospital, an institution "for the restoration of unhappy females"; was so disturbed by the problems of the patients that he wrote a treatise, *Thelyphthora,* 1780, advocating polygamy as the solution to the problem, thereby incurring so much criticism that he was forced to retire to Epsom; wrote few original hymns, but published *A Collection of Psalms and Hymns, Extracted from Various Authors,* 1760, referred to as "The Lock Collection," which was the basis for many later hymnals.

Hail, Thou once despised Jesus (alt.) (95); Lo, He comes with clouds descending (185)

Main, Hubert Platt (b. Aug. 17, 1839, Ridgefield, Conn.; d. Oct. 7, 1925, Newark, N.J.), son of the singing school teacher Sylvester Main, had scant formal education, but learned a great deal about music through his association with publishers; assisted Philip Phillips in compiling the *Methodist Episcopal Hymn and Tune Book,* 1866; was employed by William B. Bradbury (*q.v.*) in 1867 and remained with the firm throughout his lifetime (it later became Biglow and Main and was eventually purchased by Hope Publishing Co.); wrote many settings for hymns and anthems, but is remembered chiefly for his contribution as a compiler of many hymnals and gospel song books; left his personal collection of music books to the Newberry Library, Chicago.

ELLESDIE (arr.) (443, 493)

Maker, Frederick Charles (b. 1844, Bristol, Eng.; d. 1927, Bristol, Eng.) spent his entire life in Bristol, Eng., beginning his musical career as a chorister in the cathedral; served as organist in several "free" churches in the city, with 28 years at the Redland Park Congregational Church; was visiting professor of music (for 20 years) at Clifton College and conductor of the Bristol Free Church Choirs Association; at the invitation of his organ teacher, Alfred Stone, contributed several hymn tunes to *The Bristol Tune Book,* 1881; also wrote cantatas, anthems and piano compositions.

ST. CHRISTOPHER (151); INVITATION (256); REST (407)

Malan, Henri Abraham César (b. July 7, 1787, Geneva, Switz.; d. May 18, 1864, Vandoeuvres, Switz.) was schooled at the College of Geneva, where his father was a professor; was ordained in the Reformed Church, and served as pastor of the Chapelle du Temoignage in Geneva; was bold and outspoken in preaching against the universalism and formalism of the Established Church, aroused opposition and resigned from his parish; founded a chapel on his own property and preached there for 43 years; made several evangelistic tours to Belgium, Scotland, France and England, specializing in "personal soul winning"; wrote more than 1000 hymns and tunes, and published *Chants de Sion,* 1841, which greatly influenced Protestant hymn singing in France.

HENDON (144, 385)

Mann, Arthur Henry (b. May 16, 1850, Norwich, Norfolk, Eng.; d. Nov. 19, 1929, Cambridge, Eng.) was educated at Norwich Cathedral and New College, Oxford; served briefly as organist at various churches and finally (1876) went to King's College Chapel, Cambridge where he held the position with distinction for 53 years; wrote many hymn tunes, anthems and organ works; was an authority on the music of Handel (*q.v.*), and highly skilled in developing boys' choirs; was musical editor for Charles D. Bell's *The Church of England Hymnal,* 1895.

ANGEL'S STORY (506)

Mant, Richard (b. Feb. 12, 1776, Southampton, Eng.; d. Nov. 2, 1848, Ballymoney, County Antrim, Ire.) was educated at Winchester, and Trinity

College, Oxford; was ordained in the Anglican church and served several curacies; was vicar of Coggeshall, Essex and rector of St. Botolph's, Bishopsgate, London; in 1820 was consecrated Bishop of Killaloe, and transferred later to the bishoprics of Down and Connor, and Dromore; edited *The Book of Psalms in an English Metrical Version*, 1824 and *Ancient Hymns from the Roman Breviary with Original Hymns*, 1837.

God, my King, Thy might confessing (34)

March, Daniel (b. July 21, 1816, Millbury, Mass.; d. Mar. 2, 1909, Woburn, Mass.) studied at Millbury Academy and Amherst College, and graduated in theology from Yale University; became a Congregational minister, serving churches in Connecticut, New York, Pennsylvania and (for two terms totaling 26 years) in Woburn, Mass.; was greatly interested in missions and lectured frequently on his world travels; was the author of many religious works, but seems to have made only this one contribution to hymnody.

Hark, the voice of Jesus calling (493)

Marlatt, Earl Bowman (b. May 24, 1892, Columbus, Ind.; d. June 13, 1976, Winchester, Ind.), educated at DePauw University (B.A.) and Boston University (S.T.B., Ph.D.), did further graduate study at Oxford University and the University of Berlin; was professor of philosophy of religion and religious literature at Boston University and later served as dean of the School of Theology; became professor of philosophy of religion at Southern Methodist University in 1946, holding that position until his retirement in 1957; was a member of the Executive Committee of the Hymn Society of America; was associate editor of *The American Student Hymnal*, 1928, and published several books of poetry.

"Are ye able," said the Master (383)

Marsh, Charles Howard (b. Apr. 8, 1886, Magnolia, Ia.; d. Apr. 12, 1956, La Jolla, Calif.) wrote the gospel song music listed below during his early twenties; the son of a Congregational minister, was born a few months after his parents had emigrated from England; after graduating from high school, was invited by J. Wilbur Chapman (*q.v.*) to be pianist at the Winona Lake Chautauqua and Bible Conference in Indiana; after some years of study, taught at the Bible Institute of Los Angeles and then at the University of Redlands; went to France, 1926–28, to study with Isidor Phillipp, Marcel Dupré and Nadia Boulanger; returning to America, became President of the European School of Music and Art and organist-choirmaster of First Presbyterian Church in Fort Wayne, Ind.; in 1932 moved to Florida, taught organ at the Orlando College of Music, and became organist at the University of Florida in Gainesville; from 1936 until his death, served as organist-choirmaster at the St. James-by-the-Sea Episcopal Church in La Jolla, Calif.; a Fellow of the American Guild of Organists, was known also for his poetry and painting; wrote many songs, anthems and instrumental works.

CHAPMAN (128); CROWNING DAY (179)

Marsh, Donald Stuart (b. Sept. 5, 1923, Akron, Ohio) is a member of the "Avery and Marsh" duo, well known for their workshops in contemporary worship; attended Western Maryland University, the University of Houston (B.S., M.S.), and the Theodora Irvine School of Drama; since 1946 has been active professionally as an actor, director, dancer and choreographer in the New York City area; in 1960 was appointed choirmaster and Director of Arts in Christian Education at the First Presbyterian Church, Port Jervis, N.J.; is an elder in the United Presbyterian Church (U.S.A.) and a member of the Advisory Council for Discipleship and Worship for their General Assembly; is co-founder of Proclamation Productions, Inc., and has written approximately 100 hymn texts and tunes.

PORT JERVIS (573)

Marshall, W. S. No information on this composer can be found.

BLESSED QUIETNESS (192)

Martin, Civilla Durfee (b. Aug. 21, 1866, Jordan, Nova Scotia; d. Mar. 9, 1948, Atlanta, Ga.) was a small-town school teacher with some musical training; worked with her husband, Walter Stillman Martin (*q.v.*), in his evangelistic campaigns throughout the United States, and collaborated with him in writing several gospel songs.

Be not dismayed whate'er betide (421)

Martin, George Clement (b. Sept. 11, 1844, Lambourn, Berks, Eng.; d. Feb. 23, 1916, London, Eng.) studied organ with John Stainer (*q.v.*) at Magdalen College, Oxford; served as organist at Dalkeith Palace and at St. Peter's, Lutton Place, Edinburgh; in 1874 became "master of song" under John Stainer at St. Paul's Cathedral, where he later succeeded Stainer as organist; was named Professor of Organ at the Royal College of Music, 1883 and at the Royal Academy of Music, 1895; was knighted by Queen Victoria in 1897; wrote *The Art of Training Choir Boys,* which was the standard primer for years.

HOLY FAITH (335)

Martin, W. C. No information on this author can be found.

Though the angry surges roll (311)

Martin, Walter Stillman (b. 1862, Rowley, Essex Co., Mass.; d. Dec. 16, 1935, Atlanta, Ga.), educated at Harvard University, was ordained to the Baptist ministry and later joined the Disciples of Christ; for a time taught Bible at the Atlantic Christian College in North Carolina; in 1919 established his residence in Atlanta, Ga., and conducted Bible conferences and evangelistic campaigns throughout the country; with his wife, Civilla Durfee Martin (*q.v.*), wrote some gospel songs.

GOD CARES (421)

Mason, Harry Silvernale (b. Oct. 17, 1881, Gloversville, N.Y.; d. Nov. 15, 1964, Torrington, Conn.) received his education at Syracuse University and the Boston University School of Theology; was on the faculty of Auburn (N.Y.) Theological Seminary for 25 years, serving as organist and teacher of fine arts and religion; was organist of First Presbyterian Church in Auburn, and later (for 27 years) at Second Presbyterian Church.

BEACON HILL (383)

Mason, Lowell (b. Jan. 8, 1792, Medfield, Mass.; d. Aug. 11, 1872, Orange, N.J.) holds a special place in the history of church music and of music education in the United States; as a child learned to play several instruments, and at age 16, led the village choir and conducted singing schools; lived in Savannah, Ga. for a while, working in a bank, studying harmony and composition, and serving the Independent Presbyterian Church as organist; in 1827 moved to Boston and became President of the Handel and Haydn Society, and choir director of Bowdoin St. Church; in 1829 published *The Juvenile Psalmist, or The Child's Introduction to Sacred Music;* established the Boston Academy of Music (1833) and was eventually responsible for introducing music into the public school curriculum of Boston; pioneered in teaching music pedagogy for 25 years; compiled and published at least 80 music volumes which are listed in *Lowell Mason: the Father of Singing Among Children* (1946), by Arthur L. Rich; wrote more than 1100 hymn tunes and almost 500 arrangements of existing tunes, mostly from European sources.

ARIEL (arr.) (65); AZMON (arr.) (90, 346); ANTIOCH (arr.) (120); HENLEY (125, 532); HAMBURG (148); HARWELL (172); DENNIS (arr.) (207); CLEANSING FOUNTAIN (arr.) (230); BETHANY (348); OLIVET (366); NAOMI (arr.) (419); LABAN (462); MISSIONARY HYMN (472); BOYLSTON (496); SABBATH (548); MENDEBRAS (arr.) (549)

Matheson, George (b. Mar. 27, 1842, Glasgow, Scot.; d. Aug. 28, 1906, North Berwick, Scot.) was almost blind by the time he was 18 years of age, but made a brilliant record at Glasgow Academy and Glasgow University; licensed as a Church of Scotland minister, was assistant at Sandyford Church, Glasgow and then pastor of the Clydeside Church at Innellan, Argyllshire for 18 years; in 1886 was transferred to St. Bernard's Church in Edinburgh, where he remained a most popular and respected pastor until he was forced to retire (1899) because of ill health; wrote many theological and devotional volumes, and one book of verse, *Sacred Songs,* 1890.

O Love that will not let me go (351); Make me a captive, Lord (376)

Matthews, Timothy Richard (b. Nov. 4, 1826, Colmworth, near Bedford, Eng.; d. Jan. 5, 1910, Tetney, Lincs, Eng.) was educated at Bedford Grammar School and Caius College, Cambridge, and studied organ with George Elvey (*q.v.*); ordained an Anglican minister in 1853, was curate at St. Mary's, Nottingham, then rector of North Coates, Lincolnshire until he retired in 1907; composed more than 100 hymn tunes, and published *Tunes for Holy Worship* (1859), *The Village Church Tune Book* (1859), *Congrega-*

tional Melodies (1862), *Hymn Tunes* (1867), *The Village Organist* (1877), and *North Coates Supplemental Tune Book* (1878).

    MARGARET (124)

Maxwell, Mary E. is not identifiable for a certainty, but her hymn is associated with the Keswick Convention in north England. Records show that a prolific author named Mary Elizabeth Braddon was born on October 4, 1837, was educated at home by private tutors, and married John Maxwell in 1874. She died February 4, 1915 at Richmond, Surrey. The Rev. Alan Luff, Secretary of The Hymn Society of Great Britain and Ireland, has written:

> One must regret a tendency for hymn scholars to ignore the type of hymnody to be found in "Keswick." It is partly a result of a feeling that we do not have much sympathy with it and that we should therefore be led to make adverse criticisms of it. But we ought to be able to see it as a branch of hymnody that ought not be ignored, while at the same time hoping that those in sympathy with it will make their own efforts to produce the kind of background material that you are seeking.

Fortunately, this effort is being made and we have received the above information from Mr. Andrew J. Hayden of Tonbridge, Kent, England.

    How I praise Thee, precious Savior (347)

McAfee, Cleland Boyd (b. Sept. 25, 1866, Ashley, Mo.; d. Feb. 4, 1944, Jaffrey, N.H.) received his schooling at Park College, Parkville, Mo. and Union Theological Seminary; returned to Park College to teach and also served as pastor (and choir director) of the college church; 1901–12, served pastorates in Chicago and Brooklyn; was professor of systematic theology (1912–30) at McCormick Theological Seminary, Chicago, and later became secretary of the Presbyterian Board of Foreign Missions (1930–36); following his retirement in New Hampshire, remained active lecturing, preaching, teaching and writing.

    There is a place of quiet rest (342)

    McAFEE (342)

McCutchan, Robert Guy (b. Sept. 13, 1877, Mount Ayr, Iowa; d. May 15, 1958, Claremont, Calif.) was an outstanding Methodist hymnologist and author of *Our Hymnody,* 1937, the "first significant hymnal handbook in America"; received schooling at Park College (Mo.) and Simpson College (Ia.), and also studied in Paris and Berlin; taught at Baker University (Kan.) and became head (1906) of the newly-organized department of music there; in 1911 was appointed dean of the school of music, DePauw University (Ind.) and held that position until his retirement; was a leading member of commissions and committees on church music and hymnology in the Methodist church; in 1937 retired to Claremont, Calif. and remained active in conferences and lectureships; was editor of *The Methodist Hymnal,* 1935 and author of its companion, *Our Hymnody,* 1937; authored *Better Music in Our Churches* (1925), *Music in Worship* (1927), *Hymns in the Lives of*

Men (1945), *Hymns of the American Frontier* (1950) and *Hymn Tune Names: Their Sources and Significance* (1957).
ALL THE WORLD (24); CAMPMEETING (arr.) (429)

McDaniel, Rufus Henry (b. Jan. 29, 1850, near Ripley, Brown Co., Ohio; d. Feb. 13, 1940, Dayton, Ohio), educated in the public schools of Bentonville, Ohio and Parker's Academy in Claremont Co., Ohio, was licensed to preach when he was 19; later was ordained in the Christian Church (Disciples of Christ), served several pastorates in the Southern Ohio Conference, and retired in Dayton; contributed over 100 poems to hymnody, many through the collections published by The Rodeheaver Company.
   What a wonderful change in my life (281)

McDonald, William (b. Mar. 1, 1820, Belmont, Me.; d. Sept. 11, 1901, Monrovia, Calif.) at the age of 19 was a local preacher in the Methodist Episcopal Church; was active in ministry in the Maine, Wisconsin and New England Conferences and editor of the *Advocate of Christian Holiness;* edited and published: *Western Minstrels* (1840), *Wesleyan Sacred Harp* (1855), *Beulah Songs* (1870) and *Tribute of Praise* (1874).
   I am coming to the cross (270)

McGranahan, James (b. July 4, 1840 near Adamsville, Pa.; d. July 7, 1907, Kinsman, Ohio) had only a limited formal education, but quickly developed musical skills, and at age 19 was teaching music; after brief study at Bradbury's Music School, Geneseo, N.Y., was associated with J. G. Towner in music conventions and singing schools in Pennsylvania and New York; later studied with George F. Root (*q.v.*) and taught in his institutes; in 1877, after the sudden death of P. P. Bliss (*q.v.*), became song leader in the evangelistic campaigns conducted by Major D. W. Whittle (*q.v.*) in England and America; had a beautiful tenor voice and a commanding personality, and pioneered in using men's choirs in his meetings; collaborated with Ira Sankey (*q.v.*), George C. Stebbins (*q.v.*) and other musicians in many publications, including: *The Gospel Male Choir*, 2 vols. (1878, 1883), *The Choice, Harvest of Song, Gospel Choir,* and *Gospel Hymns* (Nos. 3, 4, 5 and 6).
   O, what a Savior, that He died for me (297); Far, far away, in death and darkness (487)
   CHRIST RETURNETH (178); SHOWERS OF BLESSING (249); NEUMEISTER (271); EL NATHAN (295); VERILY (297); CHRIST LIVETH (306); ROYAL BANNER (459); GO YE (487)

McIntosh, Rigdon McCoy (b. Apr. 3, 1836, Maury Co., Tenn.; d. July 2, 1899, Atlanta, Ga.) attended Jackson College, Columbia, Tenn.; studied music with L. C. and Asa Everett, and was associated with them in publishing books and teaching singing schools; in the 1860's began a 30-year relationship as music editor for the publishing house of the Methodist Episcopal Church, South; was briefly head of the Music Department of Vanderbilt University, and in 1877 accepted a similar appointment at Emory College, Oxford, Ga.; in 1895 left education and established the

R.M. McIntosh Publishing Company; was an accomplished teacher, composer, choral director and editor, whose publications include *Hermon: the Methodist Hymn and Tune Book, Prayer and Praise, Christian Hymns, Gospel Grace, McIntosh's Anthems, Glad Tidings, Living Songs* and *Songs of Service.*

PROMISED LAND (arr.) (545)

McKinney, Baylus Benjamin (b. July 22, 1886, Heflin, La.; d. Sept. 7, 1952, Bryson City, N.C.) was the most important Southern Baptist hymn writer during the first half of the 20th century; received his education at Mt. Lebanon Academy (La.), Southwestern Baptist Theological Seminary, Siegel-Myers Correspondence School of Music, and Bush Conservatory, Chicago; 1919–32, taught in the School of Music at Southwestern Baptist Seminary, Fort Worth, Tex., and was music editor for publications of Robert H. Coleman, writing a great number of gospel songs himself; resigned from the Seminary during the depression and became assistant pastor of Travis Ave. Baptist Church in Fort Worth; in 1935 became associated as music editor with the Baptist Sunday School Board, Nashville, and in 1941, was appointed secretary of the newly organized Church Music Department; died in an automobile accident; edited *Songs of Victory* (1937), *Broadman Hymnal* (1940), *Voice of Praise* (1948), and was the first editor of the monthly, *The Church Musician;* wrote words and music for 150 gospel songs, and tunes for 115 hymns written by others.

"Take up thy cross and follow Me" (473)

FALLS CREEK (473)

Medley, Samuel (b. June 23, 1738, Cheshunt, Herts, Eng.; d. July 17, 1799, Liverpool, Lancs, Eng.) was the son of a schoolteacher who was a friend of Isaac Newton; served as a midshipman in the Royal Navy and was wounded off Port Lagos, 1759; was converted after reading a sermon by Isaac Watts (*q.v.*) and joined the Eagle Street Baptist Church; pastored Baptist churches at Watford and Liverpool, the latter ministry being especially successful; edited: *Hymns* (1785), *Hymns on Select Portions of Scripture* (1785 and 1787), *Hymns* (1794), and *Hymns: The Public Worship and Private Devotions of True Christians, Assisted in Some Thoughts in Verse: Principally Drawn from Select Passages of the Word of God* (1800); is the subject of a biography, *A Memoir*, 1833, written by his daughter Sarah, and containing 44 additional hymns.

O could I speak the matchless worth (65); Awake, my soul, to joyful lays (77); I know that my Redeemer lives (166)

Meineke, Christoph (b. May 1, 1782, Oldenburg, Ger.; d. Nov. 6, 1850, Baltimore, Md.), sometimes listed as Charles Meineke, was the son of Karl Meinecke, organist to the duke of Oldenburg; in 1810 left Germany for England, then came to the United States in 1820; served as organist of St. Paul's Episcopal Church in Baltimore, Md. until his death; published *Music for the Church ... Composed for St. Paul's Church, Baltimore, by C. Meineke, Organist*, 1844.

MEINEKE (576)

Mendelssohn, Felix (b. Feb. 3, 1809, Hamburg, Ger.; d. Nov. 4, 1847, Leipzig, Ger.), one of Germany's great composers in the early 19th century, is credited with reviving interest in the music of J. S. Bach (*q.v.*); was born into a wealthy Jewish-Christian home, his father a banker, his mother a talented artist and musician who gave her children their first musical training; in 1811 moved with his family to Berlin, where all were baptized in the Lutheran church; a prodigy, made his first public appearance as a pianist at age 9, and had written five symphonies by the time he was 12; traveled widely and was feted as a brilliant performer, conductor and composer; wrote prolifically in almost every *genre* except opera—symphonies, chamber music, concertos, organ and piano music, vocal music and much sacred music, including the oratorios *St. Paul* and *Elijah;* is credited with hymn tunes that are adapted from other works.

MUNICH (arr.) (98, 219); MENDELSSOHN (106); CONSOLATION (425, 552)

Merrill, William Pierson (b. Jan. 10, 1867, Orange, N.J.; d. June 19, 1954, New York, N.Y.), converted at age 11, was successively a member of a Congregational and a Dutch Reformed Church; was educated at Rutgers College and Union Theological Seminary, and ordained to the Presbyterian ministry, 1890; served churches in Philadelphia and Chicago, and then (1911) became pastor of the Brick Presbyterian Church in New York City where he remained until his retirement in 1938; wrote many hymns as well as a number of theological books, including: *Footings for Faith* (1915), *Christian Internationalism* (1919), *The Common Creed of Christians* (1920), *The Freedom of the Preacher* (1922), *Liberal Christianity* (1925), *Prophets of the Dawn* (1927), *The Way* (1933), and *We See Jesus* (1934).

Rise up, O men of God (461); Not alone for mighty empire (521)

Messiter, Arthur Henry (b. Apr. 12, 1834, Frome, Somerset, Eng.; d. July 2, 1916, New York, N.Y.) received his early education from private tutors, and his first musical training from McKorkell and Kerfell in Northampton; in 1863 came to the United States and sang in the choir at Trinity Church, New York City; served as organist in churches in Poultney, Vt. and Philadelphia; in 1866 accepted responsibility for the music at Trinity Church, New York City, where he served for over 31 years; as a model of Episcopalian musicianship, received the honorary D.Mus. degree, St. Stephen's College, Annandale, N.Y.; edited: *Psalter* (1889), *Choir Office Book* (1891), and *Hymnal with Music as Used in Trinity Church* (1893); composed a number of anthems and wrote *A History of the Choir and the Music of Trinity Church* (1906).

MARION (14)

Miles, C. Austin (b. Jan. 7, 1868, Lakehurst, N.J.; d. Mar. 10, 1946, Pitman, N.J.) was educated at the Philadelphia College of Pharmacy and the University of Pennsylvania, and was an active pharmacist for many years; released his first gospel song, "List, 'Tis Jesus' Voice" through the Hall-Mack Publishing Company, Philadelphia, and they encouraged him to write others; in June, 1898 went to work full-time with Hall-Mack and remained for 37 years as editor and manager, continuing in an editorial capacity when the company merged with Rodeheaver in 1935; composed several cantatas and anthems, but said, "It is as a writer of gospel songs I am proud to be known, for in that way I may be of the most use to my Master whom I serve willingly although not as efficiently as is my desire."

I come to the garden alone (398)

GARDEN (398)

Milman, Henry Hart (b. Feb. 10, 1791, London, Eng.; d. Sept. 24, 1868, Sunninghill, Berks, Eng.) was the son of King George II's physician; received schooling at Eton and Brasenose College, Oxford; ordained in 1817, served churches in Reading and Westminster; was professor of poetry at Oxford University for a number of years, and in 1849 was appointed Dean of St. Paul's Cathedral; contributed 13 texts in Reginald Heber's (*q.v.*) *Hymns*, 1827; published his own collection, *Selection of Psalms and Hymns,* 1837.

Ride on! ride on in majesty! (132)

Milton, John (b. Dec. 9, 1608, London, Eng.; d. Nov. 8, 1674, London, Eng.) is best known as the brilliant blind English poet who wrote the literary masterpieces *Paradise Lost,* 1667, and *Paradise Regained,* 1671; was educated at St. Paul's School and Christ College, Cambridge; in 1649 was appointed "Latin Secretary" under Oliver Cromwell, responsible for translating letters of the British government to foreign powers; became totally blind when he was 44 years of age, but continued his work until Cromwell abdicated; escaped the scaffold, which was the fate of most Cromwell followers, because of his fame and acceptance as a writer; wrote 19 paraphrases of various psalms, intended for private devotional use; is credited with helping to develop the hymnic styles of Isaac Watts (*q.v.*) and Charles Wesley (*q.v.*).

Let us, with a gladsome mind (50)

Mohr, Joseph (b. Dec. 11, 1792, Salzburg, Aust.; d. Dec. 4, 1848, Wagrein, Aust.) will forever be remembered as author of the Christmas hymn, "Stille nacht! heilige nacht!"; was a boy chorister in the cathedral choir at Salzburg, where the Mozarts served a generation before; in 1815 was ordained in the Roman Catholic church, and went to St. Nicholas Church, Oberndorf for two years as assistant priest—here he wrote his famous carol; after several other assignments, became vicar at Hintersee (1828) and then at Wagrein (1837), where he stayed until his death.

Silent night! holy night! (117)

Monk, William Henry (b. Mar. 16, 1823, Brompton, London, Eng.; d. Mar. 1, 1889, Stoke Newington, London, Eng.) was music editor for the first three editions of the historic English hymnal, *Hymns Ancient and Modern* (1861, 1875 and 1889); first studied music with private instructors; served as organist for several London churches and was finally appointed to St. Matthias, Stoke Newington, a position he held until his death; during the same years, taught music at King's College, London, at the School for the Indigent Blind, the National Training School for Music, and Bedford College; was given the honorary D.Mus. degree, Durham University, 1882; was editor of the *Parish Choir*, 1840–1851 and contributed some 50 hymn tunes to *Hymns Ancient and Modern* (1861, 1875 and 1889).

DIX (55); VICTORY (arr.) (161); EVENTIDE (554)

Monsell, John Samuel Bewley (b. Mar. 2, 1811, St. Columb's, Derry, Ire.; d. Apr. 9, 1875, Guildford, Eng.) received his education at Trinity College, Dublin; was ordained, 1834, and served several parishes in Ireland; in 1853 went to England as vicar of Egham, Surrey and later (1870), rector of St. Nicholas, Guildford; was accidentally killed by falling masonry during roof repairs at St. Nicholas; published 11 volumes of poetry, including some 300 hymns; was a strong advocate of "more fervent and joyous" congregational singing.

Fight the good fight with all thy might (469)

Montgomery, James (b. Nov. 4, 1771, Irvine, Ayrshire, Scot.; d. Apr. 30, 1854, Sheffield, York, Eng.), the son of the only Moravian minister in Scotland, was educated at Fulneck Seminary near Leeds; made little progress in school and was dismissed because of his preoccupation with writing poetry; was apprenticed to a baker, but ran away and eventually settled in Sheffield (1792) and became associated with the *Sheffiled Register;* later became editor and owner of the newspaper and changed its name to *Sheffield Iris;* was outspoken and influential in many humanitarian causes, especially opposition to slavery; also sponsored the singing of hymns in Anglican worship, and the causes of foreign missions and The British Bible Society; wrote more than 400 hymns which appeared in his *Songs of Zion* (1822), *The Christian Psalmist* (1825), and *Original Hymns for Public, Private and Social Devotion* (1853).

Stand up and bless the Lord (22); Angels from the realms of glory (110); Go to dark Gethsemane (147); According to Thy gracious word (212); God is my strong salvation (413); In the hour of trial (418); Prayer is the soul's sincere desire (429)

Moody, May Whittle (b. Mar. 20, 1870, Chicago, Ill.; d. Aug. 20, 1963, Northfield, Mass.), the daughter of Evangelist D. W. Whittle (an associate of D. L. Moody), was actually named "Mary" but chose to be known as "May"; at age 15 attended the Girl's School founded by Moody in Northfield, Mass., and later, Oberlin College (1888–89), followed by a year at the Royal Academy of Music, London (1890–91); had a singing voice of "rare sweetness and richness of quality" and assisted her father and D. L. Moody in their evangelistic campaigns; married William R. Moody (son of the evangelist) on August 29, 1894, and they were the parents of six children, two of whom died as infants; lived at Northfield, Mass., where Will Moody was head of the Northfield Schools and the Mount Hermon Conference center founded by his father; was co-editor (with Charles M. Alexander) of *Northfield Hymnal, No. 3.*

WHITTLE (314)

Moore, Thomas (b. May 28, 1779, Dublin, Ire.; d. Feb. 25, 1852, Sloperton, Devizes, Eng.), a Roman Catholic, was widely appreciated for both his sacred and secular writings; attended Trinity College, Dublin, and studied law at Middle Temple, London; in 1804 was appointed admiralty registrar in Bermuda but, finding the position unpleasant, appointed a deputy and returned to London; was financially ruined by his deputy's embezzlement and exiled to the Continent, but returned to England (1822) after the money was repaid; wrote and published: *A Selection of Irish Melodies* (1807–34), and *Odes Upon Cash, Corn, Catholics and Other Matters* (1828); included 32 of his hymns in *Sacred Songs* (1816).

Come, ye disconsolate (423)

Moore, William has not left much record in biographical history; according to *Hymns of Our Faith*, compiled *The Columbian Harmony*, containing 180 pages of music, 17 pages of introductory instructional material, and the credit: "William Moore, West Tennessee, Wilson County, March, 1825"; signed 18 tunes in the above volume, two of which are named for his home town and the county seat—"Lebanon" and "Wilson."

HOLY MANNA (199)

Morris, Lelia Naylor (b. Apr. 15, 1862, Pennsville, Morgan Co., Ohio; d. July 23, 1929, Auburn, Ohio) moved with her family to Malta, Ohio as a child; after her father's death, with her mother and sister, opened a millinery shop just across the Muskingum River, in McConnelsville; married Charles H. Morris and the two were very active in the Methodist Episcopal Church and in holiness camp meetings; first encouraged by H. L. Gilmour, wrote more than 1000 hymns and many tunes as well, continuing even after she was old and blind.

Jesus is coming to earth again (180); If you are tired of the load of your sin (268); Nearer, still nearer (353)
SECOND COMING (180); McCONNELSVILLE (268); MORRIS (353)

Mote, Edward (b. Jan. 21, 1797, London, Eng.; d. Nov. 13, 1874, Southwark, London, Eng.), as a youth, was moved by the preaching of John Hyatt of Tottenham Court Road Chapel; became a successful cabinetmaker in a suburb of London, and was dedicated to the work of the church; wrote over 100 hymns, published in his *Hymns of Praise, A New Selection of Gospel Hymns, Combining All the Excellencies of Our Spiritual Poets, with many Originals,* 1836 (this may be the first use of the term "gospel hymn," though most of the contents were hymns of praise); in 1852 became pastor of the Baptist church in Horsham, Sussex, served for 21 years and is buried in the churchyard.

My hope is built on nothing less (313)

Moultrie, Gerard (b. Sept. 16, 1829, Rugby, Eng.; d. Apr. 25, 1885, Southleigh, Eng.), in his hymnic activity, was obviously influenced by the Oxford (high church) movement of the Anglican Church; was trained at Rugby School and Exeter College, Oxford; was ordained into the Anglican priesthood, held various chaplaincies, became vicar of Southleigh in 1869 and warden of St. James' College, Southleigh in 1873; edited and published *Hymns and Lyrics for the Seasons and Saints' Days of the Church* (1867), *Cantica Sanctorum, or Hymns for the Black Letter Saints' Days in the English and Scottish Calendars* (1880), and other volumes.

Let all mortal flesh keep silence (adapt.) (101)

Mountain, James (b. July 16, 1844, Leeds, York, Eng.; d. June 27, 1933, Tunbridge Wells, Kent, Eng.) trained for the ministry of the "Countess of Huntingdon's Connexion" (Anglican churches influenced and supported by the Countess) at Rotherham College, Nottingham Institute and Cheshunt College, with further study in Heidelberg and Tübingen, Germany; was ordained and served a pastorate at Great Marlow, but poor health interrupted his ministry; was greatly influenced by the visit of Moody and Sankey in the early 1870's and gave himself to evangelism in Britain and worldwide, 1874–89; pastored the Countess of Huntingdon's church, Tunbridge Wells, 1889–97; became a Baptist, founding St. John's Free Church at Tunbridge Wells; wrote many religious books and articles, and a number of hymn texts, but is better known for his tunes; shows the influence of Ira Sankey (*q.v.*) in his *Hymns of Consecration and Faith,* 1876.

TRANQUILLITY (394); WYE VALLEY (397); EVERLASTING LOVE (409)

Mozart, Wolfgang Amadeus (b. Jan. 27, 1756, Salzburg, Aust.; d. Dec. 5, 1791, Vienna, Aust.) has been called "the greatest musical genius in Western history"; was the son of Leopold Mozart, *kappelmeister* to the prince-archbishop of Salzburg, who recognized the talent of his children and gave them every possible advantage in education; at age six, made an extended concert tour with his father and sister, amazing audiences with his piano playing and improvisation; was widely feted throughout Europe as performer, composer and conductor but never achieved financial security; in 1782 married Constanze Weber, a cousin of Carl Maria von Weber (*q.v.*); died at age 36 from poverty and overwork; left 600 musical masterworks in all forms; may not be the source of all the hymn tunes credited to him—the authentic ones have been adapted from various compositions.

ELLESDIE (443, 493)

Mühlenberg, William Augustus (b. Sept. 16, 1796, Philadelphia, Pa.; d. Apr. 6, 1877, New York City, N.Y.) studied at the University of Pennsylvania and was ordained in the Protestant Episcopal church, 1820; served various parishes and founded the Flushing Institute (a boy's school) in 1828; established St. Paul's College in 1838; became rector of the Church of the Holy Communion, New York City, 1843; published a tract, *A Plea for Christian Hymns* (1821), which resulted in his appointment to the committee which prepared the *Prayer Book Collection,* 1826; also published *People's Psalter,* 1858 and *Poems,* 1859; died in New York City and was buried at St. Johnsland.

Savior, who Thy flock art feeding (217)

Murphy, Anne S. (b., date unknown; d. Mar. 30, 1942, Burbank, Calif.) was married to Will H. Murphy, who operated a successful pottery business in Ohio; with her husband, used wealth and influence to serve God and the church; a talented musician, singer and public speaker, was very active in the gospel ministry; in the early Depression years (*ca.* 1929) was widowed and stripped of earthly possessions, and went to live with relatives in Burbank, Calif.; was visited by composer Phil Kerr a short time before her death, and he found her serene and giving evidence of an inner peace that is the message of her song "Constantly Abiding."

There's a peace in my heart (406)
CONSTANTLY ABIDING (406)

Nägeli, Johann (Hans) Georg (b. May 26, 1768, Wetzikon, near Zurich, Switz.; d. Dec. 26, 1836, Wetzikon, Switz.) has not left a clear record in history either as to birthdate (1768 or 1773) or first name (Johann or Hans); was a pioneer music educator who strongly influenced Lowell Mason (*q.v.*), and founded a school of music in Zurich known as the Swiss Association for the Cultivation of Music; was also a music publisher who released excellent editions of the works of J. S. Bach (*q.v.*), Handel (*q.v.*), Frescobaldi, and other composers; published his theories of music education in *Gesangbildungslehre nach Pestalozzischen Grundsätzen*, 1810.

DENNIS (207); NAOMI (419)

Neale, John Mason (b. Jan. 24, 1818, London, Eng.; d. Aug. 6, 1866, East Grinstead, Sussex, Eng.) brought much of the rich treasury of ancient Greek and Latin hymns into English-language worship in the mid-19th century; was educated at Trinity College, Cambridge and ordained in 1841; in 1846 became warden of Sackville College, East Grinstead (a home for indigent old men) and remained there until his death (because of ecclesiastical opposition to his "high church" views, was made caretaker rather than chaplain, with meager compensation); was founding father of one of the first nursing homes in England, the Sisterhood of St. Margaret; a liturgical scholar and linguist, translated many early Greek and Latin hymns, which are said to be more beautiful and meaningful in English than in the original; also wrote a large number of original hymns which appear, along with the translations, in: *Mediaeval Hymns and Sequences* (1851), *The Hymnal Noted* (1852 and 1854), *Hymns of the Eastern Church* (1862), and *Sequences, Hymns, and other Ecclesiastical Verses* (1866); unrecognized by his native country, was given an honorary D.D. degree by the University of Hartford, Connecticut.

O come, O come, Emmanuel (trans.) (100); Good Christian men, rejoice (trans.) (116); Of the Father's love begotten (trans.) (122); All glory, laud and honor (trans.) (131); O sons and daughters (trans.) (160); Come, ye faithful, raise the strain (trans.) (164); The day of resurrection (trans.) (168); Are you weary, heavy laden (259); Jerusalem the golden (trans.) (536)

Neander, Joachim (b. 1650, Bremen, Ger.; d. May 31, 1680, Bremen, Ger.) has been called "the Paul Gerhardt (*q.v.*) of the German Calvinists"; received training at the Pädagogium in Bremen (where his father taught) and later at the Gymnasium Illustre; a part of the rebellious student life of his day, became convicted by the preaching of Theodore Under-Eyck in St. Martin's Church, Bremen and was converted; tutored at Frankfurt and Heidelberg, and in 1674 was appointed rector of the Latin School at Düsseldorf, sponsored by the Reformed Church; was briefly suspended from the school because of his Pietist associations and activity; in 1679 went back to Bremen to serve as an unordained assistant to Under-Eyck at St. Martin's Church; died at age 30 of tuberculosis; wrote some 60 hymns, many of which express his love of nature, and provided tunes for several; published *Geistreiches Bundes-und-Dank-Lieder,* and *A und Ω Joachimi Neandri Glaubes und Liebesübung,* 1680.

Praise to the Lord, the Almighty (43)

UNSER HERRSCHER (183); WUNDERBARER KÖNIG (375)

Neumark, Georg (b. Mar. 16, 1621, Langensalza, Thuringia; d. July 18, 1681, Weimar, Ger.) received his early education at Schleusingen and Gotha; on his way to study law at the University of Königsberg, was robbed, so was forced to take a tutorship in Kiel for two years; finally reached Königsberg and stayed five years, studying law and poetry; had several years of scant employment, but in 1652 was appointed court poet, librarian, and registrar to the Duke of Weimar, and later secretary of the ducal archives; was blind during the last year of his life; produced 34 hymns, many written in times of difficulty and misfortune; left one principal volume of sacred and secular songs, *Fortgeflantzter Musikalisch-Poetischer Lustwald,* 1657.

If thou but suffer God to guide thee (420)

NEUMARK (420)

Neumeister, Erdmann (b. May 12, 1671, Üchteritz, Ger.; d. Aug. 18, 1756, Hamburg, Ger.) was schooled at the University of Leipzig, lectured there for a period and was appointed pastor at Bibra and assistant superintendent of the Eckartsberg District; in 1704 became tutor to Duke Johann Georg's only daughter, and assistant court preacher at Weissenfels; later was senior court preacher at Sorau, then pastor of St. James' Church at Hamburg from 1715 until his death; authored some 650 hymns and is credited with originating the cantata form, with some of his texts used by J. S. Bach (*q.v.*); published *Der Zugang zum Gnadenstuhle Jesu Christo* (1705), *Evangelischer Nachklang* (1718), and *Fünffache Kirchen-Andachten* (1716), a collection of cantata texts.

Sinners Jesus will receive (271)

Newbolt, Michael Robert (b. 1874, Lambourn, Berks, Eng.; d. Feb. 7, 1956, Bierton, Bucks, Eng.) received his education at St. John's College, Oxford, and was ordained an Anglican priest in 1900; served as assistant curate at Wantage, and then as vicar of St. Mary's in Iffley; was principal of the Missionary College in Dorchester for several years; later served churches in Brighton and Chester, and was licensed to officiate in the Diocese of Oxford.

Lift high the Cross (141)

Newell, William Reed (b. May 22, 1868, Savannah, Ohio; d. Apr. 1, 1956, DeLand, Fla.) was educated at Wooster College and at Princeton and Oberlin Theological Seminaries; served several pastorates and then became assistant superintendent of Moody Bible Institute in Chicago; for many years, at the suggestion of Dwight L. Moody, held regular Bible classes in several different cities, commuting between them by train; was a popular conference speaker who published expositions of many books of the Bible.

Years I spent in vanity and pride (286)

Newman, John Henry (b. Feb. 21, 1801, London, Eng.; d. Aug. 11, 1890, Edgbaston, Eng.) was educated at Ealing and Trinity College, Oxford, and served as vicar of St. Mary the Virgin Church for 15 years; was a leader in the Oxford Movement and contributed many of their published tracts; in 1845 became a Roman Catholic and was appointed to the oratory of St. Philip Neri at Edgbaston; was rector of the newly organized Dublin Catholic University for four years, then returned to Edgbaston; in 1879 was made a cardinal of the church; wrote most of his poetry during a trip to southern Europe, and it was published in *Lyra Apostolica*, 1836.

Lead, kindly Light, amid the encircling gloom (442)

Newton, John (b. July 24, 1725, London, Eng.; d. Dec. 21, 1807, London, Eng.) went to sea with his father at age 11 and later served in the Royal Navy; captained a slave ship and, by his own admission, led a life of dissipation and wretchedness; was converted through reading *The Imitation of Christ* by Thomas à Kempis, and the experience of a stormy night at sea; was ordained an Anglican minister when almost 40 years of age, and went to Olney as curate; with William Cowper, produced the historic *Olney Hymns*, 1779, to which he contributed some 280 poems and Cowper, 68; later, was rector at St. Mary's, Woolnoth, in London; wrote this epitaph which appears on his gravestone in the churchyard at Olney: "John Newton, Clerk, Once an infidel and libertine, A servant of slaves in Africa, was by the rich mercy of our Lord and Saviour, Jesus Christ, preserved, restored, pardoned, and appointed to preach the faith he had long labored to destroy."

How sweet the name of Jesus sounds (68); I saw One hanging on a tree (146); Glorious things of thee are spoken (209); Amazing grace! how sweet the sound (288); Come, my soul, your plea prepare (431); Safely through another week (548); May the grace of Christ our Savior (589)

Nichol, Henry Ernest (b. Dec. 10, 1862, Hull, Eng.; d. Aug. 30, 1926, Skirlaugh, York, Eng.) studied civil engineering, but gave it up in favor of music; received the B.M. from Oxford, 1888; wrote primarily for Sunday School anniversary services (both words and music); often used the pseudonym "Colin Sterne," derived from the letters of his last and middle names.

> We've a story to tell to the nations (483)
> MESSAGE (483)

Nicholson, James L. (b. *ca.* 1828, Ireland; d. Nov. 6, 1876, Washington, D.C.) emigrated to the United States around 1850 and settled in Philadelphia; was active in evangelism and Sunday School work in the Wharton Street Methodist Episcopal Church; moved to Washington, D.C. in 1871 and worked as a postal clerk, continuing his church work—teaching and leading singing; died in Washington and was buried in Philadelphia.

> Lord Jesus, I long to be perfectly whole (386)

Nicholson, Sydney Hugo (b. Feb. 9, 1875, London, Eng.; d. May 30, 1947, Ashford, Kent, Eng.) received schooling at Rugby School, New College, Oxford and the Royal College of Music; was organist at Barnet Parish Church, at Lower Chapel and at Eton College, then assistant organist at Carlisle Cathedral, and organist at Manchester Cathedral and Westminster Abbey; in 1927 founded the School of English Church Music and served as Director until his death; was knighted in 1938; served as musical editor of the later editions of *Hymns Ancient and Modern;* published *Boys Choirs* (1922), *A Manual of English Church Music* (1923, with George L. H. Gardner), *Quires and Places Where They Sing* (1932) and *Peter—The Adventures of a Chorister* (1944).

> CRUCIFER (141)

Noel, Caroline Maria (b. Apr. 10, 1817, London, Eng.; d. Dec. 7, 1877, London, Eng.) began writing hymns at age 17; wrote her finest works during the last 25 years of her life when she experienced a prolonged period of illness and suffering; published *The Name of Jesus, and Other Verses for the Sick and Lonely,* 1861.

> At the name of Jesus (61)

Norris, John Samuel (b. Dec. 4, 1844, West Cowes, Isle of Wight, Eng.; d. Sept. 23, 1907, Chicago, Ill.) received his education in Canada and was ordained in the Methodist church; from 1868–78, served churches in Canada, New York and Wisconsin; became a Congregationalist in 1878, held several different pastorates and acted as conference evangelist in Wisconsin and Iowa; retired to Chicago, Illinois in 1901 where he remained until his death; wrote over 100 hymns and published one collection, *Songs of the Soul.*

> NORRIS (369)

North, Frank Mason (b. Dec. 3, 1850, New York, N.Y.; d. Dec. 17, 1935, Madison, N.J.) received the B.A. and M.A. degrees from Wesleyan University (Conn.) and was ordained in the Methodist Episcopal Church in 1872; served churches in Florida, New York and Connecticut, 1872–92; was editor of the *Christian City* and corresponding secretary of the New York Extension and Missionary Society of his denomination; in 1919 became secretary of the Board of Foreign Missions; acted as president of the Federal Council of Churches of Christ in America, 1916–20; wrote a number of hymns for special occasions.

Where cross the crowded ways of life (514)

Oakeley, Frederick (b. Sept. 5, 1802, Shrewsbury, Eng.; d. Jan. 29, 1880, London, Eng.) is principally remembered for his translation of "Adeste Fideles"; was educated at Christ Church, Oxford and made a Fellow of Balliol, 1827; was ordained in 1826 and served at Lichfield Cathedral, Whitehall, and Margaret Chapel, London; was a leader of the Oxford Movement in the Church of England and eventually became a Roman Catholic; was appointed a canon of Westminster Procathedral in 1852, and worked among the poor in that area; translated hymns from the Latin and published several volumes of prose and poetry.

O come, all ye faithful (trans.) (103)

Oatman, Johnson, Jr. (b. Apr. 21, 1856, Medford, N.J.; d. Sept. 25, 1922, Norman, Okla.) received his schooling at Herbert's Academy, Vincentown, N.J. and the New Jersey Collegiate Institute in Bordentown; was ordained in the Methodist Episcopal Church but continued as a local preacher without a permanent assignment; was active in business with his father, and later established his own insurance firm; wrote many sacred poems which were set to music by John R. Sweney (*q.v.*), William Kirkpatrick (*q.v.*), Charles Gabriel (*q.v.*), E. O. Excell (*q.v.*), and others.

There's not a friend (307); I'm pressing on the upward way (355); When upon life's billows you are tempest-tossed (569)

Ogden, William Augustine (b. Oct. 10, 1841, Franklin Co., Ohio; d. Oct. 14, 1897, Toledo, Ohio) attended community singing schools in his early years; served in the 30th Indiana Volunteer Infantry during the Civil War, then resumed his musical training under Lowell Mason (*q.v.*), Thomas Hastings (*q.v.*), E. E. Bailey, and B. F. Baker; conducted musical conventions and was known as a teacher of normal music schools; in 1887 was appointed supervisor of music for the public schools of Toledo, Ohio; wrote many gospel song melodies and edited a number of collections.

I've a message from the Lord (265)
LOOK AND LIVE (265)

Olivers, Thomas (b. 1725, Tregynon, Montgomery, Wales; d. Mar., 1799, London, Eng.) was orphaned at the age of four and grew up without much care; was apprenticed to a shoemaker, but led a restless, undisciplined life until he was converted through a sermon of George Whitefield in Bristol; in 1753 became an itinerant Methodist preacher, traveling more than 100,000 miles on horseback during 25 years of ministry; served with John Wesley (*q.v.*) and was appointed supervisor of the Methodist Press, 1775;

was discharged by Wesley in 1789 for "errors and unauthorized insertions" in the *Arminian Magazine;* retired in London.

The God of Abraham praise (36)

Olson, Ernst William (b. Mar. 16, 1870, Skåne, Sweden; d. Oct. 6, 1958, Chicago, Ill.) emigrated to America at age five and the family settled in Nebraska, then moved to Texas; graduated from Augustana College and was editor of various Swedish weekly publications for about 12 years; became associated with Engberg-Holmberg Publishing Company, Chicago (1906) and later with the Augustana Book Concern (Lutheran), where he remained more than 35 years; wrote several books, including *A History of the Swedes in Illinois;* translated 28 hymns and wrote four original texts for *Augustana Hymnal,* 1925; was a member of the hymnal committee for *Service Book and Hymnal,* 1958.

Children of the heavenly Father (trans.) (41)

Olude, Abraham Taiwo Olajide (b. July 16, 1908, Ebute-Metta, Lagos, Nigeria) was educated at Wesley College (Ibadan) and Mindola training school; as a pastor, has pioneered in the movement to exploit indigenous African music in both choir and congregational praise; toured Nigeria with his choir, demonstrating his hymns written in the African style; has also written dramas and music for schools; expressed this purpose: "It is my attempt to make singing more meaningful at worship than singing words to English tunes which make nonsense of the words used."

Jesus, we want to meet (547)

JESU A FE PADE (547)

Orr, James Edwin (b. Jan. 12, 1912, Belfast, Ire.) left his native Ireland in 1933, and has been active in worldwide evangelism ever since; was ordained an American Baptist minister in 1940; received the M.A. degree at Northwestern University, 1941 and the Th.D. from Northern Baptist Seminary, 1943; served as a chaplain in the Air Force in the southwest Pacific, 1943–46; has the D.Phil. degree from Oxford University (1948) and the Ed.D. from U.C.L.A. (1971), and honorary degrees from a seminary in India and the University of South Africa; since 1967 has been a professor in the School of World Missions at Fuller Theological Seminary, Pasadena, Calif.; has written six hymn texts and a score of books, many of them accounts of revival awakenings in church history.

Search me, O God (387)

Ortlund, Elizabeth Anne (b. Dec. 3, 1923, Wichita, Kan.) grew up on army posts where her father (Brig. Gen. Joseph B. Sweet) and mother held Bible classes for officers and their wives and led many to Christ during 40 years of service; earned her B.M. degree at the University of Redlands (Calif.) and holds the A.A.G.O. certificate of the American Guild of Organists; is married to Raymond C. Ortlund, for many years pastor of Lake Avenue Congregational Church in Pasadena, Calif.; served as organist for the "Old

Fashioned Revival Hour" broadcast, and continues on its successor "The Joyful Sound"; is the author of the booklet *Up with Worship,* and has written 80 anthems, sacred and secular solos, instrumental works, and 25 hymn texts and tunes.

The vision of a dying world (485)

Osler, Edward (b. Jan. 30, 1798, Falmouth, Eng.; d. Mar. 7, 1863, Truro, Eng.) grew up in a nonconformist home, was trained in medicine and practiced privately and in the navy for several years; in 1836 gave up his "free church" connections and devoted his time fully to religious and literary endeavors; was associated for many years with the (Anglican) Society for Promoting Christian Knowledge, and later moved to Truro where he was editor of the *Royal Cornwall Gazette* until his death; with Rev. W. J. Hall, produced the *Mitre Hymnal* (1836), to which he contributed 50 hymns and 15 psalm adaptations.

Praise the Lord! ye heavens, adore him (St. 3) (17)

Ostrom, Henry (b. date unknown; d. Dec. 20, 1941), according to a report by Wendell P. Loveless (*q.v.*), was a Methodist pastor who became convinced of the validity of the "Scofield interpretation" of scripture; beginning in 1921, was a member of the extension staff of Moody Bible Institute, Chicago, Ill. for a number of years; wrote a number of books, including *Out of the Cain-Life* (1896), *Greatness* (1904), *The Law of Prayer* (1910), and a number of hymns; is described by President James M. Gray (*q.v.*) of Moody Bible Institute in the introduction to Ostrom's *The Jew and His Mission:*

Henry Ostrom as a pastor and leader in a broader field of evangelism and Bible teaching, has been accorded a place in the confidence and affection of Christians of all denominations in the United States.

Jesus may come today (179)

Owens, Priscilla Jane (b. July 21, 1829, Baltimore, Md.; d. Dec. 5, 1907, Baltimore, Md.) was for 49 years a public school teacher, spending her entire life in Baltimore; a faithful member of the Union Square Methodist Church, wrote most of her hymns for the Sunday School; frequently released her poetry and prose in the *Methodist Protestant* and the *Christian Standard.*

We have heard the joyful sound (486)

Oxenham, John (b. Nov. 12, 1852, Manchester, Eng.; d. Jan. 24, 1941, London, Eng.) was born William Arthur Dunkerly, and trained at Old Trafford School and Victoria University in Manchester; traveled extensively in Europe, Canada and America in connection with his business; lived in the United States for two years and, returning to England, published the London edition of the *Detroit Free Press;* began writing under a pseudonym as an avocation and, because his work was so well received, eventually devoted his full time to publishing; is credited with some 40 novels and several books of poetry and prose; was long active at the Ealing

Congregational Church, London, teaching a Bible class and serving as a deacon.

Mid all the traffic of the ways (414); In Christ there is no East or West (513); Peace in our time, O Lord (519)

Palestrina, Giovanni Pierluigi da (b. 1525, Palestrina, Italy; d. Feb. 2, 1594, Rome, Italy), who derives his name from his birthplace, was a leading composer of church music in the 16th century; began as a choirboy in the Cathedral of St. Agapit, and eventually became Chapel Master of the Julian Choir in St. Peter's, Rome; is credited with 100 masses, 200 motets, offertories, hymns and other liturgical materials which are bound in 33 volumes, published by Breitkopf and Härtel, 1862–1903; because of his composing genius, is credited with rescuing Catholic church music from the restrictive reforms dictated by the Council of Trent in 1562.

VICTORY (161)

Palmer, Ray (b. Nov. 13, 1808, Little Compton, R.I.; d. Mar. 29, 1887, Newark, N.J.) received schooling at Phillips Academy and Yale University; as a Congregational minister, served churches at Bath, Me. and Albany, N.Y.; was appointed corresponding secretary of the American Congregational Union in 1865 and served until his retirement; edited *Hymns and Sacred Pieces* (1865), *Hymns of My Holy Hours and Other Pieces* (1868), and *Poetical Works* (1876); contributed a number of original hymns and translations from Latin to *Sabbath Hymn-Book* (1858); permitted no revision of his texts, and made it a habit to take no compensation for their use.

Jesus, Thou Joy of loving hearts (trans.) (91); My faith looks up to Thee (366)

Park, John Edgar (b. Mar. 7, 1879, Belfast, Ire.; d. Mar. 4, 1956, Cambridge, Me.) was trained at Queen's College in Belfast and the Royal University in Dublin, with additional study at universities in Edinburgh, Leipzig, Munich, Oxford and Princeton; was ordained a Presbyterian minister and served briefly in labor camps in the Adirondacks; spent 19 years as pastor of the Second Congregational Church in Newton, Mass.; in 1926 became president of Wheaton College, Norton, Mass., and served until retirement in 1944; wrote a number of hymns, several books, and contributed many articles to such periodicals as *The Atlantic Monthly* and *The Christian Century*.

We would see Jesus; lo! His star (125)

Parker, Edwin Pond (b. Jan. 13, 1836, Castine, Me.; d. May 28, 1925, Hartford, Conn.), educated at Bowdoin College and Bangor Theological Seminary, served the Center Church (Congregational), Hartford, Conn. for 50 years; wrote at least 200 hymns after the age of 56, and edited a number of hymn collections.

Master, no offering, costly and sweet (502)
MERCY (arr.) (194); LOVE'S OFFERING (502)

Parry, Joseph (b. May 21, 1841, Cyfarthfa, Wales; d. Feb. 17, 1903, Cartref, Penarth, Wales) was an important Welsh musician who came to America as a boy of 13 and received his first musical training in classes conducted by fellow workers in the Danville, Pa. iron works, and later attended a summer music school in Geneseo, N.Y.; returned to Wales and won several Eisteddfod contests (Swansea, 1863; Llandudno, 1864; Chester, 1866); studied at the Royal Academy of Music in London and received B.Mus. and D.Mus. degrees from Cambridge University; after a brief return to the United States (1871–73), was appointed professor of music at the University College in Aberystwyth, and finally at the University College, Cardiff; wrote oratorios, cantatas, anthems and some 400 hymn tunes.

    ABERYSTWYTH (246)

Peace, Albert Lister (b. Jan. 26, 1844, Huddersfield, Eng.; d. Mar. 14, 1912, Liverpool, Eng.), a child prodigy, was organist at the parish church of Holmfirth, York at age nine; received B.Mus. and D.Mus. degrees from Oxford and was organist of Glasgow Cathedral, 1879–97; went to St. George's Hall, Liverpool as successor to William T. Best and remained until his death in 1912; was a Fellow of the Royal College of Organists (1866) and is said to have played more dedicatory recitals on new organs than any other organist of his time; edited a number of volumes for the Church of Scotland: *The Scottish Hymnal* (1885), *Psalms and Paraphrases with Tunes* (1886), *The Psalter with Chants* (1888) and *The Scottish Anthem Book* (1891).

    ST. MARGARET (351)

Peek, Joseph Yates (b. Feb. 27, 1843, Schenectady, N.Y.; d. Mar. 17, 1911, Brooklyn, N.Y.) had no formal music training, but played the violin, banjo and piano; enlisted in the Union Army during the Civil War, giving his occupation as carpenter and farmer; in 1881 became interested in horticulture and was a very successful florist; later became an itinerant Methodist lay preacher, ministering in Maine, Florida and California; as a member of Nostrand-DeKalb Methodist Episcopal Church in Brooklyn, was fully ordained less than two months before his death.

    PEEK (337)

Pennefather, William (b. Feb. 5, 1816, Dublin, Ire.; d. Apr. 30, 1873, London, Eng.) was born of titled parents and educated at Westbury College near Bristol, and Trinity College, Dublin; was ordained in 1841, serving Anglican churches at Ballymacugh and Mellifont in Ireland; in 1848 moved to England and ministered in Aylesbury, Barnet, and East London, where he established the Mildmay Religious and Benevolent Institution, a center for religious work; produced several volumes, including *Hymns, Original and Selected,* 1872 and *Original Hymns and Thoughts in Verse,* 1873 (published posthumously).

    Jesus, stand among us (577)

Perronet, Edward (b. 1726, Sundridge, Kent, Eng.; d. Jan. 2, 1792, Canterbury, Eng.) is remembered for the text "All hail the power of Jesus' name," which is included in most English-language hymnals and in many translations; received his early education under a tutor in his father's vicarage and prepared to be a clergyman in the Church of England; was a strong evangelical whose poem *The Mitre,* 1757, attacked certain practices of the Church; associated with reformers like John and Charles Wesley (*q.v.*) and Selina, Countess of Huntingdon, but eventually withdrew from the Anglican Church; spent his last years as pastor of a dissenting congregation in a small chapel at Canterbury; wrote several volumes of poems and versified scripture.

All hail the power of Jesus' name (62, 63)

Perry, Jean (b. 1865; d. 1935). No other information on this author can be found. She is listed as the author of this hymn, but many acquaintances of Mabel Johnston Camp (composer of the music) have suggested that the author and composer are one-and-the-same, since Mrs. Camp traditionally wrote music only for her own texts. However, these birth-death dates have been given in various hymnals, and they are different from those of Mrs. Camp.

I know of a Name (92)

Peterson, John Willard (b. Nov. 1, 1921, Lindsborg, Kans.) was born into a musical family, who were members of a Mission Covenant Church and active in Christian radio; during World War II was a pilot in the Army Air Force in Asia; received training at Moody Bible Institute and American Conservatory of Music, Chicago (B.Mus., 1951); received an honorary D.D. degree (1971) from Western Conservative Baptist Seminary and the Sac.Mus.D. (1967) from John Brown University; was a staff musician, WMBI, Chicago, 1950–54; in 1954 joined Alfred B. Smith (*q.v.*) as an editor and composer for Singspiration, Inc., Montrose, Pa., and in 1963 became president of the company when it was acquired by Zondervan Publishing House, Grand Rapids, Mich.; in 1971 became "executive composer" and continues active in workshops and premieres countrywide; has edited several hymnals, including *Great Hymns of Our Faith,* 1968, and written more than 1000 texts and tunes; has published more than 25 cantatas and musicals, which have sold some six million copies.

A pilgrim was I and a-wandering (49); God of everlasting glory (56); All glory to Jesus, begotten of God (69); Marvelous message we bring (182); O what a wonderful, wonderful day (410)
SURELY GOODNESS AND MERCY (49); BRETON ROAD (56); RIDGEMOOR (69); COMING AGAIN (182); HEAVEN CAME DOWN (410); TORONTO (481)

Phelps, Sylvanus Dryden (b. May 15, 1816, Suffield, Conn.; d. Nov. 23, 1895, New Haven, Conn.) may be remembered as the father of William Lyon Phelps, author and popular English teacher at Yale; received his education at Connecticut Literary Institute, Brown University and Yale Divinity School; was ordained a Baptist minister and served the First Baptist Church of New Haven, Conn. for 28 years and Jefferson Street Baptist Church, Providence, R.I. for two years; left the pastorate to become editor of the *Christian Secretary;* published several volumes of poetry and prose, including nine editions of *The Holy Land, with Glimpses of Europe and Egypt, a Year's Tour,* 1862.

Savior, Thy dying love (345)

Pierpoint, Folliott Sandford (b. Oct. 7, 1835, Bath, Somerset, Eng.; d. Mar. 10, 1917, Newport, Eng.) took his early schooling at Bath, with higher education at Queen's College, Cambridge; for a time was master of the classics at Somersetshire College; contributed hymns to the *Lyra Eucharistica* and *The Hymnal Noted;* published several volumes of poems, including *The Chalice of Nature, Songs of Love,* and *Lyra Jesu,* 1878.

For the beauty of the earth (55)

Pigott, Jean Sophia (b. 1845, Ireland; d. Oct. 12, 1882, Leixlip, Lucan, Co. Kildare, Ire.)

Jesus, I am resting, resting (394)

Plumptre, Edward Hayes (b. Aug. 6, 1821, London, Eng.; d. Feb. 1, 1891, Wells, Somerset, Eng.) was trained at King's College, London and University College, Oxford and became a Fellow of Brasenose College; ordained in 1846, was chaplain at King's College, where he later taught pastoral theology and exegesis; also served as Dean of Queen's College, Oxford, prebendary of St. Paul's, rector of Pluckley and vicar of Bickley in Kent, and Dean of Wells; was a member of the Old Testament Revision Committee for the Revised Version of the Bible; wrote several volumes of verse, and translated many hymns.

Rejoice, ye pure in heart (14)

Pollard, Adelaide Addison (b. Nov. 27, 1862, Bloomfield, Ia.; d. Dec. 20, 1934, New York, N.Y.) was born "Sarah" but chose the name Adelaide; received her education in schools in Denmark, Ia. and Valparaiso, Ind., and the Boston School of Oratory; taught in girls' schools in Chicago and became well-known as an itinerant Bible teacher; taught at the Missionary Training School in New York City (Christian and Missionary Alliance) for eight years; was interested in missions and spent a few months in Africa before the outbreak of World War I; passed her last years in the East, still ministering, though she was in poor health most of her life; wrote a number of hymns, but only "Have Thine Own Way, Lord" has remained popular.

Have Thine own way, Lord (372)

Pollock, Thomas Benson (b. May 28, 1836, Strathallan, Isle of Man, Eng.; d. Dec. 15, 1896, Birmingham, Eng.) graduated from Trinity College, Dublin, studied medicine briefly, but took Holy Orders (1861) and became curate of St. Luke's, Leek, Staffordshire, and later at St. Thomas' in Stamford Hill, London; at St. Alban's Mission in Birmingham, served with his brother for 30 years, and succeeded him as vicar there; published *Metrical Litanies for Special Services and General Use*, 1870, and was a member of the committee which edited *Hymns Ancient and Modern*.

Jesus, with Thy Church abide (202)

Poole, William Charles (b. Apr. 14, 1875, Easton, Md.; d. Dec. 24, 1949, Lewes, Del.) was born to farming parents and was converted at the age of 11; received his education at Washington College, Chestertown, Md. and was ordained to the Methodist ministry in 1900; served various churches in the Wilmington Conference for 35 years; because of the encouragement of Charles H. Gabriel (*q.v.*), wrote many hymn texts.

Just when I need Him Jesus is near (412)

Pott, Francis (b. Dec. 29, 1832, London, Eng.; d. Oct. 26, 1909, Speldhurst, Kent, Eng.) made important contributions to hymnody through his translations from the Latin; graduated from Brasenose College, Oxford (B.A. and M.A.), was ordained in 1856 and served as curate in parishes in Somerset and Sussex; was rector of Northill, Bedfordshire for 25 years, 1866–91; was forced to retire because of deafness, and afterward was active in research and writing; was a member of the original committee for *Hymns Ancient and Modern*, 1861; edited *Hymns Fitted to the Order of Common Prayer*, 1861 and *The Free Rhythm Psalter*, 1898.

The strife is o'er, the battle done (trans.) (161)

Pounds, Jessie Brown (b. Aug. 31, 1861, Hiram, Ohio; d. 1921) was in poor health as a child, and received her early education at home; at age 15, began to submit articles to Cleveland newspapers and various religious publications; in 1896 married the Rev. John E. Pounds, pastor of the Central Christian Church in Indianapolis, Ind., who later became college pastor at Hiram, Ohio; wrote more than 400 gospel song texts, 50 librettos for cantatas and operettas, and 9 books, mostly published by James H. Fillmore (*q.v.*)

I know that my Redeemer liveth (157); Anywhere with Jesus I can safely go (328)

Prentiss, Elizabeth Payson (b. Oct. 26, 1818, Portland, Me.; d. Aug. 13, 1878, Dorset, Vt.) was a school teacher for some years; in 1845 married Dr. George Lewis Prentiss, a Presbyterian-Congregational minister, who became professor of homiletics and polity at Union Theological Seminary, New York; as a teenager, contributed to the *Youth's Companion;* published a number of works, including *Stepping Heavenward* (1869), *Religious Poems* (1873), and *Golden Hours, or Hymns and Songs of the Christian Life* (1874).

More love to Thee, O Christ (359)

Prichard, Rowland Hugh (b. Jan. 14, 1811, Graienyn, near Bala, No. Wales; d. Jan. 25, 1887, Holywell, Wales) is best known as the composer of the tune "Hyfrydol," which he wrote when about 20 years of age; spent most of his life in Bala, North Wales, where he was well-known as a choir director and amateur musician; in 1880 moved to Holywell to become an assistant loom tender at the Welsh Flannel Manufacturing Company; published *Cyfaill y Cantorion* (The Singer's Friend), 1844, which contained most of his tunes.

HYFRYDOL (99, 102, 174, 408, 512, 521)

Prudentius, Aurelius Clemens (b. 348, Spain; d. *ca.* 413) is known only from what he said about himself in a short, poetic introduction to his writings; was a Spaniard from a good family, who studied and practiced law and became a judge, and was eventually made chief of Emperor Honorius' imperial bodyguard; at age 57 was conscious-stricken because of his self-centered life, entered a monastery and spent the rest of his days in meditation, prayer and writing; left the historic volumes, *Liber Cathemerinon* (hymns for the hours of the day) and *Liber Peristephanon* (14 hymns honoring martyrs).

Of the Father's love begotten (122)

Purday, Charles Henry (b. Jan. 11, 1799, Folkestone, Kent, Eng.; d. Apr. 23, 1885, London, Eng.), during a long career, was a singer (who performed at Queen Victoria's coronation), music teacher, publisher, lecturer and conductor; was actively involved in reforming the music copyright laws; for many years served as precentor at the Scottish Church in London's Covent Garden; wrote a number of popular songs and contributed to *Grove's Dictionary of Music and Musicians;* published: *The Sacred Musical Offering* (1833), *A Few Directions for Chanting* (1855), *A Church and Home Tune Book* (1857) and *Copyright, a Sketch of Its Rise and Progress* (1877).

SANDON (44, 326)

Pusey, Philip (b. June 25, 1799, Pusey, Berks, Eng.; d. July 9, 1855, Oxford, Eng.) was trained at Eton and Christ Church, Oxford, but did not complete his degree; settled on the family estate in Berkshire and devoted himself to agriculture, public service, and writing; became a member of Parliament and was one of the founders of the Royal Agriculture Society and the London Library; was keenly interested in hymnology.

Lord of our life, and God of our salvation (395)

Quaile, Robert Newton (b. 1867, Rathkeale, Limerick, Ire.; d. July 26, 1927, Mallow, Cork, Ire.), the son of an Irish Methodist minister, attended Wesley College, Dublin, and was a business man and amateur musician in Mallow, County Cork; in the political and economic uprising in Ireland in 1920, lost all of his possessions; contributed three tunes to the English Methodist *Sunday School Hymnal,* 1910.

OLDBRIDGE (568)

Rabanus Maurus (b. 776, Mainz, Ger.; d. Feb. 4, 856, Winkel-on-the-Rhine, Ger.) was born of noble parents and educated at Fulda and Tours under Alcuin; in 803 became director of the Benedictine Abbey school at Fulda; was ordained a priest in 814 and made a pilgrimage to Palestine; became Archbishop of Mainz, 847 and later was proclaimed a saint; left extensive biblical commentaries and other scholarly works, and many Latin poems.

Come, Holy Ghost, our souls inspire (188)

Rader, Paul (b. Aug. 24, 1879, Denver, Colo., according to published reports, but his daughter Pauline Noll of Vallejo, Calif. says it was 1878 in Cheyenne, Wyo.; d. July 19, 1938, Hollywood, Calif.) was named "Daniel Paul Rader" but never used his first name; was known as one of the most powerful evangelistic preachers of his time, and described himself to newspaper reporters as an "ex-bellboy, ex-cowboy, ex-prospector, ex-football player, and ex-pugilist"; was the son of a Methodist minister, spent his boyhood in parsonages in Colorado and Wyoming, and was converted at the age of nine; studied at University of Denver and the University of Colorado, and taught in the athletic departments of the University of Puget Sound and Hamline University, St. Paul, Minn.; in academic life, lost his faith and became a defeated, discouraged man—some time later, wandering along Broadway in New York City, his conscience was stricken, and after three days alone with God his faith was restored, and he went on to become a gifted preacher; was pastor of Moody Church in Chicago, 1915–21, and followed Dr. A. B. Simpson as President of the Christian and Missionary Alliance, 1920–23; returning from a tour of many Alliance mission fields, wrote the book *Round the Round World* (1921); founded the "Big Steel Tent"—the Chicago Gospel Tabernacle—in 1922 and pastored there for 11 years; wrote texts for many hymns and some tunes, and was instrumental in founding Tabernacle Publishing Company.

We are gathered for Thy blessing (190)
TABERNACLE (190)

Ramsey, Benjamin Mansell (b. 1849, Richmond, Surrey, Eng.; d. Aug. 31, 1923, West Wittering, Chichester, Sussex, Eng.) "was for many years a well-known teacher in the Bournemouth area; a prolific composer of part-songs and pianoforte pieces and a writer of hymns and carols and on musical theory; retired from active professional life in 1916; during the last year of his life was in poor health, but organized and conducted a choral society in the village of Chichester." (From an obituary notice in the *Musical Times*, Oct. 1, 1923.)

Teach me Thy way, O Lord (379)
CAMACHA (379)

Rankin, Jeremiah Eames (b. Jan. 2, 1828, Thornton, N.H.; d. Nov. 28, 1904, Cleveland, Ohio) received his education at Middlebury College (Vermont) and Andover Theological Seminary; was ordained a Congregational minister in 1855, and served churches in New York, Vermont, Massachusetts, Washington, D.C., and New Jersey; returned to Washington, D.C. as President of Howard University, 1889; left many publications (mostly gospel songbooks) including *Gospel Temperance Hymnal* (1878), *Gospel Bells* (1883) and *German-English Lyrics, Sacred and Secular* (1897).

God be with you till we meet again (42)

Ravenscroft, Thomas (b. *ca.* 1592; d. *ca.* 1635) was a boy chorister at St. Paul's Cathedral; received the B.Mus. from Cambridge University at age 15; published many works, but is best known for his *Whole Book of Psalmes*, 1621, in which he introduced many continental tunes, and which became for many years the standard musical version of the psalter in England; is said to have initiated the practice of naming tunes after cities and other locations.

DUNDEE (33, 47)

Redhead, Richard (b. Mar. 1, 1820, Harrow, Middlesex, Eng.; d. Apr. 27, 1901, Hellingly, Eng.), during the Tractarian movement in the Church of England, pioneered in the revival of Gregorian chant; was a chorister at Magdalen College, Oxford, and studied organ with Walter Vicary; for 25 years was organist at Margaret Chapel, London (now All Saints', Margaret Street); in 1864 became organist at St. Mary Magdalen Church, Paddington, where he served for 30 years; with his pastor, Canon Frederick Oakeley (*q.v.*), was co-editor of the first Gregorian psalter used in the Anglican church, *Laudes Diurnae*, 1843; published *Ancient Hymn Melodies and Other Church Tunes*, 1853.

REDHEAD (147, 193)

Redner, Lewis Henry (b. Dec. 15, 1830, Philadelphia, Pa.; d. Aug. 29, 1908, Atlantic City, N.J.) was a very successful real estate broker in his native Philadelphia; was successively organist of four different churches including Holy Trinity, where he shared a notable ministry with rector Phillips Brooks (*q.v.*) and also was Sunday School superintendent; remained a bachelor all his life, making his home with his sister.

ST. LOUIS (121)

Reed, Andrew (b. Nov. 27, 1787, London, Eng.; d. Feb. 25, 1862, London, Eng.) is remembered as the founder of The London Orphan Asylum, The Asylum for Fatherless Children, The Asylum for Idiots, The Infant Orphan Asylum, and The Hospital for Incurables; received schooling at Hackney College and was ordained a Congregational minister in 1811; was the first pastor of the New Road Chapel (St. George's-in-the-East) and when it became too small, was responsible for building Wycliffe Chapel, remaining there until 1861; composed 21 hymns, and in 1817 published a supplement to Isaac Watts' *Psalms and Hymns*, and later, *The Hymn Book* (1842).

Holy Spirit, Light divine (194)

Reichardt, C. Luise (b. Apr. 11, 1779, Berlin, Ger.; d. Nov. 17, 1826, Hamburg, Ger.), daughter of the composer-teacher Johann Friedrich Reichardt, studied with her father and made her debut as a singer in Berlin in 1794; in 1814 settled in Hamburg and taught in a vocal academy; suffered misfortune in the death of her fiancee shortly before the wedding and later, the loss of her voice; wrote many songs, some of which remained popular for many years.

ARMAGEDDON (460)

Reinagle, Alexander Robert (b. Aug. 21, 1799, Brighton, Eng.; d. Apr. 6, 1877, Kindlington, Oxford, Eng.) was born into a family of musicians—his grandfather had been "trumpeter to the King," his father was a distinguished cellist, and his uncle (Alexander Reinagle) was a renowned pianist, composer and conductor in America; served as organist of St. Peter's in the East, Oxford, 1822–53; wrote a large amount of music and published collections of hymn tunes in 1836 and 1840.

ST. PETER (68)

Reitz, Albert Simpson (b. Jan. 20, 1879, Lyons, Kan.; d. Nov. 1, 1966, Inglewood, Calif.), in his early career, worked for the YMCA in Topeka, Kan.; traveled as soloist with evangelist Henry Ostrom (*q.v.*) for seven years; attended Moody Bible Institute, Chicago (1917–18), and was encouraged to write songs by D. B. Towner (*q.v.*); was ordained to the Baptist ministry and served churches in Wisconsin and California, remaining 26 years at Rosehill Baptist Church, Inglewood, Calif.; wrote and published over 100 hymns.

Teach me to pray, Lord (438)

REITZ (438)

Reynolds, Mary Lou (b. Dec. 15, 1924, Springfield, Mo.) attended Southwest Missouri State College and received the A.B. degree at William Jewell College in Missouri; served on the staff of First Baptist Church, Oklahoma City, Okla., 1946–47; is married to William J. Reynolds, now head of the Church Music Department, Sunday School Board, Southern Baptist Convention; was employed as an editorial assistant by Abingdon Press for five years; has written articles for church publications and supplied texts for some of her husband's music.

Praise Him, O praise him (31)

Reynolds, William Jensen (b. Apr. 2, 1920, Atlantic, Iowa) is the son of George Washington Reynolds, an evangelistic singer and church musician; was educated at Oklahoma Baptist University, Southwest Missouri State College (A.B.), Southwestern Baptist Theological Seminary (M.S.M.), Westminster Choir College and George Peabody College for Teachers (Ed.D.); served as minister of music in First Baptist Church, Ardmore, Okla., and First Baptist Church, Oklahoma City (1947–55); was employed by the Church Music Department of the Baptist Sunday School Board in Nashville, Tenn. in 1955, became music editor and later, director of editorial services; since 1971 has been head of the Church Music Department and, in that position, has been instrumental in the development of church music programs in 33,000 Southern Baptist churches; served as a member of the executive committee of the Hymn Society of America and was installed as president in 1977; was a member of the Hymnal Committee for the *Baptist Hymnal,* 1956 and General Editor of *Baptist Hymnal,* 1975; authored *Hymns of Our Faith* (companion to the 1956 edition of the *Baptist Hymnal*), *A Survey of Christian Hymnody,* 1963, and *Companion to Baptist Hymnal,* 1976; has composed many cantatas, anthems and hymn tunes.

    PASCHALL (31)

Rhodes, Sarah Betts (b. *ca.* 1829, Eng.; d. 1904, Worksop, Notts, Eng.), an active Congregationalist, was christened Sarah Betts Bradshaw and married J. Alsop Rhodes, a master silversmith in Sheffield; was gifted as a sculptress and hymn writer; after her husband's death, became headmistress of a girls' school at Worksop.

    God who made the earth (567)

Rimbault, Edward Francis (b. June 13, 1816, London, Eng.; d. Sept. 26, 1876, London, Eng.) studied first with his father, Stephen Francis Rimbault, organist of St. Giles-in-the-Fields, London and a composer of note, and later with Samuel Sebastian Wesley (*q.v.*) and William Crotch (*q.v.*); served as organist for a number of London churches, including St. Peter's, Vere Street and St. John's Wood Presbyterian Church; was an outstanding musicologist and editor of the Motet Society; received honorary degrees from universities of Harvard, Stockholm and Göttingen; edited and published music of many kinds—madrigals, ballads, anthems and services, compositions for piano and organ, etc.; produced editions of Tallis' *Cathedral Service* and *Order of Daily Service,* Este's *The Whole Book of Psalms* and Merbecke's (1550) *Book of Common Prayer Noted.*

    HAPPY DAY (239); RUTHERFORD (arr.) (535)

Rinkart, Martin (b. Apr. 23, 1586, Eilenburg, Saxony; d. Dec. 8, 1649, Eilenburg, Saxony) attended the Latin School in Eilenburg, St. Thomas School, Leipzig (where he was a foundation scholar and chorister) and the University of Leipzig, where he studied theology and poetry; served Lutheran churches at Eisleben, Erdeborn and Lyttichendorf and then became archdeacon at Eilenburg and served through the horrors of the Thirty Years' War, 1618–48; endured famine and pestilence while he gave himself and his possessions in serving others in that refugee center; officiated at as many as 40 funerals a day—possibly a total of 4500 during his lifetime; was a prolific poet, dramatist and musician, whose writings reflect his strong faith in difficult times.

    Now thank we all our God (564)

Rippon, John (b. Apr. 29, 1751, Tiverton, Devon, Eng.; d. Dec. 17, 1836, London, Eng.) was one of the most popular and influential dissenting (non-Anglican) ministers of his time; trained for the ministry at the Baptist College, Bristol; at age 22, became pastor of the Baptist church in Carter Lane, London and served until his death; made a most important contribution to hymnody in his *Selection of Hymns from the Best Authors, Intended as an*

Appendix to Dr. Watts' Psalms and Hymns (1787), which had a wide use in England and America; in 1791 published a *Selection of Psalm and Hymn Tunes from the Best Authors*, and in subsequent editions hymn tune names were added.

All hail the power of Jesus' name (adapt.) (62, 63); How firm a foundation (224)

Roberts, Daniel Crane (b. Nov. 5, 1841, Bridgehampton, L.I., N.Y.; d. Oct. 31, 1907, Concord, N.H.) was educated at Kenyon College, Gambier, Ohio, and served with the 84th Ohio Volunteers during the Civil War; was ordained a priest in the Protestant Episcopal Church (1866) and served parishes in Vermont and Massachusetts; in 1878 was appointed vicar of St. Paul's Church in Concord, N.H., where he remained until his death; was president of the New Hampshire State Historical Society for a number of years.

God of our fathers (526)

Roberts, John (b. Dec. 22, 1822, Tanrhiwfelen, Aberystwyth, Wales; d. May 6, 1877, Vron, Caernarvon, Wales), better known by his Welsh name, Ieuan Gwyllt, as a youth attended classes conducted by Richard Mills, who worked toward improving congregational singing in Wales; was a choir director at age 14 and a school teacher at 16; was ordained into the Calvinistic Methodist ministry and served churches in Aberdare and Llanberis in Capel Cock; in 1859, also founded the great music festival devoted to hymn-tunes and texts, Gymanfa Ganu; edited *Llyfr Tonau Cynulleidfaol*, 1859, the official tune book of the Calvinistic Methodists, and published *Sŵn y Iiwbili*, 1874, a translation of the Moody and Sankey hymnal.

LLANFAIR (arr.) (173)

Robinson, George Wade (b. 1838, Cork, Ire.; d. Jan. 28, 1877, Southampton, Eng.) studied at Trinity College, Dublin, and New College, St. John's Wood, London; became a Congregational minister and was co-pastor at York Street Chapel, Dublin, and later pastor at St. John's Wood, Dudley and Union Street in Brighton; published two books of verse: *Songs in God's World* and *Loveland*.

Loved with everlasting love (409)

Robinson, Robert (b. Sept. 27, 1735, Swaffham, Norfolk, Eng.; d. June 9, 1790, Birmingham, Eng.) as a youth served as a barber's apprentice; after hearing George Whitefield preach on "The Wrath to Come," struggled spiritually for three years and finally found "joy and peace in believing"; in 1758 began preaching in a Calvinistic Methodist Chapel at Mildenhall, Suffolk and later founded an independent congregation in Norwich; in 1761–90 pastored the Stone Yard Baptist Chapel in Cambridge, and was at the same time a farmer and merchant; was an eloquent spokesman for civil and religious liberty, American independence, and the abolition of slavery; wrote *A History of Baptism and Baptists* and other works.

Come, Thou Fount of every blessing (28)

Röntgen, Julius (b. May 9, 1855, Leipzig, Ger.; d. Sept. 13, 1932, Utrecht, Netherlands) was born to a Dutch father and a German mother; studied in Leipzig under Franz Lachner, Moritz Hauptmann, E. F. Richter and Carl Reinecke, and was a friend of Liszt, Brahms and Grieg; from 1877, lived in Amsterdam and was recognized as an accomplished conductor, composer, pianist, teacher and editor; was conductor of the Society for the Advancement of Musical Art from 1886; taught in the Conservatory at Amsterdam, and from 1914 to 1924 was its director; composed symphonies, concertos, operas, and music for films, and wrote a biography of Edvard Grieg (1930).

 IN BABILONE (arr.) (95)

Root, George Frederick (b. Aug. 30, 1820, Sheffield, Mass.; d. Aug. 6, 1895, Bailey's Island, Me.) was a popular American musician in the 19th century, best remembered for Civil War songs like "Tramp, Tramp, Tramp, the Boys are Marching"; became assistant organist at both Winter and Park Street churches, Boston in 1839; assisted Lowell Mason (*q.v.*) in teaching music in the Boston public schools; moved to New York in 1844 and taught in a number of institutions, including Union Theological Seminary and the New York Institute for the Blind, where Fanny Crosby (*q.v.*) was one of his pupils; studied in Paris for a year and on returning, collaborated with Miss Crosby in producing the cantata, *The Flower-Queen;* wrote for the Christy minstrel troupe under the pseudonym G. Friedrich Würzel; in 1858 moved to Chicago and was associated with his brother in the music company, Root & Cady, which suffered great losses in the Chicago Fire of 1871 and was dissolved; became affiliated with the John Church Company in Cincinnati, but kept his residence in Chicago; was involved in publishing some 75 important collections, and composed several hundred songs.

 QUAM DILECTA (578)

Roth, Elton Menno (b. Nov. 27, 1891, Berne, Ind.; d. Dec. 31, 1951, Glendale, Calif.) at the age of 12 "went forward" in an old-fashioned revival meeting in his Mennonite community and was baptized in the Wabash River; directed a church choir at age 14; attended Fort Wayne Bible School and Moody Bible Institute, and studied the higher forms of music with Dr. A. Verne Westlake and Solomon Ancis from Vienna; traveled with evangelists for a time, singing and directing the choir; taught music at Alliance Bible schools in St. Paul, Minn. and New York City, the Bible Institute of Los Angeles, Baptist Theological College and City College (Los Angeles); organized the Ecclesia Choir (1931) which toured the United States extensively; published many anthems and over 100 hymns for which he has written all the tunes, and most of the texts.

 I have a song that Jesus gave me (404)
 HEART MELODY (404)

Rousseau, Jean Jacques (b. June 28, 1712, Geneva, Switz.; d. July 3, 1778, near Paris, Fr.), of French Protestant heritage, ran away from home when he was 16 and lived an unsettled life; was a daring and creative thinker who expressed himself in music, politics and education as progressive and radical; earned his living for a number of years as a music copyist; contributed articles to Diderot's *Encyclopédie,* which were criticized by Rameau as inaccurate; in 1764 published *Dictionnaire de musique,* which became very popular and was translated into several languages; is credited with writing five operas and approximately 100 songs, most of which have been forgotten; is believed to have committed suicide at the age of 66 at Ermenonville, near Paris.

GREENVILLE (291)

Rowe, James (b. Jan. 1, 1865, Devon, Eng.; d. Nov. 10, 1933, Wells, Vt.) emigrated to the United States at age 25, married and settled in Albany, N.Y.; worked for the railroad and later was superintendent of the Hudson River Humane Society; left this work to write song texts and edit music materials, and was associated in turn with Trio Music Company (Waco, Tex.), A. J. Showalter Music Company (Chattanooga, Tenn.), and James D. Vaughan Music Company (Lawrenceburg, Tenn.); in later years moved to Vermont and worked with his artist-daughter in writing verse for greeting cards; claimed to have written more than 19,000 song texts.

Earthly pleasures vainly call me (343)

Rowley, Francis Harold (b. July 25, 1854, Hilton, N.Y.; d. Feb. 14, 1952, Boston, Mass.) received his education at Rochester University and Theological Seminary; was ordained to the Baptist ministry and served churches in Pennsylvania, Massachusetts and Illinois; was greatly interested in both human and animal welfare, and served as president of the Massachusetts Society for the Prevention of Cruelty to Animals for 35 years; wrote several volumes, including *The Humane Idea* and *The Horses of Homer;* is memorialized in the Rowley School of Humanities at Ogelthorpe University, Atlanta, Ga., named in his honor.

I will sing the wondrous story (296)

Runyan, William Marion (b. Jan. 21, 1870, Marion, N.Y.; d. July 29, 1957, Pittsburg, Kan.), the son of a Methodist minister, showed an interest in music when he was very young, and at age 12 often served as church organist; was ordained to the Methodist ministry at 21 and held various pastorates in Kansas, 1891–1903; was appointed evangelist for the Central Kansas Methodist Conference and served for some 20 years; wrote his first gospel song in 1915 and was greatly encouraged by D. B. Towner (*q.v.*) of Moody Bible Institute; in 1924 went to John Brown University, Sulphur Springs, Ark. and served as pastor of the Federated Church, and editor of the *Christian Workers' Magazine;* moving to Chicago, was associated with the Moody Bible Institute, and served as editor for Hope Publishing Company, until his retirement in 1948; received the honorary Doctor of Letters, Wheaton College (Ill.), 1948.

Lord, I have shut the door (428)
FAITHFULNESS (37); TEACH ME (370); SANCTUARY (428)

311

Sammis, John H. (b. July 6, 1846, Brooklyn, N.Y.; d. June 12, 1919, Los Angeles, Calif.) moved to Logansport, Ind. when he was 23, and became a businessman and an active Christian layman; later gave up business to serve as a YMCA secretary and, as a result, felt called to the ministry and received theological training at Lane and McCormick Seminaries; in 1880 was ordained in the Presbyterian church, and served pastorates in Iowa, Indiana, Michigan and Minnesota; moved to California in 1901 and was a faculty member of the Bible Institute of Los Angeles until his death.

> When we walk with the Lord (318)

Sandys, William (b. Oct. 29, 1792, London, Eng.; d. Feb. 18, 1874, London, Eng.) is remembered for his work in reviving interest in carols and carol singing; was educated at Westminster School and admitted to the bar in 1814, and was by avocation a musician and music researcher; had a very successful law practice, and from 1861 until his retirement was head of Sandys and Knott, Gray's Inn Square, London; among other works, published *Christmas Carols, Ancient and Modern* (1833), *Festive Songs, Principally of the 16th and 17th Centuries* (1848), and *Christmas-tide, Its History, Festivities, and Carols, with their music* (1852).

> THE FIRST NOEL (108)

Sankey, Ira David (b. Aug. 28, 1840, Edinburgh, Pa.; d. Aug. 13, 1908, Brooklyn, N.Y.) was America's most influential evangelistic musician, composer and publisher in the last half of the 19th century; received his early education in the village of Edinburgh and attended high school in Newcastle, Pa. when he moved there with his family in 1857; joined the Methodist Episcopal Church and served as Sunday school superintendent as well as choir director; after serving in the Union Army during the Civil War, returned to Newcastle and worked with his father—a collector of internal revenue; was appointed secretary, and later president of the local YMCA; while attending the international YMCA convention in Indianapolis (1870), became acquainted with Dwight L. Moody, and six months later joined him as soloist and songleader in his evangelistic work; conducted meetings with Moody throughout the United States and the British Isles for almost 30 years; published *Sacred Songs and Solos* in England, which is said to have sold more than eighty million copies, and is still in print; collaborated with P. P. Bliss (*q.v.*) and others in editing *Gospel Hymns and Sacred Songs* (1875), *Gospel Hymns No. 2* (1876), *No. 3* (1878), *No. 4* (1883), *No. 5* (1887), *No. 6* (1892), and the collected *Gospel Hymns, Nos. 1-6* (1894).

> The Lord's our rock, in Him we hide (adapt.) (322)
> HINGHAM (310); TRUSTING JESUS (320); SHELTER (322); HIDING IN THEE (400); INTERCESSION (436); SANKEY (453)

Sateren, Leland Bernhard (b. Oct. 13, 1913, Everett, Wash.), the son of a Lutheran clergyman and educator, attended the public schools of Michigan and Wisconsin, and graduated (B.A.) from Augsburg College, Minneapolis, Minn., and (M.A.) the University of Minnesota; has been active as a composer and educator since 1935, and associated with Augsburg College since 1946, and is presently chairman of the music department and director of their famous choir; has published some 300 choral works, and contributed many articles to professional magazines.

MARLEE (142)

Saward, Michael (b. May 14, 1932, Blackheath, Kent, Eng.) describes himself as an "author, journalist, hymn-writer, broadcaster, lecturer—and amateur cricketer"; received his education at Eltham College, University of Bristol (B.A.) and Tyndale Hall (Church of England Theological College); was ordained in Canterbury Cathedral in 1956 and served two curacies, 1956–64; served as Warden at Holy Trinity Inter-Church Centre, Liverpool (1964–67), Radio and Television Officer of the Church Information Office (1967–72), and since 1972 has been vicar of St. Matthew's, Fulham, London; has been very active in the area of church communications (especially radio and television), both in the Anglican Church and in interchurch conferences; has written approximately 32 hymn texts, besides booklets, newspaper articles, and a book, *Don't Miss the Party,* 1974.

These are the facts (234)

Schlegel, Katharina Amalia Dorothea von (b. Oct. 22, 1697, Ger.; d., date unknown) was one of the group who contributed to the *Cöthnische Lieder—* 29 hymns have been ascribed to her in the 1744 and 1752 collections, but only this one has been translated into English; according to Julian's *Dictionary,* was a lady attached to the ducal court at Cöthen; according to another source, may have been head of the Evangelical Lutheran nunnery at Cöthen.

Be still, my soul (324)

Schneider, Kent Edward (b. Apr. 6, 1946, Chicago, Ill.) is one of today's leading innovators in bringing jazz into worship; grew up in the Chicago area and attended Morgan Park High School, North Central College (B.A.), and Chicago Theological Seminary (M.Div.); began writing and playing jazz in 1966, and toured throughout the United States; while still a seminary student, composed the music for the best-selling record "Celebration for Modern Man" and edited the hymnal, *Songs for Celebration;* was ordained to a "ministry of celebration" in the United Church of Christ in 1970; since 1968 has been Director of the Center for Contemporary Celebration, now located in West LaFayette, Ind.; has conducted workshops at many colleges and seminaries; has written approximately 100 hymn texts and tunes, and served as consultant to the Armed Forces Chaplains Board in preparing their new *Book of Worship,* 1974.

There's a church within us, O Lord (208)

THE CHURCH WITHIN US (208)

Schuler, George Stark (b. Apr. 18, 1882, New York, N.Y.; d. Oct. 30, 1973, Sarasota, Fla.) received his training at the Chicago Musical College, Cosmopolitan School of Music, and the Moody Bible Institute, Chicago; was a member of the faculty of Moody Bible Institute for some 40 years; after retiring from Moody, served on the editorial staff of Rodeheaver Publishing Company for several years; wrote anthems and many gospel songs, and edited five songbooks and several piano and organ collections; authored some church music manuals, such as *Evangelistic Piano Playing, Gospel Song and Hymn Tune Composition,* and *Choral Directing.*

    SCHULER (505)

Schulz, Johann Abraham Peter (b. Mar. 31, 1747, Lüneburg, Ger.; d. June 10, 1800, Schwedt, Ger.) chose a musical career though his father wanted him to prepare for the ministry; at the age of 15, left home penniless to pursue musical studies with the great Kirnberger in Berlin, who taught him free of charge; later showed his gratitude to his teacher by editing his *Treatise on Pure Composition* and assisting him in the publication of *General Theory of the Fine Arts,* on which Kirnberger and Sulzer collaborated; in 1776 became director of the French Theater in Berlin; was put in charge of music under Prince Henry of Prussia at Rheinsberg (1780) and later was director of music in the court of the King of Denmark at Copenhagen (1787); returned to his native Germany in 1796 and died there in 1800; published the *Lieder im Volkston* (1785 to 1790), a collection of sacred and secular German songs, and wrote operas, oratorios and music for instruments.

    WIR PFLÜGEN (566)

Schumann, Robert Alexander (b. June 8, 1810, Zwickau, Saxony; d. July 29, 1856, Endenich, near Bonn, Ger.) studied law, but found music much more interesting and eventually overcame his mother's opposition to a musical career; studied piano with Friedrich Wieck and later married his daughter, Clara; became an accomplished pianist and composer and the editor of the well-known Czerny exercises for beginning students; injured his hand by over-strenuous practicing, which caused him to concentrate on composing, and leave it to his pianist-wife to popularize his music; developed mental instability and was committed to an asylum, where he died; founded *Die Neue Zeitschrift für Musik,* a critical journal, which is still being published; composed symphonies, chamber music, choral and organ pieces, but is best known for his solos for piano and for voice.

    CANONBURY (378)

Schütz, Johann Jakob (b. Sept. 7, 1640, Frankfort-on-the-Main, Ger.; d. May 22, 1690, Frankfort, Ger.) studied law at Tübingen, returned to Frankfort and became a distinguished and respected lawyer; was a close friend of P. J. Spener, who founded the Pietist movement in the German Lutheran Church; in later years, was influenced by J. S. Petersen and left the Lutheran communion in 1686, becoming a Separatist; published *Christliches Gedenckbüchlein,* 1675.

    Sing praise to God who reigns above (13)

Schwedler, Johann Christoph (b. Dec. 21, 1672, Krobsdorf, Silesia; d. Jan. 12, 1730, Niederwiese, Silesia) received his education at the University of Leipzig and became a popular preacher and writer of hymns; served as pastor at Niederwiese, near Greiffenberg for almost 30 years, founding an orphanage there; wrote more than 500 hymns (mostly on the themes of God's grace and the believer's confidence) and published them in his *Die Lieder Mose und des Lammes, oder neu eingerichtetes Gesang-Buch,* 1720.

Ask ye what great thing I know (144)

Scott, Clara H. (Jones) (b. Dec. 3, 1841, Elk Grove, Ill.; d. June 21, 1897, Dubuque, Iowa) attended the first musical institute held in Chicago by C. M. Cady in 1856; began teaching music at the Ladies' Seminary at Lyons, Iowa in 1859; released many of her early songs in Horatio Palmer's collections; in 1882 published *Royal Anthem Book,* the first volume of anthems by a woman, and later, other collections; met an untimely death when she was thrown from a buggy by a runaway horse.

Open my eyes, that I may see (350)

SCOTT (350)

Scriven, Joseph Medlicott (b. Sept. 10, 1819, Seapatrick, Co. Down, Ire.; d. Aug. 10, 1886, Bewdley, Rice Lake, Ont.) entered Trinity College in Dublin in 1835, but left to pursue an army career; was forced to give up his military ambitions because of poor health, and returned to Trinity College to complete his B.A. degree; moved to Canada where he taught school and served as a tutor; was a member of the Plymouth Brethren, and devoted much time to humanitarian service without remuneration; was twice denied marriage because of the tragic and premature deaths of the expected brides; in later years suffered physically and financially, with periods of great depression; died by drowning and it is not known whether it was an accident or suicide; published *Hymns and Other Verses,* 1869.

What a Friend we have in Jesus (435)

Sears, Edmund Hamilton (b. Apr. 6, 1810, Sandisfield, Mass.; d. Jan. 16, 1876, Weston, Mass.) studied at Union College, Schenectady, N.Y., and Harvard Divinity School; was ordained a Unitarian minister but believed and preached the divinity of Christ; held several pastorates in Massachusetts; co-edited the *Monthly Religious Magazine,* in which most of his hymns first appeared; wrote and published: *Regeneration* (1854), *Pictures of the Olden Time* (1857), *Athanasia, or Foregleams of Immortality* (1858), *The Fourth Gospel, the Heart of Christ* (1872) and *Sermons and Songs of the Christian Life* (1875).

It came upon the midnight clear (104)

Seiss, Joseph Augustus (b. Mar. 18, 1823, Graceham, Md.; d. 1904, Philadelphia, Pa.), the son of a miner, was educated at Gettysburg College and Seminary; became a distinguished Lutheran leader and popular preacher, holding pastorates in Virginia, Maryland, and Pennsylvania; wrote a number of books, including *Lectures on the Gospels* and *Ecclesia Lutherana.*

Fairest Lord Jesus (st. 4, trans.) (67)

Shaw, Geoffrey Turton (b. Nov. 14, 1879, London, Eng.; d. Apr. 14, 1943, London, Eng.) was a chorister in St. Paul's Cathedral under Sir George Martin (*q.v.*); studied organ under Charles Stanford and Charles Wood at Caius College, Cambridge, and served several churches; was Inspector of Music for London schools, and later, chairman of the schools' music committee of the British Broadcasting Company; followed his brother Martin in 1920 as organist at St. Mary's, Primrose Hill; composed many songs and choral works, and collaborated with his brother in editing a number of song books.

LANGHAM (516)

Shaw, Martin Edward Fallas (b. Mar. 9, 1875, London, Eng.; d. Oct. 24, 1958, Southwold, Suffolk, Eng.) was the elder brother of Geoffrey Shaw (*q.v.*); studied at the Royal College of Music; was organist at St. Mary's Church (Primrose Hill) and at St. Martin's-in-the-Fields, beginning in 1920; collaborated with Percy Dearmer (*q.v.*) in publishing several hymnals; served as Director of Music for the Diocese of Chelmsford, 1935–45; composed choral, orchestral, and chamber music; edited and published: *Additional Tunes in Use at St. Mary's, Primrose Hill* (1915), *Public School Hymn Book* (1919), *Songs of Praise* (1925) edited with Ralph Vaughan Williams (*q.v.*), and *Oxford Book of Carols* (1928).

FRENCH CAROL (arr.) (162)

Shepherd, Thomas (b. 1665, Eng.; d. Jan. 29, 1739, Bocking, Essex, Eng.) was ordained in the Church of England, but left in 1694 to become pastor of the independent Castle Hill Meeting House at Nottingham; moved to Bocking in 1700 where he first preached in a barn; after a chapel was finally built for his Bocking congregation, served there for almost 40 years.

Must Jesus bear the cross alone (495)

Sheppard, Franklin Lawrence (b. Aug. 7, 1852, Philadelphia, Pa.; d. Feb. 15, 1930, Germantown, Pa.) graduated from the University of Pennsylvania in 1872 with highest honors (a Phi Beta Kappa charter member); was put in charge of his father's foundry in Baltimore, manufacturers of stoves and heaters; served the Zion Protestant Episcopal Church as organist and vestryman, and later joined the Second Presbyterian Church and served as music director; became President of the Presbyterian Board of Publication; served on the hymnal committee for the Presbyterian *Hymnal*, 1911, and edited a Presbyterian Sunday School songbook, *Alleluia*, 1915.

TERRA BEATA (58)

Sherwin, William Fiske (b. Mar. 14, 1826, Buckland, Mass.; d. Apr. 14, 1888, Boston, Mass.) studied under Lowell Mason (*q.v.*) and became a faculty member at the New England Conservatory of Music in Boston; had great ability to organize and direct amateur choirs; was a Baptist, who was chosen by the Methodists to be their music director at the famous Lake Chautauqua Assembly in New York.

BREAD OF LIFE (220); CHAUTAUQUA (557)

Shirreff, Emily Anne Eliza (b. Nov. 3, 1814, England; d. Mar. 20, 1897, London, Eng.) was largely self-educated—a linguist with a good knowledge of history; working with her sister, devoted herself to improving education for women and actively supported the establishing of Girton College; was involved in the founding of the National Union for Improving the Education of Women of all Classes (1871); was also interested in the education of little children, and published *Principles of the Kindergarten System* (1876 and 1880) and *The Kindergarten at Home* (1884 and 1890).

Gracious Savior, who didst honor (530)

Showalter, Anthony Johnson (b. May 1, 1858, Rockingham Co., Va.; d. Sept. 16, 1924, Chattanooga, Tenn.) attended singing schools under B. C. Unseld, H. R. Palmer and George F. Root (*q.v.*), and at age 37, studied a year in Europe; published *Harmony and Composition,* 1880, in his first year of teaching; worked in a branch office of Ruebush-Kieffer Music Company in Dalton, Ga. for a time, and then founded his own company; published about 60 song books and edited the monthly periodical of his company, *The Music Teacher;* was widely known and respected as a conductor of singing schools throughout the southern states; was an elder of the First Presbyterian Church of Dalton, Ga., and for many years, their music director.

SHOWALTER (417)

Shrubsole, William (baptized Jan. 13, 1760, Canterbury, Eng.; d. Jan. 18, 1806, London, Eng.) was a chorister at Canterbury Cathedral for seven years; after two years service as organist at Bangor Cathedral, was dismissed because of his sympathy with the Dissenters; for a time, taught music privately; in 1784 became organist at Spa Fields Chapel, London, one of the chapels associated with the Countess of Huntingdon's work.

MILES LANE (63)

Shurtleff, Ernest Warburton (b. Apr. 4, 1862, Boston, Mass.; d. Aug. 24, 1917, Paris, Fr.) received his education at Boston Latin School, Harvard University and Andover Theological Seminary; served Congregational churches in California, Massachusetts and Minnesota; in 1905 took up residence in Frankfurt, Germany, where he organized the American Church; in 1906 became director of Students' Atelier Reunions, working among American students in Paris; with his wife, participated in relief work during World War I; wrote a number of books, including *Poems* (1883), *Easter Gleams* (1885), *Song of Hope* (1886), and *Shadow of the Angel* (1886).

Lead on, O King Eternal (457)

Sibelius, Jean (b. Dec. 8, 1865, Tavastehus, Finland; d. Sept. 20, 1957, Järvenpää, Finland) is recognized to have been the most famous of Finnish composers; studied under Martin Wegelius, conductor of the Finnish Opera, and later in Berlin and Vienna; taught at the Helsingfors Music Institute and Philharmonic Orchestra School; devoted himself fully to composition after receiving a grant from the Finnish government; produced symphonies, choral music, orchestral and other instrumental works; published two principal sacred collections: *Five Christmas Songs*, 1895, and *Musique religieuse*, 1927.

   FINLANDIA (324)

Silcher, Friedrich (b. June 27, 1789, near Schorndorf, Württemberg, Ger.; d. Aug. 28, 1860, Tübingen, Ger.) was a conductor and taught music both in Ludwigsburg and in Stuttgart; founded the university Choral Society and was director of music at the University of Tübingen for 43 years, beginning in 1817; is chiefly remembered for his collection of folk songs, *Sammlung deutscher Volkslieder*, published in 12 volumes; also left a *Württemberg Choralbuch, Geschichte der evangelischen Kirchengesänge* (1844), and three books of hymns.

   SO NIMM DENN MEINE HÄNDE (444)

Skoog, Andrew L. (b. Dec. 17, 1856, Värmland, Sweden; d. Oct. 30, 1934, Minneapolis, Minn.), at the age of 10, followed his father as a tailor's apprentice; emigrated to America when he was 13 years old and settled with his family in St. Paul, Minn.; had formal education only to the sixth grade, but his search for knowledge brought success in many different fields, including teaching, photography, selling, writing, publishing and printing; was a church musician (organist-choir director) in several churches in Chicago and Minneapolis; was editor-publisher of a popular Swedish language journal; wrote many hymns, hymn tunes and anthems, and edited seven hymnals, including *Evangelii Basun I* (1881) and *Jubelklangen* (1886); had a part in the first three hymnals of the Mission Covenant Church, of which *Mission Hymns* (1921) was the last.

   Day by day and with each passing moment (trans.) (561)

Sleeper, William True (b. Feb. 9, 1819, Danbury, N.H.; d. Sept. 24, 1904, Wellesley, Mass.) studied at Phillips-Exeter Academy, the University of Vermont, and Andover Theological Seminary, and was ordained to the Congregational ministry; served in home mission work in Worcester, Mass., and later in Maine, where he helped establish three churches; was pastor of Summer Street Congregational Church in Worcester, Mass. (his first mission assignment) for over thirty years; in 1883 published a book of verse, *The Rejected King, and Hymns of Jesus.*

   A ruler once came to Jesus by night (253); Out of my bondage, sorrow and night (267)

Small, James Grindlay (b. 1817, Edinburgh, Scot.; d. Feb. 11, 1888, Renfrew-on-the-Clyde, Scot.) was educated at the University of Edinburgh, ordained in the Free Church of Scotland (Presbyterian) and became pastor at Bervie, near Montrose; was keenly interested in hymnody, publishing *Hymns for Youthful Voices* (1859), *Psalms and Sacred Songs* (1859), and two books of poems.

I've found a Friend (88)

Smart, David William (b. Feb. 6, 1927, Lock Haven, Pa.) graduated from Lock Haven (Pa.) high school and Moody Bible Institute, and earned the Mus.B. and Mus.M. degrees at the American Conservatory of Music, studying composition under Leo Sowerby; has been a member of the music faculty at Moody Bible Institute, Chicago since 1957; has written many children's anthems and songs and two cantatas, and is the author of *Learning As We Sing*, a children's church music workbook.

CALDWELL CHURCH (567)

Smart, Henry Thomas (b. Oct. 26, 1813, London, Eng.; d. July 6, 1879, London, Eng.), born into a very musical family, received his early training from his father, and attended Highgate school; was largely self-taught, but served with distinction as organist of several leading London churches; became an authority on organ design and planned many outstanding installations; became totally blind when just past 50, but continued an active career; edited two hymnals: *Psalms and Hymns for Divine Worship*, 1867 and the *Presbyterian Hymnal*, 1875; was a prolific writer of music for choir and organ; also published *Choral Book*, 1856 and *Collection of Sacred Music*, 1863.

REGENT SQUARE (110, 175, 185); LANCASHIRE (168, 457, 517)

Smith, Alfred Barney (b. Nov. 8, 1916, Midland Park, N.J.) studied at Moody Bible Institute and Juilliard School of Music, and received the A.B. degree in 1943 at Wheaton College (Ill.); studied violin under Roderich Meakle and Leopold Auer, and was youth soloist with the New York Philharmonic Orchestra in 1933, and concertmaster of the Wheaton College Symphony Orchestra in 1942–43; was the founder of Singspiration, Inc., serving as president from 1941 to 1962, editing and publishing many songbooks and *Inspiring Hymns*, 1951; in 1972 founded Encore Publications, Montrose, Pa. and published *Living Hymns;* has written approximately 500 songs.

A pilgrim was I and a-wandering (49)
SURELY GOODNESS AND MERCY (49)

Smith, Elizabeth Lee (Allen) (b. 1817; d. 1898) was the daughter of Dr. W. Allen, president of Dartmouth University; in 1843 married Dr. H. B. Smith, professor at Union Theological Seminary in New York.

I greet Thee, who my sure Redeemer art (trans.) (80)

Smith, Henry Percy (b. 1825; d. 1898) was educated at Balliol College, Oxford, and became an Anglican clergyman; served as curate at Eversley (1849–51) and at St. Michael's, Yorktown, Surrey (1851–68); became vicar of Great Barton, Suffolk and later, chaplain of Christ Church, Cannes, France; was serving as canon of the Cathedral of Gibraltar at the close of his career.

MARYTON (215, 504)

Smith, Ida Reed (b. Nov. 30, 1865, near Philippi, W. Va.; d. July 8, 1951, Philippi, W. Va.) published most of her poems under the name "Ida L. Reed"; born in the hills of West Virginia, was left to care for the farm as well as her invalid mother; as a young woman, submitted verses which were printed in religious journals, and also supplied the words for many tunes that were sent to her; was bedridden for years as a result of her strenuous life; lived with the barest necessities and little financial security, until the American Society of Composers, Authors and Publishers (ASCAP) was made aware of her situation and granted a monthly income for the rest of her life "in appreciation for her substantial contribution to religious music."

I belong to the King (290)

Smith, Edward Russell (b. July 18, 1927, London, Ont., Can.) is better known by his professional name "Tedd Smith"; received music training at the Royal Conservatory of Music, London, Ont., and Catholic University, Washington, D. C.; won the gold medal for piano performance in the Peel Music Festival, and has had special training in orchestration, conducting and composition; served as director of music at the Avenue Road Church (Alliance) in Toronto (1946–50), and since 1950 has been associated with the Billy Graham Evangelistic Association as pianist; was an arranger and recording artist for RCA Victor Records; has written approximately 40 hymn texts and tunes, and has published piano works, musicals, and a cantata; composes music for films, including the recent releases, "The Hiding Place" and "Corrie."

There's a quiet understanding (204)
QUIET UNDERSTANDING (204)

Smith, Oswald Jeffray (b. Nov. 8, 1889, Odessa, Ont., Can.) is regarded as one of the greatest missionary statesmen and evangelists of our time; was educated at Canadian Bible College, McCormick Theological Seminary (Chicago) and Manitoba College; was ordained to the Presbyterian ministry and appointed pastor of the Dale Presbyterian Church, Toronto (1915–19) and later of the Alliance Tabernacle in the same city; founded the Peoples Church in Toronto, was pastor until 1959, and is presently serving as "Missionary Pastor"; has written over 1200 hymn texts and some 15 hymn tunes, published 35 books, and was editor of *The Peoples Magazine.*

Saved! Saved! Saved! (298); There is joy in serving Jesus (497)

Smith, Samuel Francis (b. Oct. 21, 1808, Boston, Mass.; d. Nov. 16, 1895, Boston, Mass.) is revered as the author of "America"; trained at Boston Latin School, Harvard University and Andover Theological Seminary; while pastor of the Baptist church in Waterville, Maine (1834–42), also taught modern languages at Waterville (now Colby) College; was pastor of the Baptist church, Newton, Mass. (1842–54); became interested in missions during his student days, and was secretary of the American Baptist Missionary Union for 15 years; visited mission fields of Asia and Europe and wrote *Rambles in Mission Fields,* 1884; wrote approximately 100 hymns, mostly for special occasions; collaborated with Baron Stowe in producing *The Psalmist,* 1843, a popular Baptist hymnal.

My country, 'tis of thee (525)

Smith, Tedd (See Smith, Edward Russell)

Smith, Walter Chalmers (b. Dec. 5, 1824, Aberdeen, Scot.; d. Sept. 20, 1908, Kinbuck, Perth, Scot.) received his education at Aberdeen Grammar School and University, and at New College, Edinburgh; in 1850 was ordained in the Free Church of Scotland and served churches in London, Glasgow and Edinburgh for a total of 44 years; 1876–94, pastored the Free High Church, Edinburgh; was elected Moderator of the Free Church of Scotland in 1893, its jubilee year; published *Hymns of Christ and the Christian Life,* 1876 and *Poetical Works,* 1902, and many other volumes.

Immortal, invisible, God only wise (35)

Smyth, Harper G. (b. Mar. 16, 1873, New York, N.Y.; d. Aug. 25, 1945, Cleveland, Ohio) studied at the Institute of Musical Art, New York and was a member of the Metropolitan Opera Company; directed church choirs in such cities as Atlanta and Indianapolis; served as song leader in meetings for the Salvation Army and Evangelist J. Wilbur Chapman; from 1913, maintained a voice studio in Cleveland, Ohio and was music director of Euclid Avenue Baptist Church; was official song leader for the National Republican Convention in Cleveland, 1924; published *Let's Adventure in Personality,* 1941 and wrote about 25 songs, but only one remains in common usage.

Is your life a channel of blessing? (509)

EUCLID (509)

Spafford, Horatio Gates (b. Oct. 20, 1828, North Troy, N.Y.; d. Oct. 16, 1888, Jerusalem, Jordan) spent his early years in New York, and later moved to Chicago and set up a successful law practice; was a very active Presbyterian layman, and served as director and trustee for the Presbyterian Theological Seminary of the Northwest (now McCormick Theological Seminary); lost most of his fortune in the Chicago fire of 1871 and later his four daughters and his son (see hymn No. 401); was for many years interested in the Holy Land, and settled in Jerusalem in 1881; founded the American Colony in that city, whose story is told by the remaining daughter, Bertha Spafford Vester, in her book, *Our Jerusalem.*

When peace like a river attendeth (401)

Sparrow-Simpson, William John (b. June 20, 1860, London, Eng.; d. Feb. 13, 1952, Great Ilford, Essex, Eng.) is best remembered as compiler of the text for John Stainer's (*q.v.*) famous oratorio, *The Crucifixion* (1887); was educated at Trinity College, Cambridge, took Holy Orders and served various churches; became Chaplain at St. Mary's Hospital, Great Ilford, 1904; besides his collaboration with John Stainer, made literary contributions in the fields of church history and theology.

Cross of Jesus, cross of sorrow (153)

Spitta, Carl Johann Philipp (b. Aug. 1, 1801, Hanover, Ger.; d. Sept. 28, 1859, Burgdorf, Ger.) showed literary aptitude at the age of eight, and as a student, wrote secular songs and verses; in his twenties, had a deep spiritual experience that led him to dedicate his gift completely to God; studied at the Gymnasium at Hanover and at the University of Göttingen; was ordained to the Lutheran ministry and served as assistant chaplain to the prison at Hamelin, and then as pastor at Wechold, near Hoya, for ten years; was appointed Lutheran superintendent of Wittingen, and later of Peine and Burgdorf; published *Psalter und Harfe,* 1833 with 61 of his hymns, and a second edition added five more; released another volume in 1843 bearing the same title, with 40 hymns.

O happy home, where Thou art loved (532)

Stainer, John (b. June 6, 1840, London, Eng.; d. Mar. 31, 1901, Verona, It.) was one of Britain's leading church musicians in the late 19th century; was a chorister at St. Paul's Cathedral, London at age 7, and became a church organist at 14; was trained at Christ Church, Oxford and St. Edmund Hall; was appointed organist at Magdalen College when he was 20, and at University College one year later; succeeded Sir John Goss as organist of St. Paul's Cathedral in 1872 and served in this capacity until failing eyesight forced him to retire in 1888; was knighted by Queen Victoria in 1888, and returned to Oxford University as professor of music until his death; wrote over 150 hymn tunes, plus anthems, cantatas and oratorios, including the well-known *Crucifixion;* in a long list of publications, co-edited *Dictionary of Musical Terms* (1879), wrote the *Music of the Bible* (1879), and was musical editor for *Church Hymnary* (1898).

THE FIRST NOEL (arr.) (108); CROSS OF JESUS (153); WYCLIFF (384)

Stanphill, Ira Forest (b. Feb. 14, 1914, Bellview, N.M.) was born of musical parents who were active in church work; attended high school and Junior College in Coffeyville, Kan.; worked in radio and crusade evangelism, and has served as pastor of Assembly of God churches in Florida, Pennsylvania and Texas; founded Hymntime Publishers which was sold to Zondervan Publishing House in 1968, and is presently a staff composer for Singspiration; has written more than 600 songs, and almost 400 have been published.

Happiness is to know the Savior (411)
HAPPINESS IS THE LORD (411)

Stead, Louisa M. R. (b. *ca.* 1850, Dover, Eng.; d. Jan. 18, 1917, Penkridge, near Umtali, Rhodesia), born in England, was converted at the age of nine, and later felt called to be a foreign missionary; came to America at age 21, and lived in Cincinnati, Ohio; at a campmeeting, volunteered for missionary service, but was not appointed because of poor health; married, but lost her husband when he drowned attempting to rescue a small child off Long Island, N.Y.; with her daughter Lily, moved to South Africa on her own and served as a missionary in the Cape Colony for 15 years; married Robert Wodehouse, a native of South Africa; in 1895, was forced by ill health to return to America, where Wodehouse served as a local Methodist pastor; returned to Rhodesia when her health improved and was appointed to the Methodist Mission at Umtali; retired in 1911 but remained in Africa until her death.

'Tis so sweet to trust in Jesus (312)

Stebbins, George Coles (b. Feb. 26, 1846, East Carlton, N.Y.; d. Oct. 6, 1945, Catskill, N.Y.) was raised on a farm in New York, and studied music in Rochester and Buffalo; moved to Chicago in his early twenties and was a clerk at Lyon and Healy Music Co., and music director at the First Baptist Church; in 1874 became music director in the Clarendon Street Baptist Church, Boston, and later at Tremont Temple in that city; in 1876 was persuaded by Dwight L. Moody to join him in evangelistic work; was associated with Moody and other leading evangelists for 25 years as song leader, choir organizer, composer, and co-compiler of many gospel song collections; collaborated with Ira Sankey (*q.v.*) and James McGranahan (*q.v.*) in preparing the 3rd, 4th, 5th and 6th editions of *Gospel Hymns;* left the autobiography, *Memoirs and Reminiscences,* 1924.

FRIEND (88); GREEN HILL (138); BORN AGAIN (253); JESUS, I COME (267); CALLING TODAY (272); ADELAIDE (372); HOLINESS (392); PROVIDENCE (478); EVENING PRAYER (558)

Stennett, Samuel (b. 1727, Exeter, Eng.; d. Aug. 24, 1795, London, Eng.), the son of a Baptist minister, was assistant to his father at the Baptist Church in Little Wild Street, Lincoln's Inn Fields, and became pastor upon his father's death; was a prominent dissenting preacher of his time, who used his influence to support the principles of religious freedom; received the honorary D.D. degree, King's College, Aberdeen, 1763; contributed some 38 hymns to John Rippon's (*q.v.*) *Selection of Hymns,* 1787.

Majestic sweetness sits enthroned (89); On Jordan's stormy banks I stand (545)

Stites, Edgar Page (b. Mar. 22, 1836, Cape May, N.J.; d. Jan. 7, 1921, Cape May, N.J.) was born into a family whose ancestors came to America on the Mayflower; served during the Civil War, and was stationed in Philadelphia in charge of feeding transient troops; later was a riverboat pilot; was an active member of the First Methodist Church of Cape May, N.J. for more than 60 years, and a local preacher, who served for a time as a home missionary; frequently used the pseudonym "Edgar Page" on his hymns.

Simply trusting every day (320)

Stockton, John Hart (b. Apr. 19, 1813, New Hope, Pa.; d. Mar. 25, 1877, Philadelphia, Pa.), born into a Presbyterian home, was converted at a

Methodist camp meeting, and became a Methodist minister; held several pastorates in the New Jersey Conference and contributed to the development of church music in each; wrote many hymns, and published two volumes: *Salvation Melodies,* 1874 and *Precious Songs,* 1875.

Come, every soul by sin oppressed (258)
GREAT PHYSICIAN (71); MINERVA (258); GLORY TO HIS NAME (289)

Stokes, Elwood Haines (b. 1815; d. 1895) is identified by Phil Kerr (*Music in Evangelism*) as "one of the founders of the Ocean Grove (N.J.) religious community, and president of the Ocean Grove Campmeeting Association." No other information is available.

Hover o'er me, Holy Spirit (195)

Stone, Samuel John (b. Apr. 25, 1839, Whitmore, Staffs, Eng.; d. Nov. 19, 1900, Charterhouse, Eng.) was educated at Charterhouse and at Pembroke College, Oxford; took Holy Orders, 1862, and became curate of Windsor; in 1874 succeeded his father as vicar of St. Paul's, Haggerston; in 1890 was appointed rector of All-Hallows-on-the-Wall, London and remained until his death; was a member of the committee which prepared the 1909 edition of *Hymns Ancient and Modern;* wrote and published *Lyra Fidelium* (1866), *The Knight of Intercession, and Other Poems* (1872), *Sonnets of the Christian Year* (1875), *Hymns* (1886), and *Order of the Consecutive Church Service for Children, with Original Hymns* (1883).

The Church's one foundation (200)

Storm, August Ludvig (b. Oct. 23, 1862, Motala, Sweden; d. July 1, 1914, Stockholm, Sweden) spent most of his life in Stockholm, where he attended elementary, trade and agricultural schools and worked as an office clerk; was converted under the ministry of the Salvation Army and later joined the corps; served as finance secretary at the Army headquarters beginning in 1892, and was later promoted to lieutenant-colonel; in 1899 was permanently crippled with a serious back disorder, but continued to carry his responsibilities until his death; was a powerful preacher and a gifted hymnist.

Thanks to God for my Redeemer (571)

Stowe, Harriet Beecher (b. June 14, 1811, Litchfield, Conn.; d. July 1, 1896, Hartford, Conn.) is best known for her novel, *Uncle Tom's Cabin,* 1852; was the daughter of Lyman Beecher, president of Lane Seminary, Cincinnati, Ohio, and sister of the famous preacher, Henry Ward Beecher; was married to a professor of language and biblical literature at Lane Seminary; published more than 40 volumes of prose, plus *Religious Poems,* 1867; contributed three hymns to her brother's *Plymouth Hymnal,* 1855.

Still, still with Thee (552)

Stowell, Hugh (b. Dec. 3, 1799, Douglas, Isle of Man, Eng.; d. Oct. 8, 1865, Salford, Eng.) received B.A. and M.A. degrees at St. Edmund's Hall, Oxford; was ordained (1823) in the Church of England, served various curacies and was then appointed rector of Christ Church, Salford in 1831, where he remained until his death; was a powerful and popular preacher who wrote "special day" hymns for Sunday School use; published *A Selection of Psalms and Hymns Suited to the Services of the Church of England,* 1831.

From every stormy wind that blows (430)

Sullivan, Arthur Seymour (b. May 13, 1842, Lambeth, London, Eng.; d. Nov. 22, 1900, Westminster, London, Eng.) is best known for his music composed for Sir W. S. Gilbert's "Savoy Operas" (Gilbert and Sullivan operettas), but opposed the use of secular tunes for church music; at age 12 became a chorister at the Chapel Royal, and at 15 had his first anthem published by Novello; studied at the Royal Academy of Music and also at Leipzig Conservatory (1858–61); held several organ positions before becoming professor of composition at the Royal Academy of Music in 1866; in addition to his tuneful operetta music, wrote anthems, hymn tunes and oratorios; edited *Church Hymns,* 1874; was knighted by Queen Victoria in 1883, and made a member of the French Legion of Honor.

ST. KEVIN (164); ST. EDMUND (356); SULLIVAN (427); ST. GERTRUDE (470)

Sumner, John B. (b. Mar. 25, 1838, Lime Hill, Pa.; d. May 9, 1918, Binghamton, N.Y.), trained at Wyoming Seminary in Pennsylvania, was ordained a Methodist minister and served many pastorates in the Wyoming Conference; also held singing schools in the east; was a gifted tenor, and with two other ministers organized the Wyoming Conference Trio, which sang at Chautauqua meetings; wrote a number of hymn tunes, but only one is still in common use.

BINGHAMTON (323)

Sweney, John R. (b. Dec. 31, 1837, West Chester, Pa.; d. Apr. 10, 1899, Chester, Pa.) showed musical gifts when he was very young, and at age 22 was teaching music in Dover, Del.; directed the Third Delaware Regiment Band during the Civil War, and afterwards was professor of music at the Pennsylvania Military Academy for 25 years; for a number of years, served as director of music at the Bethany Presbyterian Church in Philadelphia, and was a popular song leader for many summer assemblies; composed over a thousand hymn tunes and assisted in compiling some sixty collections of gospel songs, anthems, and Sunday school music, collaborating frequently with William J. Kirkpatrick.

STORY OF JESUS (130); FILL ME NOW (195); SWENEY (339); SUNSHINE (399)

Synesius of Cyrene (b. *ca.*365, Cyrene; d. *ca.*414) was born into a distinguished family of Cyrene whose lineage went back to Spartan kings; studied at Alexandria and became a Neoplatonist; converted to Christianity *ca.*400, and was elected Bishop of Ptolemais, *ca.*409; was regarded as a great statesman and a man of eloquence; wrote ten odes which have been translated, and *Hymnody Past and Present* (1937) says "they are of great interest and beauty in their presentation of Christian devotion as seen through the eyes of a Platonist philosopher."

Lord Jesus, think on me (341)

Tans'ur, William (b. *ca.* Nov. 6, 1706, Dunchurch, Warwick, Eng.; d. Oct. 7, 1783, St. Neots, Eng.) is listed as "William Tanzer, son of Edward and Joan Tanzer" in the baptismal records of Dunchurch for November 6, 1706; was an itinerant teacher of music and psalmody, who finally settled in St. Neots and became a bookseller; authored many publications, including *Harmony of Zion* (1734), *Sacred Mirth, or the Pious Soul's Daily Delight* (1739), *The Universal Harmony, containing the Whole Book of Psalms* (1743), *New Musical Grammar* (1746) and *Melodia Sacra, or the Devout Psalmist's Musical Companion* (1771).

BANGOR (133)

Tappan, William Bingham (b. Oct. 24, 1794, Beverly, Mass.; d. June 18, 1849, West Needham, Mass.) was apprenticed to a clockmaker in his early teens, and later moved to Philadelphia and worked in that profession; was very interested in the Sunday School movement, and secured a position with the American Sunday School Union, which he held until his death; in 1840 was licensed as a Congregational minister and held evangelistic campaigns throughout the United States, always emphasizing the importance of the Sunday School; published 10 volumes, including *New England and Other Poems* (1819), *Poems* (1822) and *Gems of Sacred Poetry* (1860).

'Tis midnight; and on Olive's brow (139)

Tate, Nahum (b. 1652, Dublin, Ire.; d. Aug. 12, 1715, Southwark, London, Eng.) is remembered for his association with the historic "Tate and Brady" Psalter; was the son of an Irish minister and author, and was educated at Trinity College, Dublin; wrote principally for the London stage, adapting works of others, including Shakespeare; was named Poet Laureate of England in 1692; produced his most significant contribution, *The New Version of the Psalms of David,* 1696 in collaboration with Nicolaus Brady, and this psalter was used for more than 200 years in the Church of England; was an intemperate and irresponsible man, who died in a "debtor's refuge."

While shepherds watched their flocks (119)

Tersteegen, Gerhard (b. Nov. 25, 1697, Mörs, Westphalia; d. Apr. 3, 1769, Mühlheim, Rhenish Prussia) was slated by his parents to become a Reformed Church minister, but his father's early death made university education impossible; was apprenticed to his brother-in-law, a merchant, and became a silkweaver; after five years of depression and spiritual dearth, in 1724 made a new covenant with God and signed it with his own blood; finally gave up his business, and afterward his home (called "The Pilgrim's Cottage") was open to all who needed spiritual counseling, encouraging and renewal; worked outside the Reformed church tradition, but is remembered as one of Germany's great hymnists and spiritual leaders; translated or paraphrased (in German) many classics from French and Latin sources, and wrote 111 hymns, of which about 50 have been translated into English.

God Himself is with us (375)

Teschner, Melchior (b. 1584, Fraustadt, Silesia; d. Dec. 1, 1635, Oberprietschen, Posen) was appointed cantor of the "Zum Kripplein Christi" Lutheran Church in Fraustadt in 1609, and also taught in the parish school; in 1614 moved to nearby Oberprietschen where he served as pastor, and where he was succeeded by both his son and his grandson.

ST. THEODULPH (131)

Theodulph of Orleans (b. *ca.*750; d. Sept. 18, 821, Angers) was born into a noble family (probably Italian), and became abbot of a monastery in Florence; in 781 was brought to France by Charlemagne and appointed abbot of Fleury and Bishop of Orleans; was Charlemagne's chief theologian and a proponent of education; in 818, after the emperor's death, was accused of conspiring with King Bernard of Italy against Louis I, was deposed of his bishopric and imprisoned at Angers; according to tradition, was later released by Louis (see Hymn no. 131), but he apparently died in prison, possibly from poison.

All glory, laud and honor (131)

Thompson, Will Lamartine (b. Nov. 7, 1847, East Liverpool, Ohio; d. Sept. 20, 1909, New York City, N.Y.), during his lifetime, was called "The Bard of Ohio"; received schooling at Mount Union College in Alliance, Ohio and Boston Conservatory of Music, with further study in Leipzig, Germany; established the Will L. Thompson & Company music publishing firm with offices in East Liverpool, Ohio and Chicago, Ill.; wrote many successful secular and sacred songs, and edited and published many collections.

Softly and tenderly Jesus is calling (266); Jesus is all the world to me (278)

THOMPSON (266); ELIZABETH (278)

Thomson, Mary Ann (b. Dec. 5, 1834, London, Eng.; d. Mar. 11, 1923, Philadelphia, Pa.) spent her early years in England, then came to America and married John Thomson, first librarian of the Free Library in Philadelphia; was a member of the Church of the Annunciation, Philadelphia, where her husband served as the accounting warden; wrote many poems and hymns which appeared in *The Churchman*, New York, and *The Living Church*, Chicago.

O Christian, haste, your mission high fulfilling (476)

Threlfall, Jeannette (b. Mar. 24, 1821, Blackburn, Lancs, Eng.; d. Nov. 30, 1880, Westminster, London, Eng.) was left an orphan and spent most of her life in the homes of relatives; was disabled by an accident and became a permanent invalid, but maintained exemplary love, cheerfulness and serenity; read a great deal and wrote poems and hymns without effort, sending them anonymously to various periodicals; had her collected writings published in *Woodsorrel; or, Leaves from a Retired Home* (1856), and *Sunshine and Shadow* (1873).

Hosanna, loud hosanna (134)

Thring, Godfrey (b. Mar. 25, 1823, Alford, Somerset, Eng.; d. Sept. 13, 1903, Guildford, Surrey, Eng.) was trained at Shrewsbury School and Balliol College, Oxford and ordained a priest in the Church of England in 1846; served several curacies, and in 1858 succeeded his father as rector of Alford; was prebendary of East Harptree, Wells Cathedral, 1876–93; edited and published: *Hymns and Other Verses* (1866), *Hymns Congregational and Others* (1866) and *A Church of England Hymn Book, Adapted to the Daily Services of the Church Throughout the Year* (1880), revised in 1882 with the title, *The Church of England Hymn Book.*

Crown Him with many crowns (st. 2, 3) (85)

Thrupp, Dorothy Ann (b. June 20, 1779, London, Eng.; d. Dec. 14, 1847, London, Eng.) is not well known among hymnic biographers; wrote hymns for children, many of which appeared with the pseudonym "Iota" or the initials "D.A.T." or were left unsigned; released texts in such collections as W. Carus Wilson's *Friendly Visitor and Children's Friend,* and Mrs. Herbert Mayo's *Selection of Hymns and Poetry for the Use of Infant Schools and Nurseries* (1838); edited *Hymns for the Young* (1830), in which all of the works were unsigned.

Savior, like a shepherd lead us (321)

Tisserand, Jean (b., date unknown; d. 1494, Paris, Fr.) was a Franciscan friar who founded an order for penitent women; is said to have written an office (worship service) commemorating the martyrdom of Franciscan monks in Morocco in 1220; is remembered for his Latin hymns, including the famous "O Filii et Filiae" which was published after his death.

O sons and daughters, let us sing (160)

Tomer, William Gould (b. Oct. 5, 1833; d. Sept. 26, 1896, New Jersey) received his early musical training attending singing schools and the village choir in Finesville, N.J.; began teaching school at age 17; served on the staff of General Oliver O. Howard (in whose honor Howard University is named) during the Civil War; after the war, worked as a government employee in Washington, D.C., and served as music director for Grace Methodist Episcopal Church; finally returned to New Jersey where he spent the last years of his life teaching school.

GOD BE WITH YOU (42)

Toplady, Augustus Montague (b. Nov. 4, 1740, Farnham, Surrey, Eng.; d. Aug. 11, 1778, London, Eng.) received his education at Westminster School, London and Trinity College, Dublin; was converted while a student in Ireland through a message brought by James Morris, a Methodist lay preacher; in 1762 was ordained in the Church of England and served various churches as curate before becoming vicar at Broadhembury, Devonshire in 1766; moved to London, 1775, and preached at the French Calvinist Church in Leicester Fields; was an ardent Calvinist and an outspoken, bitter critic of John Wesley (*q.v.*); published *Poems on Sacred Subjects* (1769), *Historic Proof of the Doctrinal Calvinism of the Church of England* (1774), and *Psalms and Hymns for Public and Private Worship* (1776).

Rock of Ages, cleft for me (149); Father, whate'er of earthly bliss (adapt.) (419)

Tourjée, Lizzie Shove (b. 1858; d. 1913) was the daughter of Dr. Eben Tourjée, founder of the New England Conservatory of Music; received her education in Newton, Mass. high school and Wellesley College (one year); in 1883, married Franklin Estabrook.

WELLESLEY (233)

Tovey, Herbert George (b. May 6, 1888, Melbourne, Australia; d. Mar. 20, 1972, Santa Cruz, Calif.) graduated from Moody Bible Institute, Chicago, Ill., and studied church music at the University of Southern California; during a long career, taught at Bible Institute of Los Angeles, Simpson Bible College (Seattle) and Western Bible Institute (Denver); pastored the First Baptist Church in Montebello, Calif. and was interim pastor on many occasions; wrote many hymns and gospel songs and authored *Music Levels in Christian Education;* established The Sacred Music Foundation, which published several collections and still controls some 2000 copyrights.

Give me a passion for souls, dear Lord (471)

Towner, Daniel Brink (b. Mar. 5, 1850, Rome, Pa.; d. Oct. 3, 1919, Longwood, Mo.), as a music educator at Moody Bible Institute, Chicago (1893–1919), had a profound influence on evangelical church music; received his early musical training from his father, Professor J. G. Towner, a renowned teacher and singer, and later study with John Howard, George F. Root (*q.v.*) and George J. Webb (*q.v.*); served several Methodist Episcopal churches in New York, Ohio and Kentucky as music director; became associated in evangelistic work with Dwight L. Moody in 1885; in 1893 became director of the Music Department of Moody Bible Institute, which position he held until his death; died while leading music in an evangelistic meeting in Longwood, Mo.; received the honorary Mus.D. degree from the University of Tennessee in 1900; is credited with composing over 2000 gospel songs and compiling 14 songbooks and hymnals, as well as writing textbooks on music theory and practice; is the subject of an unpublished thesis written by Perry Carroll, student at New Orleans Baptist Theological Seminary.

MOODY (240); TOWNER (250); PRICELESS (282); CALVARY (286); ONLY A SINNER (293); GLORY, I'M SAVED (301); MY ANCHOR HOLDS (311); TRUST AND OBEY (318); SECURITY (328)

Tucker, Francis Bland (b. Jan. 6, 1895, Norfolk, Va.) received his education at public schools in Lynchburg, Va., the University of Virginia, and

Virginia Theological Seminary; was ordained an Episcopal priest and has served churches in Lawrenceville, Va., Washington, D.C., and Savannah, Ga.; was a member of the committee which compiled the *Hymnal, 1940,* in which six of his hymns and translations appear.

Alone Thou goest forth, O Lord (trans.) (133)

Tullar, Grant Colfax (b. Aug. 5, 1869, Bolton, Conn.; d. May 20, 1950, Ocean Grove, N.J.), left motherless at an early age, was reared in hard circumstances by relatives; was converted at age 19 at a Methodist camp meeting; attended Hackettstown Academy for two years, was ordained to the Methodist ministry and served briefly as a pastor; for ten years was song leader for the evangelist, Major George A. Hilton; in 1893, with Isaac H. Meredith, founded the Tullar-Meredith Publishing Company, New York, publishers of church music; edited many hymnals and gospel song books, and wrote many original texts and tunes.

I've heard the King (274)

FACE TO FACE (534)

Turner, H. L. is believed to have lived in the 19th century, but no positive information is available.

It may be at morn (178)

Tweedy, Henry Hallam (b. Aug. 5, 1868, Binghamton, N.Y.; d. Apr. 11, 1953, Brattlebury, Vt.) attended Binghamton public schools and went to Phillips Andover Academy and then to Yale, with graduate work at Union Theological Seminary, New York and the University of Berlin; was ordained a Congregational minister in 1898 and served churches in Utica, N.Y. and Bridgeport, Conn.; from 1909 to 1937 was professor of practical theology at Yale Divinity School; showed his keen and functional interest in hymnody in his book, *The Minister and His Hymnal;* compiled the hymnal *Christian Worship and Praise,* 1939, and authored many other books.

Eternal God, whose power upholds (494)

Urhan, Chrétien (b. Feb. 16, 1790 near Aix-la-Chapelle, Fr.; d. Nov. 2, 1845, Belleville, Paris, Fr.) at age 15 was sent by Empress Josephine to Paris where he developed his skill, becoming an accomplished player of the violin and viola, a member of the orchestra of the Opera Française and concertmaster in 1831; also served as organist of the Church of St. Vincent de Paul; was an ascetic and very religious person, but was not known as a composer of church music, though some of his melodies have been adapted as hymn tunes.

RUTHERFORD (535)

VanDeVenter, Judson W. (b. Dec. 5, 1855 near Dundee, Mich.; d. July 17, 1939, Tampa, Fla.) attended the public schools at Dundee and Hillsdale College in Michigan; studied art and for several years taught art and penmanship in public schools; was an active Methodist Episcopal layman, felt called to the ministry and was licensed as a local preacher; held evangelistic meetings in the United States, England and Scotland; spent the last years of his life in Florida where he had an important influence on the young evangelist, Billy Graham (see *Crusade Hymn Stories.*)

All to Jesus I surrender (373)

Van Dyke, Henry (b. Nov. 10, 1852, Germantown, Pa.; d. Apr. 10, 1933, Princeton, N.J.) was an outstanding American preacher, author and educator; was educated at Brooklyn Polytechnic Institute, Princeton University, and Princeton Theological Seminary; was ordained to the Presbyterian ministry and served in Rhode Island (1879–83), and at New York City's Brick Presbyterian Church (1883–99); beginning in 1900, was Murray Professor of English Literature at Princeton University for 23 years; in 1913 was appointed U.S. minister to the Netherlands and Luxemburg by President Woodrow Wilson; served as Moderator of the Presbyterian General Assembly and as chairman of the committee which prepared the *Book of Common Worship* in 1905, and assisted in the 1931 revision; wrote many popular books, including *The Reality of Religion* (1884), *The Story of the Psalms* (1887), *The Story of the Other Wise Man* (1896), and *The Gospel for an Age of Doubt* (1896).

Joyful, joyful, we adore Thee (25)

Vaughan Williams, Ralph (b. Oct. 12, 1872, Down Ampney, Eng.; d. Aug. 26, 1958, St. Marylebone, London, Eng.) was a most significant English composer in this 20th century and strongly influenced contemporary hymnody; was the son of Arthur Vaughan Williams, an Anglican priest, and was born in the vicarage in Down Ampney; received early training in piano, violin and theory, and continued his formal education at Charterhouse School, the Royal College of Music, and Trinity College, Cambridge, with advanced music study in Berlin and Paris; served as organist and choirmaster of St. Barnabas Church, South Lambeth; was musical editor of *The English Hymnal*, 1906; co-edited—with Martin Shaw (*q.v.*) and Percy Dearmer (*q.v.*)—*Songs of Praise*, 1925 and 1931; composed six symphonies, several major works for chorus and orchestra, operas, ballets, film music, chamber music and three organ preludes on Welsh hymn tunes; was a pioneer in researching English folksong, and used many of the tunes as settings for hymns.

FOREST GREEN (arr.) (57); KING'S WESTON (61); HYFRYDOL (arr.) (102, 174, 521); QUEM PASTORES LAUDAVERE (arr.) (118); LASST UNS ERFREUEN (arr.) (166); SINE NOMINE (477, 533)

Vincent, Charles John (b. Sept. 19, 1852, Houghton-le-Spring, Durham, Eng.; d. Feb. 28, 1934, Monte Carlo) at age 11 became a chorister at Durham Cathedral and at 16, organist at Monkwearmouth Parish Church; studied at Leipzig Conservatory for two years and received B.Mus. and D.Mus. degrees from Oxford; served several parishes as organist, including Christ Church, Hampstead, and was on the faculty of Trinity College, London for many years; founded the Vincent Music Company which later became Schirmer & Company; edited *The Organist and Choirmaster* and collaborated with John Stainer and D. J. Wood in producing the *Hymnal Companion to the Book of Common Prayer* (1890), *The Chant Book Companion* and the *Anglican Organist;* composed many anthems, cantatas and an oratorio, *Ruth,* as well as secular music, largely orchestral.

PAX TECUM (arr.) (396)

Voss, Herman (b. Apr. 23, 1911, Muskegon, Mich.) attended Shaffer School of Music (Muskegon, Mich.) and Moody Bible Institute, Richard DeYoung School of Music, and Cosmopolitan School of Music, all in Chicago; has served as staff organist on radio station WMBI, Chicago, and music editor for Singspiration, Inc.; in recent years, has been a professional musician in Chicago, serving as organist and adult Bible class teacher at the First Church of the Nazarene; collaborated with Wendell P. Loveless (*q.v.*) in preparing the *Radio Songs and Choruses of the Gospel* series, and has published solo and duet books for organ and piano.

Jesus, Savior, all I have is Thine (377)

VOSS (377)

Vulpius, Melchior (b. *ca.* 1560, Wasungen, Thuringia; d. *ca.* Aug. 7, 1615, Weimar) was cantor (Lutheran) at Weimar for approximately 14 years, 1602–15; wrote many chorale melodies (published in *Cantiones Sacrae,* 1602–4) which are still in use, but is best known for his contrapuntal settings of established tunes (published in *Kirchengesänge und geistliche Lieder,* 1604); also published *Canticum beatissimae* (1605), *Ein schön geistlich Gesangbuch·* (1609), and a setting for the *Passion according to St. Matthew* (1612–14); has uncertain dates for both his birth and death, but was buried in Weimar on August 7, 1615.

GELOBT SEI GOTT (170)

Wade, John Francis (b. *ca.* 1711; d. Aug. 16, 1786, Douay, Fr.) was a devout Roman Catholic Englishman who lived many years in Douay, France, a refuge for Englishmen during the Jacobite rebellion of 1745; taught music and specialized in copying plainchant and other music for use in chapels of wealthy Roman Catholic families; collected his copied manuscripts in a volume, *Cantus Diversi pro Dominicis et Festis per annum,* 1751, now preserved at Stonyhurst College in Lancashire, England.

O come, all ye faithful (103)

ADESTE FIDELES (103)

Walch, James (b. June 21, 1837, Edgerton, near Bolton, Eng.; d. Aug. 30, 1901, Llandudno, Caernarvon, Wales) studied music with his father and later with Henry Smart (*q.v.*); became organist at Duke's Alley Congregational Church in Bolton at age 20, and served other churches (both Anglican and nonconformist) throughout his lifetime; conducted the Bolton Philharmonic Society from 1870 to 1874; in 1877 moved to Barrow-in-Furness where he was a music dealer, and honorary organist of the parish church; wrote hymn tunes and other church music.

TIDINGS (476)

Walford, William (b. 1772, Bath, Somerset, Eng.; d. June 22, 1850, Uxbridge, Eng.) within the last few years has been determined to be the author of "Sweet Hour of Prayer" (see hymn no. 434); was educated at Homerton Academy, to which he later returned as a tutor in the classics; was ordained to the Congregational ministry and served pastorates in Suffolk, Norfolk and Middlesex; wrote *The Manner of Prayer*, 1836 and an autobiography, edited by John Stoughton and published posthumously in 1851.

Sweet hour of prayer (434)

Walker, Mary Jane (Deck) (b. 1816, Bury St. Edmunds, Eng.; d. 1878, Cheltenham, Eng.) was married to Dr. Edward Walker, the first rector of Cheltenham; wrote many hymns, nine of which appeared in her husband's *Psalms and Hymns for Public and Social Worship* (1855), along with 30 by her brother, J. G. Deck, and a number by members of the new sect called "Plymouth Brethren."

Jesus, I will trust Thee (244)

Wallace, William Vincent (b. June 1, 1812, Waterford, Ire.; d. Oct. 12, 1865, Château de Bages, Fr.), of Scottish descent, received his first musical training from his father; was challenged by hearing Paganini play, and became an accomplished violinist, giving his first concert in Dublin at the age of 15; in his recital career, traveled throughout the world and had an adventure-filled life; composed seven operas (which were popular in France), wrote tunes for four hymns of John Keble (*q.v.*), a cantata, and a number of compositions for piano; because of failing eyesight, gave up writing, retired to the Pyrenees, where he remained until his death in 1865.

SERENITY (73, 216, 424)

Walter, Howard Arnold (b. Aug. 19, 1883, New Britain, Conn.; d. Nov. 1, 1918, Lahore, India) studied at Princeton University, Hartford Theological Seminary and universities in Edinburgh, Glasgow and Göttingen; taught English at Waseda University in Tokyo, Japan for a time; was assistant minister of Asylum Hill Congregational Church in Hartford, Conn., 1910–13; in 1913 joined the executive staff of the YMCA and, encouraged by John R. Mott, went to work among the Mohammedan students in Foreman Christian College in Lahore, India; died in India during an influenza epidemic.

I would be true (337)

Walter, William Henry (b. July 1, 1825, Newark, N.J.; d. 1893, New York City, N.Y.), as a boy, played the organ in Presbyterian and Episcopal churches in Newark; became organist at St. John's Chapel, St. Paul's Chapel, and Trinity Chapel, all in New York City; in 1865 was appointed organist of Columbia University, where he had previously received an honorary D.Mus. degree; published a *Manual of Church Music* (1860), *The Common Prayer, with Ritual Song* (1868), and numerous anthems and services.

FESTAL SONG (461)

Walton, James George (b. Feb. 19, 1821, Clitheroe, Lancs, Eng.; d. Sept. 1, 1905, Bradford, York, Eng.) was an English composer who edited *Plain Song Music for the Holy Communion Office,* 1874, which contained his adaptation of the tune "St. Catherine" from one of Hemy's settings in Part II of *Crown of Jesus Music,* 1864.

ST. CATHERINE (arr.) (206, 364)

Walton, W. Spencer (b. 1850; d. 1906) is known in hymnody for only this one poem; was evidently an associate of Dr. A.J. Gordon (*q.v.*) in his work in New England. No other information is available.

In tenderness He sought me (300)

Walworth, Clarence Augustus (b. May 30, 1820, Plattsburg, N.Y.; d. Sept. 19, 1900, Albany, N.Y.) graduated from Union College, Schenectady and was admitted to the bar in 1841; originally a Presbyterian, studied for the Episcopal ministry at General Theological Seminary in New York, but was influenced by the Oxford movement and became a Roman Catholic priest; was one of the founders of the Paulist Order in the United States; for his last 34 years was rector of St. Mary's in Albany; published *The Oxford Movement in America,* 1895 (which explains his conversion to Roman Catholicism), and *Andiatorocté... and Other Poems,* 1888; was blind for the last ten years of his life.

Holy God, we praise Thy name (trans.) (9)

Ward, Samuel Augustus (b. Dec. 28, 1847, Newark, N.J.; d. Sept. 28, 1903, Newark, N.J.) received musical training in New York City with Jan Pychowski and others; established a successful music store in Newark, N.J. and was involved in the musical life of the city; succeeded Henry S. Cutler (*q.v.*) as organist of Grace Episcopal Church in 1880; founded the Orpheus Club of Newark in 1889 and directed this group until 1900.

MATERNA (520)

Ware, Henry, Jr. (b. Apr. 21, 1794, Hingham, Mass.; d. Sept. 25, 1843, Framingham, Mass.) graduated from Harvard in 1812 and became a member of the faculty of Exeter Academy in New Hampshire; was ordained to the Unitarian ministry in 1817 and became pastor of the Second Unitarian Church in Boston, where Ralph Waldo Emerson served as his assistant pastor; taught at Cambridge Theological School (1830–42) as professor of pulpit eloquence and pastoral care; was editor of the *Christian Disciple,* which later became the *Christian Examiner;* left four volumes of writings which were published in 1846.

Happy the home when God is there (531)

Waring, Anna Laetitia (b. Apr. 19, 1823, Plas-y-Velin, Neath, Glamorgan, South Wales; d. May 10, 1910, Clifton, near Bristol, Eng.) was brought up in a Quaker home, but at the age of 19 joined the Church of England; published *Hymns and Meditations,* 1850 which included 19 of her own hymns (the 10th edition contained 39); was a humanitarian who often visited the Bristol prisons, and was a strong supporter of the Discharged Prisoners' Aid Society.

In heavenly love abiding (327)

Warner, Anna Bartlett (b. Aug. 31, 1824, Long Island, N.Y.; d. Jan. 22, 1915, Constitution Island, near West Point, N.Y.) wrote the famous children's hymn "Jesus Loves Me, This I Know"; made her home with her father and her sister Susan (a well-known authoress) on Constitution Island in the Hudson River; with her sister, conducted Bible classes for the cadets at West Point and was consequently buried with military honors; wrote a number of novels in which she used her pseudonym "Amy Lathrop," and two collections of verse: *Hymns of the Church Militant*, 1858 and *Wayfaring Hymns, Original and Translated*, 1869.

We would see Jesus, for the shadows lengthen (425)

Warren, George William (b. Aug. 17, 1828, Albany, N.Y.; d. Mar. 17, 1902, New York, N.Y.), though largely self-taught, was an accomplished organist who served Episcopal churches in Albany, Brooklyn and New York City; composed anthems and hymn tunes and edited *Warren's Hymns and Tunes as Sung at St. Thomas' Church*, 1888; received an honorary D.Mus. degree from Racine College (Wis.).

NATIONAL HYMN (488, 526)

Warren, Norman Leonard (b. July 19, 1934, London, Eng.) was educated at Dulwiel College and Corpus Christi, Cambridge (M.A. in music) and Ridley Hall Theological College; was ordained in the Church of England and has been vicar at St. Paul's, Leamington Spa since 1963; has written over 100 hymn tunes and published numerous booklets for evangelism; was one of the musical editors of *Psalm Praise*, 1973.

YVONNE (234); NEW HEAVEN (543)

Watts, Isaac (b. July 17, 1674, Southampton, Eng.; d. Nov. 25, 1748, Stoke Newington, London, Eng.) has been generally acclaimed as "the father of English hymnody," the first to successfully challenge the long tradition of strict psalm-singing; was educated at the Free School in Southampton and the nonconformist academy at Stoke Newington; was ordained and appointed pastor of Mark Lane Independent Chapel, London (Congregational) in 1702; because of failing health, retired in 1712 to live with the family of Sir Thomas Abney near Cheshunt, Herefordshire, serving as tutor to the children and chaplain to the family; was a brilliant scholar and produced about sixty volumes on various subjects; wrote some 600 hymns and psalm paraphrases, most of which appear in three of his collections: *Hora Lyricae* (1706), *Hymns and Spiritual Songs* (1707) and *The Psalms of David Imitated in the Language of the New Testament* (1719).

Begin, my tongue, some heavenly theme (15); Come, we that love the Lord (23); Give to our God immortal praise (29); O God, our help in ages past (48); I sing the almighty power of God (57); Join all the glorious names (70); Joy to the world! the Lord is come (120); When I survey the wondrous cross (148); Alas! and did my Saviour bleed (156, 279); Come, Holy Spirit, heavenly Dove (197); The heavens declare Thy glory, Lord (221); Come, we that love the Lord (275); My Shepherd will supply my need (325); Jesus shall reign where'er the sun (489); Am I a soldier of the cross (510); When I can read my title clear (544); Now to the King of heaven (580)

Webb, George James (b. June 24, 1803, near Salisbury, Wilts, Eng.; d. Oct. 7, 1887, Orange, N.J.), the son of a well-to-do farmer, rejected his father's plans that he become a minister; studied organ at Salisbury Cathedral with Alexander Lucas and accepted the position of organist at a church in Falmouth; came to America in 1830 and settled in Boston, where he was organist of the Old South Church for 40 years; in 1833 was appointed professor at the Boston Academy of Music where he was associated with Lowell Mason (*q.v.*); became president of the Boston Handel and Haydn Society (1840) and was well-known as a choral and orchestral conductor; edited many publications, including *The Massachusetts Collection of Psalmody* (1840), *The American Glee Book* (with Lowell Mason as co-editor, 1841), *The Psaltery* (1845), *The National Psalmist* (1848), *Cantica Laudis* (1850) and *Cantica Ecclesiastica* (1859); served as editor for *The Music Library* (1835–36) and *The Musical Cabinet* (1837–40).

WEBB (456)

Webbe, Samuel (b. 1740, London, Eng.; d. May 25, 1816, London, Eng.) was first apprenticed to a cabinet maker, and at the age of 20 turned to music; worked as a music copyist for a London publisher, which brought him to the attention of organist Carl Barbandt, who gave him lessons; was employed as organist of the Roman Catholic chapels at the Sardinian and Portuguese embassies in London, beginning in 1776; wrote a great deal of music, published in *A Collection of Sacred Music as Used in the Chapel of the King of Sardinia in London* (ca. 1793), *A Collection of Masses for Small Choirs* (1792), *A Collection of Masses and Antiphons* (1792, compiled with his son Samuel Webbe, the Younger), *Antiphons in Six Books of Anthems* (1818), and many collections of glees and catches, as well as instrumental music.

CONSOLATOR (423)

Weber, Carl Maria von (b. Nov. 18, 1786, Eutin, Ger.; d. June 5, 1826, London, Eng.) was an important composer of German national opera in the early 19th century; as the son of a theatrical impresario, acquired a great deal of stage knowledge as he traveled throughout Europe with his father; studied music with Michael Haydn and Abt Vogler; was appointed conductor of the Breslau Municipal Theater, and later held similar posts in Stuttgart, Prague, and Dresden; is famous for his operas *Der Freischütz, Preciosa, Euryanthe,* and *Oberon;* also composed symphonies, masses, cantatas and chamber music.

SEYMOUR (238, 431, 556)

Weeden, Winfield Scott (b. Mar. 29, 1847, Middleport, Ohio; d. July 31, 1908, Bisby Lake, N.Y.) is remembered as composer of the music for "I

Surrender All," whose title is engraved on his tombstone; attended public school in Ohio, and taught singing schools for a number of years before going into evangelistic work; was gifted with a fine voice and was an able song leader; late in life, lived in New York City, the owner of a small hotel in lower Manhattan; compiled several collections, including *The Peacemaker* (1894), *Songs of the Peacemaker* (1895) and *Songs of Sovereign Grace* (1897).
SURRENDER (373)

Weisse, Michael (b. *ca.* 1480, Neisse, Silesia; d. 1534, Landskron, Bohemia) was a priest in the monastery at Breslau who came under the influence of Martin Luther's writings and, with two other monks, left the Roman Catholic church; became affiliated with the Bohemian Brethren's Home in Leutomischl, Bohemia and in 1534 was admitted to their ministry, serving at Landskron, Bohemia and Fulneck, Moravia; was sent with another brother to talk with Luther about Brethren doctrine, and Luther used his hymns in Babst's *GesangBuch,* 1545; edited the first Brethren hymnbook, *Ein Neu Gesengbuchlen,* 1531.
FREUEN WIR UNS ALLE (8)

Wesley, Charles (b. Dec. 18, 1707, Epworth, Lincs, Eng.; d. Mar. 29, 1788, London, Eng.) is credited with 20 hymns in *Hymns for the Living Church,* more than any other author; was the 18th child and youngest son of Samuel and Susanna Wesley, and was educated at Westminster School and Christ Church College, Oxford; is referred to as one of the "first Methodists" since he and his brother John (*q.v.*), along with George Whitefield, formed the "Holy Club" at Oxford, based on a disciplined approach to Bible study, worship, communion and concern for the less fortunate; was ordained in the Church of England in 1735 and a year later accompanied his brother John to America as missionary to the colony in Georgia; returned to London in 1738 and met the Moravian leaders, William Law, Count Zinzendorf (*q.v.*), and Peter Böhler, under whose influence he experienced his spiritual conversion; with his brother John, traveled in evangelistic work throughout the British Isles, which led to the Great Awakening and notable spiritual, economic and political changes; was a spontaneous and prolific poet who wrote more than 6500 hymns, covering the entire span of Christian experience and theology; published 64 collections of hymns, listed in Julian's *Dictionary of Hymnology,* pp. 1259–60.

Praise the Lord who reigns above (18); Ye servants of God, your Master proclaim (19); Love divine, all loves excelling (75); O for a thousand tongues to sing (90); Come, Thou long expected Jesus (102); Hark! the herald angels sing (106); Christ the Lord is risen today (163); Hail the day that sees Him rise (173); Rejoice, the Lord is King (177); Lo, He comes with clouds descending (185); Depth of mercy! can there be (238); Jesus, Lover of my soul (246); And can it be that I should gain (248); Arise, my soul, arise! (250); I want a principle within (336); O for a heart to praise my God (346); Talk with us, Lord (432); Soldiers of Christ, arise (458); A charge to keep I have (496); Forth in Thy name, O Lord (511)

Wesley, John Benjamin (b. June 17, 1703, Epworth, Lincs, Eng.; d. Mar. 2, 1791, London, Eng.) was a leader in the Great Awakening of the 18th century, which eventually led to the birth of Methodism; received his education at Charterhouse School and Christ Church, Oxford, was ordained in the Church of England and served briefly as curate under his father; returned to Oxford as a tutor (1729–35) and joined his younger brother Charles (*q.v.*) in the activities of the "Holy Club"; spent a brief and unpleasant time as a missionary to Georgia with the specific responsibility of parish priest in Savannah; became interested in hymnody through contacts with Moravians; in 1737 published his *Collection of Psalms and Hymns*, the first hymnal printed in America; returning to England, dated his conversion from a "heart-warming experience" at a meeting in Aldersgate in 1738; in some thirty years, traveled thousands of miles on horseback in evangelistic endeavor with his brother Charles; translated at least 30 hymns, mostly from German, and wrote about 27 original hymns; with his brother Charles, co-produced and published many volumes, whose contents have been the backbone of English hymnody for almost 250 years.

Jesus, Thy blood and righteousness (trans.) (241); Jesus, Thy boundless love to me (trans.) (364); Give to the winds your fears (trans.) (422)

Wesley, Samuel Sebastian (b. Aug. 14, 1810, London, Eng.; d. Apr. 19, 1876, London, Eng.) was recognized as the outstanding English organist of his time and made notable contributions to church music; was a grandson of Charles Wesley and a chorister at Chapel Royal when he was ten years old; at 16, began his career as organist, serving in five parish churches and four cathedrals—Hereford, Exeter, Winchester and Gloucester; received both B.Mus. and D.Mus. degrees from Oxford University at the age of 29; published *The European Psalmist,* 1872, which contained over 730 hymn tunes, of which 130 were his own; also composed (liturgical-musical) services, psalm settings, anthems, glees, and organ and vocal music.

AURELIA (200, 247, 560); Unnamed tune (579)

West, Martin is a pseudonym for John F. Wilson (*q.v.*).
HINDI (332)

Westbrook, Francis (b. June 16, 1903, Croydon, London, Eng.; d. Sept. 19, 1975, Harpendon, Herts, Eng.) was educated at Trinity School (Croydon), Didsbury College (Manchester), and Manchester University, where he earned the Mus.D. degree; received special training in composition and was a Fellow of the Royal School of Church Music; from 1945 to 1971 was ministerial secretary of the Methodist Church Music Society in England, and edited the "Music Makers' Page" in the *Methodist Recorder;* was principal of the Williams School of Church Music in Harpendon, Herts from 1971 until his death; wrote approximately 20 hymn tunes, several anthems, and a Passiontide cantata, *Calvary.*

NEW HORIZONS (52)

Whelpton, George (b. May 17, 1847, Redbourne, Eng.; d. Nov. 25, 1930, Oxford, Ohio) came to the United States in 1851 at the age of four, and when he was 16, served with the Union Army in the Civil War; studied with Horatio R. Palmer at Lake Chautauqua School of Music, and became a choral director in Buffalo, N.Y., 1903-25; became associated with the Century Publishing Company, New York and edited *Hymns of Worship and Service, The Church Hymnal* and many other compilations; after many years' service, accepted a similar position with the A. S. Barnes Company.

Unnamed Tune (585); DISMISSAL (591)

Whiddington, Ada Anne (Fitzgerald) (b. 1855, England; d. Mar. 14, 1933, Hendon, Eng.) was the daughter of Richard Fitzgerald, and married Richard Whiddington; had a son, Richard, who became Cavendish Professor of Physics at Cambridge. No other information is available, but it is believed that she was affiliated with the Keswick Convention movement in England.

Not I, but Christ (381)

Whitfield, Frederick (b. Jan. 7, 1829, Threapwood, Shrops, Eng.; d. Sept. 13, 1904, Croydon, London, Eng.) received his education at Trinity College, Dublin, and was ordained in the Church of England; served churches in Otley, Kirby-Ravensworth, Greenwich, Bexley, and Hastings; wrote some thirty books of verse and prose, including *Sacred Poems and Prose,* 1861 and 1864, which contained 26 hymns.

I saw the cross of Jesus (228); There is a name I love to hear (304)

Whiting, William (b. Nov. 1, 1825, Kensington, London, Eng.; d. May 3, 1878, Winchester, Eng.) received schooling at Clapham School and Winchester College; was master of the Winchester College choristers for more than 35 years, 1842-78; wrote *Rural Thoughts and Other Poems,* 1851, and only this one hymn.

Almighty Father, strong to save (2)

Whittier, John Greenleaf (b. Dec. 17, 1807, Haverhill, Mass.; d. Sept. 7, 1892, Hampton Falls, N.H.) is acknowledged to be one of America's finest poets; was born of Quaker parents and worked on the family farm until he was 20; was largely self-taught, with a short period of study at Haverhill Academy; released his first poems in *Newburyport Free Press* in 1825 and became editor of the *American Manufacturer,* 1828; was named editor of the *New England Review* (1830), and in 1836 moved to Philadelphia where he became the editor of *The Pennsylvania Freeman,* an anti-slavery publication; published his first book, *Legends of New England,* in 1831, followed by numerous other works; once said, "I am really not a hymn writer, for the good reason that I know nothing of music," nevertheless several of his poems have found their way into common church use.

Dear Lord and Father of mankind (407); Immortal Love, forever full (424)

Whittingham, William (b. 1524, Chester, Eng.; d. June 10, 1579, Durham, Eng.) entered Brasenose College at the age of 16, was elected a Fellow of

All Souls' in 1545 and later studied in France at the University of Orleans; adopted John Calvin's (*q.v.*) views and, with John Knox, insisted on revising the Anglican Prayer Book; was appointed to draw up a Service Book which would show a compromise between the strict adherents to the Prayer Book and Calvinism; while in Geneva with Knox, turned several psalms into meter and included a total of 51 in the Service Book published in 1556; returned to England in 1560, and in 1563 became Dean of Durham; died in 1579 and was buried at Durham Cathedral, where his tomb was destroyed by the Scots in 1640.

The Lord's my Shepherd (45)

Whittle, Daniel Webster (b. Nov. 22, 1840, Chicopee Falls, Mass.; d. Mar. 4, 1901, Northfield, Mass.) moved to Chicago in his mid-teens and worked as a cashier of the Wells Fargo Bank; served with Company B of the 72nd Illinois Infantry during the Civil War and was converted after being taken prisoner, by reading the New Testament his mother had given him; was promoted to the rank of major at war's end and was thereafter known as "Major Whittle"; returned to Chicago and was treasurer of the Elgin Watch Company until 1873; became associated with D. L. Moody, who encouraged him to enter the field of evangelism; in many years of effective evangelistic work, was assisted by three capable singers: P. P. Bliss (*q.v.*), James McGranahan (*q.v.*), and George C. Stebbins (*q.v.*); wrote most of his hymns late in life, and many bore the pseudonym "El Nathan."

There shall be showers of blessing (249); Have you any room for Jesus? (adapt.) (264); I know not why God's wondrous grace (295); Once far from God and dead in sin (306); Dying with Jesus, by death reckoned mine (314); There's a royal banner given for display (459)

Wigner, John Murch (b. June 19, 1844, King's Lynn, Norfolk, Eng.; d. Mar. 31, 1911, London, Eng.) was the son of John Thomas Wigner, a Baptist minister who was one of the compilers of the Baptist volume, *Psalms and Hymns*, 1858; attended London University and was appointed to the India Home Office in London in 1867, and served until retirement; was known as a children's evangelist and a Baptist lay preacher, and was a member of the Council of the Children's Special Service Mission.

Come to the Savior now (256)

Wilkes, John Bernard (b. 1785; d. 1869) studied at the Royal Academy of Music and served as organist at several churches, including St. David's, Merthyr, and later at Llandaff Cathedral; was organist of the parish church of Monkland, near Leominster, where Henry W. Baker (*q.v.*) was vicar. (Baker was chairman of the committee which compiled the original edition of *Hymns Ancient and Modern*, 1861, and Wilkes made several contributions to that historic volume.)

MONKLAND (arr.) (50)

Wilkinson, Kate Barclay (b. 1859; d. 1928) is not a well-known individual in hymn history; according to sketchy reports, was a member of the Church of England, conducted a meeting for girls, and apparently was active in the Keswick Convention movement.

May the mind of Christ my Savior (349)

Williams, Aaron (b. 1731, London, Eng.; d. 1776, London, Eng.), a music teacher, publisher and music engraver, was clerk at the Scottish Church, London Wall; compiled and published *The Universal Psalmodist* (1763), *The Royal Harmony* (1766), *The New Universal Psalmodist* (1770), *Harmonia Coelestis* (a collection of noteworthy anthems, 6th ed., 1775) and *Psalmody in Miniature* (1778). An American edition of the *Universal Psalmodist* was published at Newburyport, Mass. by Daniel Bailey in 1769, and entitled *The American Harmony*.

ST. THOMAS (23, 203)

Williams, C. C. (b. date unknown; d. 1882)

ANY ROOM (264)

Williams, Clara Tear (b. Sept. 22, 1858, near Painesville Lake, Ohio; d. July 1, 1937, Houghton, N.Y.) is remembered by the gospel singer George Beverly Shea in a sketch in *Crusade Hymn Stories* (Hope Publishing Co., 1967); was born in the home of Thomas and Mary Evangeline (Searl) Tear, members of the Methodist Episcopal Church; after three years as a school teacher in Ohio (1879–82), joined "Sister Mary DePew" in evangelistic work, and continued in this work intermittently (and often alone) until 1890, traveling in Indiana, Michigan, Ohio, Pennsylvania and New York, and working first in Methodist Protestant churches, and later in Wesleyan Methodist groups; in 1895 married W. H. Williams, a lay preacher and they lived successively in Canton, Ohio, Massillon, Ohio, Houghton, N.Y., and Philadelphia, Pa., and finally retired in Houghton, N.Y.; wrote several hymn texts and served as consulting editor for *Sacred Hymns and Tunes Designed for use in the Wesleyan Methodist Connection*, 1900.

All my life long I had panted (283)

Williams, Peter (b. Jan. 7, 1722, Llansadurnin, Carmarthen, Wales; d. Aug. 8, 1796, Llandyfeilog, Wales) was educated at Carmarthen Grammar School and converted as a boy under the preaching of George Whitefield; was ordained at the age of 22 and became curate at Eglwys Cymmyn, where he began a school; in 1746, opposed because of his vehement preaching, left the Church of England and joined the Welsh Calvinistic Methodists as an itinerant preacher; was expelled by the Methodists on charges of heresy, so built his own chapel in Carmarthen, and continued to minister; published a volume of Welsh hymns, *Rhai Hymnau ac Odlau Ysbrydol* (1759), *Hymns on Various Subjects* (1771), an annotated Welsh Bible, and a concordance.

Guide me, O Thou great Jehovah (trans.) (448)

Williams, Robert (b. *ca.* 1781, Mynydd Ithel, Anglesey, Wales; d. 1821, Mynydd Ithel, Wales), blind from birth, passed his life as a basket-maker on the island of Anglesey; was a capable musician in the exceptional Welsh tradition, having a good voice, a good ear, and a good memory; evidently wrote hymn tunes, as was the custom of Welsh musicians.

    LLANFAIR (27)

Williams, Thomas John (b. 1869, Ynysmeudwy, Glamorgan, Wales; d. 1944, Llanelly, Wales) was a student of David Evans (*q.v.*) of Cardiff; served as organist and choirmaster of Zion Church, Llanelly, 1903–13, and at the Calfaria Church in the same community from 1913 until his death in 1944; composed many hymn tunes and some anthems.

    TON-Y-BOTEL (229, 463)

Williams, William (b. Feb. 11, 1717, near Llandovery, Wales; d. Jan. 11, 1791, Pantycelyn, Wales) was the son of a wealthy Welsh farmer who became known both as the "Sweet Singer of Wales" and "the Isaac Watts of Wales"; attended Llwynllwyd Academy to study medicine, but the preaching of Howell Harris in 1738 so challenged him, that he entered the ministry; was ordained a deacon in the Church of England and served as a curate for three years, but was refused priest's orders because of his evangelical ideas; withdrew from the Established Church and became a popular itinerant preacher for the Calvinistic Methodist Church, traveling throughout Wales for 45 years; wrote more than 800 hymns in Welsh and some 100 in English, which appeared in such collections as *Alleluia* (1745–47), *The Sea of Glass* (1752) and *Gloria in Excelsis, or, Hymns of Praise to God and the Lamb* (1771).

    Guide me, O Thou great Jehovah (trans.) (448)

Willis, Richard Storrs (b. Feb. 10, 1819, Boston, Mass.; d. May 7, 1900, Detroit, Mich.) received his education at Chauncey Hall, Boston Latin School and Yale; studied composition in Germany for six years and became an intimate friend of Mendelssohn; from 1848 to 1852 served as music critic for the *New York Tribune, The Albion* and *The Musical Times,* and from 1852 to 1864, *The Musical Times, The Musical World,* and *Once a Month;* edited and published *Church Chorals and Choir Studies* (1850), *Our Church Music* (1856), *Waif of Song* (1876), and *Pen and Lute* (1883).

    CRUSADER'S HYMN (67); CAROL (104)

Wilson, Emily Divine (b. May 24, 1865, Philadelphia, Pa.; d. June 23, 1942, Philadelphia, Pa.) was the wife of John G. Wilson, a Methodist minister who served as district superintendent in the Philadelphia Conference and finally, as pastor of the Wharton Memorial Methodist Church, Philadelphia; with her husband, regularly participated in the Ocean Grove, N.J. summer assembly; generously contributed her musical and dramatic gifts to the service of God and the church.

    HEAVEN (546)

Wilson, Hugh (b. 1766, Fenwick, Ayr, Scot.; d. Aug. 14, 1824, Duntocher, Scot.) was educated in the village school at Fenwick, and learned the shoemaking trade from his father; studied music and mathematics, and designed sundials in his spare time; after 1800 became a calculator and draftsman in the mills at Pollokshaws and then in Duntocher; was named "manager" of the Secession Church in Duntocher, and was one of the founders of the first Sunday School there; wrote and adapted many psalm tunes, but ordered the unpublished manuscripts to be burned after his death.

    MARTYRDOM (156, 212)

Wilson, Ira Bishop (b. Sept. 6, 1880, Bedford, Ia.; d. Apr. 3, 1950, Los Angeles, Calif.), with the help of an older sister, learned to play the violin and organ, and began the study of harmony while still a youth; in 1902 entered Moody Bible Institute to prepare for musical evangelism, but in 1905, accepted a position as composer and editor with the Lorenz Publishing Company, Dayton, Ohio; was a contributing editor to Lorenz's periodicals, *The Choir Leader* and *The Choir Herald,* and editor-in-chief of *The Volunteer Choir,* frequently using the pseudonym "Fred B. Holton"; wrote a large number of seasonal choir cantatas, as well as numerous anthems and hymn arrangements; moved to Los Angeles in 1930, but continued his relationship with Lorenz.

    Out in the highways and byways of life (505)

Wilson, John Floyd (b. Mar. 24, 1929, Youngstown, Ohio) has been resident editor of Hope Publishing Company since 1966, and was appointed executive editor Jan. 1, 1977; attended South High School, Youngstown, Ohio, Chicago Evangelistic Institute, American Conservatory of Music (B.Mus., 1954) and Northwestern University (M.Mus., 1959); completed additional graduate work and studied composition with Leo Sowerby and Anthony Donato; has taught music at Mountain View Bible College (Didsbury, Alberta), Fort Wayne Bible College (Ind.), Moody Bible Institute (Chicago, Ill.) and was Director of the Music Department (1964–66) at Marion College (Ind.); served as minister of music, First Methodist Church, La Grange, Ill., 1966–68; in addition to his editorial duties, directs the Student Nurses' Choir at West Suburban Hospital, Oak Park, Ill., and conducts many workshops and clinics; has written numerous hymn texts and tunes, many anthems and arrangements, and 15 full-length musicals or cantatas, including *The Son of God, Christ Triumphant, Shepherds, Rejoice!, He's Alive, Born!, Good News, World, We Are One, Let George Do It* (1975), *I Believe* (1976), *It's Music* (1976) and *The Electric Sunshine Man* (1977); authored the textbook, *Introduction to Church Music,* 1965.

    Amen, Amen (adapt.) (126); Who is this boy? (129); Jesus Christ has triumphed now! (167)

    AMEN (arr.) (126); MOUNTAIN VIEW (129); RESURRECTION (167); Unnamed Tune (584)

Winkworth, Catherine (b. Sept. 13, 1827, London, Eng.; d. July 1, 1878, Monnetier, Savoy, Fr.) is regarded as the foremost English translator of German hymns; lived most of her life near Manchester until she moved to

Clifton in 1862, to live with her father and sisters; was interested in educational and social problems, and became secretary of the association for the promotion of higher education for women in 1870; published two volumes entitled *Lyra Germanica* (1853 and 1858), *The Chorale Book for England* (1863), and *Christian Singers of Germany* (1869).

> All glory be to God on high (trans.) (10); Praise to the Lord, the Almighty (trans.) (43); In Thee is gladness (trans.) (64); From heaven above to earth I come (trans.) (111); If thou but suffer God to guide thee (trans.) (420); Now thank we all our God (trans.) (564)

Winter, Gloria Frances (b. June 14, 1938, Passaic, N.J.) is known as Sister Miriam Therese in her religious community, the Medical Mission Sisters; was educated at Bayley-Ellard Regional High School in Madison, N.J., Trinity College in Washington, D.C., Catholic University in Washington, D.C. (B. Mus., *magna cum laude*), and McMaster Divinity College in Hamilton, Ontario (M.Rel.Ed.); entered the Society of Catholic Medical Missionaries (Medical Mission Sisters) in November, 1955, and has served as Director of Public Relations for the Northeast District and Coordinator of Public Relations for the U.S.A. (1963–72), and editor of the Society's *Medical Missionary* magazine; since 1960 has been a leader in liturgy and music within the Medical Mission Sisters, and is recognized as one of the initiators of the contemporary style of sacred music; has written six Mass/Service settings and 138 songs, of which the best-known is "Joy Is Like the Rain"; has published and recorded more than ten collections of sacred music in the new style.

> Spirit of God in the clear running water (191)

> MEDICAL MISSION SISTERS (191)

Witt, Christian Friedrich (b. 1660, Altenburg, Ger.; d. Apr. 13, 1716, Altenburg, Ger.) studied music in Nüremberg, was court *kapellmeister* at Gotha, then returned to Altenburg to become director of the chapel music, which position he held until his death; was a composer of numerous dramatic and instrumental works, cantatas and hymn tunes; compiled and published *Psalmodia Sacra,* 1715.

> STUTTGART (34)

Wolf, Ellwood Shermer (b. Apr. 1, 1903, Philadelphia, Pa.) was educated in the public schools in Philadelphia, studied engineering at Drexel (University) Institute of Technology, and received degrees from Rutgers University (B.S.) and New York University (M.Mus.); was ordained to the Baptist ministry in 1934 and served pastorates in Leonardo, N.J. and Philadelphia, Pa.; after 26 years in local church ministry, was appointed assistant editorial director of Judson Press, Valley Forge, Pa. (1957); was a specialist in church music, directed the United Choral Society of N.J., and served several terms as president of the Philadelphia Chapter of The Hymn Society of America; made many contributions to hymnody, including original compositions, arrangements and orchestrations; was a member of the editorial committee, *Hymnbook for Christian Worship*, 1970; retired April 30, 1968 and is living in Oreland, Pa.

KINGSFOLD (arr.) (449)

Wood, James H. (b. Apr. 14, 1921, Rochester, Minn.) received his education at Macalester College (A.B.), Iowa University (M.A.), and Union Theological Seminary (S.M.D.); in 1951–52 was a member of the Robert Shaw Chorale; has taught at Colorado A. & M. College, Bethany College, Duke University, and Southern Baptist Theological Seminary, and is presently teaching music at Morningside College, Sioux City, Ia.; is active as a choral conductor and vocal soloist; has written many choral compositions and arrangements.

BEACH SPRING (arr.) (498)

Woodhull, Alfred Alexander (b. Mar. 25, 1810, Cranbury, N.J.; d. Oct. 5, 1836, Princeton, N.J.), the son of a Presbyterian minister, graduated from Princeton University at the age of 18, and received the M.D. degree from the University of Pennsylvania; practiced medicine at Marietta, Pa. and Princeton, N.J., and delivered lectures to the U.S. Infantry and Cavalry School which were published 62 years after his death under the title *Notes on Military Hygiene for Officers of the Line;* died suddenly at age 26, bringing a promising career to a premature end.

Great God of nations (523)

Wordsworth, Christopher (b. Oct. 30, 1807, Lambeth, London, Eng.; d. Mar. 21, 1885, Harewood, Eng.) was a nephew of the renowned English poet, William Wordsworth and the son of Christopher Wordsworth, master of Trinity College, Cambridge; was educated at Winchester School and Trinity College, Cambridge, where he was acknowledged as a scholar and athlete; was ordained in the Church of England and served as headmaster of Harrow (1836–50), vicar of Stanford-in-the-Vale, Berkshire (1850–69), archdeacon of Westminster, and in 1869 was consecrated Bishop of Lincoln; a recognized Greek scholar, wrote a commentary on the entire Bible; was a prolific and spontaneous hymnwriter who believed that "it is the first duty of a hymn to teach sound doctrine and thence to save souls"; published *The Holy Year, or Hymns for Sundays and Holy Days, and Other Occasions,* 1862, with 117 original hymns and 82 others.

O day of rest and gladness (549)

Work, John Wesley, Jr. (b. Aug. 6, 1872, Nashville, Tenn.; d. Sept. 7, 1925, Nashville, Tenn.), together with his brother, Frederick J. Work, was a leader in collecting, arranging and promoting black spirituals; graduated from Fisk University (A.B. and M.A.) and returned to teach Latin and Greek at his *alma mater;* in 1923 became president of Roger Williams University, Nashville, Tenn. and served until his death; assisted in publishing several volumes, including *Folk Songs of the American Negro,* 1907.

Go, tell it on the mountain (115)

Wreford, John Reynell (b. Dec. 12, 1800, Barnstaple, Eng.; d. 1881, St. Marylebone, London, Eng.) was trained at Manchester College, Yorkshire for the Unitarian ministry; in 1826 was appointed associate minister at New Meeting, Birmingham, but retired after five years because of voice problems; opened a school in Edgbaston, Birmingham; wrote a *Sketch of the History of Presbyterian Nonconformity in Birmingham* (1832), and *Lays of Loyalty* (1837), in acknowledgment of Queen Victoria's accession; contributed 55 hymns to J. R. Beard's *Collection of Hymns for Public and Private Worship* (1837).

Lord, while for all mankind we pray (524)

Wyeth, John (b. Mar. 31, 1770, Cambridge, Mass.; d. Jan. 23, 1858, Philadelphia, Pa.) learned the printer's trade as a youth and published tunebooks for many denominations and groups; lived and worked briefly in Santo Domingo, then in Philadelphia and Harrisburg, Pa.; with his partner, was editor of the Federalist newspaper, *Oracle of Dauphin,* for 35 years; was appointed postmaster of Harrisburg in 1793 by George Washington, but later removed by John Adams because of the "incompatibility of the office of postmaster and editor of a newspaper"; was a non-musical Unitarian, but published *Repository of Sacred Music,* 1810 and *Repository of Sacred Music, Part Second,* 1813, which sold almost 200,000 copies and contained compositions of Reed, Holden, Swann, Holyoke, Billings and others.

NETTLETON (28)

Wyrtzen, Donald John (b. Aug. 16, 1942, Brooklyn, N.Y.), the son of Jack Wyrtzen (*q.v.*), was active in the music of evangelism, radio and television from his early teens; graduated from Hampden DuBose Academy (Fla.) and Moody Bible Institute, The King's College (B.S.) and Dallas Theological Seminary (Th.M.), and did graduate work in composition at North Texas State University; was an instructor and later became chairman of the music department at Dallas Bible College, music director at Northwest Presbyterian Church, Dallas, and instructor in music at Dallas Theological Seminary; since 1970 has been associated as a composer and editor with Singspiration, Inc., Grand Rapids, Mich., and is now their Director of Special Projects; has arranged, orchestrated-and conducted several of John Peterson's (*q.v.*) musicals, and numerous sacred albums; has composed over 100 anthems and sacred songs, and several cantatas.

YESTERDAY, TODAY AND TOMORROW (284)

Wyrtzen, Jack (b. Apr. 22, 1913, New York City, N.Y.), in his early musical career in the New York City area, directed a dance band called "The Silver Moon Serenaders," and was also active in the insurance business; was converted at age 19 while playing trombone in a training camp of the U.S. Cavalry, through the testimony of one of his buddies; originated the Saturday night youth rally called "Word of Life" (often held in Madison Square Garden) which was copied all over the country by Youth for Christ; has been active in regular evangelistic broadcasts since the early 1940's and conducted youth rallies throughout New England and the East; founded

Word of Life Inn, Island Ranch and Bible Institute at Schroon Lake, N.Y., and more recently, camps and schools in Brazil, Canada, West Germany and other countries.

Yesterday He died for me (284)

Yates, John Henry (b. Nov. 21, 1837, Batavia, N.Y.; d. Sept. 5, 1900, Batavia, N.Y.) was educated in the Batavia, N.Y. Union School, became a shoe salesman, and then manager of E. L. & G. D. Kenyon (Hardware) Store; in 1886 became editor of a local paper; was a licensed Methodist preacher, but later in life was ordained as a Baptist minister and pastored West Bethany Free Will Baptist Church for seven years; published *Poems and Ballads*, 1897.

Encamped along the hills of light (453)

Young, Carlton Raymond (b. Apr. 25, 1926, Hamilton, Ohio) is the consulting editor of the Agape division of Hope Publishing Co., Carol Stream, Ill.; is the son of a Methodist minister, and attended public school in Hamilton, Ohio, the College of Music at the University of Cincinnati (B.S., 1950) and Boston University School of Theology (S.T.B., 1953); is an ordained elder in the Methodist church and served as minister of music at the Church of the Savior, Cleveland Heights, Ohio (1953-56) and Trinity Methodist Church, Youngstown, Ohio (1956-59); was associated with Abingdon Press, Nashville, Tenn. from 1959 to 1964 as director of music, in charge of music publishing and distribution; was associate professor of church music at Perkins School of Theology and the School of Arts, Southern Methodist University, Dallas, Tex., 1964-75; since 1975 has been professor of church music at Scarritt College, Nashville, Tenn.; was active in the founding of the National Fellowship of Methodist Musicians, and was director of music for the Methodist General Conference in 1966, 1968 and 1970; edited the *Methodist Hymnal*, 1966 and wrote the biographies for *Companion to the Hymnal*, 1970; is executive editor for *Ecumenical Praise* (Agape, 1977), serving with Erik Routley, Alec Wyton and Austin Lovelace on the editorial board; is active as a clinician and lecturer, and very successful as a composer, editor and compiler of sacred music.

Glory be to God the Father (adapt.) (574)
LET US BREAK BREAD (arr.) 213); Unnamed Tune (574)

Young, John Freeman (b. Oct. 30, 1820, Pittston, Me.; d. Nov. 15, 1885, New York, N.Y.) was trained at Wesleyan University, Middletown, Conn. and Virginia Theological Seminary in Alexandria; was ordained in the Protestant Episcopal church and served dioceses in Texas, Mississippi, Louisiana and New York, before being elected second bishop of Florida (1867); was keenly interested in architecture and responsible for many interesting church structures; was also involved in promoting education by establishing and re-opening schools throughout the south; published *Hymns and Music for the Young*, 1860-61 and edited *Great Hymns of the Church*, which was published posthumously in 1887 by John Henry Hopkins, Jr.

Silent night! holy night! (trans.) (117)

Zelley, Henry J. (b. Mar. 15, 1859, Mount Holly, N.J.; d. Mar. 16, 1942, Trenton, N.J.) received his early education at Mount Holly (N.J.) schools, and graduate study at Pennington Seminary and Taylor University (A.M., Ph.D., and D.D.); was ordained to the Methodist ministry and served 19 different churches in the New Jersey Conference before his retirement in 1929; wrote more than 1500 poems, hymns and gospel songs.

Walking in sunlight all of my journey (403)

Zinzendorf, Nikolaus Ludwig von (b. May 26, 1700, Dresden, Ger.; d. May 9, 1760, Herrnhut, Saxony), born to wealthy nobility, was educated at A. H. Francke's Adelspädagogium at Halle and at Wittenberg University, where he studied law; had a court post, 1721–27, but resigned and was granted a preacher's license in 1734; established a center for Moravian refugees at his estate at Herrnhut, and later devoted himself completely to the Moravian community and became their bishop in 1737; on grounds of unorthodoxy was banished from Saxony, during which time he founded colonies of Moravian missionaries in Switzerland, England, Holland, North America and the West Indies; was allowed to return to Herrnhut in 1748, and remained until his death; wrote over 2000 hymns, of which some 36 have been translated into English; had a profound influence on the lives and ministry (including the hymn writing) of John (*q.v.*) and Charles Wesley (*q.v.*).

Jesus, Thy blood and righteousness (241); Jesus, still lead on (450)

Zundel, John (b. Dec. 10, 1815, Hochdorf, Ger.; d. July, 1882, Cannstadt, Ger.), educated in his native Germany, was first organist at St. Anne's Lutheran Church of St. Petersburg (now Leningrad), Russia and bandmaster of the Imperial House Guards; came to America in 1847 and spent 30 years here, 28 of them as organist at the Plymouth Church, Brooklyn, where Henry Ward Beecher was pastor (the church was noted for quality in its preaching, organ playing and congregational singing); retired in 1880 and returned to his native Germany; published *The Choral Friend* (1852), *Psalmody* (1855), and *Christian Heart Songs* (1870); assisted Beecher in the preparation of the *Plymouth Collection* (1855), for which he wrote 28 hymn tunes.

BEECHER (3, 75)

BIBLIOGRAPHY

GENERAL REFERENCE WORKS

Blom, Eric, ed. *Grove's Dictionary of Music and Musicians*, 5th ed. 10 vols. New York: St. Martin's Press, 1954.

Blume, Friedrich, and others. *Protestant Church Music*. New York: W. W. Norton, 1974 (translation).

Dictionary of American Biography. 22 vols. New York: Charles Scribner's Sons, 1928–58.

Dictionary of National Biography. 68 vols. London, 1885–1901.

Dictionary of National Biography. Supplements 1 and 2. London, 1901 and 1902.

Fischer, Albert Friedrich Wilhelm. *Kirchenlieder-Lexicon*. Gotha: Friedrich Andreas Perthes, 1878.

Julian, John, ed. *A Dictionary of Hymnology*. New York: Charles Scribner's Sons, 1892. New York: Dover Publications, 1957 (reprint).

Koch, Edward Emil. *Geschichte des Kirchenlieds und Kirchengesangs*. Stuttgart: Chr. Belser'schen, 1866.

New Catholic Encyclopedia. 15 vols. New York: McGraw Hill Book Co., 1957.

Who Was Who in America.

Who's Who in America.

Wolff, Dr. Eugen. *Des Deutsche Kirchenlied des 16 und 17 Jahrh*. Stuttgart, n.d.

HYMNAL HANDBOOKS

Avery, Gordon. *Companion to the Song Book of the Salvation Army*, 4th ed. London: Salvationist Publishing and Supplies, 1970.

Bucke, Emory Stevens; Gealy, Fred D.; Lovelace, Austin C.; and Young, Carlton R. *Companion to the Hymnal*. New York and Nashville: Abingdon Press, 1970.

Covert, William C., and Laufer, Calvin W. *Handbook to the Hymnal*. Philadelphia: Presbyterian Board of Christian Education, 1935.

Dearmer, Percy, and Jacob, Archibald. *Songs of Praise Discussed*. London: Oxford University Press, 1933.

Farlander, Arthur; Ellinwood, Leonard; and others. *The Hymnal 1940 Companion*. New York: The Church Pension Fund, 1949.

Frost, Maurice. *Historical Companion to Hymns Ancient and Modern*. London: William Clowes and Sons, Ltd., 1962.

Haeussler, Armin. *The Story of Our Hymns*. The Handbook to the Hymnal of the Evangelical and Reformed Church. St. Louis: Eden Publishing House, 1952.

Hostetler, Lester. *Handbook to the Mennonite Hymnary*. Newton, Kansas: General Conference of the Mennonite Church of North America Board of Publications, 1949.

Kelynack, William S. *Companion to the School Hymn-Book of the Methodist Church.* London: Epworth Press, 1950.

Lightwood, James T. (ed. and revised by Francis B. Westbrook). *The Music of the Methodist Hymn-Book.* London: The Epworth Press, 1955.

Macmillan, Alexander. *Hymns of the Church, A Companion to The Hymnary of The United Church of Canada.* Toronto: The United Church Publishing House, 1935.

Martin, Hugh, ed.; Jones, J. Ithel; et al. *The Baptist Hymn Book Companion.* London: Psalms and Hymns Trust, 1962.

McCutchan, Robert G. *Our Hymnody: A Manual of the Methodist Hymnal,* 2nd ed. New York and Nashville: Abingdon-Cokesbury Press, 1942.

Moffatt, James, and Patrick, Millar. *Handbook to the Church Hymnary with Supplement,* rev. ed. London: Oxford University Press, 1927.

Parry, K. L., and Routley, Erik. *Companion to Congregational Praise.* London: Independent Press, Ltd., 1953.

Polack, William G. *The Handbook to the Lutheran Hymnal,* 3rd and rev. ed. St. Louis: Concordia Publishing House, 1958.

Reynolds, William Jensen. *Hymns of Our Faith, A Handbook for the Baptist Hymnal.* Nashville: Broadman Press, 1964.

————. *Companion to Baptist Hymnal.* Nashville: Broadman Press, 1976.

Ronander, Albert C., and Porter, Ethel K. *Guide to the Pilgrim Hymnal.* Philadelphia and Boston: United Church Press, 1966.

Seaman, William A. *Companion to the Service Book and Hymnal.* The Commission on the Liturgy and Hymnal, 1976.

Statler, Ruth B., and Fisher, Nevin W. *Handbook on Brethren Hymns.* Elgin, Illinois: The Brethren Press, 1959.

Wake, Arthur N. *Companion to Hymnbook for Christian Worship.* St. Louis, Missouri: The Bethany Press, 1970.

GENERAL HYMNOLOGY

Bailey, Albert Edward. *The Gospel in Hymns.* New York: Charles Scribner's Sons, 1950.

Barrows, Cliff, ed. *Crusade Hymn Stories.* Chicago: Hope Publishing Co., 1967.

Benson, Louis F. *The English Hymn.* New York: George H. Doran Co., 1915. (Reprint, Richmond: John Knox Press, 1962).

Brown, Theron, and Butterworth, Hezekiah. *The Story of the Hymns and Tunes.* New York: George H. Doran Company, 1906.

Clark, W. Thorburn. *Stories of Fadeless Hymns.* Nashville: Broadman Press, 1949.

Colson, Elizabeth. *Hymn Stories.* Boston: The Pilgrim Press, 1925.

Davies, James P. *Sing with Understanding.* Chicago, Illinois: Covenant Press, 1966.

Dearmer, Percy; Vaughan Williams, Ralph; and Shaw, Martin. *The Oxford Book of Carols.* London: Oxford University Press, 1928.

Douglas, Charles W. *Church Music in History and Practice.* New York: Charles Scribner's Sons, 1937. Rev. 1962 by Leonard Ellinwood.

Ellinwood, Leonard. *The History of American Church Music.* New York: Morehouse-Gorham, 1953.

Emurian, Ernest K. *Living Stories of Famous Hymns.* Boston: W. A. Wilde Co., 1955.

Erickson, J. Irving. *Twice-Born Hymns.* Chicago, Illinois: Covenant Press, 1976.

Foote, Henry Wilder. *Three Centuries of American Hymnody.* Harvard University Press, 1940.

Hall, Frederick. *Know Your Hymns?* Boston: W. A. Wilde Co., 1944.

Hutchings, Arthur. *Church Music in the Nineteenth Century.* London: Oxford University Press, 1967.

Knapp, Christopher. *Who Wrote Our Hymns?* Denver, Colorado: Wilson Foundation, 1925.

Laufer, Calvin W. *Hymn Lore.* Westminster Press, 1932.

Liemohn, Edwin. *The Chorale.* Philadelphia: Muhlenberg Press, 1953.

Mable, Norman. *Popular Hymns and Their Writers.* Independent Press Ltd., 1946–1951.

Northcott, Cecil. *Hymns We Love.* Philadelphia: The Westminster Press, 1954.

Patrick, Millar. *Four Centuries of Scottish Psalmody.* London: Oxford University Press, 1949.

———. *The Story of the Church's Song.* Scottish Churches Joint Committee on Youth, Edinburgh, 1927. Revised for American use by James Rawlings Sydnor, John Knox Press, Richmond, 1962.

Pratt, Waldo S. *The Music of the French Psalter of 1562.* New York: Columbia University Press, 1939.

Reynolds, William Jensen. *A Survey of Christian Hymnody.* New York: Holt, Rinehart and Winston, Inc., 1963.

Routley, Erik. *Twentieth Century Church Music.* New York: Oxford University Press, 1964.

———. *Hymns Today and Tomorrow.* New York: Abingdon Press, 1964.

———. *Church Music and Theology.* Philadelphia: Fortress Press, 1960.

Rudin, Cecilia Margaret. *Stories of Hymns We Love.* Chicago: John Rudin & Company, Inc., 1945.

Ryden, Ernest Edwin. *The Story of Christian Hymnody.* Rock Island, Illinois: Augustana Press, 1959.

Sheppard, W. J. Limmer. *Great Hymns and Their Stories.* London: Lutterworth Press, rev. ed., 1950.

Smith, H. Augustine. *Lyric Religion: The Romance of Immortal Hymns.* New York: D. Appleton-Century Company, 1931.

Stevenson, Robert. *Protestant Church Music in America.* New York: W. W. Norton and Company, Inc., 1966.

Sydnor, James Rawlings. *The Hymn and Congregational Singing.* Richmond: John Knox Press, 1960.

———, ed. *A Short Bibliography for the Study of Hymns.* New York: Hymn Society of America, Paper XXV, 1964.

Thompson, Ronald W. *Who's Who of Hymn Writers.* London: Epworth Press, 1967.

FOLK AND BLACK MUSIC

Buchanan, Annabel Morris. *Folk Hymns of America.* New York: J. Fischer & Brother, 1938.

Jackson, George Pullen. *Another Sheaf of White Spirituals.* Gainesville, Florida: University of Florida Press, 1952.

———. *Down-East Spirituals and Others.* Locust Valley, New York: J. J. Augustin Publisher, 1943.

———. *Spiritual Folk-Songs of Early America.* Locust Valley, New York: J. J. Augustin Publisher, 1937.

———. *White and Negro Spirituals, Their Life-Span and Kinship.* Locust Valley, New York: J. J. Augustin Publisher, 1943.

———. *White Spirituals in the Southern Uplands.* Chapel Hill, North Carolina: University of North Carolina Press, 1933. Reprinted by Folklore Associates, Inc., Hatboro, Pa., 1964.

Lovell, John, Jr. *The Forge and the Flame.* New York: Macmillan Company, 1972.

Work, John W. *American Negro Songs and Spirituals.* New York: Bonanza Books, 1940.

GOSPEL HYMNS

Emurian, Ernest K. *Forty True Stories of Famous Gospel Songs.* Natick, Massachusetts: W. A. Wilde Co., 1959.

Gabriel, Charles H. *The Singers and Their Songs.* Winona Lake, Ind.: The Rodeheaver Company, 1915.

Hall, J. H. *Biography of Gospel Song and Hymn Writers.* New York: Revell, 1914.

Kerr, Phil. *Music in Evangelism.* Glendale, California: Gospel Music Publishers, 1939.

Lillenas, Haldor. *Modern Gospel Song Stories.* Kansas City, Missouri: Lillenas Publishing Company, 1952.

Rodeheaver, Homer A. *Hymnal Handbook for Standard Hymns and Gospel Songs.* Winona Lake, Indiana: The Rodeheaver Co., 1931.

Sankey, Ira D. *My Life and the Story of the Gospel Hymns.* New York: Harper and Brothers Publishers, 1906.

Sanville, George W. *Forty Gospel Hymn Stories.* Winona Lake, Indiana: The Rodeheaver-Hall Mack Company, 1943.

Showalter, A. J. *The Best Gospel Songs and Their Composers.* A. J. Showalter Company, 1904.

Smith, Oswald J. *Oswald J. Smith's Hymn Stories.* Winona Lake, Indiana: The Rodeheaver Company, 1963.

Stebbins, George C. *Reminiscences and Gospel Hymn Stories.* George H. Doran Company, 1924.

HYMN TUNES

Frost, Maurice, ed. *English and Scottish Psalm and Hymn Tunes, c. 1543–1677.* London: Oxford University Press, 1953.

Lightwood, James T. *Hymn Tunes and Their Story.* London: The Epworth Press, 1935.

Mason, Henry L. *Hymn Tunes of Lowell Mason.* Cambridge: The University Press, 1944.

McCutchan, Robert Guy. *Hymn Tune Names, Their Sources and Significance.* New York: Abingdon Press, 1957.

Routley, Erik. *The Music of Christian Hymnody.* London: Independent Press, 1957.

Zahn, Johannes. *Die Melodien der deutschen evangelischen Kirchenlieder,* 1893. Hildesheim: G. Olms, 1963 (reprint).

ALPHABETICAL INDEX OF TUNES

ALPHABETICAL INDEX OF HYMNS
The basic listing is of first lines;
common titles are in *Italics*.

359

362